THE HOLISTIC WELLNESS BOOK BUNDLE

A Guide to Reiki, Chakra Healing, Ayurveda, The Vagus nerve and Meditation

5 in 1 Holistic health book Bundle

Monika Daniel

© **Copyright 2024** - All rights reserved. The contents of this book may not be reproduced, duplicated or transmitted without direct written permission from the author. Under no circumstances will any legal responsibility or blame be held against the publisher for any reparation, damages, or monetary loss due to the information herein, either directly or indirectly.

Legal Notice: This book is copyright protected. This is only for personal use. You cannot amend, distribute, sell, use, quote or paraphrase any part or the content within this book without the consent of the author.

Disclaimer Notice: Please note the information contained within this document is for educational and entertainment purposes only. Every attempt has been made to provide accurate, up to date and reliable complete information. No warranties of any kind are expressed or implied. Readers acknowledge that the author is not engaging in the rendering of legal, financial, medical or professional advice. The content of this book has been derived from various sources. Please consult a licensed professional before attempting any techniques outlined in this book. By reading this document, the reader agrees that under no circumstances is the author responsible for any losses, direct or indirect, which are incurred as a result of the use of information contained within this document, including, but not limited to, errors, omissions, or inaccuracies.

Table of Contents

Reiki for Beginners:..1

Chakra Healing for Beginners..119

Ayurveda for Beginners.. 242

The Vagus Nerve Unlocking the Body's Superhighway....369

Meditation For Beginners 493

About the Author

Monika Daniel, the founder of www.reikisoulacademy.com, is not just a passionate Reiki Master but also a mother of two daughters. This role has significantly influenced her practice, bringing a wealth of compassion and empathy to her work. Her understanding of the importance of nurturing and caring for oneself and others has been deepened through her motherhood journey and her dedication to holistic healing.

Monika's personal journey into the holistic side of life began in Kho Phangyang, Thailand. This journey, filled with self-discovery and growth, led her to embrace a wide array of healing modalities, with a particular focus on Reiki and energy work. Her studies and experiences have enriched her understanding of the healing potential that lies within each of us, inspiring her to share these transformative practices with others.

Monika's commitment to promoting health and wellness is not just a part of her life, it is her life. She is deeply passionate about healthy living, nutrition, and mindfulness, and she actively incorporates these principles into her daily life and teachings, inspiring others to do the same.

Monika's commitment to holistic healing extends beyond her individual practice. She is not just an organizer of retreats; she is a leader. Her passion and dedication create nurturing spaces for individuals to reconnect with themselves and experience profound healing and transformation. Her leadership in these retreats provides a sanctuary for participants to explore holistic practices, cultivate self-awareness, and embark on personal growth and empowerment journeys, instilling a sense of trust and confidence in her abilities.

With a warm heart and an unwavering commitment to the well-being of others, Monika Daniel continues to inspire and uplift those on their path to health, healing, and holistic living.

She dedicates this book to her darling daughters, Sophia and Holly, and her husband, who has supported her throughout this transformative journey.

REIKI FOR BEGINNERS:

Awaken Your Spirit to the Art and Practice of Reiki Healing

Learn About the Symbols, Affirmations, and Power of Rebalancing the Chakras

Monika Daniel

Chapter 1

Introduction to Reiki Healing

Welcome to the captivating world of Reiki healing, where ancient wisdom meets modern wellness. In this book, we embark on an enlightening journey into the art of Reiki, exploring its origins, principles, and powerful potential to transform our lives for the better.

Picture this: you're sitting in a tranquil room, surrounded by gentle music, soft candlelight, and an aura of calmness. As you close your eyes, a practitioner gently places their hands on various parts of your body, as if channeling some mystical energy. A wave of relaxation washes over you, tensions melt away, and a deep sense of peace fills your being. That is the magic of Reiki healing.

What is Reiki Healing?

Reiki is a form of healing that taps into the life-force energy that flows through all living things. The word itself is a combination of two Japanese words—"rei" meaning universal and "ki" meaning life-energy. Reiki is essentially about harnessing and channeling that powerful universal energy to promote balance, relaxation, and well-being.

During a Reiki session, a trained practitioner will use their hands to gently place them on or hover over specific areas of your body. They act as conduits to allow the healing energy to flow from the universe, through them, and into you.

The beauty of Reiki is that it's not only a physical experience but also a deeply spiritual and emotional one. As energy flows through you, it helps to release any blockages or negative emotions that may be holding them back.

One of the best things about Reiki is that it can be used to address a wide range of issues. Whether you're dealing with physical pain, stress, anxiety, emotional trauma, or simply looking to reconnect with your inner self, Reiki can help by encouraging your body to heal itself and restoring your overall well-being.

The origins of Reiki can be traced back to a Japanese Buddhist monk named Mikao Usui, who rediscovered this ancient healing system in the late 19th century. Usui believed that through the practice of Reiki, individuals could tap into this universal energy and facilitate their own healing process.

Now, here's where things get interesting. Reiki is not some far-fetched concept that requires years of rigorous training or esoteric knowledge. It's actually quite accessible and can be learned by anyone who is genuinely interested in the art of healing.

In fact, one of the most beautiful aspects of Reiki is its simplicity. By attuning yourself to the universal life force energy, you can become a vessel of healing, both for yourself and others. Imagine being able to harness this incredible force, sending waves of positive energy to support your physical, emotional, and spiritual well-being. It's a truly empowering experience!

Who Can do Reiki Healing?

Reiki can be practiced and received by people of any age, gender, or background. There are no specific qualifications or prerequisites required to practice Reiki healing. However, learning and mastering the technique often involves undergoing training or receiving attunements from a Reiki master.

Thus, Reiki healing is versatile and adaptable, making it accessible to a wide range of individuals. It can be done on yourself, on others, and even on animals and plants. This universal aspect makes it applicable to people from all walks of life and professions.

Anyone who wants to learn and practice Reiki healing can do so, regardless of their previous healing experience. Whether you are a healthcare professional, a therapist, a spiritual practitioner, or simply someone looking to enhance your own well-being, Reiki can be an invaluable tool.

Reiki practitioners believe that healing energy flows through their hands, and they use specific hand positions to direct this energy to the recipient. However, it is important to note that the energy used in Reiki healing does not come from the practitioner themselves. Instead, they act as a channel or conduit for this universal life force energy.

The beauty of Reiki healing lies in its simplicity and accessibility. Unlike traditional medical interventions, Reiki does not require any special equipment or extensive training in anatomy or physiology. This makes it an ideal option for those who are looking for a non-invasive and gentle healing modality.

Moreover, Reiki healing can be combined with other treatment methods. It is often used as a complementary therapy alongside conventional medical treatments to support the healing process. Many hospitals, clinics, and wellness centers worldwide offer Reiki as part of their integrative healthcare approaches.

One of the great advantages of Reiki is that it can be practiced both in-person and from a distance. Distance Reiki involves sending healing energy to a person who is not physically present. This makes it particularly beneficial for individuals who are unable to receive in-person treatments, such as those who are hospitalized, bedridden, or located far away.

The Benefits of Reiki Healing

Reiki healing is truly a remarkable practice that offers a multitude of benefits for both the mind and body. Here are some of the remarkable advantages of incorporating Reiki into your life:

- **Deep relaxation:** One of the primary benefits of Reiki healing is its ability to induce deep relaxation. By promoting a state of profound calmness, Reiki helps to release stress, tension, and anxiety from the body. This relaxation response not only allows you to experience a peaceful state of being but also supports your body's natural ability to heal itself.
- **Stress reduction:** In today's fast-paced world, stress has become an all-too-common companion. Reiki healing works to alleviate stress by rebalancing the energy flow in the body, which in turn enables individuals to better cope with daily challenges. Regular Reiki sessions can lead to improved stress management, a balanced mindset, and enhanced overall well-being.
- **Pain relief:** Reiki has been recognized as an effective complementary therapy for pain management. By targeting the root cause of pain, whether physical or emotional, Reiki helps to alleviate discomfort and promote healing. It is particularly useful for chronic conditions such as migraines, arthritis, fibromyalgia, and back pain, as it supports the body in its natural healing process.
- **Enhanced energy levels:** Have you ever experienced feeling depleted and low on energy? Reiki can help replenish and revitalize your energy levels by clearing blockages and restoring the flow of life force energy in the body. Many people report feeling more invigorated, focused, and rejuvenated after a Reiki session.
- **Improved emotional well-being:** Emotional balance is vital to lead a fulfilling life, but it's not always easy to achieve. Reiki healing can play a significant role in promoting emotional well-being by helping you release negative emotions, such as fear, anger, and sadness. It allows for a clearer mental state, a greater sense of self-awareness, and supports emotional healing and growth.
- **Boosted immune system:** When your energy flow is out of balance, it can have negative effects on your immune system's ability to defend against illness and disease. Reiki works to

balance the body's energy centers, thus strengthening the immune system. Regular Reiki sessions enhance the body's natural ability to heal itself, preventing illness and promoting overall health.

- **Spiritual growth:** Reiki healing is not limited to physical and emotional benefits, as it can also foster spiritual growth. It helps you reconnect with your inner self, enhancing intuition and providing a sense of purpose and clarity. Reiki can serve as a catalyst for self-discovery, self-acceptance, and a deeper connection with the universe.

Ultimately, integrating Reiki healing into your life can have transformative effects, offering relaxation, pain relief, emotional balance, improved energy levels, and promoting overall well-being. It's a practice that encourages holistic healing, and its benefits extend far beyond the physical realm.

How Reiki Works: Understanding Energy Flow

You know what Reiki is and its benefits, but how does it work?

Reiki is based on the belief that energy flows through us and is essential for our well-being. In order to understand how Reiki works, it is important to grasp the concept of energy flow and the interconnectedness of mind, body, and spirit.

Energy flow refers to the movement of life force energy, also known as Ki, Qi, or Prana, throughout our bodies. This energy is believed to be present in everything around us and within us, contributing to our vitality and overall health. When the flow of energy becomes blocked or imbalanced, it can lead to physical, emotional, or spiritual issues.

Reiki practitioners work with this energy by acting as a channel or conduit for the universal life force energy. Through gentle and intentional touch or by simply placing their hands near the client's body, they aim to rebalance and restore the energy flow.

Reiki practitioners believe that they assist in the healing process by directing and replenishing the client's energy, promoting a deep sense of relaxation and well-being. This heightened state of relaxation allows the body to activate its natural healing abilities, while also fostering emotional and mental clarity.

During a Reiki session, clients often experience various sensations such as warmth, tingling, or a soothing feeling as the energy flows through them. These sensations are subjective and can vary from person to person. However, the overall goal is to dissolve energy blockages, reduce stress, and support the body's ability to heal itself.

It's important to note that Reiki is a complementary therapy and should never replace medical advice or treatment. Instead, as expressed earlier, it can work alongside traditional medicine to promote overall wellness and support the body's healing process.

Understanding energy flow in the context of Reiki allows us to appreciate the holistic nature of healing and the vital role that balancing our energy plays in our well-being. Whether you are seeking relaxation, emotional support, or physical healing, Reiki offers a gentle and non-invasive approach to restoring harmony within ourselves.

Chapter 2

Understanding the Basics of Energy Healing

You know that Reiki is a popular and ancient healing system, and in this chapter, we will delve into the basics of understanding energy healing through Reiki. In the end, you will have an essential foundation to embark on your journey of healing and self-discovery.

The human body, just like other living things, has an invisible energy force flowing through it, known as the life force energy or ki. When this energy is abundant and freely flowing, health and vitality flourish. It is when this flow of energy becomes blocked, weakened, or imbalanced that physical and emotional ailments may arise.

Understanding the basics of energy healing in Reiki involves exploring concepts such as chakras, meridians, and the auric field, which are interconnected systems within our energetic anatomy. By gaining insight into these intricate systems, you can begin to comprehend the profound impact that energy has on your physical, emotional, and spiritual health. Moreover, you can learn techniques to clear blockages and restore balance in these energy pathways, enhancing your overall well-being and promoting optimal health.

As we progress through this chapter, we will explore the fundamental principles of Reiki, the importance of intention and mindfulness in energy healing, and practical techniques to connect with and enhance the flow of life force energy. Together, we will embark on a transformative journey that will empower you to tap into the incredible healing potential that lies within us all.

The Concept of Energy Healing

In a world where modern medicine dominates, the concept of energy healing has surged in popularity as an alternative and complementary approach to wellness. Energy healing is based on the principle that our bodies possess an innate ability to heal themselves, and that the flow of energy, or life force, through our system, is vital for maintaining overall well-being.

This fascinating practice draws from ancient traditions and offers a holistic approach to support physical, emotional, and spiritual health. In this section, we will delve into the concept of energy healing, exploring its origins, techniques, benefits, and the scientific basis behind it.

Origins and Techniques

Energy healing can be traced back to ancient civilizations such as China, India, and Egypt, where it was believed that life force energy—known as qi, prana, or chi (ki)—circulated through the body's energy pathways, or meridians. Practitioners of energy healing techniques embrace the idea that blockages or imbalances in this flow can lead to illness or discomfort.

One prominent technique in energy healing is Reiki. Developed in Japan in the early 20th century, Reiki involves the practitioner channeling energy into the patient, either by placing their hands on or near specific parts of the body. This allows the energy to flow through the practitioner's hands and into the patient, stimulating the body's natural ability to heal.

Other popular approaches include acupuncture, acupressure, and reflexology. These methods target specific points on the body—acupuncture using needles, acupressure using pressure, and reflexology utilizing foot or hand massage—to balance and restore energy flow.

Benefits and Applications

Energy healing is known to offer a wide range of benefits that extend beyond the physical realm. While results may vary from person to person, many report feeling a sense of deep relaxation, reduced stress levels, pain relief, improved sleep, increased mental clarity, enhanced emotional well-being, and a general sense of balance and harmony.

Furthermore, energy healing can be applied to multiple areas of life. It has been used to support people undergoing emotional trauma, grief, or anxiety, providing a safe space for healing and introspection. Additionally, athletes and performers often turn to energy healing to enhance their focus, performance, and recovery. Energy healing is known to aid in the healing process after surgery or injury, stimulate the immune system, and support overall vitality.

Scientific Basis

While skeptics may question the scientific basis of energy healing, there is growing evidence to suggest its efficacy. Studies have shown that energy healing can influence the autonomic nervous system, leading to relaxation, pain reduction, and improved immune system function. It is also believed that energy healing may positively impact the release of endorphins, the body's natural painkillers.

Furthermore, energy healing techniques often result in a shift in brain wave patterns, promoting a deeply relaxed state similar to meditation. This shift from a stressed state to a relaxed one may support the body's self-healing mechanism and allow it to function optimally.

Critics argue that the benefits of energy healing may be attributed to the placebo effect, where patients experience positive outcomes due to their belief in the treatment. While this may be true to some extent, the subjective experiences and reported outcomes of energy healing cannot be entirely dismissed, as they often align with the principles of holistic well-being.

Whether used as a complementary therapy alongside conventional medicine or as a standalone practice, energy healing has the potential to transform and improve lives. By recognizing and embracing the concept of energy healing, you can unlock your body's natural potential, cultivating a state of balance, harmony, and optimal well-being.

Principles of Energy Medicine

Energy medicine is a branch of alternative and complementary medicine that focuses on working with the body's energy systems to promote health, vitality, and balance. Grounded in ancient wisdom and supported by modern research, energy medicine operates on the principle that the body possesses an intricate network of energy pathways, and imbalances or blockages in this energy flow can lead to physical, emotional, and spiritual discomfort.

Energy Systems and Meridians

Energy medicine recognizes the existence of subtle energy systems within the body that play a crucial role in maintaining health and vitality. These systems, such as the Chinese meridian system or the Indian nadis, consist of pathways through which prana, qi, or life force energy flows. By stimulating and balancing these energy systems, practitioners of energy medicine seek to enhance overall health and well-being.

Qi and Life Force Energy

Central to energy medicine is the concept of Qi, referred to as prana, chi, or life force energy in different cultures and traditions. This vital energy is believed to animate and sustain all living beings. According to energy medicine, when Qi flows smoothly and harmoniously throughout the body, health and vitality thrive.

However, disruptions or imbalances in this flow can lead to a variety of physical, emotional, and spiritual issues.

Balancing and Clearing Energy Blockages

Energy medicine seeks to identify and address energy blockages or imbalances that hinder the smooth flow of vital energy. Various techniques and therapies like acupressure, acupuncture, Reiki, and chakra balancing work to clear these blockages, restore the flow of energy, and stimulate the body's self-healing abilities. By bringing balance to the energy systems, energy medicine aims to promote physical and emotional well-being.

Holistic Approach to Healing

One of the fundamental principles of energy medicine is embracing a holistic approach to healing. It recognizes that the mind, body, and spirit are interrelated and that imbalances in one area can affect the others. Energy medicine takes into account the interconnectedness of these aspects of our being and aims to restore harmony on all levels. By addressing the root causes of imbalance, energy medicine promotes holistic healing rather than just symptom management.

Individualized and Integrative Care

Energy medicine emphasizes the uniqueness of each person and the need for personalized approaches to healing. Practitioners consider a person's unique energy pattern, symptoms, and overall well-being to develop a tailored treatment plan. Moreover, energy medicine often complements conventional medicine, working alongside other modalities to create an integrative and comprehensive approach to healing and wellness.

Self-Responsibility and Empowerment

Energy medicine empowers you to take an active role in your healing journey. It encourages self-awareness, self-care practices, and techniques that you can learn and apply yourself. By fostering self-responsibility, energy medicine empowers you to heal and promotes long-term well-being and self-empowerment.

Respecting the Body's Innate Wisdom

Energy medicine recognizes that the body has an innate wisdom and intelligence that guides its healing processes. Practitioners regard symptoms as signals from the body, providing insight into the underlying imbalances. Energy medicine seeks to tap into this inherent wisdom, bringing awareness to the body's signals, and supporting the body's ability to heal itself.

Different Modalities of Energy Healing

Energy healing is a broad field that encompasses various modalities, all aimed at restoring balance and promoting well-being in the body, mind, and spirit. These modalities draw from ancient wisdom and modern understanding to tap into the body's energetic systems and facilitate healing.

In this section, we will explore some of the most popular and effective energy healing modalities, shedding light on their unique approaches.

Reiki

The subject of our book! Reiki, a Japanese healing modality, is one of the most well-known energy healing practices. It involves the channeling of universal life force energy from a practitioner's hands into the recipient's body. The gentle touch deployed in Reiki helps to dissolve energy blockages, promoting relaxation, stress reduction, and emotional balance. Reiki is often used to improve overall well-being and support the body's natural healing abilities.

Chakra Healing

Based on the ancient Eastern philosophy of energy centers in the body, chakra healing aims to balance and activate these centers. Each chakra is associated with specific organs, emotions, and aspects of life. By working with the chakras, energy healers help to remove blockages and stimulate the smooth flow of energy throughout the body. This can lead to physical, mental, and emotional healing and greater self-awareness.

Crystal Healing

Crystals have been used for healing purposes for centuries. In crystal healing, specific crystals are chosen and placed on or around the body to rebalance and harmonize the energy field. Each crystal possesses unique energetic properties, which are believed to interact with the body's energy centers, facilitating healing and emotional release. Crystal healing is known for its calming effects and ability to enhance spiritual growth.

Sound Healing

The power of sound has long been recognized as a potent healing tool. Sound healing involves using various sound sources such as singing bowls, gongs, or tuning forks to produce specific frequencies that resonate with the body's energy system. As the soothing vibrations penetrate the body, they can help release energetic blockages, reduce stress, and promote deep relaxation. Sound healing has been reported to facilitate emotional release, enhance meditation, and improve overall well-being.

Pranic Healing

Pranic healing is a non-touch energy healing technique that uses the practitioner's hands to scan, cleanse, and energize the body's energy field. It works on the principle that life force energy, known as prana, is essential for physical, emotional, and mental health. Pranic healers identify areas of energetic congestion or depletion and apply specific healing techniques to restore balance. Pranic healing is known for its ability to alleviate physical pain, speed up recovery, and address a wide range of ailments.

Quantum Healing

Quantum healing combines the principles of quantum physics with energy healing. It posits that the body's energy field can be influenced through focused intention and consciousness. By harnessing the power of the mind, practitioners can affect the energetic patterns at the quantum level, facilitating profound healing and transformation. Quantum healing is often used in conjunction with other modalities to enhance their effectiveness and catalyze personal growth.

The world of energy healing modalities is vast and diverse, offering a wide array of choices to restore balance and support their wellbeing. Whether it be Reiki, chakra healing, crystal healing, sound healing, pranic healing, or quantum healing, each modality brings its unique approach to tapping into the body's energetic systems. By exploring these different modalities, you can find the one that resonates with you and embark on a transformative healing journey toward holistic wellness.

In our next chapter, we're going to delve much deeper into the origins and history of Reiki, laying the foundations for your upcoming journey.

Chapter 3

History and Origins of Reiki

Reiki seems to have been around forever, and that's because as far as modern history goes, it has. In this chapter, let's delve into the history and origins of this famous and enlightening healing method, starting with the story of one Dr. Mikao Usui.

Dr. Mikao Usui was a humble and wise scholar from Japan, dedicated to his studies of ancient healing practices and the pursuit of spiritual enlightenment. Little did he know that his discoveries would not only change his own life but would go on to impact the lives of countless others around the world.

Born on August 15, 1865, in the village of Yago, Gifu Prefecture, Mikao Usui was a curious and introspective child. From a young age, he displayed a keen interest in learning about the human body, the mind, and the invisible energies that surrounded us all. This insatiable curiosity led him to study a wide range of disciplines, including medicine, psychology, theology, and philosophy.

As Dr. Usui delved deeper into his studies, he became increasingly dissatisfied with the conventional medical practices of his time. He realized that although modern medicine had made remarkable advancements, it often failed to address the root cause of illnesses and only treated the symptoms. This realization sparked within him a desire to find a more holistic and deeper approach to healing.

His quest for answers took him on a voyage spanning continents, as he traveled to China, India, and various other parts of Asia. Along the way, he sought out renowned scholars, healers, and spiritual masters, eager to learn from their wisdom and experience. It was during one of these journeys that Dr. Usui stumbled upon an ancient Sanskrit scripture that mentioned the secret healing techniques used by Siddhartha Gautama, the Buddha himself.

Inspired by this discovery, Dr. Usui embarked on a solitary retreat atop Mount Kurama, a sacred mountain near Kyoto. For twenty-one days and nights, he engaged in fasting, meditation, and deep introspection. On the twenty-first day, as the first light of dawn illuminated the horizon, Dr. Usui experienced a profound spiritual awakening.

In this transcendent moment, Dr. Usui received a powerful stream of healing energy flowing through the crown of his head, down into his body, and out through his hands. He discovered the art of Reiki, a Japanese word meaning "universal life-force energy" that had the potential to heal not only physical ailments but also emotional, mental, and spiritual imbalances.

Overjoyed, Dr. Usui descended from the mountain, eager to share his newfound wisdom and healing with the world. He opened the Usui Reiki Ryoho Gakkai, a society devoted to teaching and practicing this ancient art of hands-on healing. Dr. Usui's teachings were simple yet profound—by channeling the universal life-force energy, known as Reiki, one could awaken the body's innate healing abilities and bring about balance and harmony on all levels.

Word of Dr. Usui's miraculous healing spread like wildfire, and people flocked to him from near and far, seeking his guidance and treatment. Recognizing the need for trained practitioners, Dr. Usui started to pass down his teachings to a select group of students, initiating them into the practice of Reiki and empowering them to heal others.

One of his most prominent students was a woman named Hawayo Takata, a Hawaiian-born Japanese woman, who traveled to Japan seeking a cure for her chronic illness. Under Dr. Usui's guidance, Hawayo Takata not only experienced a profound healing but also became a devoted disciple, dedicated to spreading the teachings of Reiki to the Western world.

Dr. Usui's legacy continued to grow even after his passing on March 9, 1926. Today, Reiki has spread to all corners of the globe, touching the lives of millions, and igniting a spark of divine healing within each of us. The story of Dr. Mikao Usui serves as a reminder that sometimes, in our greatest moments of seeking, we find something far greater than we ever imagined—a path to healing, enlightenment, and love.

The Popularity and Development of Western Reiki

As Reiki began to spread in the West, it underwent further modifications and developments to align with the cultural context of different countries. Many Reiki Masters began incorporating elements from other healing modalities, such as crystals, sound therapy, and aromatherapy, into their Reiki practice.

During the late 20th century, several different branches of Reiki emerged, each with its unique approach and philosophy. Some of the popular variants include Karuna Reiki, Tibetan Reiki, and Seichim Reiki, each emphasizing different aspects of healing and spiritual growth.

The Evolution Continued: Reiki in the Modern Era

In recent years, Reiki has gained even more popularity in the Western world, expanding beyond individual healing sessions, and becoming integrated into hospitals and healthcare facilities. It is now commonly used as a complementary therapy alongside traditional medicine, enhancing the overall well-being of patients.

Additionally, scientific studies have begun to investigate the effects of Reiki, adding to its credibility, and leading to more acceptance within mainstream healthcare. Researchers have explored the impact of Reiki on pain reduction, stress management, and overall quality of life, providing evidence to support its efficacy as a healing modality.

Reiki has come a long way from its origins in Japan to its widespread adoption in the West. While the core principles outlined by Mikao Usui remain intact, the practice has evolved and adapted to suit the cultural context of different countries. As Reiki continues to grow in popularity, its potential to promote well-being and provide complementary support alongside traditional medicine becomes increasingly recognized and valued.

Modern Schools and Lineages of Reiki

The Usui Reiki Ryoho lineage has expanded and diversified over time, giving rise to several branches and schools. These different lineages share a common connection to Usui but emphasize different techniques, philosophies, and training methods. One such lineage is the Usui Shiki Ryoho, founded by Hawayo Takata. This lineage is known for its simplicity and focuses on hands-on healing techniques.

Another prominent modern Reiki school is the Karuna Reiki, developed by William Lee Rand. This system combines traditional Usui Reiki with additional symbols and techniques to create a more intensive healing experience. Karuna Reiki practitioners believe in the power of compassion and the healing potential of divine love.

In addition to these lineages, there are various other schools that have emerged, each offering its unique perspective on Reiki. The Holy Fire Reiki, founded by William Lee Rand, employs a combination of traditional Usui Reiki and additional spiritual practices to enhance the healing process. It is believed to be a highly refined form of energy healing, bringing warmth, love, and transformative energy to the recipient.

Another notable school is the Tibetan Reiki, which blends Reiki principles with Tibetan Buddhism practices. This lineage incorporates the use of Tibetan symbols, mantras, and meditations, aiming to facilitate deep healing on a mental, emotional, and spiritual level.

In recent years, there has been a surge in interest in the scientific aspects of Reiki. This has given rise to schools such as the Scientific

Reiki, which focuses on the scientific validation and integration of Reiki with modern medicine. Scientific Reiki practitioners strive to bridge the gap between conventional medicine and complementary healing practices by conducting research and incorporating evidence-based techniques.

The modern schools and lineages of Reiki reflect the evolving nature of this healing modality, catering to the diverse needs and interests of practitioners and clients. While they may differ in their approaches, all Reiki lineages share a common goal: to channel healing energy through the practitioner's hands to support the well-being of the recipient.

The beauty of Reiki lies in its adaptability and openness to personal interpretation. Each lineage and school offers a unique perspective, allowing practitioners to choose the path that resonates with them the most. Consequently, individuals can explore different lineages or even develop their own innovative approaches to Reiki, further expanding the possibilities and potential benefits of this healing practice.

Chapter 4

The Philosophy Behind Reiki Healing

We know that one central philosophy behind Reiki is the belief in the existence of a vital life force energy that flows through all living beings. Reiki practitioners recognize this force by various names—chi in Traditional Chinese Medicine, prana in Hinduism, or ki in Japanese—but the concept remains the same across different cultures. This energy, when balanced and free-flowing, supports optimal health and well-being. However, when this energy becomes stagnant, blocked, or depleted, it can lead to physical, emotional, or spiritual imbalances.

As we delve deeper into this chapter, we will explore these philosophical foundations of Reiki healing in greater detail. By gaining a more profound understanding of the principles that underpin this ancient practice, you will be well-equipped to harness the power of universal life energy and embark on a transformative healing journey.

Reiki as a Spiritual Practice

At its core, Reiki is not confined to any particular religion or belief system. Instead, it embraces a universal understanding that there is a vital force that connects all living things. Reiki practitioners believe that when this life force energy (chi, prana, or ki) is low or blocked, it results in physical and emotional imbalances, illness, and suffering. By channeling and directing this energy through a Reiki practitioner's hands, the practice aims to help restore balance and harmony within the recipient's being.

Reiki as a spiritual practice is grounded in the principles of love, compassion, intentionality, and mindfulness. Thus, as a practitioner, it's important to approach each session with an open heart and a genuine desire to assist in the recipient's healing journey. Through attunements and regular self-practice, you will cultivate your own energetic well-being, allowing you to act as conduits for the divine healing energy.

One of the fundamental pillars of Reiki as a spiritual practice is self-healing. Reiki encourages you to take responsibility for your own well-being by engaging in regular self-treatments. These self-healing sessions give you an opportunity to connect with your own energy centers, release emotional blockages, and enhance your overall spiritual growth. It is through these intimate encounters with your own energy that you deepen your understanding of yourself, your connection to the universe, and your purpose in life.

While self-healing is vital, Reiki also provides a profound platform for healing others. By offering Reiki to others, practitioners contribute to the healing of physical ailments, emotional wounds, and spiritual imbalances. The gentle touch of a Reiki practitioner's hands can provide a deep sense of relaxation, comfort, and peace to the recipient. As the healing energy flows through the practitioner's hands, it penetrates the body, clearing stagnant energy and promoting the natural healing response within the person receiving the treatment. This energetic exchange creates a space for profound healing and transformation to occur, touching not only the physical body but also the mind and spirit.

Reiki also serves as a powerful tool for spiritual growth and expansion. As you continue on your Reiki journey, you will develop a heightened sense of intuition, connectedness, and awareness of the subtle energies present in your surroundings. Through regular meditation and self-reflection, you can cultivate a deep sense of inner peace, attaining a state of oneness with the universe.

The practice encourages you to acknowledge you innate divinity and embrace your ability to co-create your own reality. This expansion of consciousness allows you to tap into your full potential, manifest your desires, and live a life aligned with your highest purpose.

Beyond individual healing, Reiki also holds the potential to create collective transformation. Reiki circles, where multiple practitioners come together to offer healing energy, create a powerful collective energetic field. This unified intention amplifies the healing energy, creating a space for deep healing, spiritual connection, and profound shifts to occur. Reiki circles promote a sense of community, support, and love, enhancing the overall well-being of both the individual and the group.

Overall, Reiki as a spiritual practice holds immense transformative power. Rooted in love, compassion, and intentionality, Reiki enables you to engage in self-healing, facilitate healing for others, and embark on a profound spiritual journey.

Core Principles of Reiki Philosophy

There are several core principles that form the foundation of Reiki healing. These principles provide guidance for both the practitioner and the recipient, and when practiced regularly, they can have profound effects.

- **The principle of connection:** At the core of Reiki healing is the belief in the interconnectedness of all living beings. Reiki practitioners understand that we are all connected to each other and to the universal life force energy. This principle emphasizes the importance of nurturing and valuing these connections, fostering an attitude of compassion and love toward yourself and others.
- **The principle of mindfulness:** Reiki teaches you to be fully present in the moment and aware of your thoughts, feelings, and sensations. Mindfulness allows you to cultivate a deep sense of self-awareness, enabling you to recognize and address any imbalances or blockages in your energy. By practicing

mindfulness, you can bring your focus to the present moment and provide healing energy to yourself and those around you.

- **The principle of harmony:** Reiki emphasizes the importance of finding balance and harmony within yourself and in relation to the environment. This principle recognizes that when there is an imbalance or disharmony in your energy, it can manifest as physical or emotional ailments. Reiki healing seeks to restore this balance by channeling healing energy to the areas of imbalance, promoting harmony and overall well-being.
- **The principle of gratitude:** Gratitude is a fundamental aspect of Reiki healing. Practitioners understand and appreciate the healing energy that flows through them and are grateful for the opportunity to channel it into the world. Gratitude also helps you cultivate a positive mindset and shifts your focus toward the blessings and abundance in your life. By fostering an attitude of gratitude, you invite more positivity and healing into your life.
- **The principle of intention:** Intention is a crucial element in Reiki healing, as it directs the flow of healing energy. Reiki practitioners set clear and positive intentions for the healing session, specifying the desired outcome for the recipient's well-being. This principle highlights the power of focused intention and its ability to manifest positive changes in our lives.
- **The principle of self-care:** Reiki healing emphasizes the importance of self-care as a means of maintaining and restoring your own energy. Practitioners recognize that self-care is essential for their physical, emotional, and spiritual well-being, enabling them to be more effective channels of healing energy. This principle encourages you to prioritize self-care practices, such as meditation, self-reflection, and taking time for yourself.
- **The principle of trust:** Trust is an integral part of the Reiki healing process. Both the practitioner and the recipient must have trust in the healing energy and its ability to bring

about positive change. Trust allows the energy to flow freely, creating a safe and supportive environment for healing to occur. This principle highlights the importance of trust in the healing relationship and invites you to let go of resistance and surrender to the healing process.

Harmony and Balance: The Essence of Reiki

At its core, Reiki aims to restore and harmonize the body, mind, and spirit, creating an ideal state of balance in life. This balance extends beyond the individual level and also encompasses the harmonious relationship between yourself and your surrounding environment. By understanding and embracing the essence of Reiki, you can experience a transformative journey toward achieving inner peace and holistic well-being.

To truly grasp the concept of harmony and balance within the context of Reiki, it is essential to delve into the fundamental principles that guide this ancient healing practice. The system of Reiki is based on five precepts, which serve as a moral code and a foundation for spiritual development. These precepts, when followed and internalized, can lead to a life of harmony and balance:

1. Just for today, I will not be angry.

2. Just for today, I will not worry.

3. Just for today, I will be grateful.

4. Just for today, I will do my work honestly.

5. Just for today, I will be kind to every living thing.

By embracing these precepts, you can cultivate a state of mindfulness and presence, which allows for the alignment of the body, mind, and spirit. Through the practice of Reiki, you develop a heightened sense of self-awareness, enabling you to recognize and address imbalances.

In Reiki, balance is not solely confined to the physical body. It extends to emotional well-being, mental clarity, and spiritual growth. Emotions play a vital role in your overall state of balance, as they can either energize or deplete you. Through Reiki, you can release negative emotions, such as anger, fear, and sadness, and promote a more positive emotional state.

Furthermore, Reiki aids in harmonizing the mind by calming racing thoughts and providing mental clarity. In our fast-paced modern world, where stress and anxiety are prevalent, the meditative aspect of Reiki can bring tranquility and a sense of balance to your mind.

Spiritual balance is another crucial component of Reiki. By connecting to the universal life force energy, you can tap into your inner wisdom and intuition. This connection enables you to find purpose and meaning in your lives, establishing a spiritual equilibrium that cultivates a sense of fulfillment and contentment.

Outside of the individual level, Reiki also emphasizes the importance of fostering harmony and balance in your relationships with others and the natural world. By practicing kindness, compassion, and respect towards all living beings, you can contribute to the harmonious coexistence of all creatures and the planet as a whole.

Chapter 5

Exploring the Human Energy System and Chakras

Throughout history, countless cultures and spiritual traditions have recognized that humans possess an energy system that goes beyond the realms of our physical bodies. This system, often referred to as the subtle body, encompasses a series of spinning energy centers called chakras. These chakras correspond to different aspects of our being, ranging from our physical vitality to our emotional state, and even our connection to the divine.

Our energy system, like a complex web, intertwines with every aspect of our existence. In this chapter, we'll explore the human energy field as well as the different chakras, and their associated meanings.

Introduction to the Human Energy Field

The human energy field is an intricate and complex system that surrounds and interpenetrates the physical body, consisting of various energy centers and pathways. This field, also known as the aura, is an essential aspect of your existence and plays a significant role in your overall well-being and interaction with the world around you.

To understand the human energy field, we need to delve into the concept of energy itself. We've touched upon the fact that energy is the vital force that flows through every living being, animating and sustaining life. It is an invisible force that permeates everything in the universe, connecting all living things in a web of energetic exchange.

For us humans, our energy field is not limited to the physical body alone. It extends beyond the physical boundaries and interacts with the energies of the environment, other people, nature, and even the cosmos. This interconnectedness is what enables us to sense and interact with the world on a deeper level.

The human energy field is composed of multiple layers or levels, with each layer corresponding to a different aspect of our being. These layers include the physical, emotional, mental, and spiritual aspects, each contributing to our overall state of well-being.

One of the key components of the human energy field is the chakra system. The chakras are spinning energy centers located along the spine, and they act as gateways between our physical and energetic bodies. There are seven main chakras, each associated with specific qualities and attributes. For example, the root chakra, located at the base of the spine, is associated with your sense of stability, security, and basic survival needs, while the crown chakra, located at the top of the head, is associated with your connection to higher consciousness and spiritual awareness.

In addition to the chakras, the human energy field also consists of energy meridians or channels. These channels allow the flow of vital life force energy, also known as prana or chi, throughout the body. In traditional Chinese medicine, these meridians are mapped out and used in practices such as acupuncture and acupressure to restore balance and harmony to the body's energy system.

An imbalance or blockage in the human energy field can lead to various physical, emotional, or mental health issues. When the energy flow is disrupted, it can manifest as physical pain, illness, or even psychological distress. Therefore, it is essential to maintain a healthy and balanced energy field to promote overall well-being.

It is important to remember that the human energy field is not separate from the physical body; rather, it is intimately connected to it. Your energy field is influenced by your physical health, lifestyle choices, and overall state of being. By taking care of your physical body, you also nurture your energy field, and vice versa.

What is an Aura?

An aura is a unique and invisible energy field that surrounds every living being, including plants, animals, and humans. It is often described as a luminous glow or a halo of light that emanates from the body. While it may not be physically visible to most people, some possess the ability to see and interpret auras.

The concept of the aura has been present in various cultures and belief systems throughout history. In Hinduism and Buddhism, for example, it is known as the "halo" or "nimbus" and is associated with enlightenment and spiritual awakening. In ancient Egyptian and Greek cultures, it was believed to represent a person's life force or essence.

The aura is said to consist of multiple layers, each corresponding to different levels of energy and consciousness. These layers are often depicted as different colors, with each color carrying its own meaning and significance. For example, a vibrant and bright aura might indicate vitality, while a dull or faded aura could suggest illness or emotional turmoil.

The colors of the aura are thought to reflect the person's emotional, mental, and physical state. For instance, a person with a predominantly blue aura might be known for their calm and peaceful nature, while someone with a red aura might be passionate and energetic. Different shades and combinations of colors can provide even more detailed insights into one's personality, emotions, and well-being.

The aura is not static; it can change in response to various factors such as mood, health, and environment. Negative emotions like anger, stress, or sadness can cause the aura to become murky or dim. Conversely, positive experiences, such as love, joy, or meditation, can brighten and expand the aura, making it more vibrant and luminous.

While some people naturally have the ability to perceive auras, anyone can develop the skill through practice and mindfulness. Meditation and visualization exercises are commonly used to enhance auric perception. By focusing on the body and visualizing energy flowing through it, you can begin to sense and see the subtle colors and patterns of the aura.

The study and interpretation of auras have also gained popularity in alternative healing practices, including Reiki. Practitioners believe that by sensing and manipulating the aura, they can facilitate physical, emotional, and spiritual healing. They may use techniques like aura cleansing, balancing, or chakra alignment to restore harmony and well-being.

In addition to being a tool for self-discovery and healing, the aura can also have practical applications in daily life. Understanding and recognizing the auras of others can help in building stronger relationships, as it provides insight into their emotions and intentions. It can also serve as a tool for personal growth, as you become more aware of your own energy and make conscious choices to enhance and maintain a positive aura.

Understanding Chakras and Their Functions

Chakras are energy centers within the body that play a vital role in your physical, mental, and spiritual well-being. Derived from Sanskrit, the word "chakra" translates to "wheel" or "disc," referring to the spinning vortex of energy that each chakra represents.

Let's now talk about the seven main chakras and their functions.

Root Chakra (Muladhara)

Located at the base of the spine, the root chakra is associated with your sense of stability, grounding, and survival instincts. It governs your connection to the physical world, including your basic needs for safety, shelter, and nourishment. When the root chakra is balanced, you feel secure, strong, and rooted; however, an imbalanced root chakra may manifest as fear, insecurity, or a lack of stability.

Sacral Chakra (Svadhishthana)

Situated in the lower abdomen, the sacral chakra is tied to your creativity, emotions, sexuality, and passion. It governs your ability to enjoy pleasure, embrace new experiences, and form healthy relationships. A balanced sacral chakra enhances your ability to express your emotions freely, foster intimacy, and nurture your creative endeavors. On the other hand, an imbalanced sacral chakra may lead to emotional instability, creative blockages, and a difficulty in forming genuine connections.

Solar Plexus Chakra (Manipura)

Located in the upper abdomen, the solar plexus chakra influences your self-confidence, personal power, and willpower. It is associated with your sense of identity, autonomy, and motivation. When this chakra is balanced, you have a healthy sense of self-worth, self-esteem, and personal boundaries. An imbalanced solar plexus chakra can manifest as low self-confidence, indecisiveness, or a need for external validation.

Heart Chakra (Anahata)

Situated in the center of the chest, the heart chakra is the bridge between the lower three earthly chakras and the higher spiritual ones. It represents love, compassion, forgiveness, and emotional healing. A balanced heart chakra allows you to give and receive love openly, maintain healthy relationships, and practice empathy toward yourself and others. An imbalanced heart chakra may cause feelings of resentment, jealousy, or an inability to trust others.

Throat Chakra (Vishuddha)

Located at the base of the throat, the throat chakra is associated with communication, self-expression, and truth. It governs your ability to express yourself authentically, speak your truth, and listen actively. A balanced throat chakra enables effective communication, clarity of thought, and the ability to express ideas and emotions with ease. An imbalanced throat chakra may lead to difficulties in speaking up, lack of confidence in expressing oneself, or excessive communication without meaningful content.

Third Eye Chakra (Ajna)

Situated between the eyebrows, the third eye chakra represents intuition, a higher state of consciousness, and inner vision. It governs your ability to access wisdom, make decisions based on inner knowing, and connect with your spiritual purpose. When balanced, the Third Eye chakra enhances your intuitive abilities, perception, and imagination. An imbalanced Third Eye chakra may cause feelings of disconnect from intuition, lack of clarity, or an overactive imagination.

Crown Chakra (Sahasrara)

Located at the top of the head, the crown chakra is the highest of the seven chakras, symbolizing spiritual connection, enlightenment, and transcendence. It governs your connection to the divine and the universe at large. When balanced, the crown chakra evokes feelings of unity, bliss, and a profound sense of purpose. An imbalanced crown chakra may manifest as a lack of spiritual connection, aimlessness, or ego-centered behaviors.

Understanding the functions and characteristics of each chakra can help you identify imbalances and work toward achieving harmony within yourself. Various practices, such as meditation, yoga, energy healing, and mindful living, can aid in balancing and aligning our chakras, promoting overall well-being and optimal functioning in all areas of life. Of course, Reiki is included on that list.

The Importance of Chakra Balance for Overall Well-being

When your chakras are balanced and flowing freely, it indicates a state of good health and well-being. However, various factors such as stress, emotional trauma, physical illnesses, and negative thought patterns can disrupt the flow of energy within your chakras. This imbalance can manifest as physical ailments, emotional distress, or a general sense of feeling stuck or disconnected.

Keeping your chakras balanced is therefore crucial for your overall well-being. One significant benefit of chakra balance is improved physical health. Each chakra is associated with specific organs and systems in the body, as we've explored, and when a particular chakra is blocked or imbalanced, it can result in physical symptoms related to that specific area. For example, a blockage in the throat chakra might manifest as difficulties in communication or frequent throat infections. By working to balance and cleanse your chakras, you can alleviate these physical symptoms and restore your physical health.

In addition to physical health, chakra balance also affects your emotional well-being. Each chakra is associated with specific emotions and qualities; for instance, the heart chakra is linked to love and compassion, while the sacral chakra is associated with creativity and joy. When your chakras are out of balance, the corresponding emotional qualities can become excessive or deficient. For instance, an imbalanced heart chakra might result in either an excessive attachment to others or an emotional detachment. By harmonizing your chakras, you can cultivate emotional stability and a greater sense of inner peace.

Furthermore, chakra balance has a profound impact on your spiritual growth and connection. The crown chakra, located at the top of the head, is believed to be the gateway to higher consciousness and spiritual enlightenment. When this chakra is open and balanced, you experience a deep connection with your higher self and the divine. By aligning and balancing your chakras, you can enhance your spiritual practices such as meditation, visualization, and energy healing, and deepen your connection to your inner wisdom and spiritual gifts.

So, how can you achieve and maintain chakra balance? There are various techniques and practices that can help restore harmony to our chakras. Here are a few suggestions:

- **Meditation:** Regular meditation practice is one of the most effective ways to balance your chakras. By focusing on each chakra, visualizing its corresponding color, and affirming positive qualities associated with it, you can stimulate the flow of energy and restore balance.
- **Energy healing:** Seek out energy healing modalities including Reiki, acupuncture, or sound therapy. These practices can help clear blockages and restore balance within your chakras.
- **Yoga:** Incorporate yoga poses that specifically target each chakra into your exercise routine. This can help release energy blockages and promote chakra balance.
- **Essential oils:** Use essential oils that correspond to each chakra to enhance your chakra balancing practice. Inhaling or applying these oils to specific areas can help restore balance and promote healing.
- **Crystal therapy:** Crystals are known for their ability to absorb and transmit energy. Using crystals, such as amethyst for the crown chakra or rose quartz for the heart chakra, can help balance and align your chakras.
- **Mindful breathing:** Incorporate deep, mindful breathing exercises into your daily routine. By consciously directing your breath to each chakra, you can help restore balance and release any energy blockages.

Remember, chakra balance is an ongoing process. It requires self-awareness, self-care, and regular practice to maintain optimal well-being. By making conscious efforts to balance and align your chakras, you can experience improved physical health, emotional well-being, and spiritual growth.

Chapter 6

Introduction to Symbols in Reiki Healing

Symbols form a significant part of the Reiki healing journey, acting as gateways to tap into the higher realms of energy and consciousness. These symbols hold immense power and possess the ability to magnify the flow of healing energy, allowing experienced Reiki practitioners to provide even more effective treatments.

Each symbol in Reiki is unique and carries specific meanings and intentions. They can be seen as keys that unlock certain aspects of the healing process, offering a deeper understanding and connection to the universal life force energy. By working with these symbols, you can tailor your treatments to address specific ailments or imbalances, enhancing the overall therapeutic experience.

Throughout this chapter, we will explore the meanings and applications of some of the most widely used Reiki symbols. From the empowering Cho Ku Rei, which symbolizes the power of healing and protection, to the serene Sei Hei Ki, which fosters emotional and mental balance, each symbol will be illuminated in its own radiant light.

We will dive into the origins and history of these symbols, understanding the cultural and spiritual significance behind them. Additionally, we will delve into practical exercises and techniques that will enable you to connect with and utilize these symbols to enhance your Reiki healing practice.

The Significance of Symbols of Reiki Practice

Reiki symbols are bestowed upon practitioners during their Reiki training and play a profound role in enhancing the effectiveness of treatments and facilitating spiritual growth. In this section, let's explore the significance and transformative power that symbols hold in Reiki practice.

Harnessing Intention

Symbols act as gateways to specific energies and intentions, allowing you to direct the flow of energy where it is most needed. Each symbol represents a unique aspect of healing, ranging from emotional and mental balance to spiritual growth. By activating these symbols through drawing or visualizing them, practitioners harness their power to intensify the healing energy and send it toward a specific intent. Thus, symbols serve as focal points for channeling intention and directing healing energy to the recipient.

Enhancing the Healing Process

The symbols in Reiki possess inherent frequencies and vibrations that interact with the energy field of both the practitioner and the recipient. Their presence stimulates the flow of energy, promoting deep relaxation and facilitating the body's natural healing abilities. For instance, the symbol "Cho Ku Rei," commonly known as the power symbol, aids in increasing the potency of Reiki energy, amplifying its effects during treatments. This symbol enhances focus and intention, imparting a powerful surge of energy for the recipient's healing journey.

Unlocking the Subconscious Mind

Symbols possess the ability to communicate with the subconscious mind, accessing deeply rooted emotional, mental, and spiritual blockages. During a Reiki session, symbols are consciously integrated into the healing process to address and release the underlying causes of ailments or imbalances. The symbol "Sei He Ki," often referred to as the emotional symbol, opens doors to buried emotions, traumas, and negative thought patterns, allowing them to be acknowledged and brought into the light for healing. By working in collaboration with these symbols, you can navigate the intricate labyrinth of the subconscious, promoting profound healing on multiple levels.

Connecting with Universal Wisdom

In Reiki practice, symbols are not merely tools for healing but also keys to connecting with the universal wisdom and guidance. Channeling the energy of the symbol "Hon Sha Ze Sho Nen," known as the distance symbol, enables you to transcend physical limitations, reaching out to individuals in different locations or even across time. This symbol also allows you to access Akashic records, the universal energetic archives that hold knowledge and information about past events. Through this connection, you gain insights into the root causes of imbalances and can facilitate healing and understanding beyond the confines of time and space.

Facilitating Spiritual Growth

Symbols hold immense spiritual significance, representing various facets of universal and personal transformation. The Reiki Master Symbol, often referred to as "Dai Ko Myo," encapsulates the highest level of spiritual attunement and enlightenment. It serves as a reminder of the eternal connection with the divine, empowering you to shine your inner light and embrace your true spiritual nature. By integrating these symbols into your daily practice, you not only enhance your abilities to heal but also foster your own spiritual growth and self-realization.

Overview of Reiki Symbols and Their Meanings

Here is a comprehensive guide to the top 10 Reiki symbols and their meanings. Each symbol holds a unique energy frequency that you can use to enhance your Reiki healing practice.

- **Cho Ku Rei – The Power Symbol:** This symbol represents power, protection, and the channeling of energy. It is commonly used to increase the flow of Reiki energy and to focus it wherever it is needed.

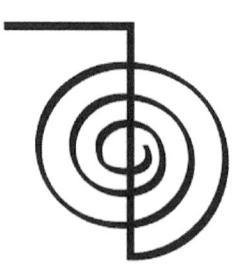

- **Sei He Ki – The Mental/Emotional Symbol:** This symbol is associated with mental and emotional healing. It helps to balance emotions, release negative patterns, and promote inner harmony.

- **Hon Sha Ze Sho Nen – The Distant Healing Symbol:** This symbol bridges the gap between time and space, enabling Reiki energy to be sent across distances. It is often used for healing past traumas, sending healing to loved ones, or connecting with past or future events.

- **Dai Ko Myo - The Master Symbol:** This symbol represents enlightenment and spiritual awakening. It brings a higher level of healing energy and is typically used for spiritual and soul healing, as well as to connect with higher levels of consciousness.

- **Raku - The Grounding Symbol:** Raku symbolizes grounding and manifestation. It helps to anchor the Reiki energy into the physical body, promoting stability, balance, and a stronger connection to the earth.

- **Zonar – The Harmonizing Symbol:** Zonar balances and harmonizes the energy centers in the body, known as chakras. It helps to release blockages, restore energy flow, and promote overall well-being.

- **Halu – The Time Symbol:** This symbol allows you to work with the past, present, and future simultaneously. It can be used to heal issues from past lives or project healing into the future.

- **Dumo – The Fire Symbol:** Dumo symbolizes the transformative power of fire. It is used to burn away negative energies and promote purification and spiritual growth.

- **Karuna – The Compassionate Symbol:** Karuna means compassion and is used for deep healing on an emotional and spiritual level. It helps to release deep-seated traumas, promote forgiveness, and awaken inner compassion.

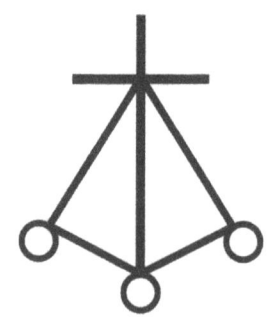

- **Shanti – The Peace Symbol:** Shanti symbolizes peace and tranquility. It is utilized to calm the mind, release stress and anxiety, and restore inner harmony.

These are some of the most common Reiki symbols. Each symbol holds its own unique energy and can be used to enhance and tailor the Reiki healing experience. Remember, the intention behind the symbol is just as important as the symbol itself, so use them with love and compassion.

Using Symbols for Healing and Empowerment

Using Reiki symbols for healing and empowerment is a wonderful way to harness the energy of Reiki. Here's a step-by-step guide on how to use Reiki symbols:

- **Learn the symbols:** First, make sure you have received the necessary training and attunements in Reiki. This will help you understand and connect with the symbols better. There are various symbols used in Reiki, such as the Power Symbol (Cho Ku Rei), the Mental/Emotional Symbol (Sei He Ki), and the Distant Healing Symbol (Hon Sha Ze Sho Nen).

- **Activate your Reiki energy:** Focus on your breath and imagine a warm and loving energy flowing into your body. Allow yourself to become fully present and centered in this moment. You can also perform a few minutes of self-Reiki to activate your energy.

- **Draw the symbols:** Using your hand or visualize it mentally, draw the symbol(s) in front of you or over the area you wish to heal or empower. Repeat the name of the symbol three times to create a strong connection and intention.

- **Intend healing and empowerment:** State your intention clearly, either aloud or silently. For example, if you're healing a physical ailment, you could say, "I invite healing energy to flow through me and into this area for the highest good." If you're seeking empowerment, you could say, "I welcome the strength and confidence that this symbol represents into my life."

- **Send Reiki energy:** Imagine or visualize a stream of loving, healing energy flowing from the symbol and into the intended person, situation, or yourself. You can picture this energy in any way that feels right to you, such as a gentle white or golden light. Trust that the Reiki energy will flow where it is needed most. Don't worry, this is also something we're going to delve into far more in coming chapters.

- **Trust the process:** Let go of any attachment to the outcome and trust that the Reiki energy is doing its work. Stay open to any insights or sensations you may receive during the process.

Remember, Reiki symbols are powerful tools, but it's your intention and connection to the Reiki energy that truly creates the healing and empowerment. Practice regularly, and with time and experience, you'll develop a deeper understanding of how to utilize these symbols effectively for your own personal growth and the benefit of others.

Chapter 7

Learning the Power of Affirmations in Reiki Practice

Affirmations serve as a vital tool in energy healing, enabling you to access the deep reservoirs of positive thoughts and beliefs that reside within you. By nurturing and reshaping your inner dialogue, you can manifest transformative change in your physical, emotional, and spiritual well-being.

Therefore, by combining the principles of Reiki with the practice of affirmations, you can amplify its healing potential and accelerate the manifestation of positive outcomes.

In this chapter, we will explore various aspects of affirmations in Reiki healing, beginning with the understanding of how affirmations work and their role in reprogramming your subconscious mind.

The Role of Affirmations in Reiki Healing

Affirmations are powerful tools that can help rewire our thought patterns and beliefs. By consciously choosing positive words and phrases, you can gradually shift your mindset and create a more supportive and uplifting mental environment. In the context of Reiki healing, affirmations become even more potent as they work in conjunction with the flow of universal energy.

- **Aligning intention with energy:** Reiki healing focuses on balanced energy flow within the body. Affirmations act as a bridge between your intention and the universal life force energy. By intentionally infusing affirmations with positive energy, you can enhance the healing process and create a more profound impact on the recipient.

- **Clearing negative belief systems:** Reiki healing aims to create harmony by identifying and addressing disharmony in the energy system. Affirmations play a crucial role in this process as they help identify and reframe negative beliefs. For example, if someone is struggling with self-doubt, affirmations like "I am confident and worthy" can help them transform their thoughts and beliefs, opening the path to healing and self-acceptance.

- **Enhancing self-awareness:** Affirmations encourage you to become more aware of your thoughts and beliefs, allowing you to consciously choose positive statements that resonate with your true essence. By using affirmations, you can assist clients in exploring their inner landscape and replacing self-limiting beliefs with empowering ones. This process cultivates self-awareness, leading to personal growth and transformation.

- **Amplifying the power of intent:** Intent is a focal point in Reiki healing. Affirmations serve as a means to amplify this intention. When you incorporate affirmations into your healing sessions, you are intentionally programming positive thoughts and energy into the process. This augments the strength of your intentions and enhances the healing experience for both you and the recipient.

- **Promoting positive mind-body connection:** Reiki healing recognizes the interconnectedness of mind, body, and spirit. Affirmations aid in strengthening the mind-body connection by promoting positive thoughts and beliefs. By repeating affirmations such as "I am healthy and vibrant," you encourage your body to respond accordingly, fostering an overall state of well-being.

Crafting Effective Affirmations for Healing

Let's discuss the key elements of crafting effective affirmations for Reiki healing and provide ten examples to inspire your practice.

- **Positive language:** Affirmations should always be expressed in positive language. Instead of focusing on what you want to release or heal, channel your energy toward what you wish to manifest. For example, instead of saying, "I am no longer feeling anxious," rephrase it as "I am calm and at peace."
- **Present tense:** Phrase your affirmations in the present tense, as if they are already happening. By doing so, you align your mind and energy with the desired outcome. For instance, say "I am radiating vibrant health," rather than "I will become healthy."
- **Keep it personal:** Tailor your affirmations to your specific needs and desires. Use first-person pronouns such as "I" or "my" to make the affirmation feel more personal and relevant. For example, say "I am filled with love and compassion," rather than "People love and respect me."
- **Emotional connection:** Affirmations should evoke positive emotions and resonate with your heart. The more emotionally connected you are with the affirmation, the more impact it will have on your overall well-being. Choose words that truly resonate with your intentions and evoke positive feelings within you.

Now, let's explore ten examples of affirmations for reiki healing:

- "I am a vessel of healing energy, bringing love, light, and peace to myself and others."
- "Every breath I take fills me with vibrant health, vitality, and wellness."
- "I release all negative thoughts and emotions, embracing a state of inner calm and serenity."
- "I am open to receiving the abundance and prosperity that the universe has in store for me."
- "Divine love flows through me, healing and harmonizing my body, mind, and spirit."
- "I embrace forgiveness, letting go of past pains, and allowing unconditional love to guide me."
- "My body is a temple of divine energy, and I treat it with love, respect, and gratitude."

- "Every day, I wake up filled with joy and gratitude for the endless possibilities that lie ahead."
- "I choose to release all fears, doubts, and insecurities, and instead, I embrace my inner strength and power."
- "I am surrounded by loving, supportive, and positive energies that uplift and nourish my soul."

Remember, these affirmations are just starting points. Feel free to modify and personalize them to best resonate with your own intentions and healing journey. You can also create new ones based on specific situations or challenges you may be facing.

Also incorporate these affirmations into your daily practice, repeating them with intention and belief. Consider creating a sacred space where you can easily access and recite your affirmations, such as on a mirror or in a personal journal. The more you immerse yourself in these positive statements, the more they will become ingrained in your subconscious mind, fostering healing and transformation.

Incorporating Affirmations into Reiki Sessions

We've already established that when combined with Reiki, affirmations can facilitate deep healing and create powerful shifts in your energy and thought patterns.

There are several ways to incorporate affirmations into a Reiki session. You can begin by inviting your client to set an intention or focus for the session. This intention can then be turned into a positive affirmation that is repeated throughout the session. For example, if the client's intention is to release fear and cultivate inner peace, the affirmation could be: "I am letting go of fear and embracing inner peace."

As the Reiki energy flows through the client's body, you can use affirmations to enhance the healing process. For instance, if you sense a blockage in the client's heart chakra, you can ask them to repeat affirmations focused on love, compassion, and forgiveness such as, "I am opening my heart to love and compassion. I release all past hurts and embrace forgiveness."

In addition to verbal affirmations, visual affirmations can also be incorporated into a Reiki session. You can use visual aids, such as cards or images with positive affirmations, to help the client focus on specific areas of healing. These visual affirmations can be placed near the client or held by you during the session, allowing the energy to flow through them and into the client.

Another powerful way to incorporate affirmations in Reiki is through the use of symbols. Reiki symbols are sacred symbols that hold specific energies and can be used to enhance healing. You can incorporate symbols into affirmations, drawing them or visualizing them while repeating positive statements. This combination of symbols and affirmations can deepen the healing process and bring about profound transformation.

It's important to remember that affirmations should always be positive, uplifting, and aligned with the client's highest good. They should focus on what the client wants to manifest rather than what they want to avoid or release. Affirmations stated in the present tense, as if they are already true, have a particularly powerful effect on the subconscious mind.

During a Reiki session, you can guide the client in saying affirmations aloud or silently to themselves. This helps to reinforce the positive messages on a conscious level, while the Reiki energy works on a deeper, energetic level. Affirmations can also be repeated after the session or as part of a daily practice, to continue the healing process and to reinforce the positive changes that have been initiated.

Clients who experience Reiki sessions with affirmations often report feeling more empowered, lighter, and more aligned with their true selves. They may notice shifts in their thought patterns, behavior, and overall outlook on life. By incorporating affirmations into Reiki sessions, you can enhance your ability to facilitate healing and support your clients' journey toward wholeness.

Chapter 8

Initiating Your Reiki Journey: Self-Healing Techniques

Self-healing is a fundamental aspect of Reiki, as it empowers and enables you to take charge of your own healing process. By embarking on this journey, you will develop a deep connection with yourself, discover inner healing potentials, and pave the way for personal growth and transformation.

Throughout this chapter, we will explore various self-healing techniques that you can incorporate into your daily routine. From scanning your body for energy imbalances to using Reiki symbols and meditative practices, you will learn how to become your own healer and facilitate healing on a holistic level.

The Importance of Self-Healing in Reiki

When you think of Reiki, the image of a practitioner using healing touch immediately comes to mind. However, what often goes unnoticed is the crucial role self-healing plays.

Self-healing in Reiki refers to the process of applying Reiki techniques to yourself in order to achieve physical, emotional, and spiritual healing. As a Reiki practitioner, it is imperative that you prioritize your own well-being so that you can better serve others. By taking the time to address your own needs, you establish a strong foundation from which you can offer healing energy to others.

The Benefits of Self-Healing

- **Enhanced sensitivity and awareness:** Engaging in self-healing practices allows you to develop a deep sense of self-awareness. Through the regular practice of Reiki on oneself, you become more attuned to your own energy, noticing subtle shifts and imbalances within your body. This heightened sensitivity not only benefits you but also enhances your ability to identify and address energy imbalances in others.

- **Self-care and stress reduction:** In today's fast-paced world, it is easy to neglect your own well-being. However, self-healing in Reiki provides you with an opportunity to prioritize self-care and reduce stress. By turning inward and dedicating time to healing yourself, you can release tension, restore balance, and cultivate a sense of inner peace. This, in turn, has a positive ripple effect on all aspects of your life.

- **Personal growth and transformation:** Self-healing through Reiki offers you the chance to embark on a journey of personal growth and transformation. By delving into your own healing process, you gain insights into subconscious patterns, past traumas, and limiting beliefs. Through self-reflection and self-healing, old wounds can be mended, freeing you to step into your full potential and become more effective healers.

- **Improved intuition and healing abilities:** Regular self-healing practice enhances your intuition and strengthens your healing abilities. By consistently working on yourself, you develop a deep understanding of the energy flow within your body. This intimate connection allows you to better recognize and interpret the energy of others, ultimately leading to more precise and effective healing sessions.

- **Deepening connection with universal energy:** Self-healing serves as a powerful way to strengthen your connection with Universal Energy, the source of Reiki healing. As you dedicate time to your own healing, you harmonize your energy with the universal life force, expanding your capacity to flow healing energy not only to yourself but also to others. The more attuned you become, the greater the impact you can have on your clients.

As you can see, the benefits of self-healing extend far beyond you, positively impacting the healing journey of those you serve.

Techniques for Self-Reiki Treatment

So far, we've talked about Reiki offering a powerful tool for self-healing. In this section, we will explore a range of techniques that you can utilize to amplify your own self-healing abilities through Reiki.

Basic Hand Placement

Sit or lie comfortably in a quiet space. Place your hands gently on your body, starting with your head, and work your way down. Allow the healing energy to flow through your hands, spending a few minutes in each position. Trust your intuition to guide you to the areas that need attention the most.

Scanning Technique

Begin by hovering your hands a few inches above your body. Slowly move your hands over your body from head to toe, feeling the energy field or any sensations such as warmth, tingling, or coolness. Pay attention to areas that feel different or need healing. Once identified, place your hands directly on those areas and allow the energy to flow.

Chakra Balancing

Sit comfortably and close your eyes. Visualize a ball of healing light at the base of your spine, starting with the root chakra. Move your hands to the corresponding chakra points on your body (root, sacral, solar plexus, heart, throat, third eye, and crown), spending a few minutes on each. Allow the energy to flow and visualize each chakra balancing and harmonizing.

Aura Cleansing

Stand or sit comfortably and visualize a protective bubble of light around you. Gently sweep your hands around your body, a few inches away, in a sweeping motion from head to toe. As you do this, imagine any negative or stagnant energy being released and replaced with fresh, healing energy.

Emotional Healing

Identify any emotions or situations that are causing you stress or discomfort. Place one hand on your heart chakra and the other hand on the area where you feel the tension or discomfort in your body. Allow the Reiki energy to flow, bringing healing and balance to your emotional well-being.

Intention Setting

Before beginning your self-Reiki practice, set a clear intention for what you wish to achieve. It could be physical healing, stress relief, or simply a sense of overall well-being. Focus your energy and thoughts on this intention throughout the session, allowing the Reiki energy to facilitate its manifestation.

Distance Healing

You can send Reiki energy to loved ones, situations, or places that need healing, regardless of physical proximity. Visualize the person or situation in your mind and hold your hands in prayer position, imagining the Reiki energy flowing to them. Trust that the energy will reach its destination and provide healing and comfort.

Breath Connection

Combine deep breathing techniques with Reiki for enhanced relaxation and energy flow. As you inhale, visualize drawing in healing energy, and as you exhale, imagine releasing any tension or negative energy. Coordinate your breath with the movement of your hands, allowing the energy to synchronize with your breath.

Reiki Infused Water

Fill a glass of water and hold it between your palms. Close your eyes and imagine the healing energy flowing from your hands into the water. Visualize the water being infused with the positive, healing properties of Reiki. Drink the water slowly, savoring the energy it carries, and allow it to nourish your body and soul.

Self-Reiki Before Bed

Before going to sleep, practice self-Reiki to release any built-up stress or tension from the day, promoting a deep and restful sleep. Perform any of the above techniques or simply place your hands on your body, intending to release and let go of any negativity. Allow the Reiki energy to lull you into a state of deep relaxation, allowing for maximum rejuvenation.

Learning to perform self-Reiki treatments empowers you to take an active role in your own healing and well-being. These ten techniques provide a starting point for your self-Reiki practice, allowing you to tap into the healing energy whenever you need it most. Trust your intuition, set clear intentions, and allow the Reiki energy to flow through you, bringing balance, relaxation, and overall harmony to your mind, body, and spirit.

Establishing a Self-Care Routine with Reiki

Incorporating the healing energy of Reiki into your self-care routine can greatly enhance your experience and deepen the connection with your mind, body, and spirit. Let's explore what to include in a self-care routine with Reiki and how to incorporate its principles effectively.

Creating a Sacred Space

To enhance the efficacy of self-healing with Reiki, it is essential to create a conducive environment. Designate a tranquil space in your home or any space where you feel at peace. Cleanse and declutter the area to encourage relaxation and invite positive energy.

Consider using essential oils, candles, or soothing music to further enhance the ambiance. By doing this, you establish a sacred space where you can focus solely on your self-healing practice.

Grounding and Centering

Grounding is a fundamental aspect of self-healing through Reiki. Begin by finding a comfortable seated position or standing with your feet shoulder-width apart. Close your eyes and take a few deep breaths, allowing your body to relax. Visualize your body connecting with the earth, as though roots are anchoring you to the ground. This technique helps you establish a sense of stability and connection, enabling the free flow of healing energy.

Self-Reiki Hand Positions

Reiki operates through the use of specific hand positions that help direct energy flow. To facilitate self-healing, explore different hand placements on your body during your practice. Begin by placing your hands on your head, inviting energy to flow through the crown and promoting clarity and relaxation. Move your hands to your throat, chest, and solar plexus, fostering harmony and balance within these areas. Lastly, direct the energy to your abdomen, pelvis, and legs, promoting a sense of grounding and stability.

Visualization and Intention

Intention is a powerful force that can greatly enhance the effectiveness of self-healing. Combine your Reiki practice with visualization techniques to manifest and direct energy towards specific areas of concern. For example, if you are experiencing physical pain, close your eyes and visualize a soothing, golden light enveloping and healing the affected area. Intentionally directing healing energy through visualization empowers your self-healing journey.

Chakra Alignment

The chakra system is deeply connected to our well-being and can greatly influence our physical, emotional, and spiritual health. Reiki can aid in balancing and aligning the chakras, promoting improved energy flow throughout the body. Utilize hand positions specifically designed for each chakra, meditating on opening, and harmonizing them. Through this practice, you can unlock energy centers, fostering self-healing potential.

Reiki Infused Self-Care

Integrate Reiki into your daily self-care routines to enhance its effect on your well-being. Incorporate Reiki-infused bath rituals, where you can visualize healing energy enveloping you as you soak in warm water. Use Reiki symbols over your skincare products or create a sacred healing space during your meditation or yoga sessions. Infusing self-care practices with Reiki amplifies their rejuvenating effects, allowing for deeper healing on all levels.

Journaling and Reflection

Take the time to journal about your self-healing journey with Reiki. Document your experiences, observations, and any emotions that arise during your practice. Regularly review your journal to track progress, spot patterns, and gain insights into your healing process. This self-reflection can be profound, providing valuable guidance as you continue on your path to self-healing.

Regular Practice and Adaptation

To fully benefit from your self-care routine with Reiki, it is essential to maintain consistency and adapt it to suit your evolving needs. Reiki can be integrated into your daily routine, even if it's just for a few minutes each day.

Experiment with different techniques, such as incorporating Reiki symbols into your practice or using specific hand positions to target specific areas of your body. As you become more comfortable, you can also explore practicing Reiki on others or seeking professional treatments to enhance your self-care routine.

Chapter 9

Connecting with Reiki Energy: Attunements and Empowerment

Attunements are sacred initiations that allow you to become a conduit for the Reiki energy. They tune your energy field to resonate with the frequency of Reiki, enabling you to channel this divine healing energy effortlessly. In this chapter, we will explore the process of receiving attunements, understanding their significance, and how they create a sacred bond between you and Reiki.

Furthermore, we will dive into the concept of empowerment. Empowerments are rituals that help you connect with specific energies within the Reiki system, such as the symbols and mantras. They enhance your capacity to work with the various facets of Reiki energy, ensuring a greater level of healing, manifestation, and personal growth.

Through the guidance provided in this chapter, you will gain a deeper understanding of attunements and empowerments, allowing you to fully tap into the vast potential of the Reiki energy.

Understanding Reiki Attunements

Attunements are an integral part of the practice and understanding of Reiki.

At its core, an attunement is a powerful energetic initiation that opens you up to the flow of Reiki energy. It is often described as a spiritual awakening or a deepening of your connection to the universal life force. Attunements can be considered as a key that unlocks the door to the Reiki healing system.

During an attunement, the Reiki Master, who is experienced and trained in the practice, performs a series of rituals or ceremonies to help you attune with the energy within. These rituals are often conducted in person, although remote attunements are also possible. The specific process may vary between different Reiki lineages and Masters, but the intention remains the same—to align you with the Reiki energy.

One of the primary goals of an attunement is to cleanse and balance the energetic system of the practitioner. It helps to clear any blockages, release stagnant energy, and establish a harmonious flow within your energy field. This process allows you to become a clear and open channel for the universal life force energy, enabling you to conduct healing energy to yourself and others.

Attunements also activate your energy centers or chakras, bringing them into alignment and increasing their vibrational frequency. The chakras act as gateways or receptors for the universal life force, and when they are attuned, they become more sensitive and receptive to the healing energy. This heightened sensitivity allows you to perceive and work with the energy in a more refined and intuitive manner.

Furthermore, attunements create a connection between the you and the lineage of Reiki Masters who came before you. Reiki is passed down from teacher to student, with each attunement serving as a link in an unbroken chain of energy transmission. This connection to the lineage adds depth and integrity to your practice, as you are drawing upon the accumulated wisdom and experience of those who have practiced Reiki before you.

Attunement is not a one-time event but rather a lifelong process of growth and development. Each attunement builds upon the previous one, deepening your connection to the Reiki energy and expanding your ability to channel and use it effectively. It is not uncommon to experience an increase in sensitivity to energy, as well as a heightened spiritual awareness, following an attunement.

The effects of an attunement can vary from person to person. Some people may experience immediate shifts, such as increased energy flow or a sense of lightness and peace. Others may undergo a more gradual transformation, with the attunement serving as a catalyst for personal growth and healing over time. Thus, it is important to note that the attunement process is unique to each person and should be respected as such.

It is also worth mentioning that attunements are not exclusive to Reiki practitioners. Other energy healing modalities, such as Seichim or Karuna Reiki, also utilize attunements to activate and align the practitioner's energy system with the specific healing frequency of that modality. These attunements serve a similar purpose of opening the practitioner to the flow of higher vibrational energies, allowing them to connect with and channel these energies for healing purposes.

The Process and Benefits of Receiving Attunements

Now you know what attunement is, let's explore the process and benefits of receiving attunements in Reiki, shedding light on the transformative journey it offers when seeking healing and personal growth.

The Attunement Process

Let's quickly recap: Attunements are typically performed by a Reiki master who has undergone extensive training and received attunements themselves. The process typically involves a one-on-one session or a small group setting, where the attunement ceremony takes place. Although the specific rituals may vary between Reiki lineages, the underlying principles of attunement remain consistent.

- **Preparation:** Prior to the attunement, it is suggested that you engage in a period of self-reflection and set clear intentions for their Reiki journey. This can involve meditation, journaling, or any other practice that helps focus the mind and cultivate receptivity to the attunement energy.

- **Cleansing rituals:** The Reiki master may perform a series of cleansing rituals to create a sacred and energetically pure space. These can include burning sage or incense, using symbols or mantras to invoke protective energies, and setting a peaceful ambiance through soothing music or candles.
- **Connection and alignment:** The Reiki master then initiates you into the Reiki energy by acting as a conduit. Through gentle touch or non-contact methods, the master establishes a connection, aligning your energy with the universal life force energy. Various hand positions may be used, as the master channels the energy into specific points on your body, corresponding to the seven major energy centers or chakras.
- **Empowerment:** The attunement ceremony often includes the introduction of sacred symbols that hold profound healing and transformative power in Reiki. The master shares these symbols with you, teaching you how to draw and utilize them for healing purposes. These symbols serve as keys to accessing different frequencies of healing energy, amplifying the effectiveness of Reiki practice.
- **Integration:** Following the attunement, you may experience a period of adjustment and integration. It is common to encounter physical, emotional, or spiritual shifts as the attunement energy begins to settle. These changes can vary widely, ranging from heightened sensitivity and emotional release to feelings of lightness, clarity, and increased vitality. The length and intensity of integration vary from person to person, but compassionate self-care during this phase is highly encouraged.

Benefits of Receiving Attunements in Reiki

- **Enhanced healing abilities:** Attunements awaken your innate healing abilities, allowing you to channel Reiki energy for both self-healing and healing others. You become a conscious channel for healing energy, promoting physical, emotional, and spiritual well-being.

- **Deepened connection to universal energy:** Attunements facilitate a profound connection to the universal life force energy, enabling you to access an endless source of healing energy. This connection enhances your sense of interconnectedness and promotes a greater understanding of the unity of all living things.
- **Stress reduction and relaxation:** Receiving attunements in Reiki can induce a deep state of relaxation, activating the parasympathetic nervous system and reducing the effects of chronic stress. This can lead to improved sleep, reduced anxiety, and an overall increased sense of calm and well-being.
- **Spiritual growth and personal transformation:** Attunements ignite a spiritual awakening within, inviting you to explore your inner landscape and cultivate a deeper understanding of yourself. This journey often leads to personal transformation, increased self-awareness, and a greater sense of purpose and direction in life.
- **Energetic protection and self-care:** Attunements in Reiki equip you with powerful tools to protect and maintain your energetic well-being. You can use Reiki symbols to create energetic shields, cleanse and balance your own energy field, and support your overall health and vitality.

Receiving attunements in Reiki is an empowering and transformative process that opens you to the healing power of universal life force energy. Attunements in Reiki offer a beautiful and transformative journey, supporting you in your pursuit of holistic well-being and a balanced life.

Aftercare and Integration Following Attunements

Attunements can be a transformative experience, where an energy exchange occurs, allowing you to align with higher frequencies and harness newfound abilities. As you begin your journey with your attunement, it is important to focus on aftercare and integration to optimize your experience and support your continued personal growth.

Aftercare involves taking care of yourself physically, emotionally, and energetically following an attunement. It is crucial to honor the powerful energy shift that has taken place and allow yourself time to integrate and adjust to the higher frequencies. Here are some essential practices to consider for your aftercare:

- **Rest and hydration:** Attunements can be energetically intense experiences that may leave you feeling tired or drained. It is important to prioritize rest and ample hydration to support your body's healing process and aid in the integration of the new energies.
- **Grounding and earthing:** Connect with the earth's energy to ground yourself after an attunement. Walk barefoot on grass, meditate outdoors, or practice grounding exercises like visualizing roots extending from your feet into the earth. This helps stabilize and balance your energy, bringing you back into the present moment.
- **Journaling:** Documenting your experiences and insights in a journal can be a powerful tool for integration. Write down any emotions, thoughts, or visions that arise during or after your attunement. This practice can assist in gaining clarity, understanding, and processing of the energetic shifts that have occurred.
- **Self-care practices:** Engage in activities that promote self-care and nourishment. This can include indulging in relaxing baths, practicing mindfulness and meditation, engaging in gentle exercise, or enjoying hobbies that bring you joy and fulfillment. By prioritizing self-care, you create a nurturing environment for your energy to settle and harmonize.
- **Seek support:** It's essential to connect with others who have undergone similar attunements or who can provide guidance and support during your integration process. Seek out like-minded individuals, energy healers, or spiritual mentors who

can provide insight, encouragement, and clarity. Community support can be invaluable during this transformative journey.

Integration is the process of assimilating the energies and aspects of the attunement into your daily life. It involves bridging the gap between the energetic shift and practical application in your physical reality. Here are some creative and practical ways to integrate your attunement experiences:

- **Energetic clearing and balancing:** Regularly cleanse and balance your energy field through practices like energy healing sessions, meditation, Reiki itself, or other energetic modalities. This helps maintain the energetic alignment achieved during the attunement and supports ongoing integration.

- **Mindfulness and presence:** Cultivate mindfulness and presence in your daily life. Be conscious of your thoughts, emotions, and actions, and consciously choose alignment with the higher frequencies accessed through your attunement. This awareness can be instrumental in integrating the attunement's benefits into your daily experiences.

- **Visualization and affirmations:** Utilize the power of visualization and affirmations to reinforce the energetic shifts and intentions that came with the attunement. Visualize yourself embodying the new energies or use affirmations to reprogram your subconscious mind and align with the qualities you desire to embody.

- **Creative expression:** Engage in creative outlets to allow the energies from the attunement to flow through you. Paint, draw, dance, write, or play an instrument as a means of expressing and integrating the new frequencies. Creativity can be a powerful avenue for channeling and manifesting the energies within you.

- **Service and contribution:** Share the gifts and insights you've gained through your attunement by serving others. Offer healing sessions, teach workshops, or simply be a beacon of light and love in your community. By sharing your experiences, you help anchor the higher frequencies in the world and contribute to the collective consciousness.

Remember, integration is an ongoing process that requires patience, self-compassion, and willingness to surrender to the transformation unfolding within you. Each person's integration journey is unique, and it is essential to honor and trust your own timing and process.

At each step of the way, embrace the growth, expansion, and personal empowerment that come with your attunement. Embrace your newfound abilities, trust your intuition, and continue to cultivate self-love and self-care as you integrate these energies into your daily life. The aftercare and integration practices mentioned above will support you tremendously on your journey of self-discovery and spiritual evolution. Embrace this beautiful opportunity and enjoy the infinite possibilities that await you.

Chapter 10

Harnessing the Power of Symbols in Healing Sessions

A little earlier, we talked about the main symbols used in Reiki healing. In this chapter, we're going to take it a step further and talk about harnessing the power of those symbols in your Reiki practice.

Symbols have been used throughout history as powerful tools to convey meaning and communicate concepts that are often difficult to express in words alone. Reiki symbols serve as energetic gateways that allow you to tap into deeper layers of healing and unlock hidden potentials.

When used intentionally, symbols have the remarkable ability to amplify the flow of Reiki energy, intensifying its impact on both you and the recipient. These sacred symbols act as bridges connecting the conscious mind to the vast realm of universal energy. They serve as focal points for intention, enabling you to direct the healing energy precisely where it is needed most.

Not only do symbols enhance the flow of energy, but they also provide you with a unique tool for intention setting, visualization, and manifestation. Each symbol holds a specific vibration and resonance, offering an array of possibilities for tailoring your Reiki practice to address specific issues, goals, or intentions.

Symbolic Activation in Reiki Sessions

We know that one of the key elements in Reiki is the use of symbols, which act as potent tools for amplifying the healing energy. In this guide, we will explore the process of activating symbols in Reiki healing in detail.

Understand the Reiki Symbols

Before diving into the activation process, it is essential to have a thorough understanding of the symbols used in Reiki healing. There are three commonly taught symbols in traditional Usui Reiki: the Cho Ku Rei, the Sei He Ki, and the Hon Sha Ze Sho Nen. Each symbol holds its unique purpose and energy, enhancing specific aspects of the healing process. Here's a quick reminder:

- **Cho Ku Rei (Power Symbol):** This symbol is often used to increase the power and intensity of Reiki energy. It helps in grounding, protection, and manifestation.
- **Sei He Ki (Mental/Emotional Symbol):** The Sei He Ki symbol aids in emotional and mental healing. It is frequently used to balance emotions, release negative thought patterns, and promote emotional harmony.
- **Hon Sha Ze Sho Nen (Distance Healing Symbol):** This symbol enables you to send Reiki energy across time and space, facilitating distant healing sessions.

Attune Yourself to Reiki Energy

To activate and utilize the symbols effectively, it is crucial to be attuned to Reiki energy by a qualified Reiki Master. Attunements open up your energy channels and increase your receptivity to the healing energy of the symbols. Attunements create a sacred connection between you and the symbols, allowing you to tap into their inherent power more effectively.

Connect With the Symbols

Once you are attuned to Reiki, it's time to establish a personal connection with the symbols. This connection strengthens your intention and enhances your ability to channel their energies. Spend some time meditating on each symbol, holding the image mentally or physically. Visualize the symbol radiating light and energy, feel its vibration, and allow its essence to resonate within your being.

Practice Drawing the Symbols

To activate the symbols, learn to draw them accurately. Begin by practicing until you can recreate each symbol confidently and without hesitation. Use a pen and paper, or if you prefer, draw them with your finger in the air. Remember, intention is more crucial than perfect artistic skill. Focus on imbuing each stroke with your intention to activate the symbol's energy.

Charging the Symbols

To fully activate the symbols in Reiki healing, you need to give them energy and charge them with intention. There are various ways to charge the symbols, and practitioners often develop their techniques depending on personal preference. Here are a few commonly practiced methods:

- **Verbal affirmations:** Stand or sit in a relaxed position, holding the symbol with your hands in front of you. Silently or aloud, repeat the symbol's name along with a positive affirmation. For example, while focusing on the Cho Ku Rei symbol, say, "Cho Ku Rei, empower my healing abilities and amplify Reiki energy."
- **Visualizations:** Close your eyes and visualize the symbol in your mind's eye. See it pulsating with vibrant energy, illuminating with light and love. Envision the symbol's energy flowing into your heart center, merging with your own energy. With intent, perceive your entire being radiating with the symbol's energy.
- **Breathwork:** Take a few deep breaths, allowing yourself to enter a state of relaxation. As you exhale, visualize, or imagine the symbol appearing in front of you. With each inhalation, imagine drawing the symbol into yourself, filling your entire

being with its energy. Exhale and envision the energy infusing your aura and surrounding space.

Activating symbols is a personal and sacred process that deepens your connection to the healing energy of Reiki. Remember, intention, focus, and dedication are key to harnessing the transformative energy that symbols in Reiki offers.

Techniques for Symbolic Healing

Symbolic healing and application techniques play a crucial role in enhancing the effectiveness of Reiki sessions. These techniques involve the use of sacred symbols, visualization, intention setting, and intuition to facilitate deeper healing and to address specific issues.

In this section, we will explore some of these advanced techniques in detail and discuss their practical application in Reiki sessions.

- **Symbolic Scanning:** Prior to the treatment, you can use your intuitive abilities to scan the client's energy field using symbols. By visualizing symbols such as the Cho Ku Rei or Sei He Ki, you can identify areas of imbalance or blockages within the body.
- **Symbol infusion:** During a Reiki session, you can visualize or draw the symbols over specific body parts, chakras, or areas that require focused healing attention. The symbols act as a catalyst, intensifying and directing the healing energy to the targeted areas.
- **Symbolic healing grid:** By using symbols, you can create a healing grid by placing your hands or crystals with symbols in specific formations on the client's body. This technique helps in channeling Reiki energy to multiple areas simultaneously, creating an overall harmonizing effect.
- **Intention setting and visualization:** Intention and visualization are crucial elements in advanced symbolic

healing techniques, as they aid in directing the healing energy with focused intent.

- **Intention-based symbol healing:** You can set specific intentions while working with symbols. For instance, while using the Sei He Ki symbol to address emotional healing, you may specifically intend to release past traumas or promote self-love and acceptance for the client.

- **Visualization for deep healing:** Through visualization, you can create imagery that supports the healing process. Visualization techniques can include envisioning the affected area returning to its natural state of balance or seeing the symbols radiating healing energy throughout the body and aura.

- **Enhanced intuition and instinctive healing:** As you become more advanced in Reiki healing, you will rely more on your intuition and instinctive healing abilities. This involves trusting and following your inner guidance during sessions.

- **Intuitive symbol selection:** During a session, you may be guided to select and use different symbols that are not typically associated with a particular issue. This intuitive selection allows for a personalized approach, where the energy of the symbols resonates with the specific needs of the client.

- **Instinctive hand placements:** As you become more experienced, you may deviate from traditional hand placements, allowing your hands to be drawn intuitively to areas needing additional healing. Intuition guides you to trust what your hands sense, enhancing the overall healing experience.

By incorporating sacred symbols, intention setting, visualization, and intuition, Reiki becomes a more interactive and personalized healing modality. The use of these techniques allows you to address specific issues, intensify the healing energy, and create a profound impact on the physical, emotional, and spiritual well-being of your recipients. With dedication and practice, you can unlock the full potential of advanced symbolic healing, contributing to the overall advancement of Reiki as a transformative healing modality.

The Importance of Time

As with any skill, learning Reiki healing takes time, patience, and practice to develop proficiency in Reiki. Giving yourself ample time to learn and allowing your skills to grow naturally is of utmost importance when embarking on this profound journey. Some of the techniques mentioned in this chapter will be out of reach for a while, and as you advance in your practice, you'll learn to rely upon your intuition more and find you have more success.

It's about taking baby steps.

One of the primary reasons for allowing yourself time when learning Reiki is to build a strong foundation. Learning the art of Reiki involves not only understanding the techniques but also developing a deep connection with the universal life force energy. By taking it slow, you have the opportunity to acquaint yourself with the energy and understand its intricate workings. This process allows you to align yourself with the Reiki principles and develop a sense of presence and intuition, which are essential for the effective practice of Reiki.

Another significant advantage of allowing yourself time is that it gives you the opportunity to explore and experiment with different techniques and approaches. Reiki is a versatile practice that can be adapted to meet individual needs. By giving yourself the freedom to explore various techniques, you can discover what resonates with you the most and tailor your practice accordingly. This helps in deepening your understanding of Reiki and ultimately enhances your ability to heal and transform energy.

Embracing patience in your Reiki learning journey also allows for the integration of personal growth and self-discovery. As you delve deeper into the world of Reiki, you might find that it not only heals others but also acts as a catalyst for your own healing and personal transformation. By giving yourself time, you create space for self-reflection and introspection, allowing for the exploration of any internal blockages or limiting beliefs that may hinder your growth. This self-awareness facilitates personal growth, leading to a more profound connection with the universal life force energy.

Furthermore, taking your time nurtures a sense of authenticity and genuineness in your practice. With the abundance of information available in books and online resources, it can be tempting to rush, but remember that this is a lifelong skill you're attempting to learn, and a more measured approach will bring greater results for both you and those you help in the future.

Chapter 11

Exploring Advanced Reiki Techniques

As you expand your knowledge and skills in Reiki, you will discover that there are a multitude of advanced treatments available, each providing a unique approach to healing the mind, body, and spirit. These treatments offer an opportunity to explore different aspects of Reiki energy, allowing you to tap into the vast potential of this ancient healing art.

Throughout this chapter, we will explore a variety of advanced Reiki techniques, such as distance healing. You can also explore the use of symbols and mantras to amplify your healing energy, as well as the incorporation of essential oils, sound therapy, and sacred geometry into your treatments.

Whether you are a seasoned Reiki practitioner looking to expand your repertoire or a curious beginner intrigued by the possibilities of advanced healing techniques, this chapter will be a valuable resource for you.

Beyond Basic Hand Placements: Advanced Techniques

As you progress on your Reiki journey, you will discover that your hands are not just mere conduits of energy, but powerful instruments capable of creating profound shifts in the energetic body. Get ready to unlock a whole new level of healing as we explore advanced hand techniques that will not only deepen your connection with the universal life force, but also bring about transformative healing for yourself and others.

Let's explore 10 advanced hand placement techniques:

Head and Neck Technique

- Start by positioning yourself beside the recipient's head.
- Place your hands gently on either sides of their temple, allowing your fingers to naturally rest on the sides of their skull.
- Send Reiki energy by visualizing a pure white light flowing steadily from your palms into their head.
- Hold this position for approximately five minutes, or until you feel a sense of balance and relaxation.

Upper Chest and Heart Technique

- Stand at the recipient's side and gently place your hands on the upper part of their chest, just above the heart area.
- Keep your fingers relaxed, allowing them to naturally curve around the contour of their chest.
- Visualize Reiki energy radiating from your palms and penetrating into the recipient's heart area, promoting deep emotional healing and balance.
- Maintain this position for around five to ten minutes, or until you sense a harmonious energy flow.

Abdomen Technique

- Begin by standing at the recipient's side and place your hands on their abdomen, just below the navel.
- Relax your fingers, allowing them to naturally rest on their stomach.
- Imagine Reiki energy flowing from your palms into their abdominal region, promoting physical and emotional well-being.
- Continue this hand placement for five to ten minutes or until you feel a sense of warmth and relaxation.

Kidney Technique

- Position yourself slightly behind the recipient and place your hands on both sides of their lower back, just above the waist.
- Keep your fingers relaxed and gently rest them on the area around the kidneys.
- Envision Reiki energy flowing through your palms and into the recipient's kidneys, promoting balance and revitalization.
- Maintain this position for approximately five minutes or until you notice a soothing energy flow.

Throat Technique

- Stand behind the recipient and place your hands on both sides of their throat.
- Allow your fingers to naturally rest on the sides of their neck, being careful not to apply excessive pressure.
- Visualize Reiki energy flowing from your palms and into their throat area, encouraging clear communication and self-expression.
- Hold this position for five to ten minutes, or until you sense a calming and balanced energy flow.

Third Eye Technique

- Position yourself slightly above the recipient's head and place your hands on both sides of their forehead.
- Let your fingers naturally rest over their brow, focusing on the area between their eyebrows.
- Visualize Reiki energy streaming steadily from your hands and into their third eye area, promoting intuition, clarity, and spiritual awareness.
- Continue this hand placement for five to ten minutes or until you perceive a deep sense of tranquility and mental clarity.

Solar Plexus Technique

- Stand beside the recipient and place your hands on their upper abdomen, just below the rib cage.
- Keep your fingers relaxed and lightly rest them on the stomach area.
- Imagine Reiki energy flowing from your palms and into their solar plexus region, promoting confidence, personal power, and emotional balance.
- Maintain this position for five to ten minutes or until you feel a gentle and comforting energy flow.

Sacral Technique

- Position yourself beside the recipient and place your hands on their lower abdomen, just below the navel.
- Relax your fingers, allowing them to naturally rest on the area around their sacral chakra.
- Visualize Reiki energy flowing from your palms into their sacral region, promoting creativity, emotional healing, and the release of any blockages.
- Hold this position for approximately five minutes or until you perceive a warm and soothing energy flow.

Hands-On Hara Technique

- Stand behind the recipient and place your hands on their lower abdomen, slightly below the navel.
- Relax your fingers, allowing them to naturally rest on the hara area.
- Envision Reiki energy flowing from your palms and into their hara, promoting grounding, stability, and a sense of centeredness.
- Maintain this position for five to ten minutes or until you sense a balanced and grounded energy flow.

Full Body Technique

- Begin by standing at the recipient's side and place your hands lightly on their shoulders.
- Slowly move your hands down along their body, following an imaginary line from their shoulders to their feet.
- Visualize Reiki energy flowing through your palms and into their entire body, promoting overall well-being, harmony, and balance.
- Continue this technique for approximately ten to fifteen minutes, ensuring that you cover all areas of the recipient's body.

Remember, when practicing Reiki, always trust your intuition and adapt these hand placement techniques as needed to best suit the recipient's individual needs.

Distance Healing with Reiki

Distance healing with Reiki is a powerful and fascinating aspect of this ancient Japanese energy healing technique. Despite physical barriers, time zones, and geographical distances, Reiki practitioners are able to channel healing energy to individuals who are not physically present. This incredible ability to transcend space and time opens up a world of possibilities for those seeking healing and balance.

At its core, Reiki is based on the concept of universal life force energy. Practitioners are trained to tap into this energy and channel it, with the intention of promoting physical, emotional, and spiritual healing. Through the use of symbols and specific hand positions, Reiki practitioners connect with this energy and direct it to the recipient, whether they are in the same room or miles away.

Distance healing with Reiki operates on the principle that energy is not confined to physical proximity. Just as radio signals and internet waves can travel across vast distances, so too can Reiki energy. Time and space become irrelevant, as the intention and focus of the practitioner are what ultimately matter in this powerful healing modality.

There are several ways in which you can perform distance healing. One common method is through the use of a surrogate, such as a stuffed animal or a photograph. You can hold or place their hands on the surrogate, visualizing the recipient and channeling the healing energy to them. This method is particularly useful when working with animals or young children, who may not be able to sit still for a traditional hands-on session.

Another method of distance healing involves visualization. You can mentally connect with the recipient, imagining them in a peaceful and relaxed state. By visualizing the recipient receiving the healing energy, you can effectively transmit the energy across any distance. This method is often used when the recipient is unable to physically participate in a session, such as when they are in a hospital or on the other side of the world.

Technology has also played a significant role in distance healing with Reiki. With the advent of video calling platforms, you can now conduct sessions remotely, providing a more personalized and interactive experience. By seeing and hearing the recipient, you can establish a stronger connection and better understand their individual needs. This method allows for real-time feedback, ensuring that the energy is being transmitted accurately and effectively.

One important aspect of distance healing with Reiki is the consent and openness of the recipient. Energy healing works best when the recipient is willing to receive and accept the healing energy. It is important for the recipient to be in a relaxed and receptive state, ready to embrace your healing intentions.

The benefits of distance healing with Reiki are vast and varied. Physical ailments, such as chronic pain or illnesses, can be addressed and potentially alleviated. Emotional imbalances, anxiety, and stress can be eased, promoting a sense of calm and well-being. Spiritual growth and self-discovery are also common outcomes of distance healing sessions, as the energy works to align and balance.

Despite its intangible nature, distance healing with Reiki has been reported to have profound effects on both the practitioner and the recipient. Many recipients have reported feeling a warmth or tingling sensation during a session, while others have experienced a deep sense of relaxation and peace. Others have reported shifts in their physical or emotional well-being, as the energy works to clear blockages and restore balance.

Incorporating Crystals and Sound Healing into Reiki

Incorporating crystals and sound healing into Reiki can enhance the overall energy healing experience, helping to balance and align the body, mind, and spirit. By combining these powerful healing modalities, you can tap into the vibrational frequencies of crystals and sound to deepen the healing effects of Reiki.

Crystals, with their unique energetic properties, have been used for centuries for their healing abilities. Each crystal possesses its own vibrational frequency, which can resonate with and support specific areas of the body and energy centers, known as chakras. When combined with Reiki, crystals can amplify and direct healing energy towards specific intentions, enhancing the healing process.

To begin incorporating crystals into a Reiki session, it is essential to choose the right crystals that align with the energy centers and intentions of the recipient. For example, amethyst can be used to promote spiritual growth and enhance intuition, while rose quartz can help to heal emotional wounds and promote self-love. Clear quartz, known as the master healer, can be used to amplify the healing energy of Reiki and other crystals.

During a crystal-infused Reiki session, crystals can be placed strategically on or around the body to align with the chakras or areas of specific concern. You can intuitively select the crystals or use pendulum dowsing to determine the most appropriate crystals for the session. You can also hold the crystals during the Reiki treatment to infuse their energy into the healing process.

Here are ten crystals commonly used in Reiki and their corresponding purposes:

- **Clear Quartz:** Known as the master healer, it amplifies energy and cleanses blockages, enhancing the overall healing process.
- **Amethyst:** Promotes spiritual growth and awareness, bringing a sense of calmness and tranquility. It aids in connecting with higher consciousness during Reiki sessions.
- **Rose Quartz:** Often called the "stone of love," it helps heal emotional wounds, promoting self-love, forgiveness, and compassion for oneself and others.
- **Citrine:** Known as the "stone of abundance," it attracts positivity, prosperity, and success. It enhances self-confidence and motivation in Reiki sessions.
- **Carnelian:** Boosts energy levels and activates the Sacral Chakra, promoting creativity, motivation, and vitality. It helps balance emotions and enhances passion.
- **Selenite:** Encourages clarity of mind, purification, and spiritual growth. Selenite is often used to cleanse energy fields and spaces before and after Reiki sessions.
- **Black Tourmaline:** Shields against negative energies, providing protection and grounding for both the practitioner and the client. It helps transmute negative energy into positive vibrations.
- **Lapis Lazuli:** Enhances intuition, psychic abilities, and spiritual insight. Lapis Lazuli promotes inner peace, wisdom, and clear communication during Reiki sessions.

- **Green Aventurine:** Provides emotional balance, harmony, and healing. It helps release fears and anxieties, promoting a sense of well-being and soothing energy.
- **Labradorite:** A powerful stone for spiritual awakening and transformation. Labradorite enhances intuition, psychic abilities, and connection to higher realms during Reiki sessions.

Remember, while crystals can complement Reiki practices, it is essential to choose the crystals that resonate with you personally. Trust your intuition in selecting the crystals that provide the most healing and supportive energies for your Reiki sessions.

Sound Healing

Sound healing, on the other hand, utilizes the power of vibrations and frequencies to assist in healing and balancing the body, mind, and spirit. Sound can be produced through various instruments such as singing bowls, tuning forks, drums, or even the human voice. The vibrations of sound can penetrate deep into the body, promoting relaxation, stress reduction, and energetic harmony.

Incorporating sound healing into a Reiki session can be done in several ways. One approach is to have a trained sound healer play the singing bowls or tuning forks near or on the body of the recipient during the Reiki treatment. The resonating sound vibrations can help to clear energy blockages, balance the chakras, and facilitate deep relaxation.

Another way to introduce sound healing into Reiki is through using vocal toning or chanting. You can use your voice to create specific sounds or tones that correspond to the energy centers or intentions of the recipient. This technique helps to activate and balance the chakras while enhancing the flow of Reiki energy.

It is important to note that while incorporating crystals and sound healing into Reiki can enhance the overall healing experience, these modalities should not replace the traditional practice of

Reiki. Instead, they serve as complementary tools that can deepen and enhance the healing process.

When blending these methods together, it is crucial to create a harmonious and sacred space for the healing session. Clearing the space with sage or Palo Santo, setting intentions, and creating a serene atmosphere through soft lighting, gentle music, or aromatherapy can all contribute to an optimal healing experience.

As with any healing practice, it is important to approach crystal and sound healing with respect, proper training, and in alignment with ethical guidelines. Ultimately, the combination of Reiki, crystals, and sound healing can create a potent healing synergy, supporting you and your clients on their journey toward wholeness and well-being.

Chapter 12

Deep Dive into Chakra Healing and Balancing

A little earlier in the book, we talked about the main chakras and what they represent. In this chapter, let's delve deeper into chakra healing and understand how to incorporate it into your Reiki practice.

Originating from ancient Indian spiritual traditions, chakras are powerful energy centers located within our subtle body. Of course, chakras are believed to be spinning vortexes of energy that correspond to different aspects of our physical, emotional, and spiritual selves. There are seven major chakras, each associated with specific colors, elements, and qualities.

Understanding the chakra system is essential for achieving holistic wellness. When our chakras are balanced and energized, the vital life force, known as prana, flows freely through our body, enabling us to experience optimal health, emotional stability, and spiritual growth. However, when any of our chakras become blocked or imbalanced, disruptions occur, leading to various physical and emotional ailments.

Before we talk about how to work with chakras, let's recap on the main ones:

- **The Root Chakra (Muladhara):** Located at the base of the spine, it represents our foundation, stability, and feeling grounded. It is associated with the color red and governs our sense of security and survival instincts.

- **The Sacral Chakra (Svadhisthana):** Positioned in the lower abdomen, it influences our emotions, passion, and creativity. The sacral chakra is associated with the color orange and plays a role in our relationships, sensuality, and self-expression.
- **The Solar Plexus Chakra (Manipura):** Located in the upper abdomen or stomach area, this chakra is responsible for our personal power, confidence, and self-esteem. Represented by the color yellow, it governs our willpower, motivation, and sense of purpose.
- **The Heart Chakra (Anahata):** Positioned in the center of the chest, it represents love, compassion, and emotional balance. The heart chakra is associated with the color green or pink and influences our ability to give and receive love, along with our connections to others.
- **The Throat Chakra (Vishuddha):** Situated at the throat region, it governs communication, self-expression, and authenticity. The throat chakra is represented by the color blue and influences our ability to express ourselves clearly, speak our truth, and listen attentively.
- **The Third Eye Chakra (Ajna):** Positioned between the eyebrows, it is associated with intuition, perception, and spiritual awareness. The third eye chakra is represented by the color indigo and facilitates our inner wisdom, imagination, and higher consciousness.
- **The Crown Chakra (Sahasrara):** Located at the top of the head, it symbolizes our connection to the divine, spirituality, and enlightenment. Associated with the color violet or white, it governs our sense of purpose, higher consciousness, and the integration of our entire being.

These chakras harmoniously work together, keeping the energy flowing freely throughout our bodies. Balancing and aligning them can promote overall well-being and enhance various aspects of our lives. Remember, taking care of both your physical and energetic bodies lead to a more harmonious existence.

Techniques for Chakra Assessment and Diagnosis

By now, you know that it is essential to keep your chakras balanced and aligned to promote a healthy and harmonious life. Chakra assessment and diagnosis plays a crucial role in identifying any energy imbalances or blockages within these energy centers. In this section, we will explore some detailed techniques for conducting a thorough chakra assessment and diagnosis.

Visualization and Intuition

One of the primary techniques for chakra assessment is visualization and tapping into your intuition. This technique involves closing your eyes and visualizing each of the seven main chakras, starting from the root chakra and moving upwards to the crown chakra. Pay close attention to any sensations or images that come to mind as you focus on each chakra. Trust your intuition, as it may guide you to areas that require attention or healing.

Hand Sensing

Another effective technique for chakra assessment is hand sensing. Begin by finding a quiet and comfortable space. Close your eyes, take deep breaths, and center yourself. Gently extend your receptive hand, keeping it relaxed and open. Slowly move your hand towards your body, about 5 to 6 inches away from each chakra. Pay attention to any variations in temperature, pressure, or tingling sensations you may feel in your hand as you scan each chakra. Note any inconsistencies or areas that may require further examination.

Pendulum Dowsing

Pendulum dowsing is a technique that utilizes a small, weighted object, such as a crystal pendant, attached to a string or chain. This technique allows you to tune into the energy flow of each chakra. Hold the pendulum over each chakra, maintaining a relaxed state of mind. Observe the direction and movement of the pendulum as it interacts with each chakra. Clockwise rotation indicates a balanced and open chakra, while counterclockwise or erratic movements may suggest energy imbalances or blockages.

Aura Photography

Modern technology has brought about an innovative technique for chakra assessment known as aura photography. Aura photography uses specialized equipment to capture the energy field (aura) surrounding the body. By analyzing the colors, density, and patterns within the aura, practitioners can identify specific areas of imbalance or disharmony. Aura photography offers a visual representation of the chakras and can be an effective diagnostic tool.

Energy Scanning

Energy scanning is a technique that involves running your hands or fingertips slowly over the body, searching for areas of energy disruption or imbalance. Start from the head, moving down towards the feet, being mindful of any sensations, heat, coldness, or changes beneath your fingertips. Pay close attention to any areas that feel denser, stagnant, or devoid of energy. These are signals of potential chakra imbalances that may require further examination.

Muscle Testing

Muscle testing, also known as applied kinesiology, is a technique used to assess the energy flow and strength of individual chakras. With the help of a partner, stand or sit in a relaxed position. Have your partner gently touch each of your chakras while maintaining a constant pressure. As they touch each chakra, you will resist their pressure by pushing against it. Observe if you can easily resist the pressure or if there is a change in your strength, which may signify a chakra imbalance.

Chakra Balancing Tools

Another technique for chakra assessment involves the use of tools designed specifically for balancing and diagnosing these energy centers. These tools include chakra stones, crystals, tuning forks, and essential oils. By utilizing these tools, you can identify areas that require attention by noting any changes in energy levels, vibrations, or sensations in response to their use. These tools can also provide valuable insights into the overall health and alignment of your chakras.

Incorporating these detailed techniques for chakra assessment and diagnosis into your holistic well-being routine can assist in maintaining and promoting a balanced energy system. Remember, it is vital to approach the assessment process with an open mind and trust your intuition.

Chakra Balancing Practices and Their Effects

Chakra balancing practices are ancient techniques that involve aligning and harmonizing the body's energy centers, or chakras. These practices can help restore balance and promote overall well-being. In this section, we will explore 10 different chakra balancing practices and their effects. While all of these methods can be used, you may find that some call out to you more than others.

- **Meditation:** Meditation is a widely practiced technique that involves quietening the mind and focusing on the breath. When it comes to chakra balancing, meditation plays a crucial role. By focusing on each chakra, one can visualize its vibrant color and imagine the energy flowing freely through it. Regular meditation has been shown to calm the mind, reduce stress, and enhance overall energy flow.
- **Yoga:** Yoga combines physical postures, deep breathing, and meditation, making it a powerful practice for chakra balancing. Different yoga poses target specific chakras, promoting healing and balancing their energy. For example, Child's Pose stimulates the root chakra, while Cobra Pose can activate the heart chakra. Yoga enhances flexibility, strength, and overall physical and mental well-being.
- **Sound healing:** Sound has a profound impact on our energy centers. Sound healing involves using different frequencies and

vibrations to balance the chakras. Instruments such as Tibetan singing bowls, crystal bowls, and tuning forks can be used to produce specific tones. As the sound waves wash over the body, they help align and clear any blockages in the chakras. This practice promotes deep relaxation, reduces anxiety, and enhances the flow of energy.

- **Aromatherapy:** Aromatherapy utilizes essential oils derived from plants to promote healing and balance. Certain essential oils have specific properties that resonate with each chakra. For example, lavender oil is associated with the crown chakra and helps calm the mind and promote spiritual connectedness. Using essential oils through diffusers, massages, or baths can help restore balance and unleash the chakras' potential.

- **Crystals and gemstones:** Crystals and gemstones have unique energetic vibrations that can be used to activate and balance the chakras. Each chakra responds to specific stones, such as amethyst for the crown chakra or citrine for the solar plexus chakra. Placing these stones on the corresponding chakras during meditation or wearing them as jewelry can enhance energetic flow and promote healing.

- **Reiki:** While we're focusing on Reiki throughout this book, let's include it as part of this list as a way to balance chakras in practice. Of course, Reiki is a form of energy healing that involves the transfer of universal life force energy through the practitioner's hands. By channeling this energy, blockages in the chakras can be cleared, allowing for the free flow of energy. During a reiki session, the practitioner places their hands on or above the client's body, promoting relaxation, reducing pain, and restoring balance.

- **Color therapy:** Each chakra is associated with a specific color, and exposing oneself to these colors can have a profound effect on balancing the energy centers. Color therapy involves visualizing or surrounding oneself with these colors or using colored lights on the body. For example, surrounding oneself with blue light can support the throat chakra, enhancing communication and self-expression.

- **Breathwork:** Conscious breathwork techniques such as alternate nostril breathing, or the 4-7-8 breath can help balance and align the chakras. By bringing attention to the breath and consciously inhaling and exhaling, the energy flow can be balanced, promoting relaxation and stress reduction. Breathwork can also help release any emotional or energetic blockages in the chakras.
- **Nature connection:** Connecting with nature can have a grounding and healing effect on the chakras. Spending time outdoors, walking barefoot on grass, hugging trees, or even gardening can help balance the root chakra, promoting a sense of stability and security. Nature connection allows us to tap into the earth's energy and align our own energy centers.
- **Affirmations and mantras:** Affirmations and mantras are positive statements that can help reprogram the mind and shift energy towards balance. When used in combination with chakra healing, affirmations and mantras can target specific chakras. For instance, repeating "I am worthy of love" can support healing and balancing the heart chakra. Regularly using positive affirmations can transform negative thought patterns and promote overall chakra alignment.

Chakra balancing practices offer a holistic approach to healing and promoting overall well-being. Whether through meditation, yoga, sound healing, aromatherapy, crystals, or any of the other mentioned techniques, you can tap into the power of your energy centers to restore balance, enhance vitality, and maintain a sense of harmony in your mind, body, and spirit. Experiment with these practices to find what resonates with you and create your own unique chakra balancing routine.

Chapter 13

Integrating Reiki into Daily Life: Practical Applications

When you integrate Reiki into your daily routine, you open yourself up to a myriad of benefits. One of the most remarkable aspects of Reiki is its ability to not only alleviate physical pain and ailments but also nurture our emotional and spiritual well-being. By engaging with Reiki regularly, you can experience a profound sense of relaxation, release stress, and achieve a greater sense of inner peace.

Integrating Reiki into your daily lives also empowers you to take an active role in your own healing process. Through self-healing techniques, you can tap into the unlimited reservoir of healing energy that resides within you, accessing your innate power to promote health and harmony. Whether it is through self-treatments, meditation, or incorporating Reiki principles into your thoughts and actions, you become a catalyst of positive change in your life.

Additionally, your intuitive abilities and awareness are enhanced through regular Reiki use. This allows you to develop a deeper connection with yourself and those around you, fostering compassion, empathy, and understanding. Reiki teaches you to be present in the moment and appreciate the subtle energies that surround you, enabling you to live more consciously and authentically.

In this chapter, we will explore various ways to incorporate Reiki into your daily life. From morning rituals to bedtime practices, from workplace rejuvenation techniques to mindful eating, we will discover how Reiki can infuse every aspect of your existence with healing energy and profound transformation.

Using Reiki for Stress Reduction and Relaxation

In today's fast-paced and demanding world, stress has become an inevitable part of our lives. Finding ways to manage stress effectively is essential for maintaining a healthy mind and body.

Let's explore practical steps on how to utilize this practice for stress reduction and relaxation.

Preparing Yourself:

Before beginning a Reiki session, it is crucial to create a serene and peaceful space. Ensure that the room is tidy, well-ventilated, and free from distractions. Dimming the lights and playing soft, calming music can enhance the atmosphere and aid relaxation. It is also helpful to create a warm and comfortable environment by adjusting the temperature and providing soft cushions or blankets for the recipient.

Starting the Reiki Session:

- Begin by centering yourself. Take a few deep breaths, inhaling positivity and exhaling any tension or negativity. Focus on your intention to bring relaxation and stress reduction.
- Gently knock three times on the door of the room to energetically signal that you are entering a sacred space. This practice promotes respect and mindfulness.
- Stand near the recipient's head and visualize a connection between yourself, the earth, and the universal energy source. This connection will serve as a conduit for the flow of Reiki energy throughout the session.
- Place your hands in the Gassho position, with palms together in a prayer-like gesture, and take a moment to set your intention for the session. This can be as simple as a silent

affirmation, such as "May this Reiki session bring deep relaxation and stress reduction to (recipient's name)."
- Open the session by stating your intention out loud, addressing the higher powers or the recipient directly. For example, "I invoke the healing powers of Reiki to promote deep relaxation and stress reduction for (recipient's name)." This verbal acknowledgement sets the tone and invites the healing energy to flow.

The Reiki Hand Positions:

During a Reiki session, a series of hand positions are used to channel the energy into the recipient's body. These positions generally start from the head and progress towards the feet. It is essential to keep your hands relaxed, palms slightly cupped, and fingers together.

- **Head positions:** Starting with your hands above the recipient's head, allow the energy to flow down through your palms onto the head, face, and neck. After several minutes, move on to the other head positions, covering the temples, ears, and back of the head.
- **Neck and shoulder positions:** Place your hands gently on the shoulders or sides of the neck, allowing the energy to penetrate and release any tension. Move your hands down the shoulders and upper arms, directing the energy along the outer and inner parts.
- **Back positions:** Continue by placing your hands on the recipient's upper back, one slightly higher than the other. Gradually move your hands downward in parallel lines, covering the entire back. Focus on areas where tension or stress may be stored, providing extra attention and care.
- **Front positions:** Move to the front of the recipient, starting with hands over the heart area. Allow the energy to flow into the chest, abdomen, and pelvis. Progress downwards, covering the lower abdomen, hips, and upper thighs.

- **Conclusion:** Once you have completed the front positions, return to the recipient's head. Stand near their feet and send the energy down their body, ensuring that the energy has circulated through the entire system. Thank the universe or any higher powers you believe in for their assistance and guidance in the healing process.

Closing the Reiki Session:

- Gradually remove your hands from the recipient's body, ensuring a gentle transition.
- Take a few moments to ground yourself by placing your hands on the ground, visualizing any excess energy dissipating into the earth.
- Express gratitude to the higher powers or the recipient for their participation in the healing session. Offer a few kind and encouraging words to support their journey towards relaxation and stress reduction.
- Step out of the room, gently closing the door behind you. Symbolically, you are sealing the healing energy within the space and allowing the recipient to absorb its benefits.

Performing Reiki on Yourself

- **Find a quiet and peaceful space:** Start by finding a quiet and comfortable space where you can sit or lie down undisturbed. Make sure you have enough room to stretch out and relax.
- **Set the intention:** Close your eyes, take a few deep breaths, and set the intention to release stress and bring relaxation to your mind and body. Visualize yourself surrounded by a warm, healing light.
- **Hand placement:** Begin by placing your hands gently on your body, starting from the top of your head. You can also hold your hands slightly above your body if that feels more comfortable. The important thing is to listen to your intuition and go with whatever feels right to you.

- **Energy flow:** Allow the universal life force energy to flow through your hands and into your body. Imagine this energy flowing through you, clearing any energy blockages, and promoting relaxation.
- **Move through chakra points:** Spend a few minutes on each chakra point, starting from the crown of your head and moving down to the base of your spine. Simply place your hands on each area and feel the warmth and healing energy radiating from your palms.
- **Stay mindful:** As you perform self-reiki, keep your mind focused on the present moment. Try not to worry about the past or future. Instead, concentrate on the warmth and relaxation you're experiencing.
- **Trust your intuition:** If you feel drawn to a particular area of your body, spend more time there. Trust your intuition and let it guide you. It knows exactly where you need healing the most.
- **Take your time:** There's no rush when practicing self-reiki. Take your time and give yourself the gift of relaxation. You can spend as little as a few minutes or as long as you like. Experiment and see what feels best for you.
- **Gratitude and closure:** Once you've completed your self-reiki session, express gratitude for the healing energy you've received. Take a few moments to savor the relaxation and peace you've cultivated within yourself.

Reiki for Emotional Healing and Mental Clarity

Having covered stress and relaxation, let's now explore how to perform Reiki specifically for emotional healing and mental clarity. Whether you are a seasoned Reiki practitioner or a beginner, these step-by-step instructions will help you harness the healing energy of Reiki to promote emotional well-being and mental clarity.

Preparing Yourself and the Space:

- Find a quiet and comfortable space where you can perform your Reiki session. Ensure the room is well-ventilated and clutter-free.
- Ground and center yourself using deep breathing exercises. Relax your body and bring your mind into a calm and focused state.
- Cleanse the energy of the room by burning sage, incense, or using any preferred method of energy cleansing.
- Set your intention for the Reiki session. Focus on promoting emotional healing and mental clarity.

Preparing Your Reiki Tools:

- Ensure that you have a Reiki table, a comfortable mat, or a chair where the recipient can relax during the session.
- Gather any additional tools you may prefer to use during the session, such as crystals, essential oils, or soothing music that promotes relaxation.
- If you are using crystals, cleanse and charge them before the session according to your preferred method (e.g., sunlight, moonlight, water, etc.).

Basic Hand Positions:

- Position yourself near the recipient, standing or sitting, as feels comfortable for you.
- Beginning with the crown of the head, move your hands slowly towards the recipient's body, about 2-4 inches away, making gentle hovering motions.
- Use your intuition to guide you to the areas that need the most attention. Trust your instincts and allow your hands to naturally gravitate towards those areas.
- Keep your hands in each position for a few minutes or until you sense the energy flowing freely to that area.

- Note that hand positions can vary depending on the recipient's needs and comfort level. Adapt and adjust as necessary.

Scanning the Energy Field:

- To scan the recipient's energy field, hover your hands a few inches above their body from head to toe.
- Move your hands slowly and feel the energy field of the recipient. Pay attention to any areas where you feel imbalances, blockages, or temperature changes, as these can indicate areas in need of healing.
- Spend extra time in areas that feel unusually warm, cold, or dense, allowing Reiki energy to flow and promote healing.
- Trust your intuition, as it will guide you to the areas that require the most attention.

Releasing Emotional Blockages:

- As you encounter areas of emotional blockages, visualize them being surrounded and filled with healing Reiki energy.
- Use your hands to gently sweep away the negative energy or stagnant emotions from these areas, allowing them to be released and replaced with positive healing energy.
- Continue to move your hands, using circular motions, to facilitate the healing energy flow through these areas.
- Encourage the recipient to take deep breaths and imagine letting go of any emotional attachments or negative thoughts.

Balancing and Rejuvenating the Mind:

- When focusing on mental clarity, bring your attention to the recipient's head area.
- Gently place your hands on the sides of the head, or hover them above, and infuse the energy of Reiki to balance and rejuvenate the mind.
- Visualize the recipient's thoughts becoming clear and calm, free from any mental clutter or stress.

- Remind the recipient to relax and let go of any thoughts that may arise during the session, allowing the healing energy to clear their mind.

Closing the Session:

- Once you feel that the healing session is complete, gently remove your hands from the recipient's body.
- Thank the universal life force energy, your higher self, and any spiritual guides that you work with, for the healing support provided during the session.
- Offer gratitude to the recipient for allowing you to share Reiki energy with them.
- Give the recipient time to slowly come back to their surroundings before discussing their experience or offering any additional guidance.

Performing Reiki on Yourself

Here's a guide on how to perform Reiki on yourself to facilitate emotional healing and mental clarity:

- **Find a quiet and comfortable space:** Begin by finding a quiet and peaceful space where you can relax without any disturbances. It could be a room, a comfortable corner, or even outdoors, as long as you feel at ease.
- **Set your intentions:** Take a few moments to set your intentions for the Reiki session. This helps focus your energy on emotional healing and mental clarity. You can close your eyes, take some deep breaths, and visualize yourself transforming into a state of emotional balance and mental clarity.
- **Assume a comfortable position:** Sit or lie down in a position that is comfortable for you. It's essential to be at ease, so you can fully concentrate on the practice without any physical discomfort.
- **Activate Reiki energy flow:** With your hands resting gently on your lap or next to your body, close your eyes and take a

few deep breaths. Begin by visualizing a bright, warm light surrounding you, symbolizing the universal life force energy or Reiki. You can imagine this light entering through the top of your head and flowing throughout your body.

- **Place your hands:** Starting from your head, place your hands gently on different areas of your body, keeping them in each position for a few minutes. Some common hand positions include placing your palms on your forehead, the sides of your head, the back of your head, your heart, your stomach, and your hips. Follow your intuition and give attention to any specific areas that feel tense or in need of healing.

- **Focus your mind:** While your hands are placed on each position, bring your attention to that specific area of the body. Take deep breaths and imagine the Reiki energy flowing through your hands, bringing emotional healing and mental clarity to that part of your body. You can also repeat affirmations silently, such as "I release emotional blockages" or "I cultivate mental clarity."

- **Allow the energy to flow:** Remember, Reiki is a gentle and profound healing practice that works in harmony with your body's natural energy. While your hands are placed, trust that the energy will flow to where it's needed most for emotional healing and mental clarity. Avoid forcefully trying to change or manipulate the results and instead, allow the Reiki energy to do its work.

- **Complete the session:** After you have placed your hands on all the desired positions, take a few moments to thank the Reiki energy for its healing and supportive presence. Gradually bring your awareness back to your surroundings by wiggling your fingers, toes, and slowly opening your eyes.

Reiki for Physical Health and Well-being

Before we delve into how to perform Reiki for physical health and wellbeing, it is important to note that Reiki should not replace traditional medical treatment. It can, however, serve as a complementary therapy that works alongside conventional medicine.

- **Ground yourself:** Start by grounding yourself to establish a strong connection with the earth's energy. You can accomplish this by sitting or standing comfortably, closing your eyes, and taking a few deep breaths. Visualize roots growing from your feet, connecting you to the Earth's core and drawing in its healing energy.
- **Hand positions:** When performing Reiki on others, it is recommended to follow a predetermined set of hand positions. Start by placing your hands gently on the recipient's head, allowing the energy to flow through your hands and into their body. Move your hands systematically through each position, covering areas such as the temples, ears, base of the skull, neck, shoulders, chest, abdomen, hips, knees, and feet. Remember to maintain a light touch and allow the energy to flow naturally.
- **Energy sensations:** As you perform Reiki, be open to the sensations you may experience. You may feel warmth or tingling in your hands, or you may perceive shifts in energy or emotions. Trust these sensations as signs that the energy is working and flowing through you and the recipient.
- **Focus on problem areas:** If the recipient has specific physical concerns, spend extra time and attention on these areas. Use your hands to channel Reiki energy directly onto these points, allowing the healing energy to penetrate deeply into the affected areas.
- **Closing the session:** When you feel the Reiki session is complete, gently remove your hands and offer gratitude for the healing energy that has flowed through you. Advise the recipient to take their time before getting up, as they may feel relaxed or light-headed after the session.

Post-Reiki Session:

- **Hydrate:** Encourage the recipient, and yourself if applicable, to drink plenty of water following a Reiki session. This aids in

the detoxification process and helps to energize and rehydrate the body.
- **Rest and reflect:** After a Reiki session, it's important to rest and allow the body to integrate the healing energy. Some individuals may experience a shift in energy, emotions, or physical sensations, so taking time for relaxation and reflection is beneficial.
- **Follow-up:** Depending on the recipient's specific needs, it may be beneficial to schedule regular Reiki sessions. Each person's healing journey is unique, and consistent Reiki can help maintain balance and promote ongoing physical health and wellbeing.

Here's a step-by-step guide on how to perform Reiki on yourself for physical health and wellbeing:

- **Find a quiet and peaceful space:** Start by finding a quiet and peaceful space where you won't be disturbed. This helps create an environment conducive to relaxation and focus.
- **Get comfortable:** Sit or lie down in a comfortable position. You can use pillows and blankets to support your body and ensure you're completely at ease.
- **Set your intention:** Before you begin, take a moment to set your intention for the session. It can be something like "I am open to the healing energy of Reiki for my physical health and well-being."
- **Activate Reiki energy:** Hold your hands in front of your heart, with your palms facing each other. Imagine a warm and bright light emanating from the center of your chest and visualize it flowing into your hands. This activates the Reiki energy.
- **Begin with self-healing hand positions:** Place your hands gently on different areas of your body, using the following hand positions as a guide:
- **Crown:** Place your hands on the top of your head.
- **Third Eye:** Position your hands over your forehead, between your eyebrows.

- **Throat:** Rest your hands lightly on your throat.
- **Heart:** Place your hands on your chest, near your heart.
- **Solar Plexus:** Position your hands just above your navel.
- **Sacral:** Rest your hands just below your navel.
- **Root:** Place your hands on your pelvic area.
- **Channel the energy:** As you place your hands on each position, imagine the healing energy flowing from your palms into the corresponding area. Picture any tension or discomfort being dissolved and replaced with a sense of relaxation and balance.
- **Spend time on areas of concern:** If you have specific areas of concern, such as an injury or pain, spend extra time gently holding your hands there, allowing the energy to focus on that part of your body.
- **Trust your intuition:** While following the suggested hand positions and general guidelines is helpful, remember that your intuition and personal connection to Reiki are important. Feel free to adjust your hand positions or additional areas to focus on based on what feels right for you.
- **Conclude the session:** After spending time on all the hand positions or as long as you feel is necessary, slowly bring your session to a close. Express gratitude for the healing energy and the benefits received.

Remember, practicing regularly will help you develop a deeper connection with the energy and maximize the benefits for your physical health and overall well-being.

Chapter 14

Enhancing Reiki Practice with Meditation and Mindfulness

Meditation, a practice of calming the mind and cultivating self-awareness, acts as a powerful ally in your Reiki journey. By stepping into a state of deep relaxation and mindfulness, you create an ideal environment for energy work to thrive. Amidst the stillness, you can tune into your intuition, heighten your sensitivity to energy, and open yourself to a heightened connection with the universal life force. Through meditation, you can also cultivate a sense of grounding, presence, and clarity, which are invaluable qualities for any Reiki practitioner.

Mindfulness, the art of being fully present in the moment, is another transformative practice that can supercharge your Reiki sessions. By cultivating an attitude of non-judgmental awareness, you can become attuned to the subtle shifts in energy and the healing process unfolding before you. Mindfulness allows you to engage with your Reiki practice with more clarity, compassion, and authenticity, while fostering a deeper connection with your clients.

When combined with meditation and mindfulness, Reiki can unlock even greater possibilities. In this chapter, let's explore how these different practices work hand-in-hand.

The Synergy of Reiki and Meditation

In today's fast-paced world, stress and imbalance have become the norm for many people. Fortunately, various holistic practices have emerged to help restore equilibrium and promote overall well-being. Two such practices, Reiki and meditation, have gained significant popularity in recent years. Both techniques work synergistically to enhance spiritual growth, foster self-awareness, and facilitate healing on multiple levels.

Let's dig deeper into the profound synergy between Reiki and meditation, shedding light on their individual benefits and explaining how their combined practice can lead to deep inner harmony and healing.

While Reiki and meditation are powerful in their own right, combining these practices boosts their efficacy and potential benefits. The synergy between Reiki and meditation lies in their shared focus on energy, intention, and relaxation.

- **Energy alignment:** Reiki and meditation both seek to balance the energy flow within the body. Of course, when practicing Reiki, you act as a conduit for universal life force energy, channeling it into the recipient's body to dissolve energy blockages and promote healing. Meditation, on the other hand, allows you to connect with your inner energy, becoming aware of any imbalances and facilitating their own energy alignment. By practicing both techniques, you can enhance your ability to sense energy imbalances and cultivate self-healing capabilities.
- **Intention and focus:** The power of intention is central to both Reiki and meditation. During a Reiki session, your direct your intention toward promoting healing, while the recipient aligns their intentions with their desired outcomes. Similarly, meditation cultivates focused intention, guiding you toward your desired state of being. The combination of Reiki and meditation magnifies intention, enabling you to tap into your subconscious mind and manifest positive changes in your life.

- **Deep relaxation and healing:** Reiki and meditation share a common goal of facilitating relaxation and providing a space for deep healing. Reiki sessions often induce a state of deep relaxation, allowing recipients to release stress, tension, and emotional blockages. Meditation, through its calming and centering effects, promotes relaxation and activates the body's natural healing processes. When practiced together, Reiki and meditation create a harmonious environment that encourages profound healing on physical, emotional, and spiritual levels.

Overall, Reiki and meditation are complementary practices that work synergistically to promote holistic healing, self-awareness, and spiritual growth. The combination of Reiki's energy healing and meditation's mindfulness and focus creates a powerful synergy that enhances the benefits of each practice.

Incorporating Reiki into meditation practice deepens your connection to universal life force energy while amplifying the intention and relaxation experienced during meditation. By embracing the synergy between Reiki and meditation, you can unlock your inner harmony, foster self-healing, and embark on a transformative journey towards overall wellness and balance.

Mindful Approaches to Reiki Practice

Reiki is not just about transferring energy from the practitioner to the recipient, but it also involves using mindful approaches to enhance the overall experience for both parties involved. Mindfulness, essentially the practice of being fully present and aware, can be seamlessly integrated into Reiki sessions, deepening the healing process, and leading to transformative experiences.

In this section, let's explore some of the mindful approaches that can be applied within Reiki practice.

- **Cultivating presence:** The foundation of any mindful practice begins with cultivating presence. As a Reiki practitioner, it is essential to be fully present and focused in the moment, both physically and mentally. This means being aware of your body, breath, and emotions, as well as observing the environment and the recipient's energy. Take a few moments before each session to ground yourself, connect with your breath, and set your intention to be fully present.

- **Non-judgmental mind:** Mindfulness teaches you to observe without judgment. When practicing Reiki, this principle applies not only to the recipient but also to yourself as a practitioner. Avoid labeling any sensations or emotions that arise during the session as "good" or "bad." Instead, observe them with curiosity and an open mind. By cultivating a non-judgmental attitude, you create a safe space for the recipient to fully delve into their own healing process without fear of being judged.
- **Active listening:** Mindful Reiki practice involves active listening on multiple levels. Firstly, listen to the recipient's words and concerns before the session begins, allowing them to openly express their intentions and needs. Secondly, during the session, listen to the recipient's non-verbal cues such as body language, facial expressions, and energy. By being attentive to the recipient's needs and responding accordingly, the healing experience becomes more personalized and profound.
- **Intuitive awareness:** Mindful Reiki practice encourages the development of intuitive awareness. Tap into your intuition and allow it to guide your hands during the session. Trust the sensations and insights that arise as you move through the recipient's energy field. Intuition can help you identify areas that require additional attention, allowing the healing energy to flow where it is most needed.
- **Deepening breath:** The breath is a powerful tool for grounding and deepening the Reiki experience. Encourage the recipient to take slow, deep breaths throughout the session. As a practitioner, synchronize your breath with the recipient's, creating a subtle connection and fostering a sense of harmony. Pay attention to your breath as well, allowing it to anchor you

in the present moment and flow through you as you channel healing energy.

- **Mindful touch:** Touch is an integral part of Reiki practice. Mindful touch entails being fully present and attentive during each contact with the recipient's body. Focus on the sensations in your hands, consciously feeling the warmth and energy being exchanged. Maintain a light touch that respects the recipient's boundaries and comfort level. Each touch should be intentional, offering healing energy with love and compassion.

- **Reflective practice:** After each Reiki session, engage in reflective practice to deepen your understanding and connection with the healing process. Spend some time journaling about your experience, noting any insights, emotions, or observations that arise. Reflecting on your sessions allows you to learn from each encounter, discover patterns, and assess your growth as a Reiki practitioner.

- **Self-care:** Lastly, self-care is an essential component of mindful Reiki practice. As a practitioner, ensure that you prioritize your own well-being and maintain Balance between giving and receiving. Take time for self-Reiki sessions to replenish your own energy. Engage in activities that bring you joy and relaxation, as these will contribute to enhancing your presence and energy during Reiki sessions.

Incorporating mindful approaches into Reiki practice can significantly deepen the healing experience for both you and the recipient. By embracing the mindful approaches mentioned in this section, Reiki sessions can become more meaningful and impactful, fostering holistic healing on physical, emotional, and spiritual levels.

Guided Meditation Practices for Reiki Practitioners

Guided meditation is a powerful tool that can greatly enhance your Reiki practice. By combining the healing energies of Reiki with the deep relaxation and focus of meditation, you can elevate your abilities and tap into a heightened state of awareness and connection.

In this section, we will delve into the essence of guided meditation practices specifically designed for Reiki practitioners. We will explore different techniques, benefits, and how they can be seamlessly incorporated into a Reiki session.

Benefits of Guided Meditation for Reiki Practitioners

Guided meditation offers several remarkable benefits. Firstly, it helps to cultivate a deep sense of relaxation, quieting the mind and centering the energy. This state of calmness allows you to connect with your clients on a more profound level, thereby enhancing the effectiveness of the Reiki energy transfer. Guided meditation also aids in reducing stress and anxiety, which is especially beneficial for clients who may have specific concerns or emotional blockages.

Moreover, guided meditation can help to enhance your intuitive abilities by creating a space of inner stillness and receptivity. This heightened awareness allows you to better perceive the subtle energy flows within the client's body, further improving your ability to target specific areas requiring healing. Additionally, by incorporating guided imagery and visualization techniques during meditation, you can awaken and utilize your imagination, enabling powerful symbolic healing experiences and profound transformative shifts within yourself and your clients.

Techniques for Guided Meditation in Reiki Practice

Breath Awareness Technique: Begin by guiding the client to focus on their breath, gently bringing their attention to each inhalation and exhalation. Encourage slow, deep breaths to cultivate relaxation. As they become more centered, you can then guide the client through various affirmations or intentions that align with the Reiki session's goals.

Body Scan Technique: With this technique, you guide the client's attention to different parts of their body, focusing on any tension or areas of discomfort. By bringing awareness to these areas and using Reiki energy, you can help release physical and emotional blockages and promote healing.

Chakra Balancing Technique: This technique aims to harmonize and balance the client's energy centers or chakras. You can guide the client's attention to each chakra individually, using guided imagery and visualization to visualize the chakra spinning and vibrant with energy. The Reiki energy amplifies the effects of this technique, facilitating the restoration of balance and flow within the client's energy system.

Journey Visualization Technique: This technique involves guiding the client through a visualization journey, creating a safe and serene landscape in their mind's eye. You can guide them to encounter various symbols or beings that represent their healing and personal growth. Reiki energy can be infused into these visualizations to deepen their impact and facilitate powerful inner transformations.

Incorporating Guided Meditation into Reiki Sessions

By creating a meditative atmosphere and facilitating a focused state, you can enhance the client's receptiveness to the healing energies and create a deeper sense of relaxation.

Before beginning the Reiki session, spend a few minutes guiding the client through a brief meditation, utilizing any of the techniques mentioned above. This allows for the establishment of a calm and grounded state before the energy transfer commences.

During the Reiki session, continue to guide the client through visualizations or affirmations, encouraging them to remain present and open to the healing energies. This can help in maintaining the client's focus and deepen their experience by connecting with the energy on a conscious level.

By incorporating these techniques into your practice, you can tap into a deeper understanding of energetic healing, expand your intuitive abilities, and create a profound space for transformation and growth. The fusion of guided meditation and Reiki opens up a world of possibilities, allowing you to create a truly holistic and transformative healing experience for all those seeking your care.

Chapter 15

Conclusion – Continuing Your Reiki Journey: Further Resources and Next Steps

Our journey through the fascinating world of Reiki has brought us to a profound understanding and appreciation for this ancient healing practice. Throughout this book, we have delved into the history, origins, principles, techniques, and benefits of Reiki, granting us a comprehensive view of its transformative power.

One of the most remarkable aspects of Reiki is its ability to go beyond conventional medicine and touch the realms of energy and spirituality. By harnessing universal life-force energy, you are able to facilitate healing on physical, emotional, and spiritual levels. We have witnessed the incredible harmony and balance that Reiki brings to us, promoting overall well-being and connecting us to our inner selves.

Reiki is a beacon of hope in our fast-paced and stressful modern lives. It provides you with an opportunity to pause, breathe, and reconnect with your inner essence. By aligning your energy centers, Reiki allows you to release blockages, negative emotions, and stagnant energy, paving the way for vitality, clarity, and peace to flow through your being.

Throughout this journey, we have explored the different techniques used in Reiki, such as hand positions, distant healing, and the use of symbols. Each technique serves as a tool to channel healing energy, harmonize the chakras, and address specific ailments or conditions. The flexibility and adaptability of Reiki make it an accessible and versatile practice for anyone seeking to enhance their well-being or support the healing process.

Furthermore, Reiki is not limited to the individual level; it holds the potential for collective healing and transformation. By sending distant healing to loved ones or even places or situations in need, you tap into the interconnectedness of all beings. This realization opens up infinite possibilities for healing on a global scale and fostering a world filled with compassion, love, and understanding.

The spiritual dimension of Reiki cannot be overlooked either. As you embark on this journey, you come face to face with your own spirituality, discovering your higher self and connecting with the divine. Reiki becomes a medium through which you can deepen your spiritual connection and uncover the brighter aspects of your own existence. It facilitates personal growth, self-awareness, and empowers you to live from a place of authenticity and love.

Of course, Reiki also intertwines with other holistic practices and modalities, complementing and enhancing their effects. Whether combined with massage therapy, meditation, yoga, or aromatherapy, Reiki amplifies the benefits of these practices, creating a harmonious synergy. The integration of Reiki into mainstream healthcare systems is also gaining recognition and acceptance, as its positive effects on patients become increasingly evident.

The Journey Ahead

As we come to the end of this book, it is essential to acknowledge the incredible potential within you to become a catalyst for healing and change. Reiki is not limited to a select few; it is available to all who are willing to embrace it. By becoming attuned to Reiki energy and committing to your personal practice, you gain the ability to self-heal and support others on their healing journey.

In essence, Reiki invites you to reclaim your innate power as a healer, empowering you to contribute positively to the well-being of yourself and the world around you. It teaches you to radiate love, compassion, and healing energy, serving as a reminder that you are an integral part of a greater whole.

As we close this book, carry the profound wisdom of Reiki in your heart and spirit, allowing it to guide you toward a life of balance, harmony, and fulfillment. May Reiki continue to empower you to embrace your true self, heal your wounds, and spread love and healing wherever you go.

It's now time to embark on your own personal journey with Reiki. Take the first step in attaining your attunement and immerse yourself in the transformative energy that awaits you. Let the exploration of Reiki be a continual source of growth, self-discovery, and healing.

Continuing Education and Advanced Training in Reiki

As you deepen your understanding and experience with Reiki, you may seek continuing education and advanced training to expand your knowledge, skills, and mastery. Before we close this book, let's explore the importance of continuing your education, the various avenues available for advanced training, and the benefits of embarking on this journey of growth and development.

Continuing education in Reiki is not only beneficial for personal growth but also for professional development. It allows you to deepen your understanding of Reiki's principles, techniques, and applications. By acquiring new knowledge and skills, you can confidently address a wider range of physical, emotional, and spiritual issues in yourself and/or your clients.

- **Expanding your knowledge base:** Continuing education provides you with the opportunity to explore various aspects of Reiki that may not have been covered in your initial training. Advanced courses delve deeper into topics such as energy anatomy, chakra balancing, and distance healing, expanding your understanding of how energy works and how it can be utilized for healing purposes.

- **Strengthening your skills:** Reiki is not just about the transfer of healing energy but also about your ability to intuitively navigate the energetic field. Advanced training enhances your skills in sensing, interpreting, and channeling energy, enabling you to be more effective healers. You gain a deeper understanding of hand positions, symbols, and mantras, empowering you to provide targeted and customized healing sessions.
- **Mastering different Reiki systems:** There are multiple Reiki systems and lineages, each with its unique techniques and approaches. By pursuing advanced training, you can explore different systems like Usui, Karuna, or Tibetan Reiki. Learning from different lineages broadens your perspective and allows for a more holistic approach to healing. It also opens up opportunities to incorporate other modalities or create personal blends of Reiki techniques.

Avenues for Advanced Training

There are several avenues and resources available to expand your Reiki knowledge and skills.

- **Reiki Master Teachers:** Reiki Master Teachers (RMTs) offer advanced training, attunements, and certifications. They have reached the highest level in their Reiki lineage and are equipped to guide practitioners on their journey towards mastery. RMTs often offer workshops, retreats, and mentorship programs to further develop your skills and understanding.
- **Reiki Associations and Organizations:** There are numerous Reiki associations and organizations that provide resources, workshops, and conferences for continuing education. These events bring together Reiki practitioners from various backgrounds, offering opportunities for networking, exchanging knowledge, and learning from experienced instructors. Attending these gatherings can be a valuable

experience for both personal growth and professional development.

- **Online Courses and Webinars:** In today's digital age, online courses and webinars have become a popular platform for learning. Many experienced Reiki practitioners and trainers offer virtual workshops, allowing you to access advanced training from the comfort of your own home. These online resources often include recorded lectures, demonstrations, and interactive forums for questions and discussions.

Finding Reiki Communities and Support Networks

One of the best places to start your search for Reiki communities and support networks is online. The internet has made it easier than ever to connect with people who have similar interests, and Reiki is no exception. There are numerous websites, forums, and social media groups dedicated to Reiki where you can find a wealth of information, share experiences, and connect with fellow practitioners from all over the globe.

One popular online platform for Reiki enthusiasts is social media. Platforms like Facebook, X/Twitter, Instagram, and LinkedIn have dedicated Reiki groups where you can connect with practitioners and teachers. Simply search for relevant keywords like "Reiki community," "Reiki support," or "Reiki practitioners" to get started. Joining these groups will allow you to engage in discussions, ask questions, and even find local Reiki events or training opportunities.

In addition to social media, there are several Reiki-specific websites and forums where you can find a community of like-minded individuals. Websites like The Reiki Association, Reiki.org, and International Center for Reiki Training have forums where you can interact with other practitioners, seek advice, and find Reiki events happening in your area. These platforms also often have directories that list certified Reiki practitioners and teachers, making it easy for you to find someone to connect with or receive treatment from.

Another great way to find Reiki communities is by attending local Reiki events, seminars, and workshops. Many cities offer Reiki shares or healing circles where practitioners come together to practice and share experiences. These events often attract a diverse group of practitioners, ranging from beginners to advanced healers, providing a supportive and nurturing environment for all. Attending these events not only allows you to connect with fellow practitioners but also provides an opportunity to expand your knowledge and skills through workshops and presentations by experienced Reiki teachers.

To find local Reiki events, you can search online event listings, sign up for Reiki newsletters, or reach out to Reiki teachers and practitioners in your area. They may be aware of upcoming events or regular meetups that you can attend. Additionally, consider contacting holistic healing centers, yoga studios, or wellness retreats in your area, as they often host Reiki events or have Reiki practitioners on their team.

Another avenue to explore is joining Reiki membership organizations or associations. These organizations are dedicated to promoting Reiki as a healing practice and often offer numerous benefits to their members, including access to a network of practitioners, ongoing education, resources, and opportunities for professional development. By becoming a member of such organizations, you can connect with like-minded individuals, stay up-to-date on the latest developments in the field, and even gain credibility as a certified Reiki practitioner.

One well-known Reiki membership organization is the Reiki Membership Association founded by the International Center for Reiki Training. They provide a directory of professional Reiki practitioners, teachers, and masters, making it easier for you to find and connect with others in your area. Additionally, the organization offers benefits such as liability insurance, group

Conclusion – Continuing Your Reiki Journey: Further Resources and Next Steps

rates on products and services, and opportunities to attend Reiki conferences and workshops.

In addition to online platforms, local events, and membership organizations, consider seeking out personal recommendations. If you have friends or acquaintances who have experience with Reiki, ask them if they are aware of any Reiki communities or support networks in your area. Personal recommendations can often lead to valuable connections and introductions to individuals who share your passion for Reiki.

Overall, enhancing your practice will only bring added results. Take all of this knowledge and move forward with your journey, safe in the knowledge that you will not only benefit yourself, but many others too.

References

Admin, T. (2023, November 23). *Balancing The Body’s Energy Flow with Reiki*. Chester Wellness Centre. https://www.chesterwellnesscentre.co.uk/balancing-the-bodys-energy-flow-with-reiki/

Admin, W. (2023, June 14). *Chakra balancing with Reiki- 4 things you should know*. Omega Hub. https://omegahub.co.uk/reiki-healing/chakra-balancing/#:~:text=By%20placing%20their%20hands%20on,flow%20throughout%20the%20energy%20centres.

Administrator, R. (2019, September 10). *What is Reiki?* Reiki. https://www.reiki.org/faqs/what-reiki

Administrator, R. (2020, May 26). *What is the History of Reiki?* Reiki. https://www.reiki.org/faqs/what-history-reiki

Adminrtr. (2022, April 5). *How to remember the Reiki hand positions*. Reiki Therapy Resources. https://www.reikitherapyresources.com/hand-positions/

Amanda, & Amanda. (2019, November 15). *Empowerment or attunement*. New Earth Energies. https://newearthenergies.org/empowerment-or-attunement/

Bedosky, L. (2023, January 17). *Reiki: How this energy healing works and its health benefits*. EverydayHealth.com. https://www.everydayhealth.com/reiki/

Chakra Balancing & Reiki | The Breathing Space. (2023, May 11). The Breathing Space. https://breathingspaceyogastudio.co.uk/chakra-balancing-and-reiki/

Department of Health & Human Services. (n.d.). *Reiki*. Better Health Channel. https://www.betterhealth.vic.gov.au/health/conditionsandtreatments/reiki#:~:text=The%20underlying%20philosophy%20of%20reiki,feel%20more%20relaxed%20and%20peaceful.

Gibbons, K. (2021, March 19). *What is Reiki Meditation? - Meditation Magazine*. Meditation Magazine. https://www.meditationmag.com/blog/what-is-reiki/

Grundy, E. H. (2023, May 29). *Self-healing and self-attunement with Reiki*. The Reiki Centre. https://www.reiki-centre.com/post/self-healing-and-self-attunement-with-reiki

Holland, K. (2023, April 18). *What is an aura? and 15 other questions, answered*. Healthline. https://www.healthline.com/health/what-is-an-aura

Jones, H. (2024, March 2). *Reiki: Everything you need to know*. Verywell Health. https://www.verywellhealth.com/reiki-therapy-6362562

Kendall, J. (2019, July 5). *Reiki meditation*. Reiki. https://www.reiki.org/articles/reiki-meditation

King, T. (2015, September 29). *Attunements and Empowerments: What is the Difference? | Reiki Evolution*. Reiki Evolution | Learn Original Japanese Reiki for Peace & Inner Calm. https://www.reiki-evolution.co.uk/attunements-and-empowerments-what-is-the-difference/

Lisapowers. (2022, November 30). *How I perform a Reiki session - Lisa Powers - official site*. Lisa Powers - Official Site. https://lisapowers.co/how-i-perform-a-reiki-session/

Marshall, L. (2024, February 29). *Reiki Symbols: meaning and drawings of each*. Drawings Of. . . https://drawingsof.com/reiki-symbols/

mindbodygreen. (2022, September 23). *What everyone should know about energy healing*. Mindbodygreen. https://www.mindbodygreen.com/articles/surprising-facts-about-energy-healing

mindbodygreen. (2023a, May 11). *Everything you've ever wanted to know about the 7 chakras in the body*. Mindbodygreen. https://www.mindbodygreen.com/articles/7-chakras-for-beginners

mindbodygreen. (2023b, June 15). *Reiki Symbols & Their Meanings: Everything you need to know*. Mindbodygreen. https://www.mindbodygreen.com/articles/reiki-symbols-meanings

Newman, T. (2023, June 14). *Everything you need to know about Reiki*. https://www.medicalnewstoday.com/articles/308772#:~:text=The%20word%20%E2%80%9CReiki%E2%80%9D%20means%20%E2%80%9C,injury%20or%20even%20emotional%20pain.

Nunez, K. (2020, August 24). *How to use Reiki principles to Boost Well-Being*. Healthline. https://www.healthline.com/health/reiki-principles

Rand, W. (2019, July 5). *Reiki and affirmations*. Reiki. https://www.reiki.org/articles/reiki-and-affirmations

Reiki Flow. (2024, March 30). *Home - Reiki Flow*. https://reikiflow.ie/

Rmt. (2024, February 26). *Affirmations for Reiki Practitioners: To honour your Reiki Practice*. Reiki

Healing Association. https://reikihealingassociation.com/affirmations-for-reiki-practitioners-to-honour-your-reiki-practice/

Shah, P., & Shah, P. (2023, July 6). *I’m a Reiki Master Teacher, and Here’s How I Practice Self-Healing on a Regular Basis*. Well+Good. https://www.wellandgood.com/reiki-self-healing/

Stelter, G. (2023, February 13). *A beginner's guide to the 7 chakras and their meanings*. Healthline. https://www.healthline.com/health/fitness-exercise/7-chakras#Chakra-101

The history of Reiki. (n.d.). Georgiana Monckton Reiki. https://www.georgianamoncktonreiki.com/the-history-of-reiki.php#:~:text=Reiki%20is%20a%20method%20of,Dr%20Mikao%20Usui%20rediscovered%20it.

Tnn. (2019, August 16). *5 most effective energy healing techniques and how they work*. The Times of India. https://timesofindia.indiatimes.com/life-style/health-fitness/home-remedies/5-most-effective-energy-healing-techniques-and-how-they-work/articleshow/70698807.cms

Walsh, S. (2022, September 14). *10 traditional Reiki hand positions you should know*. Protectivity - Insurance. https://www.protectivity.com/knowledge-centre/10-traditional-reiki-hand-positions-you-should-know/

Welch, A. (2023, July 11). *What is energy healing?* EverydayHealth.com. https://www.everydayhealth.com/integrative-health/energy-healing/guide/

What Is Reiki, and Does it Really Work? (2024, March 19). Cleveland Clinic. https://health.clevelandclinic.org/reiki

Wikipedia contributors. (2024a, February 5). *Aura (paranormal)*. Wikipedia. https://en.wikipedia.org/wiki/Aura_(paranormal)

Wikipedia contributors. (2024b, March 31). *Reiki*. Wikipedia. https://en.wikipedia.org/wiki/Reiki

CHAKRA HEALING FOR BEGINNERS

Harness the Power of Your Vagus Nerve and the Chakras to Unlock Inner Energy and Achieve Balance

MONIKA DANIEL

Chapter 1

Introduction to Chakra Healing

Welcome to the exciting world of chakra healing. Get ready to dive deep into the mystical realm of your energetic centers and discover the transformative power within you.

Chakra healing is rooted in ancient Eastern traditions, focusing on restoring balance and alignment to the body, mind, and spirit. Picture your chakras as spinning wheels of energy, each responsible for different aspects of your well-being. From grounding and stability to creativity and intuition, these energy centers are vital to your overall health and happiness.

Before we embark on this adventure together, it's important to note that chakra healing is not just about wearing crystals or practicing yoga (although those can definitely be part of it!). It goes much deeper than that. It's about understanding the interconnectedness of your body and mind and learning to cultivate harmony within.

Throughout this book, we'll explore each chakra in detail, learning how to recognize imbalances and blockages that may be affecting your life. We'll uncover powerful techniques, such as meditation, affirmations, and energy healing, to restore energy flow within your chakras.

The History of Chakra Healing

Let's delve into the origins and evolution of chakra healing, exploring its historical ties to various cultures and its interconnectedness with Ayurveda - the ancient Indian system of medicine. Get ready to uncover the stories behind the alignment of energy within the body and the profound impact it continues to have on modern holistic healing.

Origins of Chakra Healing

The roots of chakra healing lie in ancient Vedic scriptures, known as the Vedas, originating in India over 5,000 years ago. These sacred texts introduced the concept of energy centers within the human body, suggesting that these centers play a crucial role in maintaining physical, mental, and spiritual well-being.

According to Vedic teachings, the human body contains seven primary chakras, with each chakra corresponding to distinct physiological and psychological functions. These energy centers are said to be located along the spine, from the base to the crown of the head. Each chakra is associated with a specific color, element, sound, and psychological state, forming a complex system that influences our overall health.

Evolution and Cultural Influences

As chakra healing evolved, it spread across various cultures and regions. In ancient Egypt, the concepts of the chakras can be traced in their teachings on the "Ka" or life force. Similarly, Traditional Chinese Medicine emphasizes the flow of vital energy known as "Qi," which shares similarities with the principles of chakra healing.

The emergence of Ayurveda brought new dimensions to the practice of chakra healing. Ayurveda recognizes that imbalances within the chakras can lead to physical and emotional ailments. Thus, restoring balance to these energy centers became crucial to Ayurvedic healing.

Chakra Healing in Ayurveda

Ayurveda employs various techniques to restore balance and harmony to the chakras. These include lifestyle modifications, dietary guidelines, herbal treatments, yoga, meditation, and the use of specific sound vibrations (mantras). Ayurvedic practitioners assess the state of an individual's chakras by observing physical symptoms, emotional patterns, and energy imbalances.

Over centuries, chakra healing transcended geographical boundaries and gained global recognition. In recent times, it has found its place in the realm of modern holistic healing practices. With a growing interest in spiritual and alternative approaches to wellness, chakra healing has garnered a dedicated following, integrating seamlessly with various modalities such as Reiki, crystal healing, and aromatherapy.

Science and Chakra Healing

While chakra healing remains a subject of debate within scientific circles, some modern studies have explored the potential benefits of these practices. These studies often examine correlations between energetic imbalances and physical or emotional disturbances, providing a basis for further investigation into the efficacy of chakra healing.

Overview of the Chakras and Their Significance

There are seven main chakras, starting from the base of the spine and going up to the crown of the head. Each chakra has its own unique qualities and is associated with specific organs, emotions, and states of being. They're like energetic powerhouses that contribute to our overall balance and harmony.

Now, why are these chakras significant, you ask? Well, picture them as the fuel stations of our energetic system. When our chakras are open and balanced, the energy flows freely, allowing us to feel vibrant, grounded, and at ease. On the other hand, if a chakra is blocked or imbalanced, it can lead to physical, emotional, or spiritual disturbances. By understanding and working with our chakras, we can identify areas that need attention and use various healing techniques, such as meditation, yoga, or energy work, to keep them in tip-top shape.

Before we delve into how to work with your chakras for healing and overall well-being, let's do a brief run-through of each one and its significance. However, remember that we will delve into the chakras in much more detail in a later chapter. This part is simply to help you understand how many chakras there are and what they do.

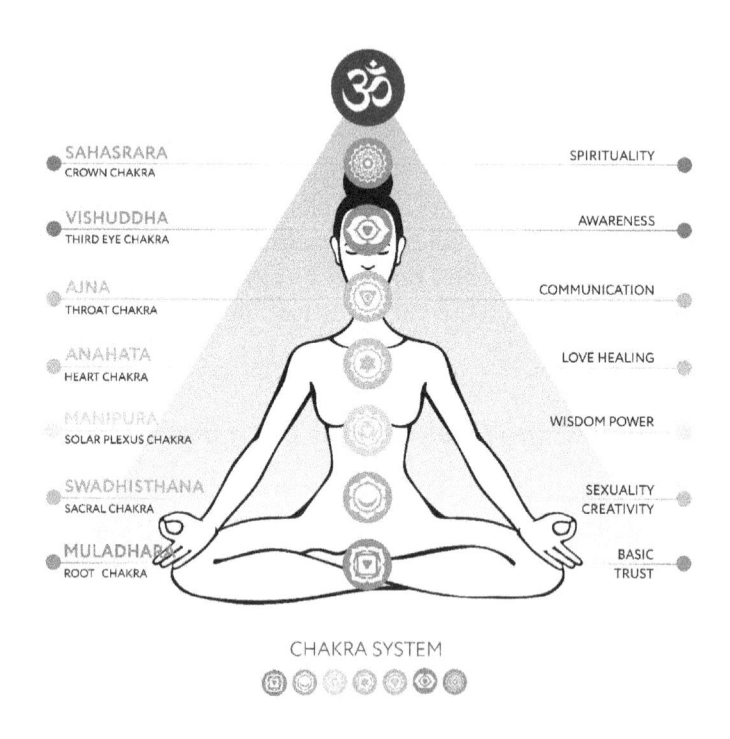

```
SAHASRARA          SPIRITUALITY
CROWN CHAKRA

VISHUDDHA          AWARENESS
THIRD EYE CHAKRA

AJNA               COMMUNICATION
THROAT CHAKRA

ANAHATA            LOVE HEALING
HEART CHAKRA

MANIPURA           WISDOM POWER
SOLAR PLEXUS CHAKRA

SWADHISTHANA       SEXUALITY
SACRAL CHAKRA      CREATIVITY

MULADHARA          BASIC
ROOT CHAKRA        TRUST
```

CHAKRA SYSTEM

Root Chakra (Muladhara)

- **Location:** Base of the spine
- **Significance:** Represents stability, grounding, and survival instincts
- **Personality:** Solid as a rock, this chakra provides a strong foundation for your energy system. It keeps you rooted and

balanced like a trustworthy friend, always there to support you.

Sacral Chakra (Svadhisthana)

- **Location:** Lower abdomen, below the belly button
- **Significance:** Associated with creativity, sexuality, and passion
- **Personality:** This chakra adds a splash of color and playfulness to your energy. It's like the vibrant artist who encourages you to embrace pleasure, embrace your desires, and explore your creative side.

Solar Plexus Chakra (Manipura):

- **Location:** Upper abdomen, below the chest
- **Significance:** Governs self-confidence, personal power, and willpower
- **Personality:** Think of this chakra as your cheerleader, boosting your self-esteem and motivation. It radiates a warm, fiery energy, empowering you to step into your own strength and embrace your personal power.

Heart Chakra (Anahata)

- **Location:** Center of the chest
- **Significance:** Associated with love, compassion, and emotional healing
- **Personality:** This chakra is all about spreading love and kindness, like a gentle hug or a comforting presence. It helps you connect with others on a deeper level and embrace unconditional love for yourself and others.

Throat Chakra (Vishuddha)

- **Location:** Throat
- **Significance:** Governs communication, self-expression, and truth

- **Personality:** The throat chakra is like your own personal spokesperson, helping you express yourself clearly and authentically. It encourages you to speak your truth and share your thoughts, just like an eloquent and trustworthy friend who always has your back.

Third Eye Chakra (Ajna)

- **Location:** Between the eyebrows (center of the forehead)
- **Significance:** Associated with intuition, inner wisdom, and spiritual insight
- **Personality:** The third eye chakra acts like your wise guru, bringing clarity and insight to your life. It opens the door to your inner wisdom and helps you make intuitive decisions like a guiding light leading the way.

Crown Chakra (Sahasrara)

- **Location:** Top of the head
- **Significance:** Represents spiritual connection, higher consciousness, and enlightenment
- **Personality:** The crown chakra is like your spiritual cheerleader, connecting you to the divine and expanding your consciousness. It fills you with a sense of wonder and awe, like a trusted guide leading you toward enlightenment.

Remember, each of these chakras contributes to your energy system's overall balance and harmony. Embrace their unique qualities, lean on them when needed, and allow their positive energy to flow through you.

What Does Science Say About the Chakras?

The world of chakras and chakra healing is a fascinating topic that brings together ancient wisdom and modern scientific inquiry.

We know that chakras, originating from ancient Indian philosophy, are said to be spinning wheels of energy located along the vertical axis of the human body. While the existence and functioning of chakras cannot be directly measured or observed through conventional scientific methods, some researchers have delved into this mystical realm, attempting to understand the potential mechanisms behind chakra healing.

It's important to note that these explorations often fall into alternative or complementary medicine, complementing rather than contradicting conventional medical practices.

One area of scientific interest is their relationship to the nervous system. Chakras are thought to correspond to crucial nerve plexus centers in the body, which are responsible for transmitting electrical signals and regulating bodily functions. Certain studies suggest stimulating specific nerve plexuses associated with various chakras may positively affect health and well-being. Although these findings are preliminary and more research is needed, they provide a starting point for further investigations into the intricate connection between chakras and our physiological systems.

Another aspect of chakra healing that warrants scientific consideration is the potential influence of energy fields. Energy fields are electromagnetic or bioelectric currents that flow through and around the human body. These energy fields can be measured using various techniques, such as biofeedback and Kirlian photography. Some researchers hypothesize that chakras may act as energy transformers or transmitters, facilitating the flow and balance of energy within our bodies. Chakra healing techniques aim to restore balance and alleviate physical and emotional disturbances by promoting the harmonious circulation of energy.

Furthermore, current scientific research emphasizes the vital role of the mind-body connection in overall health and well-being. Chakra healing techniques often involve meditation, visualization, and affirmations to promote self-awareness and a positive mindset. Meditation has been extensively studied and proven to have numerous physical and psychological benefits, such as reducing stress, improving cognitive function, and fostering emotional well-being. These findings support the idea that practices centered around chakras, which seek to improve mental states, can profoundly affect our overall health and sense of inner harmony.

Additionally, proponents of chakra healing often underscore the importance of energy flow throughout the body. Science acknowledges the significance of proper blood circulation, nerve conduction, and electrical activity in maintaining optimal health. Some chakra healing techniques, such as yoga and tai chi, aim to enhance physical movement and flexibility, promoting a better energy flow throughout the body. Engaging in these practices not only stimulates the physical body but also affects our mental and emotional well-being, reinforcing the interconnectedness of our entire being.

While science has made strides in exploring the potential ins and outs of chakra healing, it is worth noting that its traditional roots often involve spiritual and metaphysical dimensions that lie beyond the scope of scientific inquiry. Nevertheless, the growing field of mind-body medicine recognizes the profound impact of consciousness, emotions, and belief systems on health outcomes. By harmonizing our energy centers, chakra healing seeks to align our mind, body, and spirit—an integrative approach that complements modern medical practices.

The Concept of Inner Energy and Balance

The concept of inner energy and balance is a fascinating topic that has been explored and discussed by philosophers, spiritual leaders, and individuals seeking to find harmony within themselves and their surroundings. It is a concept seen across various cultural traditions, from ancient Eastern practices such as Chinese medicine and yoga to Western notions of mindfulness and self-awareness.

At its core, the idea of inner energy and balance is centered on the belief that each person possesses a unique life force or energy that flows within them, affecting their physical, mental, and emotional well-being. You might have heard this energy referred to as qi, prana, or vital force. Maintaining a sense of balance within this energy is seen as essential to achieving optimal health and overall harmony in life.

To fully understand the concept, it is important to recognize that the human body is considered a miniature version of the universe itself, reflecting the same principles of energy and balance that govern the world around us. Just as the sun and moon, day and night, and yin and yang have their own interplay, our inner energy is also subject to fluctuations and the need for harmony.

Imagine standing on the shore of a tranquil lake; your reflection mirrored in the stillness of the water. This picturesque scene is a metaphor for the balance we strive for in our lives. Just as ripples disrupt the mirror-like surface, external factors such as stress, negative emotions, and poor lifestyle choices can disturb the delicate balance of our inner energy.

Cultivating and maintaining a sense of inner balance requires several techniques. One important aspect is taking care of our physical bodies. Regular exercise, a balanced diet, and sufficient rest all contribute to nurturing our inner energy. By engaging in activities that promote physical wellness, we allow our energy to flow freely throughout our bodies, revitalizing and harmonizing our being.

In addition to physical well-being, mental and emotional aspects play a crucial role in achieving inner balance. The mind is a powerful force capable of shaping our perceptions and experiences. By practicing mindfulness and cultivating positive thoughts, we can create an internal environment that is conducive to balance and well-being. Being aware of our emotions, processing them in a healthy manner, and fostering positive relationships also contribute to this state of equilibrium.

Creativity is another avenue through which we can channel our inner energy and achieve balance. Engaging in artistic pursuits such as painting, writing, or playing a musical instrument allows us to tap into our creative potential and express ourselves meaningfully. This creative outlet brings about a sense of satisfaction and helps us connect with our inner selves and release any pent-up energy or emotions.

Remember, achieving and maintaining inner balance is not a static state but an ongoing journey. Life is filled with challenges, and external factors are constantly evolving. However, by staying attuned to our inner energy and regularly assessing its flow, we can adjust and adapt accordingly to restore balance when necessary.

Testimonials to Increase Your Interest

In this section, let's delve into the world of chakra and vagus nerve healing by showcasing compelling testimonials from people who have experienced transformative effects in their lives. These testimonials highlight the power and effectiveness of these practices, giving rise to hope, inspiration, and a deeper understanding of their potential benefits.

Sarah's Story: Awakened Energy Centers

"I was feeling emotionally drained, struggling with anxiety, and lacking motivation in life. That's when I decided to explore chakra healing techniques. After working with a chakra healing practitioner, I felt a profound shift in my energy centers. I noticed increased positivity, better emotional stability, and enhanced creativity. The practice helped me cultivate a sense of self-awareness and balance that transformed my approach to relationships and daily life. Chakra healing acts as an energetic reset button, awakening dormant potentials within us."

David's Journey: Embracing the Vagus Nerve Activation

"As someone who has dealt with chronic stress and anxiety for years, discovering the power of vagus nerve healing was a revelation. Through techniques such as deep breathing exercises, meditation, and mindfulness practices, I gradually activated my vagus nerve and experienced an incredible shift in my overall well-being. The constant feeling of unease diminished, replaced by a sense of calm and tranquility. My sleep improved, my digestion normalized, and my ability to manage stress skyrocketed. Vagus nerve healing gave me back control over my life, and I am eternally grateful for this newfound peace."

Anna's Transformation: Connecting Body and Mind

"Living with chronic pain due to an accident left me feeling deeply frustrated and hopeless. Seeking an alternative to conventional medicine, I focused on chakra and vagus nerve healing. Through a combined approach, I started experiencing miracles. By aligning my chakras and activating my vagus nerve, I felt a profound connection between my body and mind. The pain gradually subsided, and I regained mobility. I learned to listen to my body's needs and developed a deep sense of compassion towards myself. Chakra and vagus nerve healing have opened doors to a life full of possibilities and personal growth."

Michael's Empowering Journey: Restoring Inner Harmony

"After years of working a high-stress job, I found myself mentally and emotionally depleted. The unrelenting demands took a toll on my health and overall happiness. Seeking a path to renewal, I began exploring chakra healing. Through this practice, I discovered the power of balancing my energy centers. I gradually released emotional blockages and gained clarity as I delved deeper into chakra healing. I became more attuned to my inner self, embracing self-love and fostering healthier relationships with others. Chakra healing has empowered me to find my own rhythm and restore inner harmony."

Emily's Reboot: Enhancing Self-Expression

"As an artist, connecting with my creativity is vital for my work. However, I went through a phase where I felt creatively stagnant and struggled to express myself. Enter chakra and vagus nerve healing. By aligning my chakras and activating my vagus nerve through daily practices and meditation, I experienced a remarkable transformation. The floodgates of creativity opened. Ideas flowed effortlessly, and my ability to communicate effectively increased. It was like finding a well of inspiration within myself that I had long forgotten. Chakra and vagus nerve healing reignited my creative spirit and balanced all aspects of my life."

These testimonials provide real-life snapshots of how chakra and vagus nerve healing have positively impacted individuals' journeys toward holistic well-being. Through activating and balancing energy centers and the vagus nerve, these practices have helped individuals overcome emotional and physical challenges, find inner harmony, unleash creativity, and embrace a renewed sense of self.

Remember, these are personal experiences, and each individual's journey will be unique. The power of chakra and vagus nerve healing lies in its potential to unlock our inner potential and lead us to a more fulfilling and balanced life.

Chapter 2

Understanding the Vagus Nerve

In the world of chakra healing, the vagus nerve plays a vital role. Its name may sound a bit peculiar initially, but trust me, there's nothing vague about it! The word "vagus" actually derives from Latin, meaning "wandering" - an apt description for this nerve that meanders through the depths of our bodies, connecting our brain, facial muscles, throat, heart, lungs, digestive system, and more.

Anatomy and Function of the Vagus Nerve

The vagus nerve, also known as the tenth cranial nerve, is one of the longest nerves in the human body. It originates in the brainstem's medulla oblongata and extends all the way down to various organs in the chest and abdomen, including the heart, lungs, and gastrointestinal tract.

The vagus nerve is an essential component of the parasympathetic nervous system, which promotes a relaxed state and restores balance after moments of stress or excitement. It plays a crucial role in regulating various bodily functions, bringing peace and tranquility to your inner world.

One of its primary duties is to regulate heart rate. The vagus nerve delivers signals to the sinoatrial node, often referred to as the heart's natural pacemaker. These signals help slow down heartbeats, ensuring a steady rhythm and preventing our hearts from going on a wild rollercoaster ride. So, next time you find yourself in a moment of calm, remember to thank your vagus nerve for keeping your heart in check.

Not only does the vagus nerve have a say in matters of the heart, but it also has a profound effect on our respiratory system. It plays a role in controlling the muscles involved in respiration, helping us take those deep, relaxing breaths after a stressful day or during meditation.

The vagus nerve also plays an integral role in digestion, stimulating the release of gastric juices, enzymes, and acids that aid in breaking down the foods we eat.

Let's not forget about the vagus nerve's role in sensory perception. It carries sensations from the throat, larynx, and other organs back to the brain, allowing us to experience the world around us. Have you ever felt that tantalizing tickle in your throat that made you burst into a fit of laughter? Well, you have your vagus nerve to thank for that delightful sensation!

In addition to its sensory duties, the vagus nerve also plays a role in our facial expressions. It contributes to our ability to smile, frown, and show various other expressions that add color and emotion to our interactions.

The Role of the Vagus Nerve in Chakra Healing

We know that the vagus nerve is one of the longest cranial nerves in our body, traveling from our brainstem to various organs, including our heart, lungs, and digestive system, and even reaching down to our lower abdomen. It plays a crucial role in regulating various bodily functions and also serves as a communication link between our brain and the rest of the body.

So, how does the vagus nerve come into play when it comes to chakra healing? Well, imagine the vagus nerve as a superhighway of communication that connects our energetic chakra centers with our physical body. It carries the electrical impulses that control bodily functions and the subtle energy that flows through our chakras.

The vagus nerve bridges our chakras and our physical body, allowing the flow of energy to pass freely and facilitating chakra healing. It serves as a messenger, delivering vital information from our chakra centers to our brain and vice versa.

Think of it this way: if your heart chakra, which is located in the center of your chest, is imbalanced, the energy flow in that area might be sluggish, affecting your emotions, relationships, and ability to give and receive love. When the vagus nerve detects an imbalance in this chakra, it plays its part as a diligent messenger and sends signals to your brain.

The brain then sends signals back to the chakra center, activating the vagus nerve's "healing mode." This can result in increased blood flow, improved heart rate variability, reduced inflammation, and enhanced overall well-being. In other words, the vagus nerve helps restore balance and harmony to your heart chakra, allowing the energy to flow freely once again.

As the vagus nerve communicates with our chakra centers, it also connects with our parasympathetic nervous system, which is responsible for our body's rest, relaxation, and repair responses. As it stimulates this system, the vagus nerve promotes deep relaxation, reduces stress, and supports our body's natural healing process.

It's important to note that chakra healing is a holistic practice that encompasses various techniques and modalities. Working directly with the vagus nerve is just one piece of the puzzle. Other practices like meditation, yoga, breathwork, energy healing, and mindfulness all contribute to chakra healing and overall well-being. We will delve into these things in much more detail as we move through this book.

Isn't it fascinating how these ancient spiritual practices intertwine with our modern understanding of the nervous system? The vagus nerve truly plays a pivotal role in connecting our energy centers and physical body, supporting chakra healing and contributing to our overall vitality.

The Benefits of Vagus Nerve Stimulation

The vagus nerve might enjoy the anonymity of being one of the least known nerves in our body - but don't let that fool you! It is a true superstar, connecting our brain to various organs in what seems like an intricate communication network. This extraordinary nerve has been hailed as the key to unlocking numerous health benefits.

But what is vagus nerve stimulation? It is a therapeutic technique that involves sending gentle electrical impulses to the vagus nerve, bolstering its activity and positively influencing various bodily functions. Thanks to advancements in medical research, this novel form of treatment has gained significant attention over the years.

Now, let's delve into the plethora of benefits that vagus nerve stimulation brings to the table.

- **Mood booster:** Have you ever experienced those down-in-the-dumps days when even a ray of sunshine couldn't lift your spirits? Vagus nerve stimulation has shown promise in combating depression and enhancing mood. By stimulating the nerve, it triggers the release of mood-regulating neurotransmitters like serotonin and norepinephrine, acting as a natural antidepressant.
- **Inflammation reduction:** We all know inflammation can be quite a troublemaker, causing various diseases and discomfort. However, studies suggest that vagus nerve stimulation can help reduce inflammation throughout the body, thereby potentially alleviating symptoms of conditions like arthritis, Crohn's disease, and even asthma.
- **Improved heart health:** Vagus nerve stimulation can lend a helping hand in keeping our ticker happy and healthy. By stimulating the vagus nerve, it has been shown to lower heart rate and blood pressure, reducing the risk of cardiovascular ailments.

- **Memory enhancer:** Recent research suggests that this wonder technique has the potential to boost memory and enhance cognitive performance.
- **Seizure tamer:** This therapeutic approach has shown promising results in reducing the frequency and severity of seizures in individuals with epilepsy.
- **Healing sleep:** Vagus nerve stimulation might just be your ticket to a good night's sleep. Studies suggest that this technique can improve sleep quality, helping combat insomnia and other sleep disorders.

How to Meditate

Throughout the following chapters, I'm going to suggest meditation several times. Not only does meditation help with balancing your chakras, but it's also ideal for stimulating your vagus nerve, too. But not everyone finds meditation easy.

So, before we move toward more practical advice, let's examine how to meditate. By the end, you'll see it's not as complicated as you think.

To begin your meditation journey, find a quiet, comfortable space where you won't be easily disturbed. Sit in a position that allows you to be both relaxed and alert, such as the classic cross-legged pose or even sitting on a chair with your feet planted firmly on the ground. Remember, there is no "correct" way to sit for meditation - find what works best for you.

Now that you are settled close your eyes and take a few deep breaths, inhaling slowly through your nose and exhaling through your mouth. Let go of any tension you may be holding in your body, allowing your muscles to relax. As you breathe deeply, focus on the present moment, letting go of any thoughts or distractions.

An overly active mind is one of the most common blocks to progress in meditation. Don't be discouraged if you find it challenging to quiet your thoughts. Instead, acknowledge the presence of these thoughts and gently guide your attention back to your breath. Picture your breath entering and leaving your body, noticing the sensations with each inhalation and exhalation. Remember, the purpose of meditation is not to be thought-free but rather to cultivate a sense of mindfulness and awareness.

Another obstacle you may encounter is restlessness or physical discomfort. This may manifest as an itch, a sore joint, or the sudden urge to change positions. Whenever you feel these sensations arise, try not to react immediately. Instead, bring your attention to the discomfort, observing it without judgment. In time, you may find that the discomfort fades or becomes more tolerable. Of course, if you experience severe pain, adjusting your posture or seeking medical advice is essential.

When it feels like your meditation practice is not progressing as you had hoped, doubt and frustration may creep in. This is perfectly normal. Remember, meditation is a journey, and progress can sometimes be subtle and gradual. It's crucial to approach your practice with patience and kindness for yourself. Acknowledge the small victories, no matter how insignificant they may seem. Celebrate the moments of clarity or the periods where you can anchor your attention on your breath for a few seconds longer than before.

If you find it challenging to maintain motivation for meditation, consider introducing variety into your practice. Experiment with different styles of meditation, such as guided meditations or focusing on specific points of the body. Alternatively, you could try practicing meditation in diverse settings - perhaps outdoors in nature or a softly lit room. Breaking the monotony and exploring new approaches can help rekindle your interest and enthusiasm.

Connecting with a like-minded community can also be a powerful source of support and inspiration. Consider joining meditation classes or groups where you can share your experiences and learn from others. Engaging with a community of meditators can provide valuable insights, accountability, and encouragement as you navigate your own meditation journey.

Lastly, remember that meditation is not about achieving a specific result or becoming an expert overnight. The true essence of meditation lies in the process and the willingness to show up and be present with yourself. It's about cultivating a sense of self-awareness, inner calm, and compassion for yourself and others.

So, as you embark on your meditation practice, remember these tips. Overcoming blocks to progress may require patience, determination, and a gentle touch of self-compassion. Stay focused, be open to the unexpected, and remember that the journey itself holds countless treasures. Happy meditating!

Chapter 3

The Seven Main Chakras

In our first chapter, we briefly explored the seven chakras. In this chapter, we're going to delve deeply into each one. Why? Because understanding the concept of chakras can be a powerful tool in promoting holistic healing.

Remember, the chakras are believed to be energy centers within the body that correspond to different aspects of our physical, emotional, and spiritual well-being. By gaining knowledge about these energy centers, we can identify imbalances and work towards restoring harmony within ourselves.

Each chakra is associated with specific qualities and characteristics. For example, the root chakra, located at the base of the spine, is connected to feelings of stability, grounding, and security. If one is experiencing feelings of fear or insecurity, focusing on balancing the root chakra can be beneficial.

Similarly, the heart chakra represents love, compassion, and emotional well-being. When this chakra is out of balance, it can result in difficulties with relationships, self-acceptance, or an inability to express love. By understanding the heart chakra and its functions, one can actively work to heal and balance these areas.

Understanding the chakras also opens the door to various healing modalities that can be used to restore balance. Techniques such as meditation, energy healing, yoga, and even color therapy can be utilized to align and activate the chakras. Additionally, recognizing and addressing energetic blockages in the chakras can release emotional traumas and promote overall well-being.

Incorporating the understanding of chakras into our healing journey provides a framework for self-growth and self-awareness. It allows us to delve deeper into our emotions, thoughts, and experiences, guiding us toward inner peace and self-empowerment.

So, let's start with the first chakra!

The Root Chakra

The root chakra, also known as the Muladhara in Sanskrit, is the foundation of our being. Located at the base of the spine, it is associated with our sense of security, stability, and connection to the physical world. The root chakra is like the roots of a tree, providing a strong and stable anchor from which we can grow and thrive.

The primary function of the root chakra is to keep us grounded and secure. When this energy center is balanced, we feel a deep sense of stability within ourselves and the world around us. We can trust in the process of life, knowing that we are supported and protected. Additionally, a balanced root chakra allows us to feel a sense of belonging and connection to our physical bodies and the Earth itself.

Associated with the root chakra are the elements of earth and gravity. Earth represents the grounding energy that helps us stay connected to the present moment and the physical world. It enhances our sense of stability, resilience, and practicality. Gravity, on the other hand, symbolizes the force that keeps us grounded and rooted. It reminds us to stay in touch with our physical bodies and not get lost in our thoughts or fantasies.

There are some signs that indicate a balanced root chakra. Your root chakra is likely well-balanced if you feel secure, stable, and comfortable in your body and environment. You will likely have a strong sense of self and a deep connection to the physical world. You feel safe, supported, and grounded in your life.

However, an imbalanced root chakra can manifest in various ways. Feeling anxious, fearful, or constantly on edge could be a sign of an overactive root chakra. On the other hand, if you tend to feel disconnected from your body, spacey, or lack a sense of stability, your root chakra may be underactive.

An overactive root chakra may also lead to stubbornness, materialism, and an excessive need for control. On the other hand, an underactive root chakra may result in a lack of motivation, low self-esteem, and difficulty manifesting abundance in your life.

To balance and heal the root chakra, it is important to focus on activities and practices that help cultivate a sense of stability and safety. Grounding exercises, such as spending time in nature, walking barefoot, or gardening, can be very beneficial. Engaging in physical activities that connect you with your body, such as yoga or tai chi, can also help to balance the root chakra.

Incorporating earthy and grounding foods into your diet, such as root vegetables and foods rich in protein, can also support the root chakra. Additionally, using grounding essential oils like patchouli, vetiver, and cedarwood during aromatherapy can help balance the root chakra.

Remember, an imbalanced root chakra is nothing to worry about – it simply indicates that your energy needs a little tender love and care. By focusing on activities and practices that connect you with the stability and security of the Earth, you can bring your root chakra back into balance and enjoy a deep sense of groundedness and stability in your life.

The Sacral Chakra

Nestled just below the navel, the sacral chakra is vital for our emotional well-being, creativity, and passion.

Often referred to as Svadhishthana in Sanskrit, it is the center of pleasure, sensuality, and emotions, and it plays a crucial role in our self-expression and ability to nurture ourselves and others.

This radiant energy fuels our desires, relationships, and artistic endeavors.

To fully comprehend the essence of the sacral chakra, we must explore its associated elements - water and the color orange. Water symbolizes fluidity, adaptability, and our ability to navigate the ever-changing tides of life. Just like water, the sacral chakra encourages us to go with the flow, fostering flexibility and resilience. The vibrant hue of orange signifies enthusiasm, joy, and positivity, capturing the essence of the sacral chakra's zest for life.

When this energy center is in harmony, it allows our creativity to blossom, igniting our passions and bringing a sense of overall well-being. Signs of a balanced sacral chakra may include an ability to express ourselves freely, a healthy emotional state, a strong sense of pleasure and sensuality, and the capacity to form fulfilling and nurturing relationships. Embracing change becomes natural, and we radiate a vibrant zest for life.

If the sacral chakra experiences imbalance, it may manifest in various ways. An inhibited sacral chakra can result in a lack of creative inspiration, feeling emotionally stuck or distant, difficulty in forming and maintaining healthy relationships, and an overall sense of dissatisfaction or suppression of our desires. On the other hand, an overactive sacral chakra may lead to impulsiveness, emotional volatility, addictive behaviors, and a tendency to prioritize pleasure-seeking above all else.

To help balance the sacral chakra, take a soothing bath or swim, allowing yourself to feel the immense joy and freedom water offers. Engaging in activities that kindle your creativity, such as painting, dancing, or writing, can also help harmonize your sacral chakra.

Additionally, grounding exercises like meditation, yoga, or mindfulness can provide a stable foundation for the sacral chakra's energies. Seeking therapy or working with a qualified energy healer may also prove valuable in releasing emotional blocks and fostering self-acceptance.

Solar Plexus Chakra

The solar plexus chakra, also known as Manipura in Sanskrit, is an incredibly important energy center located just above the navel. With its vibrant yellow color, this chakra holds a special place in the body's energetic system.

Imagine this chakra as your own personal sun, radiating warmth and power throughout your being. It is linked to the element of fire, which embodies transformation, passion, and the spark of creativity. Just like a flame, the solar plexus chakra ignites your personal power, guiding you toward success and self-confidence.

When this chakra is balanced, you'll feel like you're on top of the world. You'll exude self-assurance, have a strong sense of your identity, and be motivated to pursue your dreams. You'll be full of zest and enthusiasm, radiating a charming and magnetic energy that others can't help but be drawn to.

When the solar plexus chakra is underactive, you might feel insecure, lack confidence, or struggle with decision-making. It's like someone turned down the brightness on your personal sun, leaving you feeling a bit dull.

On the other hand, an overactive solar plexus chakra can make you excessively controlling, dominating, or prone to angry outbursts. It's as if someone turned up the heat a little too much, and now you're feeling the burn.

You can explore various activities to nourish and revitalize your solar plexus chakra. Engaging in physical exercise, like yoga or dance, will help you maintain a healthy body, instill a sense of discipline, and increase your confidence.

Practicing mindfulness and meditation can also work wonders for the solar plexus chakra. And let's not forget the importance of nourishing your body with a balanced diet. Foods rich in yellow hues, like bananas, corn, and pineapple, can help stoke the fire in your solar plexus chakra. Sip a chamomile tea to calm your digestive system and promote a healthy energy flow.

Heart Chakra

The heart chakra, also known as Anahata in Sanskrit, is the fourth energy center in the body's chakra system. This chakra is located in the center of the chest, near the heart, and is associated with the color green. The heart chakra is a magical and vital energy hub that plays a significant role in our emotional well-being and relationships.

Functionally, the heart chakra serves as a bridge between the lower three chakras, which are primarily focused on physical and earthly matters, and the upper three chakras, which are associated with spiritual and higher states of consciousness. It acts as a center of balance, connecting the physical and spiritual aspects of our being.

The heart chakra is associated with the element of air, which represents freedom, movement, and breath. Air embodies lightness and expansion; through the heart chakra, the energy of love, compassion, and joy flows freely, like a gentle breeze that clears any tension or negativity.

A balanced heart chakra is characterized by a deep sense of love and connection, not only towards oneself but also towards others and the world at large. Individuals demonstrate compassion, empathy, and kindness when the heart chakra is in harmony. They possess the ability to forgive themselves and others and can maintain healthy and loving relationships. In essence, a balanced heart chakra fosters harmonious and joyful interactions with the world around us.

On the other hand, an unbalanced heart chakra can manifest in various ways. When the heart chakra is deficient or blocked, individuals may experience feelings of loneliness, isolation, or a lack of empathy. They may struggle to form meaningful connections and relationships and may even exhibit a tendency towards selfishness or emotional coldness. Conversely, an excessive or overactive heart chakra can lead to co-dependency, possessiveness, and an overwhelming need for approval from others. It can manifest as an inability to set healthy boundaries and constantly seeking external validation.

A balanced heart chakra is marked by a genuine sense of love, acceptance, and compassion towards ourselves and others. You may notice a deep connection and appreciation for nature, as well as a desire to help and nurture others. Relationships are based on mutual respect, trust, and emotional support.

On the other hand, an unbalanced heart chakra may present itself through various symptoms. These can include being overly critical of ourselves or others, feeling emotionally disconnected, having difficulty expressing emotions, or experiencing an intense fear of intimacy or commitment. Other signs may include a tendency to seek constant validation, being overly possessive or jealous, or developing a fear of rejection.

Engaging in self-care activities, such as meditation, yoga, and journaling, can help you reconnect with your heart center. Additionally, practicing acts of love and kindness towards yourself and others can work wonders.

Throat Chakra

The throat chakra, also known as the Vishuddha chakra, is the fifth primary chakra in the human body. Located at the base of the throat, this chakra is associated with sound, communication, and self-expression. It plays a vital role in helping us express our thoughts and emotions and communicate with others effectively.

Functionally, the throat chakra governs everything related to communication. It empowers us to speak our truth with confidence and authenticity. When the throat chakra is balanced, we can effortlessly express our thoughts and emotions, listen attentively, and find the right words to convey our message. It allows us to use our voice to create harmony and understanding in our relationships and interactions.

The element associated with the throat chakra is sound. Sound is a powerful medium through which we express ourselves and connect with others. Sound vibration facilitates communication and allows energy to flow freely through the chakra. Chanting mantras, listening to uplifting music, or even speaking kind words can help activate and balance this chakra.

A balanced throat chakra is characterized by clear and truthful communication. People with a harmonious throat chakra speak confidently, without fear of judgment or rejection. They are excellent listeners, empathetic, and possess a strong sense of integrity. These individuals effortlessly express their creativity and have a knack for self-expression, whether through art, music, or writing.

However, an imbalanced throat chakra can manifest in several ways. When the throat chakra is overactive or "blanched," individuals may experience excessive talkativeness, an incessant need to be heard, and a tendency to dominate conversations. This can lead to a lack of harmony and understanding with others. Additionally, an overactive throat chakra can manifest physically as a sore throat, throat infections, or voice-related issues.

On the other hand, an underactive or unbalanced throat chakra can lead to difficulties in expressing ourselves. People with an underactive throat chakra may struggle with speaking up, fear judgment or rejection, or struggle to articulate their thoughts and emotions. They may doubt their own ideas and opinions, leading to self-censorship. Physically, an underactive throat chakra can manifest as hoarseness, a weak voice, or difficulties in swallowing.

Several practices can be implemented to restore balance to the throat chakra. First and foremost, it is crucial to cultivate self-expression and authentic communication. This can be done through journaling, creative writing, or engaging in open and honest conversations. Additionally, practicing active listening and speaking with kindness and compassion can enhance the throat chakra's energy.

Sound therapy is also a powerful tool for balancing the throat chakra. Experimenting with mantras, humming, or even singing can help release blockages and restore energy flow. Surrounding ourselves with positive and uplifting music can also have a beneficial effect on the throat chakra.

Third Eye Chakra

The third eye chakra, also known as Ajna in Sanskrit, holds a special place in the chakra system. Nestled between the eyes, this energy center is often symbolized by an indigo-colored lotus flower with two petals, representing duality and the ability to perceive both the physical and non-physical worlds.

Functionally, the third eye chakra is responsible for our intuition, imagination, and higher knowledge. It acts as our inner guide, providing insight, clarity, and foresight in our lives. When in balance, it gives us a clear vision of our life's purpose and connects with our inner wisdom. It enhances our perception, allowing us to see beyond the surface and tap into the subtle energies at play. A balanced third eye chakra empowers us to trust our intuition, make decisions confidently, and navigate through life with a deep sense of knowing.

The element of light is closely tied to the third eye chakra, representing illumination and enlightenment. Just as light allows us to see the physical world, the third eye chakra helps us perceive the metaphysical realms. Meditation is a practice often recommended to awaken the third eye chakra, as it invites stillness, focus, and a deep connection with the inner self. Journaling, dreamwork, and engaging in creative activities are also beneficial in nurturing the imagination and expanding the intuitive abilities associated with this chakra.

When the third eye chakra is balanced, you may notice several signs in your life. You have a strong intuition and can easily trust and act upon your gut feelings. You possess a vivid imagination and a genuine interest in exploring the unknown. Your dreams are rich and symbolic, providing valuable insights into your waking life. You have a deep sense of purpose and are driven to pursue your passions. People may seek your advice or guidance due to your ability to provide thoughtful and intuitive solutions. Overall, life feels harmonious, and you clearly envision where you are headed.

On the other hand, an imbalanced third eye chakra can manifest in various ways. If it is overactive, you may experience excessive daydreaming, a tendency to live in a world of illusions, and difficulties distinguishing between reality and fantasy. You may become overwhelmed by psychic experiences or feel consumed by fear and paranoia. Conversely, if your third eye chakra is underactive, you may struggle with a lack of imagination, rigid thinking, and feeling disconnected from your intuition. Decision-making becomes challenging, and you may feel a lack of purpose or direction in life.

But don't worry! There are many ways to bring the third eye chakra back into balance. Engaging in mindfulness practices such as meditation and deep breathing exercises can help quiet the mind and enhance your intuitive abilities. Surround yourself with indigo-colored objects, such as clothing or crystals like amethyst or lapis lazuli, to promote balance in this energy center. Spending time in nature, particularly under the night sky, can also stimulate the third eye chakra.

Crown Chakra

The crown chakra, also known as Sahasrara in Sanskrit, is the seventh and highest chakra in the body's energetic system. It is located at the top of the head and is associated with the color white or violet. It is often represented as a thousand-petaled lotus flower, symbolizing its limitless and expansive nature.

The crown chakra connects us to our higher selves and the divine. It functions as a gateway to spiritual unity and cosmic consciousness. When this chakra is balanced and fully open, we experience a deep sense of inner peace, spiritual insight, and a profound connection to something greater than ourselves.

One of the primary functions of the crown chakra is to facilitate the flow of universal energy into our being. Here, we tap into the infinite well of wisdom, knowledge, and spiritual guidance. This chakra allows us to transcend the physical world's limitations and experience a higher level of consciousness.

In addition to its spiritual functions, the crown chakra also plays a role in our overall well-being. It regulates the functioning of the upper brain and the pituitary and pineal glands, which are responsible for hormonal and circadian rhythm regulation. A balanced crown chakra can enhance our overall mental and physical health.

When the crown chakra is balanced, we experience a deep sense of connectedness to the universe and an understanding of our purpose in life. We may feel a sense of clarity, inspiration, and inner peace. Our intuition becomes stronger, and we can better trust in the flow of life. We have a deep sense of knowing and can tap into higher levels of consciousness.

On the other hand, an unbalanced crown chakra can manifest in various ways. If it is overactive, we may feel disconnected from our physical body and earthly matters. We may become excessively focused on spirituality or lose touch with reality. We may experience a lack of grounding and struggle with practical matters.

If the crown chakra is underactive, we may feel disconnected from our spiritual selves and have difficulty accessing higher levels of consciousness. We may feel lost, confused, or lack a sense of purpose. We may also struggle with anxiety, depression, or a sense of spiritual emptiness.

There are several ways we can balance and activate the crown chakra. Meditation is a powerful practice that allows us to quiet the mind, expand our consciousness, and open ourselves up to spiritual insights. Surrounding ourselves with the color white or violet, such as through clothing or home decor, can help to stimulate and balance this chakra.

Spending time in nature, particularly in open spaces or near bodies of water, can also benefit the crown chakra. Engaging in activities that promote spiritual growth and self-discovery, such as yoga or energy healing, can help activate and balance this chakra.

Now you have a detailed overview of each chakra, let's delve into the techniques you can use to help heal yourself. We'll take each chakra in turn.

MULADHARA
Sanskrit: मूलाधार

ROOT CHAKRA

Chapter 4

The Root Chakra and Grounding Techniques

Let's start with the root chakra, the first energy center located at the base of the spine, at the perineum. It is associated with the color red and represents our foundation, stability, and survival instincts. As we already know, the root chakra is responsible for grounding us in the Earth, allowing us to feel connected and secure in our physical bodies and the world around us. It is like the roots of a tree, providing stability and support so that we can grow and thrive.

The significance of the root chakra cannot be overstated, as it forms the basis for our overall well-being. When this chakra is balanced, we feel a sense of safety, security, and groundedness. We are able to move through life with stability and confidence, trusting in our ability to meet our basic needs and navigate challenges. However, if the root chakra becomes blocked or imbalanced, we may experience feelings of fear, insecurity, and instability.

This can manifest in physical symptoms such as lower back pain, digestive issues, or a weakened immune system. By working on opening and balancing the root chakra, we can enhance our sense of stability and security, laying a solid foundation for our overall energy system.

Guided Practices for Grounding and Stability

To restore harmony to the root chakra, it is essential to incorporate a range of grounding practices into our daily lives. Here are some effective grounding exercises for you to try.

Walking Barefoot in Nature:

1. Find a natural environment such as a garden, park, or beach.
2. Remove your shoes and socks, allowing your feet to make direct contact with the Earth.
3. Take slow, deliberate steps while consciously observing the sensations in your feet.
4. Tune in to the textures, temperature, and energy of the ground beneath you.
5. As you walk, breathe deeply and visualize roots extending from the soles of your feet, grounding you to the earth.

Yoga and Grounding Poses:

1. Find a quiet and comfortable space where you can practice yoga.
2. Begin with Mountain Pose (Tadasana) by standing tall with your feet hip-width apart.
3. Distribute your weight evenly across both feet and engage your leg muscles for stability.
4. Visualize a strong connection between your feet and the ground, imagining roots growing deep into the Earth.
5. Hold the pose for several deep breaths, focusing on grounding energy flowing up into your body.

Grounding Meditation:

1. Sit comfortably in a quiet space, either on the floor or in a chair.
2. Close your eyes and take a few deep breaths, allowing yourself to relax.

3. Bring your attention to your breath, focusing on the inhalation and exhalation.
4. Visualize a red glowing ball of energy at the base of your spine, representing your root chakra.
5. Imagine roots extending downwards from the ball, anchoring you to the Earth's core.
6. Stay in this meditation for as long as you feel comfortable, allowing the grounding energy to flow through your body.

Connection with Nature:

1. Spend time outdoors, whether it's in a park, garden, or forested area.
2. Find a comfortable spot to sit or lie down, close your eyes, and take a few deep breaths.
3. Listen to the sounds of nature around you, such as the rustling of leaves or birds chirping.
4. Feel the cool breeze or warmth of the sun on your skin, allowing yourself to become fully present in the moment.
5. As you connect with the natural world, envision the Earth's grounding energy entering your body and restoring balance to your root chakra.

Essential Oils and Grounding:

1. Choose grounding essential oils such as patchouli, vetiver, or cedarwood.
2. Dilute a few drops of the essential oil in a carrier oil such as coconut or jojoba oil.
3. Rub the diluted oil mixture onto the soles of your feet, focusing on gentle, circular motions.
4. As you apply the oil, take a moment to breathe in its aroma, allowing it to calm and ground your energy.

Incorporating these grounding practices into your daily routine can restore balance and stability to your root chakra. Remember, consistency is key, so make an effort to practice these exercises regularly. As you cultivate greater grounding and stability, you will find yourself more connected to the present moment, more self-assured, and better equipped to navigate life's challenges. Embrace the power of grounding and enjoy its positive transformation to your overall well-being.

Integrating Vagus Nerve Stimulation for Enhanced Grounding

By incorporating vagus nerve stimulation techniques into grounding exercises, we can enhance the connection to our root chakra, thereby deepening our grounding and promoting overall balance. To that aim, let's explore some exercises incorporating vagus nerve stimulation for enhanced grounding with the root chakra.

Breathing Exercises:

Deep, diaphragmatic breathing is a simple yet powerful technique to stimulate the vagus nerve and promote grounding. Breathing isn't difficult, so follow these steps to incorporate this exercise into your grounding routine:

1. Find a comfortable seated position, placing your hands on your lower abdomen.
2. Inhale deeply through your nose, allowing your breath to expand your belly rather than your chest.
3. Exhale slowly through your mouth, allowing your belly to gently contract.
4. As you continue to breathe deeply, visualize a warm, grounding energy flowing down from the base of your spine into the Earth.
5. Repeat this breathing exercise for 5-10 minutes, allowing yourself to sync with your breath's rhythmic flow fully.

Chanting with Root Chakra Affirmations:

Chanting or vocalizing root chakra affirmations vibrates the vocal cords, activating the vagus nerve and promoting a sense of grounding and stability. Here's how you can incorporate this technique into your grounding practice:

1. Find a quiet space where you feel comfortable and safe.
2. Sit or stand with a tall spine, ensuring that your feet are firmly planted on the ground.
3. Take a few deep breaths to center yourself.
4. Choose a root chakra affirmation that resonates with you. For example, "I am grounded and secure in my connection to the Earth."
5. Start chanting or repeating the affirmation aloud, allowing the vibrations to flow through your entire body, particularly the area around your throat and neck where the vagus nerve is located.
6. Continue chanting for at least 5-10 minutes, feeling the grounding energy of the affirmation spreading through your entire being.

Ear Massage and Acupressure:

Massaging or stimulating specific acupressure points around the ears can activate the vagus nerve and support grounding. Follow these steps to perform an ear massage and acupressure technique:

1. Begin by locating a point called Shen Men on the outer part of your ear. It is the small triangular fossa just above the earlobe. Gently massage this point in circular motions for about 1-2 minutes.
2. Move your fingers slightly upward to a point called Point Zero. It is the hollow at the center of the upper curvature of your ear. Apply gentle pressure with your thumb for 1 minute, focusing on slow and intentional breathing.

3. Next, slide your fingers along the crease behind your ear, slowly massaging the area. This releases tension and promotes relaxation.
4. Finish by gently pulling your earlobes downward a few times while taking deep breaths. This stimulates the vagus nerve and encourages grounding.

Nature Connection Meditation:

Spending time in nature is a powerful way to support grounding. Combining nature's connection with a calming meditation can further stimulate the vagus nerve and deepen our root chakra grounding. Follow these steps to perform a nature connection meditation:

1. Find a peaceful outdoor location, such as a park or garden.
2. Sit comfortably with your back straight and relax your body.
3. Begin focusing on your breath, allowing it to become steady and deep.
4. Gently bring your attention to the sounds, smells, and sensations around you, immersing yourself in the present moment.
5. Take a few moments to notice the sensations in your body as it connects with the Earth beneath you. Visualize roots extending from the base of your spine, anchoring deep into the ground.
6. Spend as much time as you need in this meditative state, feeling the energy of the Earth supporting your grounding and stability.
7. When you feel ready, slowly return to the present moment with gratitude for the grounding experience.

As you practice these techniques, remember to approach them with an open heart and a sense of curiosity, allowing the power of the vagus nerve to guide you deeper.

Affirmations for the Root Chakra

If you've never tried affirmations before, you're in for a treat!

Put simply, affirmations are positive statements that help rewire the mind and shift our perspective toward a desired outcome. They provide a means to challenge negative and limiting beliefs, replacing them with empowering thoughts. Affirmations for the root chakra strengthen our foundation, boost confidence, and foster a sense of security. Regularly practicing them can help restore balance and awaken the potential of this energy center.

To use affirmations for the root chakra effectively, creating a quiet and peaceful space where you feel comfortable is important. Begin by taking a few deep breaths, relaxing, and releasing any tension. Visualize a warm, grounding energy at the base of your spine, connecting you to the earth beneath you.

As you recite each affirmation, focus on the physical sensations you feel in your body. Notice the area of your root chakra and imagine it becoming increasingly vibrant and balanced. Repeat the affirmations several times, believing in their power to transform your thoughts and emotions.

Here are ten affirmations specifically crafted to support the root chakra:

- I am safe and secure in my body, and I trust the process of life.
- I am deeply rooted, and I am strong and stable.
- I am worthy of abundance, and I welcome prosperity into my life.
- I release fear and embrace a life filled with courage and resilience.
- I am deeply connected to the Earth and honor its wisdom and guidance.
- I am grounded and centered, and I face challenges with confidence.

- I am grateful for the stability in my life, and I attract positive experiences.
- I am deserving of love and support, and I create healthy boundaries.
- I trust my instincts and make decisions that align with my highest good.
- I am a divine being here to manifest my purpose in this world.

By consistently practicing these affirmations, you will gradually align your thoughts, emotions, and energy with the frequency of the root chakra. As a result, you will cultivate a deep sense of stability, security, and self-confidence.

Remember, affirmations are most effective when repeated regularly, so make them a part of your daily routine and witness the positive changes they can bring to your life.

SVADHISHTHANA
Sanskrit: स्वाधिष्ठान

SACRAL CHAKRA

Chapter 5

The Sacral Chakra and Emotional Balance

Located just below the navel, the sacral chakra, also known as Svadhisthana in Sanskrit, is a vital energy center within our bodies. It holds immense power, deeply influencing our emotions, sexuality, desires, and creative expressions. In this exploration, we delve into the magnificent influence and significance of the sacral chakra on our emotional well-being and creative processes.

The sacral chakra is the second primary chakra, connecting the physical and spiritual realms while governing our emotional and creative energies. It functions as a gateway for self-expression, sensuality, and the ability to experience joy in life. When this chakra is balanced and activated, it positively affects our emotions and nurtures our creative potential.

The sacral chakra acts as the energetic epicenter of our emotions. It governs our ability to maintain emotional balance, experience pleasure, and manage relationships with others and ourselves. A well-functioning sacral chakra facilitates the processing and integration of emotions, leading to a healthier and happier emotional state.

Furthermore, the sacral chakra encourages us to be in touch with our feelings and to embrace emotional vulnerability. By allowing ourselves to feel deeply, we create a space for emotional healing and personal growth. It empowers us to release any emotional blockages and cultivate a state of emotional harmony.

Linked to the sacral chakra is the vital life force energy that lies within each of us — our sexual energy. The energy of this chakra fuels our creative potential, manifesting in various forms such as art, writing, music, and innovation. Harnessing and channeling this creative energy allows us to tap into our innate talents and unleash our creative expressions.

When our sacral chakra is vibrant and unblocked, sexual energy flows freely, stimulating our creative juices. It encourages us to embrace our sensual nature and indulge in pleasurable experiences, setting the stage for inspiration and imaginative exploration.

Cultivating Creativity through Sacral Chakra Activation

It is essential to balance and energize the sacral chakra to enhance creativity. Various practices and techniques can aid in this process, including:

- **Movement and dance:** Engaging in dance and movement practices, such as yoga, belly dancing, or simply swaying to music, can help activate and unblock the sacral chakra. The rhythmic movements serve as a catalyst for unlocking creativity and inviting a free flow of energy.
- **Creative and expressive arts:** Engaging in artistic activities such as painting, writing, music, or any other form of creative expression can stimulate the sacral chakra. These activities provide an outlet for emotional release, helping to clear blockages and ignite inspiration.
- **Connecting with nature:** Immerse yourself in the beauty of nature and allow its serene energy to inspire and uplift you. Spending time near water bodies, such as lakes or oceans, can be particularly beneficial, as water is profoundly connected to the sacral chakra.
- **Sensory exploration:** Engaging in activities that evoke pleasure and stimulate the senses, such as indulging in aromatherapy, enjoying a luxurious bath, or exploring various textures through touch, can reignite the sacral chakra's creative flame.

Techniques for Emotional Healing and Balance

We know that the sacral chakra, located just below the navel, is associated with our emotions, creativity, passion, and sexuality. When this chakra is balanced, we experience a sense of harmony in these areas of our life. So, what can we do to bring that balance back?

Practicing mindfulness and meditation is one technique to promote emotional healing through the sacral chakra. Take a few moments each day to sit in a quiet space, close your eyes, and focus your attention on the area around your sacral chakra. Imagine a glowing orange light radiating from that area, balancing and clearing any emotional blockages. Breathe in deeply and exhale, releasing any tension or negative emotions you may be holding onto.

Engaging in creative activities is another fantastic way to heal and balance the sacral chakra. From painting and drawing to dancing and singing, anything that allows you to express yourself creatively can bring immense healing. So, pick up that paintbrush, turn up the music, and let your inner artist shine!

Incorporating aromatherapy can also be incredibly beneficial for sacral chakra healing. Consider using essential oils like orange, jasmine, or ylang-ylang, which have been known to enhance creativity, boost mood, and stimulate the sacral chakra. Take a moment to inhale the pleasant aroma and let it envelop you, heightening your emotional well-being.

Don't forget about the power of movement! Engaging in activities like yoga, tai chi, or dancing can help release any stagnant energy, increase vitality, and restore balance to the sacral chakra. So, put on your favorite tunes and let your body sway to the rhythm of life – your sacral chakra will thank you.

Finally, embracing your sensuality and exploring your desires in a healthy and consensual manner is crucial for sacral chakra healing. This can involve connecting intimately with a partner or simply acknowledging and accepting your own desires without judgment. Remember, positively embracing your sexuality can do wonders for your emotional well-being.

By incorporating these techniques into your daily routine, you'll be well on your way to attaining emotional healing and balance through the power of the sacral chakra. So go forth, unleash your creativity, and let your emotions flow freely.

The Role of the Vagus Nerve in Emotional Regulation

The vagus nerve and the sacral chakra are a dynamic duo in the realm of emotional regulation. These two powerhouses work tirelessly to ensure our emotional well-being remains in balance. So, let's dive into the fascinating role of the vagus nerve and its collaboration with the sacral chakra in this 1000-word section!

If the vagus nerve had a theme song, it would be "Under Pressure" by Queen and David Bowie because this nerve certainly knows a thing or two about keeping us composed in the face of stress.

So, what happens when the vagus nerve and the sacral chakra join forces? Well, they form a powerful alliance that enables us to navigate the ups and downs of life with grace and poise.

The vagus nerve acts as the vigilant guardian, constantly scanning our body for signs of distress. When it detects stress or danger, it sends signals to our brain, triggering the well-known fight-or-flight response. But here's where things get interesting. The vagus nerve also possesses another superpower – the ability to activate the relaxation response. This response helps us relax, calm down, and restore our emotional equilibrium.

Enter the sacral chakra, stage right. This energetic center plays a vital role in emotional regulation, acting as the control center for our emotions. When the sacral chakra is balanced and aligned, we experience a smooth flow of emotions, creativity, and a healthy expression of our sensuality.

But sometimes, life throws us a curveball, and our emotional equilibrium wavers. Here's where our dear vagus nerve steps in, activating the relaxation response and assisting the sacral chakra in finding its balance. It's like having a trusty sidekick by your side, ready to lend a helping hand when emotions start to run wild.

Together, the vagus nerve and the sacral chakra work in perfect synchrony to regulate our emotions. When stress triggers the fight-or-flight response, the vagus nerve steps in to calm things down, ensuring that our emotions don't spiral out of control. It's like having a skilled conductor leading an emotional symphony, guiding us to a place of peace and tranquility.

But wait, there's more! This dynamic duo also aids in releasing emotional blockages that may hinder our emotional well-being. With its expertise in connecting different organs, the vagus nerve helps release tension stored in our bodies, promoting a sense of emotional release and freedom. Meanwhile, the sacral chakra knocks on the door of our emotions, inviting us to explore and express our feelings in a healthy and balanced way.

So, dear reader, the vagus nerve's role in collaboration with the sacral chakra is truly awe-inspiring. They work tirelessly to regulate our emotions, ensuring we can navigate life's highs and lows with ease and grace. Imagine them as the ultimate power couple, supporting each other and helping us achieve emotional harmony.

Affirmations For the Sacral Chakra

To help you continue working with the sacral chakra, here are ten affirmations you can use:

- I embrace my emotions and allow myself to feel deeply and authentically.

- My creative energy flows freely, allowing me to express myself fully and joyfully.
- I trust my intuition and follow its guidance to create a balanced life.
- I am deserving of pleasure, joy, and abundance in all aspects of my life.
- I release any guilt or shame surrounding my sexuality, embracing it as a sacred and beautiful gift.
- I welcome and embrace change as it brings growth and new opportunities into my life.
- I have a healthy relationship with my emotions, allowing them to flow without becoming overwhelmed or suppressed.
- I am in tune with my passion and harness its power to manifest my dreams and desires.
- I honor my unique creativity and allow myself to explore new ideas and express myself freely.
- I am connected to my sensuality and experience pleasure in a balanced and respectful way.

MANIPURA

Sanskrit: मणिपूर

SOLAR PLEXUS CHAKRA

Chapter 6

The Solar Plexus Chakra and Personal Power

The solar plexus chakra holds a significant role in our sense of self-confidence and personal power. This chakra radiates a vibrant energy that empowers us to be bold, assertive, and connected to our inner strength.

Imagine the solar plexus chakra as the sun within our being, fueling us with the courage to face life's challenges and the determination to manifest our dreams. It's like having a constant cheerleader cheering you on from deep within your core!

This chakra acts as our energetic power station, providing us with the necessary life force and fuel to take charge of our lives and stand tall in our truth. When the solar plexus chakra is balanced and spinning harmoniously, our self-confidence blossoms, and we exude an undeniable aura of personal power.

However, the solar plexus chakra loves to be nurtured. Just as a plant needs sunlight and water to grow, our sense of self-confidence and personal power thrives on self-care, positive affirmations, and embracing our authenticity.

When our solar plexus chakra is strong and harmonized, we naturally radiate charisma and magnetism. People are drawn to us like bees to honey, captivated by our self-assurance and unmistakable aura of personal power. We become the shining stars of our own lives, embracing our uniqueness and fearlessly sharing our authentic selves with the world.

Practices to Boost Self-Esteem and Personal Power

By focusing and balancing the energy in this chakra, we can enhance our self-esteem and tap into our inner strength. Here are some exercises and practices you can use to do just that.

Solar Plexus Meditation:

1. To start, find a quiet and comfortable place to sit. Close your eyes, take a few deep breaths, and allow your body to relax.
2. Visualize a bright, warm, golden light glowing in your solar plexus region. As you inhale, imagine this light expanding and filling your entire torso, radiating confidence and personal power.
3. With each exhale, let go of any self-doubts or limiting beliefs.
4. Stay in this meditation for 15 minutes, focusing on the strength and vitality of your solar plexus chakra.

Solar Plexus Breathing:

1. Breathing exercises can help energize and balance the solar plexus chakra. Sit comfortably and place one hand on your belly and the other over your solar plexus.
2. Take a deep breath in through your nose, allowing your belly to expand, and feel the energy flowing into your solar plexus.
3. As you exhale through your mouth, release any tension or negative energy stored in this area.
4. Repeat this belly breathing technique for 10 minutes, focusing on the sensation of energy flowing in and out of your solar plexus.

Visualization and Power Pose:

1. Imagine yourself in a situation where you feel confident and empowered. Visualize yourself standing tall, shoulders back, head held high, radiating self-assurance.

2. As you imagine this, strike a power pose - stand up straight, hands on your hips, and take a few deep breaths.
3. Feel the energy coursing through your body, igniting your solar plexus chakra.
4. Practice this visualization and power pose for five minutes whenever you need an instant self-esteem boost.

Journaling:

1. Grab a journal and spend 15 minutes reflecting on your thoughts and emotions related to self-esteem and personal power.
2. Write about any insecurities or doubts you may have and then come up with positive affirmations or counter-arguments to debunk these beliefs.
3. Focus on the strengths and accomplishments that make you feel powerful and proud.
4. By journaling regularly, you'll gain insights into your self-esteem journey and foster a more positive self-image.

Remember, building self-esteem and personal power is an ongoing process. Consistency is key, so incorporate these exercises into your daily routine.

Enhancing Vagus Nerve Function for Inner Strength

By combining the vagus nerve with the stimulation of the solar plexus chakra, we can unlock a deeper sense of inner strength. Let's explore some exercises to help you in this journey.

Chanting "RAM":

Chanting is an effective way to activate and balance the solar plexus chakra while gently stimulating the vagus nerve. The sound of the mantra "RAM" resonates with the energy of the solar plexus chakra, fostering a sense of personal power and strength.

1. Find a quiet and comfortable space where you can sit or lie down.
2. Close your eyes and take a few deep breaths to center yourself.
3. Begin chanting "RAM" out loud, focusing on the vibrations in your throat and chest.
4. Let the sound of the mantra fill your awareness, allowing it to reverberate throughout your body.
5. Continue chanting for at least five minutes, gradually prolonging the duration as you progress.

Abdominal Self-Massage:

The solar plexus chakra is closely connected to the physical sensations in our abdomen. By gently massaging this area, we can further stimulate the solar plexus chakra and enhance vagus nerve function.

1. Lie down on your back and expose your abdomen.
2. Apply a small amount of massage oil or lotion to your hands, rubbing them together to warm them up.
3. Place your hands on your abdomen, just below the ribcage.
4. Apply gentle pressure in a circular motion, moving clockwise around your navel.
5. As you massage, visualize warm, golden energy radiating from your hands into your solar plexus chakra.
6. Continue massaging for at least five minutes, focusing on any areas of tension or discomfort.

Nadi Shodhana Pranayama (Alternate Nostril Breathing):

Nadi Shodhana Pranayama, or alternate nostril breathing, is a powerful technique that balances the left and right hemispheres of the brain while stimulating the vagus nerve. This practice promotes mental clarity, emotional stability, and inner strength. It's also not as complicated as it sounds!

1. Sit comfortably with your spine erect and your eyes closed.

2. Bring your right hand to your face and fold your index and middle fingers toward your palm, extending your thumb, ring finger, and pinky finger.
3. Close your right nostril with your thumb and inhale deeply through your left nostril.
4. Close your left nostril with your ring finger and exhale slowly through your right nostril.
5. Inhale through your right nostril, then close it with your thumb, opening your left nostril.
6. Exhale through your left nostril and continue this pattern for at least five minutes.

Consistency is key in enhancing vagus nerve function and activating the solar plexus chakra. Incorporate these exercises into your daily routine, starting with shorter durations and gradually increasing as you progress. Be patient with yourself, and trust that with regular practice, you will begin to develop a more profound sense of inner strength and resilience.

Affirmations for the Solar Plexus Chakra

In our last section, we talked about how affirmations are useful for helping to unblock and balance chakras. We also talked about how to use them. As we move through these chapters, I will give you affirmations for each chakra. So, here are ten affirmations you can use to balance and activate your solar plexus chakra:

- I am worthy of love and respect.
- I am confident and capable of achieving my goals.
- I am empowered to make my own choices and decisions.
- I deserve success and abundance in all areas of my life.
- I am worthy of receiving the blessings that come my way.
- I trust in my own abilities to navigate through challenges and obstacles.
- I embrace my uniqueness and shine my light authentically.

- I am strong, courageous, and resilient.
- I release all fears and doubts that hold me back from my true potential.
- I am surrounded by positive, supportive, and empowering relationships.

Combining these affirmations with visualization exercises can enhance their effectiveness. Close your eyes, take a few deep breaths, and imagine a vibrant yellow energy spinning in your solar plexus area. As you repeat your affirmations, visualize this energy growing brighter and expanding, filling your entire body with confidence, self-assurance, and personal power.

ANAHATA

Sanskrit: अनाहत

HEART CHAKRA

Chapter 7

The Heart Chakra and Love

The heart chakra is associated with love, compassion, and emotional balance. The heart chakra plays a vital role in our ability to form and maintain healthy relationships, as it serves as a bridge between our lower chakras (associated with earthly desires and emotions) and our higher chakras (associated with spiritual connection and awareness).

The heart chakra is commonly referred to as the seat of love. It radiates with unconditional love, inviting us to experience deep connections with ourselves and others. When this chakra is balanced and open, it allows for the free flow of love and compassion, leading to nurturing and fulfilling relationships.

One of the significant aspects of the heart chakra is its connection to self-love. We must learn to love ourselves before we can truly love others. The heart chakra helps us recognize our worth and value as individuals, promoting a healthy sense of self-esteem and self-acceptance. It encourages us to embrace our strengths and weaknesses, fostering a deep understanding of self-compassion.

When our heart chakra is blocked or imbalanced, it can manifest in various ways that hinder our ability to form healthy relationships. For example, if the heart chakra is deficient, we may struggle with feelings of unworthiness or have difficulties trusting others. We may find receiving love challenging or being vulnerable, creating barriers in our relationships.

On the other hand, an excessive heart chakra may cause us to place too much emphasis on others' needs, neglecting our own. We may become overly dependent on external validation or seek love and validation in unhealthy ways. This imbalance can lead to codependence and an inability to establish healthy relationship boundaries.

The heart chakra enables us to experience deep and transformative love in relationships. It allows for emotional intimacy, where we can connect with our partners profoundly. When the heart chakra is balanced, we can love others without expectations or conditions, fostering healthy and nurturing relationships.

The heart chakra also empowers us to experience love and compassion beyond romantic relationships. It connects us to a greater sense of universal love, allowing us to extend kindness and empathy towards all beings. It fuels our desire to positively impact the world, promoting acts of service and generosity.

Methods for Opening and Balancing the Heart Chakra

Opening and balancing the heart chakra is essential for nurturing love, compassion, and connection in our lives. Let's explore some effective methods to open and balance the heart chakra so you can start grabbing the rewards for yourself.

Heart-Centered Meditation:

One popular technique for opening and balancing the heart chakra is through heart-centered meditation.

1. Find a quiet and comfortable place to sit with your back straight and relaxed.
2. Close your eyes and take a few deep breaths to center yourself.
3. Imagine a beautiful green glowing light in the center of your chest, the energy of your heart chakra.
4. As you continue to breathe, bring your attention to this area, feeling warmth and love expanding with each breath.

5. Visualize this radiant light expanding beyond your body, enveloping your surroundings, and filling you with a sense of love and compassion.

Heart-Opening Yoga Poses:

Practicing heart-opening yoga poses can help release tension and blockages in the chest area, allowing energy to flow freely through the heart chakra. Some beneficial poses include Cobra Pose (Bhujangasana), Camel Pose (Ustrasana), and Bridge Pose (Setu Bandhasana).

1. Start by lying on your mat, face down, with your feet hips-distance apart.
2. Place your hands beneath your shoulders and gently press your palms into the ground to lift your chest, engaging your back muscles while keeping your lower body relaxed.
3. If you are comfortable, you can deepen the stretch by lifting your torso and slightly arching your back.
4. Remember to breathe deeply and listen to your body, allowing it to guide you into a comfortable and safe stretch.

Heart-Opening Essential Oils:

Using essential oils is another excellent way to facilitate the opening and balancing of the heart chakra. Ylang-Ylang, Rose, and Jasmine are known for their heart-opening properties.

1. To use essential oils, find a quiet space and sit comfortably.
2. Place a few drops of your chosen oil on your palms, rub them together, and bring your hands toward your face.
3. Take a deep breath in, inhaling the scent, and slowly exhale.
4. Repeat this process a few times, allowing the aroma to uplift your spirit and create a sense of harmony and openness within your heart.

Heart-Centered Journaling:

Writing can be a powerful tool for self-reflection and opening the heart.

1. Grab a journal or a piece of paper and pen, finding a comfortable and quiet space to sit.
2. Start by taking a few deep breaths to calm your mind.
3. Set an intention to connect with your heart energy as you begin writing.
4. Journaling prompts could include exploring what love and compassion mean to you, reflecting on acts of loving-kindness, or expressing gratitude for the love in your life.
5. Let your thoughts flow freely, without judgment or expectation.

By pouring your thoughts and emotions onto paper, you create space for greater clarity, understanding, and self-compassion.

Vagus Nerve Techniques for Fostering Compassion and Connection

In our fast-paced and technology-driven world, fostering compassion and connection can sometimes feel like an uphill battle. However, by combining the power of the vagus nerve techniques and the heart chakra, we can tap into a wellspring of empathy and enhance our ability to form meaningful connections with others.

Let's look at a few exercises and practices to help you activate and balance your heart chakra, cultivating compassion and deepening human connection.

Exercise 1: Heart-Centered Breathing:

1. Find a quiet and comfortable space where you can sit or lie down.
2. Close your eyes and take a few deep breaths to relax your body and calm your mind.

3. Place your hand gently over your heart area, tuning into the sensation of touch.
4. Begin to focus your breath on your heart area, imagining each inhale and exhale traveling in and out of your heart.
5. As you continue to breathe in this heart-centered manner, visualize your breath as a soothing, warm light filling your heart space.
6. With each inhale, imagine this light expanding and radiating compassion and love outward.
7. Allow yourself to feel the warmth and connection within your heart, letting go of any tension or resistance.
8. Practice heart-centered breathing for at least 5 minutes, gradually extending the duration as you become more comfortable with the exercise.

Loving-Kindness Meditation:

1. Find a comfortable seated position and close your eyes.
2. Take a few deep breaths to center yourself and bring your attention to the present moment.
3. Start by directing loving-kindness towards yourself. Repeat the following phrases silently or aloud: "May I be happy. May I be healthy. May I be safe. May I live with ease."
4. After a few minutes, shift your focus to a loved one, family member, or friend. Repeat the phrases, substituting "I" with their name: "May [their name] be happy. May [their name] be healthy. May [their name] be safe. May [their name] live with ease."
5. Gradually expand your circle of compassion to include acquaintances, strangers, and even those with whom you may have difficulties. Send loving-kindness to all beings: "May all beings be happy. May all beings be healthy. May all beings be safe. May all beings live with ease."
6. Continue this meditation for as long as you like, allowing feelings of compassion and connection to flow freely.

Heart-Centered Visualization:

1. Find a quiet space where you can sit comfortably.
2. Close your eyes and take a few deep breaths to settle into a relaxed state.
3. Visualize a rosebud in the center of your chest. Imagine this bud slowly opening, revealing a vibrant and radiant heart-shaped flower.
4. As the flower blooms, visualize soft pink light radiating from it and expand it to encompass your entire body.
5. Feel this loving energy infusing every cell and fiber of your being, permeating your thoughts, emotions, and actions.
6. Picture tendrils of light stretching out from your heart, connecting with the hearts of those around you, intertwining and creating a web of compassion and connection.
7. Sit in this visualization for a few minutes, basking in the warmth, love, and interconnectedness it brings.

As you continue to practice these exercises, you'll find the power of the vagus nerve and heart chakra working harmoniously within you, creating a more compassionate and connected existence.

Affirmations for the Heart Chakra

Innkeeping with the affirmations we used in the previous chakras, let's look at ten affirmations that can help open and balance your heart chakra:

- My heart is open and receptive to giving and receiving love in abundance.
- I am worthy of love, and I deserve to experience deep and meaningful connections.
- I forgive myself and others, releasing any past hurts and allowing love to flow freely.
- I am grateful for all the love and joy that surrounds me; I attract loving relationships into my life effortlessly.

- I embrace compassion and kindness, radiating love towards myself and others.
- I trust in the wisdom of my heart, knowing that it always guides me towards what is best for my highest good.
- I am connected to the universal energy of love, and it flows through me effortlessly, nurturing my soul.
- I listen to my heart's desires and follow them with courage and authenticity.
- I release any fears or blocks that prevent me from fully experiencing love; my heart is open and free to love without limitations.
- I am a magnet for love; I attract loving and nurturing people into my life, creating harmonious and fulfilling relationships.

Repeat these affirmations daily, either silently or out loud, to help balance and strengthen your heart chakra and cultivate an abundance of love in your life.

VISHUDDHA
Sanskrit: वशिुद्ध

THROAT CHAKRA

Chapter 8

The Throat Chakra and Communication

The throat chakra is a vital energy center in our bodies that plays a crucial role in self-expression and communication. Located at the base of our throat, it bridges our thoughts, emotions, and the external world.

Picture yourself standing in front of a crowd, ready to express your thoughts and ideas or perform a piece of art. The ability to effectively communicate and convey your message relies heavily on the health and balance of your throat chakra. This energy center is associated with the color blue, symbolizing clear communication, authenticity, and self-expression.

When the throat chakra is open and aligned, you will feel comfortable expressing yourself honestly and authentically. Words flow effortlessly, allowing you to articulate your thoughts with clarity and conviction. You become a master of communication, conveying your ideas and emotions accurately to others. People may find it easy to connect with your words, drawing them in with your charisma and natural charm.

However, the throat chakra can easily become imbalanced. Stress, fear, and trauma can hinder its proper functioning, leading to difficulties in expressing oneself. Have you ever experienced that feeling of a lump in your throat when trying to say something important or being uncomfortable speaking in front of a group? These are signs of an imbalanced throat chakra.

When the throat chakra is blocked, communication breaks down. You may struggle to find the right words, stutter, or even remain completely silent when you wish to speak up. This lack of self-expression can leave you feeling frustrated, misunderstood, and disconnected from others. It's like a radio station with a weak signal, making it challenging for others to tune into your frequency.

If this happens to you, don't worry. There are various methods to heal and balance the throat chakra, enabling the free flow of self-expression and fostering effective communication.

As the throat chakra harmonizes and opens, you will experience a profound transformation in your communication skills. This newfound clarity amplifies your ability to express your desires, needs, and boundaries effectively. Your interactions with others become more meaningful as you confidently, assertively, and respectfully articulate your thoughts and emotions.

A balanced throat chakra promotes active listening and empathy, which are essential to healthy communication. You create a safe space for open and honest dialogue when fully present and receptive to others. You foster connections and build stronger personal and professional relationships by actively listening and understanding.

Exercises to Clear and Activate the Throat Chakra

Let's talk about some exercises that can help clear and activate your throat chakra, allowing you to express yourself with confidence and authenticity.

Pranayama Exercise:

Breathing exercises are a powerful way to connect with the throat chakra.

1. Begin by sitting comfortably, cross-legged, or on a chair with a straight spine.
2. Close your eyes and take a few deep breaths in through your nose, and slowly exhale through your mouth.

3. Visualize a calming blue light filling your throat as you inhale, and as you exhale, imagine all the stagnation and blockages leaving your body.
4. Repeat this breathing exercise for a few minutes, feeling the air as it travels in and out of your throat.

Lion's Roar:

Let's awaken the roar within!

1. Sit up straight and take a deep breath in through your nose.
2. As you exhale forcefully through your mouth, open your mouth wide while sticking your tongue out and stretching it downwards towards your chin.
3. Let out a powerful "aahh" sound, just like a lion announcing its presence.
4. Feel the vibrations in your throat as if you are releasing any unexpressed emotions or thoughts that might be blocking your throat chakra.
5. Repeat this exercise three to five times, allowing your voice to be heard in the world.

Vocal Toning:

1. Begin by humming gently, feeling the vibration in your throat.
2. Gradually, let the sound travel up to your mouth as if chanting a melodious tune.
3. As you continue, experiment with different vowel sounds like "ah," "ee," and "oh."
4. Focus on maintaining a smooth, resonant tone.
5. Allow your voice to flow freely, being aware of any sensations in your throat.
6. Continue for a few minutes, relishing in the blissful vibrations.

Chakra Mantra Meditation:

Meditation is a precious gift for chakra healing, and it's no different for the throat chakra.

1. Find a comfortable position and close your eyes.
2. Take a few deep breaths, and as you exhale, silently repeat the mantra "HAM," which corresponds to the throat chakra.
3. Visualize a brilliant blue light radiating from your throat, calming and clearing any blockages.
4. Let the mantra resonate and reverberate within you, allowing it to dissolve any resistance or unexpressed thoughts.
5. Continue this peaceful practice for at least five minutes, basking in the divine energy of your throat chakra.

Creative Journaling

1. Grab a pen and a journal and allow your thoughts to flow freely onto the pages. Write without judgment, allowing your authentic voice to surface.
2. Explore your emotions, dreams, desires, and aspirations. This exercise helps untangle any hidden emotions and stimulates self-expression, promoting a healthier throat chakra.
3. Remember, there's no right or wrong way to journal – just let your thoughts and words pour out onto the paper.

Sing Your Heart Out:

Singing is a profound way to open and activate your throat chakra.

1. Choose a song that resonates with you or uplifts your spirits.
2. Sing with gusto, allowing your voice to carry your emotions. Let your soul be liberated through song, whether in the shower, in your car, or on a karaoke night with friends.
3. Feel the joy, freedom, and release as you connect with the power of your voice.

Remember, be patient and honor your own pace. Allow your unique voice to be heard and expressed authentically in the world. You are now equipped with the tools to unlock your throat chakra's power and confidently express yourself. Bravo!

Using the Vagus Nerve to Support Healthy Communication

So, how can we stimulate and strengthen the vagus nerve to enhance our communication skills? The good news is that some simple exercises can help you do just that. Let's explore a few of them.

Humming and Chanting:

Humming and chanting produce vibrations that stimulate the vagus nerve, helping to release tension and activate the relaxation response.

1. Find a quiet space, take a deep breath, and begin to hum or chant a soothing sound or mantra.
2. Allow the sound to resonate within you, feeling the vibrations in your chest and throat.
3. Explore different pitches and tones and continue for a few minutes.

This exercise can help calm your mind, reduce stress, and enhance your communication clarity.

Cold Water Splash:

This exercise might sound a bit unconventional, but it has proven to be an effective way to stimulate the vagus nerve.

Splash cold water on your face, focusing on your eyes and the area around your sinuses. The sudden sensation of the cold water triggers a physiological response that activates the vagus nerve.

This exercise helps to increase alertness, improve focus, and enhance communication.

Laughter Yoga:

Laughter is contagious and an excellent way to activate the vagus nerve.

1. Engage in a laughter yoga session by finding a comfortable position and laughing out loud.
2. Start with fake laughter, and soon it will transform into genuine laughter.
3. Allow yourself to let loose and embrace the joy of laughter.

Not only does this exercise improve communication, but it also boosts mood and promotes overall well-being.

Social Engagement:

Engaging in social interactions and fostering meaningful connections is a natural way to activate the vagus nerve. Practice active listening, maintain eye contact, and be genuinely present in conversations. Show empathy, ask open-ended questions, and be attentive to non-verbal cues.

By practicing these social engagement skills, you will find that your communication becomes more effective and fulfilling.

Affirmations For The Throat Chakra

By this point, it should come as no surprise that there are affirmations you can use for every single chakra in the body. Let's look at ten you can use for your throat chakra.

- I express myself clearly and confidently, allowing my truth to flow freely from my throat chakra.
- My voice is a powerful tool, and I use it to inspire, motivate, and uplift others.

- I am open and receptive to receiving and expressing love, kindness, and compassion through my words.
- I trust in my unique creative expression, knowing it is a powerful force for positive change.
- My thoughts and words are in harmony, bringing clarity and coherence to all my communication.
- I release any fear or self-doubt, trusting that my ideas and opinions are valuable and worthy of being heard.
- My throat chakra is balanced and aligned, enabling me to communicate with integrity and authenticity.
- I speak my truth with love and respect, honoring the power of my words and their impact on others.
- I am a skilled listener, fully present and attentive when others speak, allowing for deep understanding and connection.
- I release any past experiences that may have hindered my expression and embrace the freedom and joy of fully expressing my unique voice.

AJNA
Sanskrit: आज्ञा
THIRD-EYE CHAKRA

Chapter 9

The Third Eye Chakra and Intuition

The third eye chakra, also known as the Ajna chakra, is the sixth primary chakra in the subtle body, located between the eyebrows in the middle of the forehead. It is associated with intuition, inner vision, and clarity of thought.

First things first, what is intuition? Intuition can be defined as the ability to understand or know something without the need for conscious reasoning. It feels like a gut feeling, a hunch, or a sense of knowing that goes beyond logic. The third eye chakra is a conduit for higher wisdom, connecting the physical world with the spiritual realm and unlocking our intuitive abilities.

When the third eye chakra is balanced and aligned, our intuition becomes more accessible. We can tap into our innate wisdom and make decisions from a place of clarity and inner knowing. Our intuition acts as a guide, steering us in the right direction and helping us navigate life's challenges.

The third eye chakra connects us to our intuition and allows us to perceive the world on a deeper level. It allows us to see beyond the physical realm and perceive subtle energies, emotions, and spiritual insights. This expanded awareness helps us gain a deeper understanding of ourselves and others, enabling us to make more informed and empathetic decisions.

How to Listen to Your Intuition

We know that we should listen to our gut feeling or our intuition, but sometimes that can be very hard to do, especially if you're unsure whether it's intuition or paranoia speaking. However, when tuning in to your third eye chakra, it's important to be open to your intuition and allow it to guide you.

In a world filled with constant external noise and distractions, it becomes increasingly crucial to tap into our inner compass and listen to our intuition. In the end, our intuition holds the key to understanding ourselves better and making decisions aligned with our deepest desires and values.

If you struggle to listen to your gut, let's take a look at some practices to help you tune in a little more.

Cultivating Self-Awareness:

Listening to your intuition starts with developing self-awareness. Take time to reflect on your thoughts, emotions, and physical sensations without judgment. Engage in practices such as mindfulness meditation, journaling, or simply spending quiet time alone to connect with your inner self. By becoming aware of your own internal landscape, you create a solid foundation for honing your intuitive abilities.

Trusting Your Gut:

Intuition often speaks to us through our gut feelings or "gut instincts." Learn to recognize and trust these gut reactions. When faced with a decision, pay attention to the initial response that arises within you. It might manifest as a subtle feeling of ease or discomfort. Trusting your gut allows you to tap into your innate wisdom beyond logical reasoning, guiding you towards choices aligned with your authentic self.

Tune Into Your Body:

Our bodies are powerful messengers of intuition. Pay attention to physical sensations that arise when making choices or engaging with different people or situations. Does a particular decision make your heart race with excitement, or does it leave you feeling drained? Does your body feel light and relaxed when you meet someone aligned with your values, or does it tense up in their presence? By tuning into these bodily signals, you can gain insights into what resonates with your intuition.

Recognize Patterns and Synchronicities:

Intuition often reveals itself through patterns and synchronicities in our lives. Notice recurring themes, symbols, or coincidences that catch your attention. Keep a journal to record these events, allowing you to reflect on their deeper meanings over time. By recognizing patterns and synchronicities, you can uncover hidden messages that your intuition is trying to communicate.

Practice Active Listening:

Active listening is a skill that can greatly enhance your ability to listen to your intuition. When engaging in conversations, be fully present and attentive to both verbal and non-verbal cues. Pay attention to how you feel during interactions. Do you sense a genuine connection? Does the conversation excite or drain you? By practicing active listening, you can sift through external influences and access your intuition's guidance.

Embrace Silence and Stillness:

In our fast-paced world, the silence and stillness of solitude are often underrated. Create regular moments for quiet contemplation, away from the noise and distractions of everyday life. Whether through meditation, walks in nature, or simply sitting in a peaceful place, embrace silence and stillness to nourish your intuition. It is within these serene moments that we often receive the clearest intuitive insights.

Cultivate an Open Mind:

To listen to your intuition effectively, cultivate an open mind. Embrace curiosity and embrace the unknown. Allow yourself to explore different perspectives and possibilities. An open mind facilitates the reception of intuitive guidance and helps to overcome biases or preconceived notions that may hinder your decision-making process.

Follow Your Passions:

Passion and intuition are closely intertwined. When you engage in activities or pursuits that ignite a fire within you, your intuition naturally aligns with your passions. Pay attention to the activities that bring you joy, fulfillment, and a sense of purpose. By following your passions, you tap into an abundant source of intuitive wisdom and guidance.

Practices for Enhancing Intuitive Abilities and Insight

To help you boost your intuition and seek guidance, let's explore some exercises and practices that can help cultivate balance in the third eye chakra.

Meditation for Third Eye Activation:

1. Sit comfortably in a quiet space and gently close your eyes.
2. Take a few deep breaths, allowing your body to relax.
3. Visualize a radiant indigo light at the center of your forehead, where your third eye is located.
4. Imagine this light growing brighter with each breath, pulsating with energy.
5. Stay with this visualization for a few minutes, focusing on the feeling of expansion and connection to your intuition.

Journaling to Tap into Intuition:

Keeping a journal can be a valuable practice to deepen your intuitive connection. Set aside a few minutes each day to write down your intuitive hunches, dreams, or synchronistic experiences. Reflecting on these entries will help you recognize patterns and develop trust in your intuitive abilities.

Guided Visualization for Intuitive Exploration:

1. Find a quiet space and play a guided visualization or meditation specifically designed to stimulate intuitive insights.
2. Allow the soothing voice to guide you through vivid imagery, encouraging your third eye to awaken and expand.

These visualizations can open the doors to your inner wisdom and intuitive guidance.

Crystal Healing for Ajna Balancing:

Certain crystals can be used to support the activation and balance of the third eye chakra. Choose crystals like amethyst, lapis lazuli, or clear quartz and place them over your third eye while meditating or lying down. As you breathe deeply, visualize the crystal's energy integrating with your third eye, opening and balancing it.

Sound Healing and Chanting:

Sound has a profound impact on our energetic being. Take time to listen to binaural beats, healing frequencies, or nature sounds that aid in activating and balancing the third eye chakra. Additionally, you may explore chanting sacred mantras such as "Om" or "AUM," directing the sound to resonate within your forehead.

Engaging in Creative Practices:

Creativity is a powerful way to tap into our intuition. Engage in artistic endeavors such as drawing, painting, writing poetry, or playing a musical instrument. Allow the creative process to flow naturally, trusting your instincts rather than focusing on the outcome. This practice stimulates the intuitive faculties, resulting in profound insights and inspiration.

Connecting with Nature:

Nature has a way of grounding our energy and opening us up to spiritual realms. Spend time in natural surroundings, such as forests, parks, or by the ocean. Take mindful walks, observing the beauty around you. Allow yourself to become fully present, letting your senses absorb the subtle energies of nature, awakening your intuitive connection.

The Vagus Nerve's Role in Sharpening Intuition

The influence of the vagus nerve extends beyond its primary physiological functions, as it also forms a crucial bridge between the brain and the gut - referred to as the "gut-brain axis." This connection suggests that the vagus nerve plays a significant role in regulating our emotional responses, including our capacity to access and process intuitive information.

We know that intuition is an inherent, subconscious process that allows us to make quick decisions without consciously analyzing all the available information. While intuition has long been associated with mysticism, recent scientific studies suggest that it may be grounded in neurobiology, including the communication between the brain and the gut via the vagus nerve.

One aspect that makes the vagus nerve particularly intriguing in relation to intuition is its connection to the enteric nervous system (ENS) - often referred to as the "second brain." The ENS is a complex network of neurons embedded in the walls of the digestive system, comprising over 100 million nerve cells, more than the spinal cord contains. This intricate network communicates directly with the brain via the vagus nerve, giving rise to the possibility that gut instincts and intuitions may stem from the communication between the ENS and the brain.

Vagal Tone and Intuition

Vagal tone refers to the degree of activation and efficiency of the vagus nerve. When the vagal tone is high, it indicates active and healthy nerve functioning, enabling better emotional regulation, stress reduction, and even heightened intuitive capabilities. On the other hand, low vagal tone correlates with increased susceptibility to anxiety, depression, and difficulties with emotional regulation.

Studies have suggested that people with higher vagal tone exhibit an enhanced ability to listen to and trust their gut feelings, leading to improved decision-making. High vagal tone allows for smoother communication between the gut and brain, allowing the transmission of both physiological and intuitive signals. This optimal communication enables individuals to access and interpret subtle cues and information more accurately, providing the basis for confident, intuitive decision-making.

Enhancing Vagal Tone and Strengthening Intuition

The good news is that vagal tone is not fixed and can be actively enhanced through various practices aimed at lowering stress and promoting relaxation. These practices include deep breathing exercises, meditation, yoga, and engaging in activities that promote positive social connections and emotional well-being.

By incorporating these techniques into our lives, we can cultivate a healthier vagus nerve and harness its potential to sharpen our intuitive capabilities.

Deep breathing exercises, such as diaphragmatic breathing, stimulate the vagus nerve, signaling the body to transition into a state of rest and relaxation. Incorporating mindfulness meditation into our daily routine can also enhance vagal tone, as it focuses our attention and calms the mind, allowing for clearer access to intuitive thoughts and feelings. Meanwhile, engaging in regular physical exercise, particularly activities like yoga that emphasize breath control and movement, can positively impact both vagal tone and overall well-being.

Affirmations For The Third Eye Chakra

On your journey toward trusting your intuition, affirmations can be a great tool. Here are ten affirmations to help open and balance your third eye chakra.

- I am open and receptive to the wisdom and intuition of my third eye chakra.
- My third eye is clear and balanced, allowing me to see the truth in all situations.
- I trust my inner guidance and follow it with confidence and clarity.
- My intuition is strong and accurate, guiding me towards my highest good.
- I easily tap into my higher knowledge and wisdom through my third eye chakra.
- I am connected to my intuition and use it to make wise decisions in my life.
- My third eye chakra is balanced, allowing me to perceive the world from a higher perspective.
- I honor and trust my intuitive abilities, knowing they are a valuable asset in my life.
- My third eye chakra is open and free of any blockages, allowing the flow of divine insights.
- I embrace and nurture my psychic abilities, using them for the benefit of myself and others.

SAHASRARA
Sanskrit: सहस्रार
CROWN CHAKRA

Chapter 10

The Crown Chakra and Spiritual Connection

Now, let's turn our attention to the crown chakra.

Situated at the crown of the head, the Crown Chakra, also known as Sahasrara, is the gateway to the spiritual realm. It is like the pinnacle of a great tower, connecting us to the divine energy that flows through the universe. With its ethereal violet hue, it is no wonder that this chakra embodies spirituality, transcendence, and enlightenment.

At its core, the Crown Chakra serves as a conductor of cosmic energy, funneling it into the entirety of our being. This energy nourishes our mind, body, and spirit, fostering a harmonious equilibrium that allows us to look beyond the confines of the material world. When balanced, it acts as a vessel for spiritual enlightenment, opening our minds to a higher consciousness and connecting us to the universal energy that permeates all things.

For those who seek spiritual connection and a glimpse into the vastness of our existence, understanding the Crown Chakra is paramount. It is in this divine center that the proverbial key to enlightenment resides. As we explore its significance, let me be your astute guide on this profound journey.

Imagine the Crown Chakra as a lotus flower, delicately unfolding its petals as we delve deeper. Each petal represents a different facet of spiritual enlightenment, and it is in their harmonious alignment that we can achieve a truer connection to the divine.

The first petal of this celestial lotus represents pure consciousness. In order to achieve enlightenment, one must first attain a state of pure awareness, transcending the limitations of our physical form. This awareness allows us to perceive and understand the interconnectedness of all things, removing the barriers that separate us from the divine.

The second petal, inner peace, is essential in our quest for spiritual connection. It is only through a calm and tranquil mind that we can truly silence the chatter of everyday life and open ourselves to the wisdom of the universe. In this stillness, we are able to hear the whispers of our inner self, guiding us towards a more enlightened existence.

As we progress through the petals, we come across the third one: surrendering the ego. This crucial step involves relinquishing our attachment to our self-identity, allowing ourselves to dissolve into the vastness of the cosmos. Only by transcending ego-driven desires can we truly let the divine energy flow through us unimpeded and limitless.

The fourth petal represents divine love and compassion—a concept that seems simple yet holds tremendous power. By opening our hearts to love and compassion, we become conduits for universal energy. This altruistic love radiates outward, connecting us with others and allowing us to transcend the boundaries of our own existence.

As we approach the final petal, we encounter spiritual wisdom. This wisdom is not obtained through bookish knowledge but through direct experience and spiritual insight. It is the light that illuminates our path, guiding us toward a deeper understanding of our purpose and the interconnectedness of all things.

When all the petals are aligned and harmonious, the Crown Chakra blossoms in its full glory, paving the way for spiritual connection and enlightenment. In this state, we become receptive to the cosmic energy that surrounds us, allowing us to experience a profound connection with the universe and everything within it.

Now, don't be disheartened if you feel overwhelmed by the complexities of this journey. Understanding the Crown Chakra's role in spiritual connection and enlightenment is a lifelong endeavor. With patience, dedication, and a humble heart, you can gradually align this magnificent chakra, allowing it to guide you toward a more profound spiritual connection.

Remember, practice makes perfect, and when it comes to working with the crown chakra, that's a certain truth.

Techniques for Achieving Spiritual Balance and Connection

On your journey toward achieving spiritual balance and connection, there are many exercises and techniques you can use. Let's explore some of the most effective.

Create a Serene Space for Grounding:

1. Find a quiet and serene space where you can comfortably sit or lie down undisturbed. This could be a cozy corner in your home or a peaceful spot outdoors. Make sure you feel relaxed and at ease in this space.
2. Take a few deep breaths and feel yourself grounded in the present moment.
3. Imagine roots growing from the soles of your feet, connecting you deep into the earth.
4. Visualize this grounding energy, stabilizing you and providing a strong foundation for your spiritual journey.

Meditation and Mindfulness:

1. In your comfortable space, close your eyes and bring your attention to your breath.
2. Focus on the natural rhythm of your inhalations and exhalations.
3. As thoughts arise, gently acknowledge them and let them go, bringing your focus back to the breath.

This practice of mindfulness helps calm the mind and cultivate inner peace.

Visualization and Imagery:

1. Envision a beautiful violet or white light pouring down from the universe, entering through the top of your head, and filling your entire body.
2. Visualize this light expanding and radiating, clearing any blockages and aligning your crown chakra.
3. Feel a strong sense of connection to the divine and universal energy.

Sound Healing and Music:

Immerse yourself in soothing sounds or uplifting music that resonates with your spiritual journey. This could include chanting, Tibetan singing bowls, or gentle instrumental music. Allow the vibrations to wash over you and elevate your energy, promoting balance and connection within your crown chakra.

Gratitude and Journaling:

Take a moment to express gratitude for the divine guidance and wisdom you've already received in your life. Reflect on the blessings and spiritual growth you've experienced. Consider keeping a journal to document your spiritual journey, insights, and experiences along the way.

Remember, the path to spiritual balance and connection with your crown chakra is unique to you. Feel free to explore additional practices that resonate with your personality and preferences. Stay authentic to your journey and enjoy the beautiful transformation that comes with embracing your spiritual self.

Integrating Vagus Nerve Practices for Spiritual Well-being

In recent years, the connection between the vagus nerve and our overall well-being, including spiritual health, has gained attention. The vagus nerve is the longest and most complex nerve in our body, playing a crucial role in regulating various bodily functions.

It is also intimately tied to the crown chakra, which is associated with spiritual connection and enlightenment.

Let's take a look at some practical exercises and practices that can help balance the vagus nerve and stimulate the crown chakra, enhancing spiritual well-being.

Diaphragmatic Breathing:

This is a technique that can be used with most chakras, but in this case, it can help stimulate the vagus nerve and lead to spiritual health. Let's remind ourselves how to do it.

1. Find a quiet and comfortable space where you won't be disturbed. Sit or lie down in a relaxed position.
2. Place one hand on your chest and the other on your abdomen, just below your ribcage.
3. Take a slow, deep breath in through your nose, allowing your abdomen to expand. Focus on filling your lower lungs while keeping your chest relatively still.
4. Exhale slowly through your mouth, allowing your abdomen to deflate. Pay attention to the sensation of your breath leaving your body.
5. Repeat this diaphragmatic breathing technique for 5-10 minutes, gradually increasing the duration as you feel more comfortable. Allow your breath to become slow, rhythmic, and relaxed.

Meditation and Visualization:

1. Find a peaceful and comfortable space where you can sit undisturbed. Close your eyes and take a few deep breaths to center yourself.
2. Imagine a bright, shimmering white light above your head, representing the crown chakra. Visualize this light flowing down and entering the top of your head, gradually expanding and filling your entire body.

3. As you continue to breathe slowly and deeply, imagine this white light radiating throughout your body, bringing clarity, peace, and spiritual connection to every cell.
4. Stay in this meditative state for as long as you feel comfortable. You can set a timer or allow yourself to naturally come out of the meditation when ready.

Chanting and Toning:

1. Sit comfortably with your back straight and take a few deep breaths to relax.
2. Choose a simple mantra or sacred sound that resonates with your spiritual practice or beliefs. Examples include "Om," "Aum," or "Ah."
3. Begin chanting or toning the chosen sound, either out loud or internally. Focus on feeling the vibration of the sound, starting from your throat and resonating throughout your entire body.
4. Repeat the chant for several minutes, allowing the sound to cleanse and activate your crown chakra. Feel the energy flowing upward, connecting you to the divine.

Conscious Walking in Nature:

1. Find a calm, natural environment where you can take a leisurely walk. This could be a park, a beach, or a forest.
2. As you start walking, pay attention to the sensations in your body and the connection you have with the earth beneath your feet. Slow down and be present in each step.
3. Take mindful breaths, focusing on the rise and fall of your chest and the rhythm of your footsteps. Allow your mind to quiet as you immerse yourself in the beauty of nature.
4. With every step, imagine you are absorbing the tranquil energy of the earth, allowing it to flow up through your body and open your crown chakra. Feel the connection between your spiritual self and the greater universe.

5. Continue this conscious walking for as long as you wish, allowing your mind to become clear and receptive to spiritual insights and inspiration.

Remember, these exercises are meant to support your spiritual well-being, but they should be practiced with intention and regularity. Find a routine that works for you, and as you engage in these practices, let your intuition guide you.

Affirmations to Work With the Crown Chakra

Here are ten affirmations you can use to activate and balance the crown chakra.

- "I am divinely connected to the universal consciousness, and my crown chakra is open and balanced."
- "I trust in the wisdom of the universe to guide me, and I surrender any limitations to my highest self."
- "I am open to receiving divine insights and guidance for the highest good of all."
- "I embrace my spiritual journey and honor the higher realms of consciousness."
- "My crown chakra is a channel for pure, divine energy. I allow it to flow freely and harmoniously through me."
- "I release all attachments to ego and embrace the oneness of all beings."
- "I radiate love, compassion, and gratitude, creating a deep sense of unity and harmony within and around me."
- "I am connected to my higher self, and I trust its guidance to lead me towards enlightenment and spiritual growth."
- "I am a vessel for divine wisdom, and I use it to inspire and uplift others."
- "I acknowledge my unique expression of consciousness, and I strive to align my thoughts, words, and actions with my highest self."

Chapter 11

Daily Practices for Chakra and Vagus Nerve Health

In our fast-paced and often stressful world, taking care of our physical and mental well-being is of vital importance. One effective way to achieve this balance is by incorporating practices that promote the maintenance of our chakras and vagus nerve.

Developing a daily routine centered around chakra and vagus nerve maintenance can help us feel centered, grounded, and at peace, enabling us to navigate life with ease and grace.

Now, let's start by designing a daily routine that incorporates practices aimed at chakra and vagus nerve maintenance. Remember, consistency is key, so finding a routine that works for you and sticking to it is essential.

Step 1 – Yoga Stretching

Begin your mornings with a gentle yet energizing activity like yoga or stretching. These practices help awaken and balance the chakras while also activating the vagus nerve. As you move through each pose, envision the energy flowing freely through your chakra centers, enhancing their strength and vitality.

Here is a good yoga routine to try:

- Begin by finding a quiet and peaceful space where you can practice without distractions. You can use a yoga mat or a comfortable surface.

- Start with a few minutes of deep breathing to center yourself. Close your eyes and take slow, deep breaths, inhaling through your nose and exhaling through your mouth. This will help calm your mind and bring focus to your practice.
- Begin with gentle neck rotations. Sit or stand with a straight back and slowly rotate your head in a clockwise direction for 5-10 rotations, and then repeat in a counter-clockwise direction.
- Move on to shoulder rolls. Stand with your feet hip-width apart, relax your shoulders, and roll them forward in a circular motion for 5-10 rounds. Then, reverse the direction and roll them backward.
- Now, it's time to warm up your spine with cat-cow stretches. Come down to all fours with your hands directly under your shoulders and knees under your hips. Inhale, arch your back and lift your chest and tailbone towards the ceiling (cow pose). Exhale, round your back, tuck your chin towards your chest and draw your navel in towards your spine (cat pose). Flow through these movements 5-10 times, syncing your breath with the movement.
- Transition into a seated position for seated forward bends. Extend your legs in front of you and flex your feet. Inhale, raise your arms overhead and then exhale as you fold forward over your legs, reaching for your feet or shins. Stay here for a few breaths, gently releasing any tension in your spine and hamstrings.
- Next, move into a seated twist to activate your core and stimulate the solar plexus chakra. Bend your right knee and cross your left foot over the right knee. Place your left hand on the floor behind you for support, and on an inhale, lift your right arm up and twist your torso to the left. Hold for a few breaths, feeling the twist in your spine. Repeat on the other side.
- Transition to a downward-facing dog pose to energize the entire body and stimulate circulation. From all fours, tuck your toes, lift your hips towards the ceiling, and straighten your legs as

much as comfortable. Spread your fingers wide, engage your core, and relax your neck. Take a few deep breaths here.

- From down dog, gently drop to your knees and sit back on your heels for a child's pose. Extend your arms forward and rest your forehead on the mat. Breathe deeply, allowing the pose to relax your mind and deeply stretch your lower back.

Step 2 – Chakra Meditation

Following your morning movement routine, dedicate some time to meditation. Find a quiet and comfortable space where you can sit undisturbed for at least 10-15 minutes.

- Close your eyes, take a few deep breaths, and bring your attention inward.
- Visualize each chakra and imagine cleansing and clearing any blockages or stagnation that may be present.
- As you do this, also direct some focus towards activating the vagus nerve by consciously slowing down your breathing, allowing your body and mind to relax.

Step 3 – Crystal Healing

After your meditation session, consider incorporating a chakra-balancing practice such as crystal therapy into your routine. You can place crystals that resonate with each chakra on corresponding areas of your body. By doing so, you engage your senses and create an environment conducive to healing and alignment.

To help you understand which crystal to use and where here is a list of each chakra and its corresponding crystals.

1. Root Chakra (Muladhara):

- Red Jasper: Supports grounding, stability, and courage.

- Smoky Quartz: Aids in releasing negative energy and promoting grounding.

- Hematite: Enhances vitality, strength, and stability.
- Black Obsidian: Supports emotional grounding and protection.

2. Sacral Chakra (Svadhishthana):

- Carnelian: Boosts creativity, passion, and sensuality.
- Orange Calcite: Enhances motivation, joy, and personal power.
- Sunstone: Encourages confidence, vitality, and self-expression.
- Peach Moonstone: Supports emotional healing and balance.

3. Solar Plexus Chakra (Manipura):

- Citrine: Amplifies personal power, abundance, and confidence.
- Yellow Jasper: Enhances self-esteem, courage, and optimism.
- Tigers Eye: Boosts motivation, clarity, and focus.
- Golden Tiger Eye: Supports willpower, assertion, and strength.

4. Heart Chakra (Anahata):

- Rose Quartz: Encourages love, compassion, and emotional healing.
- Green Aventurine: Enhances harmony, vitality, and growth.
- Rhodonite: Supports forgiveness, compassion, and self-love.
- Green Jade: Boosts emotional balance, abundance, and harmony.

5. Throat Chakra (Vishuddha):

- Sodalite: Encourages clear communication and intuition.
- Lapis Lazuli: Enhances self-expression, wisdom, and truth.
- Blue Lace Agate: Supports calming energy and clear communication.
- Aquamarine: Boosts communication, soothing energy, and self-expression.

6. Third Eye Chakra (Ajna):

- Amethyst: Enhances intuition, spiritual awareness, and clarity.

- Labradorite: Boosts psychic abilities, insight, and spiritual connection.

- Purple Fluorite: Supports mental clarity, spiritual discernment, and focus.

- Sodalite: Encourages intuition, insight, and deep meditation.

7. Crown Chakra (Sahasrara):

- Clear Quartz: Amplifies spiritual connection, clarity, and energy flow.

- Amethyst: Enhances divine connection, spiritual insight, and higher awareness.

- Selenite: Supports spiritual growth, purification, and connection to higher realms.

- Clear Calcite: Boosts spiritual awakening, energy flow, and consciousness.

Step 4 - Pranayama

Midway through your day, take a break to practice pranayama, an ancient yogic breathing technique. By consciously regulating your breath, you activate the vagus nerve, promoting a sense of calm and relaxation.

- Inhale deeply through your nose for a count of four
- Hold your breath for four counts
- Exhale slowly through your mouth for a count of eight
- Repeat this cycle for a few minutes, allowing a deep sense of calm to wash over you

Step 5 – Mindful Eating

Mindful eating can be a great practice for chakra and vagus nerve healing. Here are some steps to incorporate mindful eating into your routine:

- **Establish a peaceful environment:** Find a quiet and comfortable space to eat your meal. Make sure there are no distractions like screens or noise.
- **Create a nourishing meal:** Prepare a balanced meal with fresh, whole foods that provide a variety of nutrients. Include foods that are known to support chakra and vagus nerve healing, such as leafy greens, fruits, nuts, seeds, and foods rich in omega-3 fatty acids.
- **Engage your senses:** Before you start eating, take a moment to observe the colors, smells, and textures of your food. Engage your senses by appreciating the beauty and aroma of your meal.
- **Express gratitude:** Before you take the first bite, express gratitude for the meal in front of you and for the nourishment it will provide your body. This can be a simple mental acknowledgment or a spoken expression of gratitude.
- **Slow down and savor each bite:** Take small, mindful bites and chew your food thoroughly. Pay attention to the flavors and textures as you eat. Pause between bites and appreciate the sensation of eating.
- **Monitor your body's signals:** Pay attention to your body's hunger and fullness cues. Eat until you feel satisfied and avoid overeating. This helps maintain a healthy balance and promotes better digestion.
- **Stay present and focused:** Be fully present with your meal, noticing any thoughts, sensations, or emotions that arise. If your mind wanders, gently bring your attention back to the present moment.
- **Listen to your body:** As you eat mindfully, listen to your body's feedback. Notice how certain foods make you feel, both

physically and emotionally. Adjust your choices accordingly to support your chakra and vagus nerve healing.

Step 6 – Bathe in Essential Oils

In the evening, wind down with a warm bath infused with essential oils. Allow the healing properties of the oils to soothe your senses while simultaneously imagining the warm water washing away any residual stress or energetic impurities. As you relax, reflect on your day and express gratitude for the opportunities it presented to grow and nurture yourself.

Here are the ideal essential oils to use with each chakra.

- **Root Chakra (Muladhara):** Cedarwood, Patchouli, Vetiver, Frankincense
- **Sacral Chakra (Svadhisthana):** Orange, Ylang Ylang, Clary Sage, Sandalwood
- **Solar Plexus Chakra (Manipura):** Lemon, Peppermint, Bergamot, Rosemary
- **Heart Chakra (Anahata):** Rose, Lavender, Geranium, Eucalyptus
- **Throat Chakra (Vishuddha):** Chamomile, Peppermint, Eucalyptus, Blue Tansy
- **Third Eye Chakra (Ajna):** Lavender, Frankincense, Clary Sage, Helichrysum
- **Crown Chakra (Sahasrara):** Frankincense, Lavender, Sandalwood, Rose

Remember to always dilute essential oils with a carrier oil before applying them to the skin or a bath and consult with a certified aromatherapist if you have any specific concerns or questions.

Step 7 - Journaling/Reading

Before you drift off to sleep, spend a few minutes journaling or engaging in a relaxing activity such as reading. Journaling allows you to release any lingering thoughts or emotions and brings clarity to your mind.

Reading, on the other hand, transports you into different worlds and opens your imagination, subtly stimulating and balancing the chakras.

Building a daily routine for chakra and vagus nerve maintenance not only benefits your physical and mental well-being but also nourishes your soul. It's essential to tailor these practices to suit your needs and preferences. Experiment and explore various techniques, and don't be afraid to add your own personal touch to the routine.

Remember, a routine is not set in stone, and you can always modify it as you go along. The key is to find what resonates with you and brings you joy and peace. So, here's to finding your own unique pathway to chakra and vagus nerve maintenance.

Meditation, Breathwork, & Mindfulness Exercises

Meditation, breathwork, and mindfulness are key aspects of incorporating chakra healing into your lifestyle. We've covered a couple of easy exercises, but let's delve into some extra ones here so you always have something to refer back to.

Meditation Exercises

Chakra Balancing Meditation

- Sit in a comfortable position, close your eyes, and take a few deep breaths to relax.
- Begin by focusing on your root chakra, located at the base of the spine. Visualize a bright red color and imagine it spinning

- in a clockwise direction. As you visualize the color, repeat the affirmation, "I am grounded and secure."
- Shift your attention to the sacral chakra, located just below the navel. Visualize a vibrant orange color and imagine it spinning in a clockwise direction. Repeat the affirmation, "I am creative and passionate."
- Move up to the solar plexus chakra, located in the upper abdomen. Visualize a radiant yellow color spinning in a clockwise direction. Repeat the affirmation, "I am worthy and confident."
- Focus on the heart chakra, located in the center of the chest. Visualize a serene green color spinning in a clockwise direction. Repeat the affirmation, "I am open to love and compassion."
- Shift your attention to the throat chakra located in the throat area. Visualize a peaceful blue color spinning in a clockwise direction. Repeat the affirmation, "I express myself with authenticity and clarity."
- Move up to the third eye chakra, located in the middle of the forehead. Visualize a deep indigo color spinning in a clockwise direction. Repeat the affirmation, "I trust my intuition and inner wisdom."
- Lastly, focus on the crown chakra located at the top of the head. Visualize a luminous violet color spinning in a clockwise direction. Repeat the affirmation, "I am connected to divine wisdom and peace."
- Take a few moments to sit in this balanced state, feeling the energy flow through each chakra.
- When you're ready, gently open your eyes.

Vagus Nerve Activation Meditation

- Sit or lie down comfortably, allowing your body to relax completely. Take a few deep, slow breaths to settle your mind.

- Begin by bringing your awareness to your breath. Inhale deeply through your nose, expanding your belly. Exhale slowly through your mouth, releasing any tension or stress. Imagine exhaling all the way down to your feet, grounding yourself in the present moment.
- Place your right hand on your belly, just below your ribcage. Focus on the sensation of your breath as you inhale, feeling your belly rise. As you exhale, feel your belly gently descend. Continue this deep, mindful breathing for a few more cycles.
- Now, bring your attention to your heart area. Visualize a warm, soothing light surrounding your heart. As you inhale, imagine breathing in this healing light, allowing it to fill your entire chest. As you exhale, release any tension or negativity from your heart space.
- Shift your focus to the area behind your ears, where the vagus nerve is located. Visualize a gentle, flowing river of energy running from this area down to your belly. As you inhale, imagine this river of energy becoming brighter and more vibrant. As you exhale, feel any blockages or tension being released and carried away by the flow.
- As you continue to breathe, expand your awareness to the rest of your body. Imagine this river of energy flowing through your arms, down to your fingertips. Feel a sense of relaxation and renewal spreading throughout your body with each breath.
- Stay in this relaxed state for as long as you like, allowing the healing energy to permeate your entire being. When you're ready, gently bring your awareness back to the present moment.

Chakra Breathwork Meditation

- Sit in a comfortable position with your spine straight and your palms facing up, resting on your thighs. Close your eyes and take a few deep breaths to relax.
- Start by inhaling deeply through your nose. As you do, envision a bright, healing light entering through your crown

- chakra at the top of your head and moving down through each chakra in your body.
- Hold your breath briefly as you focus on each chakra, starting from the crown chakra and moving down to the root chakra. With each chakra, visualize the corresponding color.
- Exhale slowly and intentionally through your mouth, releasing any tension or negative energy from each chakra. As you exhale, visualize any blockages or stuck energy being carried away and dissolved into the earth.
- Repeat this process, taking slow, deep breaths for several cycles. With each inhalation and exhalation, imagine your chakras becoming more balanced, vibrant, and aligned.
- After a few minutes, allow your breath to return to its natural rhythm. Sit in stillness for a moment, feeling the energy flowing freely through your chakras and the sense of peace and renewal it brings.
- When you're ready, gently open your eyes, bringing the positive energy and balance you cultivated during the meditation into your day.

Breathwork Exercises

Chakra Balancing Breath

- Sit in a comfortable position, close your eyes, and take a deep breath in through your nose.
- As you inhale, imagine a white light entering your body from the top of your head.
- Visualize this light flowing down through each chakra, starting from the crown to the base.
- As you exhale, imagine any stagnant energy or negativity leaving your body through your feet.
- Repeat this visualization for a few minutes, focusing on each chakra as you go along.

Vagus Nerve Activating Breath

- Sit in a comfortable position and take a deep breath in through your nose.
- Slowly exhale through your mouth, making a soft "haaa" sound as you do.
- After fully exhaling, pause for a moment before taking another deep inhale.
- Repeat this pattern, focusing on the rhythm of your breath and the sound you make while exhaling.

This exercise activates the vagus nerve, promoting relaxation, calmness, and overall well-being.

Alternate Nostril Breathing

- Sit comfortably and place your left hand on your left knee, palm facing up.
- With your right hand, bring the index and middle finger to the space between your eyebrows.
- Close your right nostril with your thumb and take a deep breath in through your left nostril.
- Close your left nostril with your ring finger and release your thumb from the right nostril as you exhale slowly through that side.
- Inhale through the right nostril, close it with your thumb and exhale through the left nostril.
- This is one round. Repeat for 5-10 rounds, focusing on the flow of breath and the balancing effect it has on your energy centers.

Mindfulness Exercises

Chakra Visualization

- Find a quiet and comfortable space where you can sit or lie down.

- Close your eyes and take a few deep breaths to relax your body and mind.
- Start by focusing on your root chakra located at the base of your spine. Imagine a radiant red light glowing at the base, slowly expanding and spinning, bringing a sense of grounding and stability.
- Move your attention to your sacral chakra, envisioning an orange light swirling in a circular motion, awakening creativity and passion within you.
- Gradually move up to your solar plexus chakra, imagining a vibrant yellow light radiating confidence and personal power.
- Continue this process with each chakra, visualizing a green light at the heart chakra, a sky-blue light at the throat chakra, an indigo light at the third eye chakra, and finally, a violet light at the crown chakra.
- While visualizing each chakra, focus on balancing and harmonizing its energy, allowing any blockages to be released.

Heart-Centered Gratitude

- Sit comfortably and place both hands over your heart.
- Take a few deep breaths, focusing on the rise and fall of your chest.
- As you breathe, think of three things you are grateful for.
- Allow the feeling of gratitude to envelop your heart center, visualizing a warm green light radiating from this area, symbolizing the heart chakra.
- With each breath, imagine this light expanding and flowing freely, promoting healing and balance within your heart chakra.

Body Scan Meditation

- Find a comfortable position, either sitting or lying down, and close your eyes.

- Start by bringing your attention to your breath, focusing on its steady rhythm.
- Take a few moments to ground yourself and relax.
- Begin scanning your body from head to toe, paying attention to any sensations, tensions, or discomfort.
- As you bring awareness to each area, breathe deeply and send waves of relaxation to those areas.
- Visualize the healing energy flowing through you, melting away any blockages or pain.
- Be gentle with yourself as you explore each part of your body. If you encounter areas of tension, focus your breath on that area, allowing the muscles to relax and release any stored stress.
- Move slowly and mindfully, feeling the interconnectedness between your mind, body, chakras, and the vagus nerve.
- Conclude the practice by taking a few moments to appreciate your body's ability to heal and restore itself.
- Open your eyes, feeling refreshed, balanced, and attuned to the harmonious energy within you.

Chapter 12

Nutrition and Lifestyle for Energy Balance

We know that chakras can be pictured as colorful energy wheels situated along the spine, each corresponding to different aspects of our physical, emotional, and spiritual existence. These chakras absorb and distribute energy throughout our body, and their balance is crucial for our overall well-being. But did you know that our diet also plays a vital role in energizing and supporting these chakras?

Nourishing our body with wholesome, nutrient-dense foods helps maintain the vibrancy and balance of our chakras.

Foods and Habits That Support Energetic Balance

Maintaining a healthy and balanced energy system is crucial for overall well-being, and one way to achieve this is by taking care of our chakras and vagus nerve. By incorporating certain foods and habits into our daily routine, we can support a harmonious balance in our chakras and vagus nerve function. Let's explore some of these practices.

Starting with the basics, incorporating a whole foods diet is essential for supporting overall health, including the energetic balance of chakras and vagus nerve. Eating a variety of colorful fruits and vegetables provides a wide range of nutrients and antioxidants that support the optimal functioning of our body. Think vibrant green leafy vegetables like spinach and kale, antioxidant-packed berries, and nutrient-dense foods like avocados and sweet potatoes. By nourishing our bodies with the right nutrients, we can enhance the flow of energy in our chakras and promote vagus nerve relaxation.

When it comes to individual chakras, there are specific foods associated with each energy center that can support their balance. For example, to nourish and energize the root chakra located at the base of the spine, incorporating grounding foods like root vegetables, legumes, and proteins can be beneficial. These include foods such as beets, carrots, lentils, beans, and lean meats. Such foods provide stability and nourishment to help us feel more rooted and connected to the earth.

Moving up the chakra system, the sacral chakra located in the lower abdomen can be supported by incorporating vibrant orange foods. Fruits like oranges, mangoes, and peaches, as well as vegetables like carrots and sweet potatoes, can help enhance creativity, passion, and emotional well-being.

In the solar plexus chakra, which is connected to personal power and confidence, incorporating yellow foods can support its energetic balance. Foods like bananas, corn, yellow bell peppers, and turmeric contain the color and nutrients associated with this chakra, promoting self-esteem and a strong sense of self.

The heart chakra, which is all about love, compassion, and emotional healing, can benefit from consuming green foods. Leafy greens like kale and spinach, as well as broccoli, green apples, and herbs like parsley and cilantro, can help foster a sense of love and emotional balance.

Moving higher up, the throat chakra is associated with communication and self-expression. To support this, blue foods like blueberries, kelp, and blue spirulina can be consumed. These foods nourish the throat area not only physically but also energetically, promoting clear communication and self-expression.

Next, the third eye chakra, which is related to intuition and spiritual connection, can be supported by consuming purple foods. Foods like purple grapes, purple cabbage, purple sweet potatoes, and blueberries can enhance the energetic balance of this chakra, promoting clarity of thought and inner wisdom.

Lastly, the crown chakra, which represents our connection to the divine and spiritual realm, can be supported by consuming white and light purple foods. Foods like cauliflower, garlic, ginger, and onions contain the essence of this chakra, promoting spiritual growth, awareness, and connection.

In addition to incorporating the right foods, certain habits can also support the balance of chakras and vagus nerve function. Regular physical activity, such as yoga or any form of exercise, can help release stagnant energy and promote the overall flow of energy in our body. This can enhance the energetic balance of our chakras and also support the healthy functioning of the vagus nerve.

We know that practicing mindfulness and meditation is another habit that can support chakra and vagus nerve balance. Taking a few minutes each day to sit in stillness, focusing on your breath, can help calm the mind and promote relaxation. This, in turn, can support the optimal functioning of our chakras and the vagus nerve, enhancing our overall energetic balance.

Remember, incorporating these foods and habits into your daily routine is not a quick fix but rather a holistic approach to supporting the balance of your chakras and vagus nerve. As with any changes to your diet or lifestyle, it is always beneficial to consult with a healthcare professional or nutritionist, especially if you have any specific health concerns or conditions.

So, let's embark on this nourishing journey towards chakra and vagus nerve energetic balance, one colorful plate and mindful step at a time. Your energy system will thank you, and you'll be well on your way to a more vibrant and harmonious life!

Detoxification and its Benefits for Overall Well-being

In our fast-paced, modern world, it is all too easy to find ourselves living in a toxic bubble. From the polluted air we breathe to the processed foods we consume, our bodies are constantly bombarded with various toxins that can adversely affect our overall well-being. That's where detoxification comes in - a natural and effective way to give our bodies a fresh start and regain balance.

Detoxification, in simple terms, is a process of eliminating harmful substances from our bodies. It is not just about following trendy juice cleanses or extreme diets; instead, it is a holistic approach that supports our body's natural detoxification mechanisms. By optimizing the function of organs such as the liver, kidneys, and lymphatic system, detoxification helps to eliminate toxins, reduce inflammation, boost energy levels, enhance mental clarity, and promote optimal wellness.

One of the most notable benefits of detoxification is the ability to improve our immune system. Clearing out toxins allows our immune system to function more efficiently, which in turn helps us ward off illnesses and infections more effectively. A healthy immune system is crucial for maintaining overall health and vitality, and detoxification plays a key role in supporting its optimal function.

Furthermore, detoxification can also have a positive impact on our digestive system. The modern diet, often high in processed foods, unhealthy fats, and added sugars, can wreak havoc on our digestive health. By eliminating these toxins and incorporating whole, nutrient-dense foods into our diets, we can promote better digestion and nutrient absorption. This, in turn, can help alleviate digestive issues such as bloating, constipation, and indigestion, allowing us to feel lighter and more energetic.

Detoxification isn't just about physical health but also has profound benefits for our mental and emotional well-being. The buildup of toxins over time can contribute to cognitive fog, sluggishness, and even mood imbalances. By undergoing a detoxification regimen, we can experience mental clarity, increased focus, and improved mood, which can positively impact our productivity, creativity, and overall quality of life.

It doesn't end there. Detoxification can also support weight management efforts. As we eliminate toxins from our bodies, our metabolism can become more efficient, which may lead to weight loss or weight maintenance. By adopting a clean, whole foods-based diet during the detoxification process, we also reduce the intake of empty calories and unhealthy fats, further supporting our weight management goals.

It's important to note that detoxification is not a quick fix or a one-time solution. Instead, it should be seen as a lifestyle choice aimed at creating long-term results. Incorporating regular detoxification practices into our lives, such as drinking plenty of water, eating a nutritious diet, exercising regularly, and practicing stress-reducing techniques like meditation or yoga, can help us maintain a healthy, toxin-free body.

Now, I must remind you that while detoxification is undeniably beneficial, it is important to approach it wisely and with caution. Always consult with a healthcare professional or a qualified nutritionist before embarking on any detoxification program, especially if you have any underlying health conditions or are taking medications. They can guide you in choosing the right approach that suits your individual needs, ensuring a safe and effective detoxification experience.

Chapter 13

Long-term Healing and Personal Growth

Life is an extraordinary adventure, and through embracing the process of healing and nurturing personal growth, we unlock the door to an ever-evolving, fulfilling existence.

When we embark on a path of long-term healing, we lay the groundwork for profound transformation. It begins by acknowledging that life's challenges and wounds are not insurmountable barriers but rather opportunities for growth. By facing our internal struggles head-on, we create the space to heal and thrive, fortified by newfound strength and resilience.

Here's the thing- healing is not a destination but a lifelong journey. It becomes a daily practice, a commitment to self-care, and a relentless pursuit of understanding ourselves on a deeper level. As we gradually mend the wounds of our past, we discover a sense of clarity, inner peace, and an enhanced appreciation for life's simplest joys.

We also need to focus on personal growth - expanding our horizons, pushing boundaries, and discovering the infinite depths of our potential. By consciously nurturing personal growth, we step out of our comfort zones, embrace new experiences, and are rewarded with a profound sense of personal empowerment.

Ultimately, personal growth unveils our true essence, allowing us to peel away the layers of self-doubt and embrace the brilliance that lies within. It encourages us to develop new skills, cultivate healthy habits, and continuously learn from life's diverse experiences. As we grow, we unleash our creativity, take risks, and become architects of our own destinies. The journey is exhilarating, and the rewards are limitless.

To push that point home even further, let's take a look at the benefits that long-term healing and personal growth bring into our lives:

- **Increased self-awareness:** As we embark on a journey of healing, we develop an increased understanding of our emotions, desires, and patterns of behavior. This self-awareness allows us to make conscious choices that align with our true selves, leading to a more fulfilling and authentic existence.
- **Enhanced relationships:** By nurturing our personal growth, we cultivate deeper connections with others. We become better listeners, empathizers, and communicators. Our newfound emotional intelligence enables us to foster healthier, more meaningful relationships, creating a ripple effect of positivity in our lives and the lives of those around us.
- **Heightened resilience:** Long-term healing and personal growth grant us the ability to bounce back from life's setbacks with grace and resilience. We develop coping mechanisms and a greater capacity to overcome adversity, transforming challenges into catalysts for growth.
- **Improved mental and emotional well-being:** Through the pursuit of healing and personal growth, we actively take care of our mental and emotional well-being. We develop self-compassion, adopt mindfulness practices, and let go of self-limiting beliefs, resulting in reduced stress and anxiety and an overall improved sense of happiness.
- **Accomplishment of goals:** Personal growth fuels our desire to set and achieve goals that align with our authentic selves. We develop clarity of purpose and gain the confidence needed to manifest our dreams into reality. Every triumph becomes a testimony to our growth and motivates us to continue striving for greatness.

When you think about it, long-term healing and personal growth are gifts that keep on giving. It holds the power to transform our lives from the inside out, paving the way for self-discovery, self-love, and a more meaningful existence. So, embrace the adventure with open arms, be gentle with yourself, and remember that each step forward is progress.

Sustaining Chakra and Vagus Nerve Health Over the Long-Term

Starting your chakra and vagus nerve healing journey is one thing, but you need to keep it going and sustain it over the long term. Doing so will allow you to grab the benefits for many years to come.

Here are some tips to help you do just that.

Think of Yourself as a Cactus

Imagine your chakra system as a garden of exotic cacti, each one representing a particular energy point. Just as these prickly wonders need tender care, nurturing yourself is crucial for sustaining your chakra and vagus nerve healing.

Set aside daily self-care routines, such as practicing mindfulness, meditation, or engaging in activities that bring you joy and inner peace. Remember, even a fuzzy cactus needs a little hydration - stay hydrated!

Dance Like Nobody's Watching

Movement and physical activity play a vital role in maintaining chakra balance. Engage in exercises like yoga, tai chi, or dance to promote energy flow throughout your body. Unleash your inner Beyoncé or Michael Jackson if you feel like it – dancing is a joyful expression that enhances your creative energies.

Nature's Warm Embrace

Mother Nature is the ultimate healer and a powerful ally on your journey. Spend time outdoors, bask in sunlight, take peaceful walks in the park, or find solace in the sound of crashing waves. Let the serenity of nature's symphony help you release any stagnant energy while reconnecting with your inner self.

Nourish Your Body and Soul

Food isn't just about satisfying hunger; it can also boost your chakra healing process. Incorporate nutrient-rich foods into your diet, such as fresh fruits, vegetables, whole grains, and lean proteins. Consider exploring Ayurvedic or traditional Chinese medicine principles to understand how different foods can support specific chakras. Don't forget to treat yourself to a piece of dark chocolate or a bowl of your favorite comfort food occasionally – balance is the key!

Detox Your Surroundings

Creating a harmonious environment is essential for balancing your chakras and ensuring sustainable healing.

Surround yourself with positive energy by decluttering your physical space and allowing fresh air to circulate. Introduce elements like crystals, essential oils, or soothing colors that resonate with each chakra to enhance the healing process. Don't be afraid to add some personality and quirkiness to your personal sanctuary!

The Power of Sound and Vibration

Sound therapy, such as chanting, singing bowls, or listening to specific frequencies, can help tune and clear your chakras. Explore different forms of sound healing that resonate with you personally. You might find yourself humming along to your favorite song while simultaneously aligning your energy centers!

Seek Out Supportive Souls

Connecting with like-minded individuals or joining a supportive community can be incredibly beneficial in maintaining long-term chakra healing. Engage in spiritual discussions, attend workshops, or join online forums to share experiences and gain insights from others on a similar journey.

Developing meaningful connections can offer guidance, support, and a sense of belonging.

Get Your Beauty Sleep

Sleep is a form of sacred rejuvenation, allowing your body to heal and restore balance. Ensure you get enough restful sleep each night to support your chakras.

Create a calming nighttime routine by indulging in a warm bath, reading a book, or meditating before bed. Remember, your dreams deserve to be as colorful and vibrant as your chakras!

As you continue your journey toward sustained chakra and vagus nerve healing, remember to embrace your uniqueness and infuse your personality into each step. Celebrate the progress you make along the way, as growth is a beautiful and ever-evolving process. By nurturing yourself, embracing nature, engaging in movement, and seeking support, you are fostering a harmonious balance that will benefit you in the long run.

Setting Goals for Continued Personal Growth and Healing

Life is a beautiful and complex journey, filled with ups and downs, triumphs and challenges. Along this journey, personal growth and healing play integral roles in our pursuit of self-discovery and fulfillment. It is a process of constantly evolving, learning, and setting goals that serve as stepping stones toward becoming the best version of ourselves.

Goals are like roadmaps, guiding us through the twists and turns of life and providing a sense of direction and purpose. They empower us to identify our desires, prioritize our values, and challenge ourselves beyond our comfort zones. While the journey toward personal growth and healing is unique for each of us, here are some helpful strategies and steps to assist you on your path.

- **Define your values and priorities:** Begin by pondering what truly matters to you in life. Reflect on your core values and the principles that guide your decisions. This will help you align your goals with who you are at your core, ensuring that they are meaningful and fulfilling.

- **Imagine yourself at the end of your life:** Visualize yourself looking back and reflecting on what truly brought you joy and fulfillment. What experiences and achievements would you want to have as part of your life story? With this clarity, you can begin to craft goals that are in harmony with your values and priorities.

- **Be specific and measurable:** When setting goals, it is essential to be clear and specific about what you want to achieve. Vague goals tend to lack focus and can easily become overwhelming. Instead, break down your larger aspirations into smaller, manageable tasks that can be measured and tracked. For example, instead of setting a goal to "get fit," be more specific by stating, "I will go to the gym three times a week and complete a 30-minute workout." This specificity helps create a sense of accountability and progress.

- **Set realistic and attainable goals:** While it is always good to dream big, it is equally important to set goals that are realistic and attainable. Setting yourself up for success is essential to maintain motivation and momentum. Consider your current circumstances, resources, and time availability. It is okay to challenge yourself, but ensure that your goals are within reach. For instance, if you have never run before, it might be more realistic to aim for completing a 5K race rather than a marathon for your first ambitious fitness goal.

- **Break goals into steps:** To avoid feeling overwhelmed by the magnitude of your goals, break them down into smaller, achievable steps. Each step becomes a mini goal that you can pursue with focused determination. Taking the example of fitness, if your ultimate goal is to run a 5K race, start by setting shorter-term goals like jogging for five minutes without stopping, gradually increasing the duration as you progress. This approach allows for incremental growth, giving you a sense of accomplishment along the way.
- **Enlist support:** Recognize that personal growth and healing are journeys that don't have to be traversed alone. Seek support from friends, family, or professionals who can guide, encourage, and inspire you. Share your goals with trusted individuals who can hold you accountable and provide a support system when challenges arise. Surround yourself with positive influences and seek out communities or groups that share similar aspirations. Together, you can learn from one another, celebrate successes, and offer solace in times of setbacks.
- **Embrace failure as a learning opportunity:** Failure is not an endpoint; it is an opportunity for growth and invaluable learning. It teaches us resilience, adaptability, and problem-solving skills. When setting goals, recognize that setbacks will inevitably occur. Instead of viewing failures as personal shortcomings, reframe them as stepping stones towards success. Analyze what went wrong, learn from the experience, and adjust your approach accordingly. Remember, failure is not the opposite of success - it is an essential part of the journey.
- **Celebrate small victories:** Personal growth and healing are not linear processes. Celebrating small victories along the way is crucial for maintaining motivation and building momentum. Acknowledge and reward yourself for each milestone and goal achieved, regardless of how insignificant they may seem. Treat yourself to something special, share your accomplishments with loved ones, or take a moment to reflect on the progress

made. These celebrations cultivate a positive mindset and foster resilience in the face of challenges.
- **Embrace continuous learning:** The quest for personal growth and healing is a lifelong process. Embrace the mindset of a perpetual learner and seek opportunities to expand your knowledge and skills. Read books, attend workshops, take online courses, or engage in activities that stretch your comfort zone. Be open to new experiences, perspectives, and wisdom. Remember, personal growth is not limited to external achievements but also encompasses inner transformation and self-awareness.

Remember, you hold the power to shape your destiny. With determination, perseverance, and nurturing self-compassion, you will pave the way for a life filled with growth, healing, and infinite possibilities. Combining chakra healing with your life's goals will take you even closer to achieving the so-called impossible.

Building a Supportive Community and Resources for Ongoing Support

If you are a seasoned practitioner or a curious beginner, one thing is for sure: having a supportive community and access to resources for ongoing support are essential for your chakra healing journey.

In this section, we'll explore how you can build and nurture a community that will uplift and empower you. We will also discover the plethora of resources available to enhance your understanding and practice of chakra healing.

First and foremost, let's talk about the importance of building a supportive community. Surrounding yourself with like-minded individuals who share your passion for chakra healing can be incredibly empowering. Their energy, experiences, and knowledge can serve as inspiration and guidance throughout your journey. But how do you go about building this community?

One way is to join local chakra healing groups or workshops in your area. These gatherings are not only a fantastic opportunity to meet fellow enthusiasts but also a chance to learn from experienced practitioners. Many cities offer regular meetups or workshops where you can connect with others who share your interest in chakra healing. These events often include interactive sessions, group discussions, and even guest speakers who can share their wisdom and insights. So, don't hesitate to join one – you never know the wonderful connections you might make!

For those seeking a more virtual community, the internet is your friend. There are numerous online forums, social media groups, and even dedicated platforms specifically designed for chakra healing enthusiasts. These platforms allow you to connect with people from all over the world, providing a diverse range of perspectives, experiences, and techniques that can greatly enrich your own practice. Become an active participant in these online communities – ask questions, share your experiences, and offer support to others. Not only will you receive invaluable advice and encouragement, but you'll also be able to contribute to the growth and development of the community as a whole.

Now, let's explore the wealth of resources available to enhance your understanding and practice of chakra healing. From books to podcasts, online courses to workshops, the possibilities are endless!

Books serve as a treasure trove of knowledge, providing comprehensive insights into chakra healing. Some notable titles include "Wheels of Life" by Anodea Judith, "Eastern Body, Western Mind" by Anodea Judith, and "The Sevenfold Journey" by Anodea Judith and Selene Vega. No, I'm not an Anodea Judith fan. Why do you ask? These books cover various aspects of chakra healing, including the energetic system, the connection between mind and body, and practical techniques for balancing your chakras.

If you prefer audio content, podcasts could be your new best friend. Look for podcasts that focus on chakra healing or related topics. They often feature interviews with experts, discussions on different techniques, and personal stories of transformation. Some popular options include "Chakra Girl Radio," "The Chakra Activation System," and "Chakra Healing with Affirmations and Science."

Another avenue worth exploring is online courses and workshops. Many reputable websites offer in-depth courses led by experienced chakra healing practitioners. These courses cover everything from the basics for beginners to advanced techniques for more seasoned practitioners. With the convenience of online learning, you can access these courses at your own pace and from the comfort of your own home. So, grab your favorite herbal tea, cozy up with your laptop, and get ready to deepen your knowledge!

Lastly, attending workshops and retreats can be a transformative experience. These gatherings often bring together a community of chakra-healing enthusiasts and offer immersive experiences that can take your practice to the next level. Check out local listings or search online for upcoming workshops or retreats near you that resonate with your interests and needs. These events usually provide a blend of practical techniques, insightful discussions, and even opportunities for personal healing and growth.

Conclusion

Your Path to Inner Energy and Balance

As we bring this transformative journey of chakra and vagus nerve healing to a close, it is my utmost pleasure to reflect upon the incredible impact these practices can have on our overall well-being. Throughout this book, we have explored the intricate connection between our chakras—the energy centers within our bodies—and the vagus nerve—a vital pathway that connects our organs, breath, and emotions.

From the beginning, we embarked on a quest to understand the ancient wisdom of the chakra system and the symbiotic relationship it shares with the vagus nerve. Together, they form a profound network within our being, interweaving physical, emotional, and spiritual aspects of our lives. As we delved deeper into this exploration, we uncovered a fascinating tapestry of knowledge that has the power to transform and heal.

Through practical exercises and meditative techniques, we have laid the foundation for aligning and harmonizing our chakras, empowering ourselves to navigate life with greater ease and balance. By understanding the distinct qualities and energies associated with each chakra, we have equipped ourselves with the tools to identify and address any imbalances that might hinder our well-being.

One of the most significant revelations on this journey has been the recognition of the vagus nerve's pivotal role in directing the body's response to stress, as well as its influence on our emotions, digestion, and overall health. By cultivating an awareness of this crucial nerve and nurturing its optimal functioning, we have taken a huge stride toward achieving physical and emotional resilience.

As we progressed through our exploration, we discovered that the practices of chakra and vagus nerve healing complement one another perfectly. Just as the chakras store our emotional imprints, the vagus nerve acts as a conduit for the release and integration of these emotions. By combining the practices of chakra balancing with vagus nerve stimulation, we unlock the potential for deep healing on multiple levels.

Throughout our journey, we also dwelled upon the power of breath and its profound impact on our overall well-being. By harnessing the simple yet potent act of conscious breathing, we realized that we hold within us the key to unlocking our own healing potential. Breathing with intention and awareness not only calms the nervous system but also supports the vital flow of energy in our chakras.

Throughout this book, we have emphasized the importance of approaching our healing journey with patience, self-compassion, and self-acceptance. Healing is a lifelong process, and there is no one-size-fits-all solution. Our uniqueness shines through in every aspect, and what works for one individual may not resonate with another. It is in honoring our unique journeys that we truly embrace healing in its most authentic form.

Remember, healing is not a destination but an ongoing process of growth and self-discovery. As you integrate the teachings and practices shared within these pages, may you find solace in knowing that you possess the innate wisdom to heal and transform. Embrace the power within you, for it is within your reach.

A Hint of Encouragement

Embarking on the path of chakra and vagus nerve healing is a powerful journey that can bring profound transformation to your mind, body, and spirit. It is a process that requires dedication, patience, and a willingness to dive deeper into your own being. As you begin this journey, it is essential to remember that progress may not happen overnight. But fear not! In this section, we will cover some tips and guidance to help you overcome obstacles and keep going, even when the road gets tough.

Embrace the Learning Process

Learning about chakras and vagus nerve healing is like opening a door to a treasure trove of wisdom and self-discovery. However, it is important to approach this journey with an open mind and a readiness to learn.

Expect that you will encounter new concepts, terminology, and practices that might seem complex at first. Take it one step at a time, allowing yourself the space to absorb the knowledge and integrate it into your life gradually.

Remember, learning is a beautiful journey, and every step you take brings you closer to a deeper understanding of yourself and your healing potential.

Set Realistic Expectations

It is vital to acknowledge that healing, particularly in terms of chakra and vagus nerve work, is a holistic process that occurs over time. Be patient and avoid putting unnecessary pressure on yourself to achieve quick results.

Healing requires consistency, dedication, and a gentle, compassionate approach towards yourself. Celebrate each small milestone along the way, and remember that every effort you make, no matter how small, contributes to your overall progress.

Find Your Support System

Surrounding yourself with a supportive and like-minded community can be instrumental in maintaining motivation and overcoming challenges. Seek out individuals who share your interest in chakra and vagus nerve healing. Connect with local or online groups, attend workshops, or participate in forums where you can exchange ideas, seek advice, and share experiences.

Having people who understand your journey can be immensely empowering and help you stay on track even when faced with obstacles.

Customize Your Practice

There is no one-size-fits-all approach when it comes to chakra and vagus nerve healing. Each individual is unique, and what works for one person may not work for another. It is essential to be fluid and adaptable in your practice, experimenting with different techniques and adapting them to suit your specific needs. Pay attention to your body, mind, and emotions, and adjust your healing practices accordingly.

By customizing your practice, you will be better able to maintain consistency and evoke positive change in your life.

Cultivate Mindfulness and Patience

Chakra and vagus nerve healing involve delving into the depths of your being, addressing blockages, and releasing stagnant energy. This process requires mindfulness and patience.

Cultivate a daily practice of mindfulness, focusing on the present moment and your intentions for healing. Be patient with yourself, understanding that change happens at its own pace. Trust the process and allow yourself the space needed for transformation to unfold naturally.

Self-Care is Essential

As you journey toward chakra and vagus nerve healing, it is crucial to prioritize self-care. Nurture yourself physically, emotionally, and spiritually. Incorporate practices such as meditation, yoga, breathwork, journaling, or spending time in nature into your routine. Engage in activities that bring you joy and promote overall well-being. By caring for yourself, you create a loving and supportive environment for healing to occur.

Remember, the path of chakra and vagus nerve healing is a transformative and rewarding journey. Although progress may not come overnight, your dedication will yield beautiful and lasting results. Stay determined, believe in yourself, and trust that healing is an ongoing process. You have all the strength within you to navigate this journey with grace and resilience.

References

How to meditate in ten minutes - Headspace. (n.d.). Headspace. https://www.headspace.com/articles/how-to-meditate-in-ten-minutes

I Had My Chakras Balanced—Here's Exactly What Happened. (2022, April 15). *Byrdie.* https://www.byrdie.com/chakra-balancing-treatment-5185835

Jain, R. (2024, May 9). *Complete Guide To The 7 Chakras: Symbols, Effects & How To Balance | Arhanta Yoga Blog. Arhanta Yoga Ashrams.* https://www.arhantayoga.org/blog/7-chakras-introduction-energy-centers-effect/

Jain, V. (2023, October 30). *Did you know the colour of your food can keep your Chakras healthy? A Reiki expert tells you more.* Healthshots. https://www.healthshots.com/healthy-eating/nutrition/did-you-know-the-colour-of-your-food-can-keep-your-chakras-healthy-a-reiki-expert-tells-you-more/

Mindfulness exercises. (2022, October 11). Mayo Clinic. https://www.mayoclinic.org/healthy-lifestyle/consumer-health/in-depth/mindfulness-exercises/art-20046356#:~:text=Mindfulness%20is%20a%20type%20of,mind%20and%20help%20reduce%20stress.

Professional, C. C. M. (n.d.). *Vagus nerve.* Cleveland Clinic. https://my.clevelandclinic.org/health/body/22279-vagus-nerve

Skarda, E., & Skarda, E. (2022, July 29). *I was a skeptic of Chakra Balancing…And then I tried it.* Yoga Journal. https://www.yogajournal.com/yoga-101/chakras-yoga-for-beginners/i-was-a-skeptic-of-chakra-balancing-and-then-i-tried-it/

Stelter, G. (2023, February 13). *A beginner's guide to the 7 chakras and their meanings.* Healthline. https://www.healthline.com/health/fitness-exercise/7-chakras#Chakra-101

The 7 Chakras for Healing and Energy. (2023, December 1). WebMD. https://www.webmd.com/balance/what-are-chakras

Vagus nerve stimulation - Mayo Clinic. (2023, April 18). https://www.mayoclinic.org/tests-procedures/vagus-nerve-stimulation/about/pac-20384565

Wikipedia contributors. (2024, June 12). *Chakra.* Wikipedia. https://en.wikipedia.org/wiki/Chakra

Yugay, I. (2024, June 6). *9 Chakra healing power moves to K.O. negative energy and ignite your inner sunshine.* Mindvalley Blog. https://blog.mindvalley.com/chakra-healing/

AYURVEDA FOR BEGINNERS

A Complete Guide to Understanding and Embracing Ancient Wisdom for Modern Well-Being and Balance

MONIKA DANIEL

Chapter 1

Introduction to Ayurveda

Welcome to the wonderful, spiritual, and fascinating world of Ayurveda. Right now, you might not know too much about this ancient practice, but by the end of this book, you'll know enough to embark on your own journey.

So, to help you get started, let's roll back to the beginning.

Ayurveda, often referred to as the "Science of Life," is a holistic system of medicine that originated in ancient India over 5000 years ago. The word Ayurveda comes from the Sanskrit words "ayur," meaning life, and "veda" meaning knowledge, emphasizing the interconnectedness of body, mind, and spirit in the maintenance of health and well-being.

The origins of Ayurveda can be traced back to the Vedas, the ancient scriptures of India, where the principles of Ayurveda were first documented. The fundamental texts of Ayurveda, known as the Charaka Samhita and the Sushruta Samhita, were compiled around 1000 BC and are considered the foundational texts of Ayurvedic medicine.

At its core, Ayurveda recognizes the importance of maintaining balance to achieve optimal health and prevent disease. Imbalances are believed to be the root cause of illness and disease, and Ayurvedic treatments aim to restore this balance through a combination of dietary modifications, herbal remedies, lifestyle changes, and therapeutic practices.

In addition to its focus on the individual, Ayurveda also places a strong emphasis on prevention, promoting healthy lifestyle practices such as daily routines, seasonal detoxification, and mindfulness practices to maintain overall well-being.

Over the centuries, Ayurveda has evolved and adapted to different cultures and regions, gaining recognition as a comprehensive system of medicine that encompasses not only physical health but also mental, emotional, and spiritual well-being. Today, Ayurveda is practiced worldwide, offering a unique perspective on health and healing that continues to inspire and influence the field of holistic medicine.

As we delve deeper into the world of Ayurveda, we'll uncover a treasure trove of wisdom that has withstood the test of time, offering a holistic approach to health and wellness that is as relevant and effective today as it was thousands of years ago. The principles of Ayurveda remind us of the interconnectedness of all aspects of our being and the importance of nurturing harmony within ourselves and our environment.

Philosophical Foundations: The Core Principles of Balance and Harmony

Picture this: Imagine a serene garden filled with vibrant flowers swaying gently in the breeze. In this peaceful setting, the principles of Ayurveda come to life, rooted in the idea that true health and well-being stem from a harmonious balance of mind, body, and spirit.

At the heart of Ayurveda lies the concept of the three doshas – Vata, Pitta, and Kapha. These doshas represent the fundamental energies that govern all biological functions within the body. Just like the elements of nature – air, fire, water, earth, and ether – each dosha carries its own unique qualities and characteristics.

Vata, embodying the elements of air and ether, governs movement and communication in the body. It is associated with qualities such as creativity, flexibility, and enthusiasm. Pitta, aligned with the elements of fire and water, governs transformation and metabolism. It is characterized by qualities like intensity, focus, and determination. Kapha, representing the elements of earth and water, governs structure and stability. It exudes qualities of nurturing, strength, and resilience.

In Ayurveda, the key to maintaining health and well-being lies in keeping these doshas in a state of balance. When any one of the doshas becomes excessive or deficient, it can lead to imbalances and, ultimately, disease. By understanding our unique constitution, or "prakriti," we can tailor our lifestyle, diet, and daily routines to support our individual needs and promote optimal health.

It's a little like your body as a finely tuned instrument, with each dosha playing its own melody in perfect harmony. When all three doshas are in balance, you experience a sense of vitality, clarity, and inner peace. It's like finding the perfect rhythm in a symphony of life, where every note blends seamlessly into the next.

Ayurveda teaches us to listen to our body's subtle cues and to be attuned to the ebb and flow of our inner landscape. Just as the seasons change, so too do the dynamics of our doshas. By adapting our lifestyle and habits according to these natural rhythms, we can align ourselves with the cyclical nature of existence.

In the quest for balance and harmony, Ayurveda offers a treasure trove of holistic practices, from herbal remedies and dietary recommendations to yoga, meditation, and pranayama (breathwork). Each of these modalities serves as a tool for cultivating self-awareness and fostering inner equilibrium.

As you explore the philosophical foundations of Ayurveda, you begin to see your body not as a separate entity but as an integral part of the intricate web of life. You realize that true health is not merely the absence of disease but a state of vibrant well-being that emanates from a deep sense of balance and wholeness.

By embracing the core principles of balance and harmony in Ayurveda, you embark on a transformative journey of self-care and self-discovery. You learn to cultivate a deeper connection with your body, mind, and spirit, nurturing a sense of wholeness that transcends the boundaries of individuality.

The Benefits of Ayurveda

Now that we know what Ayurveda is, let's talk about its incredible benefits and how it promotes health and well-being.

Personalized Approach:

- Ayurveda recognizes that each individual is unique and has a specific mind-body constitution known as doshas (Vata, Pitta, and Kapha).
- By identifying your dosha through a consultation with an Ayurvedic practitioner, you can tailor your diet, lifestyle, and wellness routines to suit your specific needs.

Emphasis on Prevention:

- Ayurveda focuses on preventing disease by maintaining balance in the body through practices such as yoga, meditation, and herbal remedies.
- By understanding your dosha and following Ayurvedic lifestyle guidelines, you can proactively prevent imbalances and health issues.

Natural Healing:

- Ayurveda utilizes natural remedies derived from herbs, minerals, and plants to address health concerns.
- These natural remedies are gentle on the body and promote healing without the harmful side effects often associated with synthetic medications.

Mind-Body Connection:

- Ayurveda recognizes the interconnectedness of the mind, body, and spirit in maintaining overall health.

- Practices such as meditation and pranayama (breathwork) are used to calm the mind, reduce stress, and promote emotional well-being.

Holistic Wellness:

- Ayurveda considers all aspects of your life, including diet, exercise, sleep, and mental health, in promoting holistic well-being.
- By addressing imbalances in all areas of life, Ayurveda aims to create harmony and vitality in the body.

Improved Digestion:

- Ayurveda places great emphasis on the importance of digestion in overall health.
- By following a diet tailored to your dosha and incorporating digestive spices and herbs, you can improve digestion and nutrient absorption.

Detoxification:

- Ayurveda promotes the practice of seasonal detoxification to eliminate toxins accumulated in the body.
- Through practices such as Panchakarma, a detox program involving therapies like massage and herbal cleanses, you can reset your body and promote optimal health.

Enhanced Energy Levels:

- By aligning with your natural doshic balance and incorporating Ayurvedic practices into your daily routine, you can experience increased energy levels and vitality.
- Ayurveda helps to remove blockages in the body's energy channels, known as nadis, allowing for improved energy flow.

Stress Reduction:

- Ayurveda offers various techniques, such as meditation, yoga, and stress-relieving herbal remedies, to help you manage and reduce stress.

- By addressing the root causes of stress and promoting relaxation, Ayurveda aids in maintaining mental clarity and emotional balance.

As you can see, Ayurveda is a comprehensive system of healing that offers a wealth of benefits for promoting health and well-being. From personalized approaches to natural remedies, Ayurveda provides you with the tools to achieve balance in mind, body, and spirit.

Modern Relevance

Let's explore how Ayurveda's ancient wisdom continues to be relevant in our modern world! Ayurveda, with its holistic approach to health and well-being, has stood the test of time and continues to be a valuable resource in contemporary health practices. Here's how Ayurveda fits seamlessly into our modern lifestyles:

- **Mind-Body Connection:** In today's fast-paced world, the importance of the mind-body connection is increasingly recognized in mainstream healthcare. Ayurveda's emphasis on the interconnectedness of physical health, mental well-being, and emotional balance aligns perfectly with modern approaches to holistic health.
- **Personalized Medicine:** The rise of personalized medicine and integrative healthcare has brought Ayurveda to the forefront as a valuable tool for understanding individual health needs. Ayurvedic principles of doshas help individuals customize their diet, lifestyle, and wellness routines to optimize their health outcomes.
- **Natural Remedies:** With our growing interest in natural and holistic healing modalities, Ayurveda's reliance on natural remedies derived from herbs, minerals, and plants resonates with modern consumers seeking non-invasive health solutions. Ayurvedic herbs and supplements are increasingly gaining popularity for their effectiveness and minimal side effects compared to synthetic medications.

- **Preventive Healthcare:** As the focus shifts towards preventive healthcare and wellness promotion, Ayurveda's emphasis on maintaining balance in the body to prevent disease is particularly relevant. Ayurvedic practices such as yoga, meditation, and seasonal detoxification offer practical tools to take charge of our health and well-being proactively.
- **Stress Management:** We all know how stressful modern society has become, and because of that, stress management has become a crucial aspect of overall health. Ayurveda's holistic approach to stress reduction through practices like meditation, pranayama, and herbal remedies provides effective tools for us to combat stress and promote mental resilience.
- **Digestive Health:** With digestive issues on the rise due to poor diet and lifestyle choices, Ayurveda's focus on improving digestion through dietary recommendations tailored to one's dosha is highly relevant. Ayurvedic principles of mindful eating and digestion-enhancing spices offer practical solutions for improving gut health and nutrient absorption.
- **Integrative Wellness:** Ayurveda seamlessly integrates with other wellness practices such as yoga, acupuncture, and mindfulness meditation to create a comprehensive approach to health and well-being. By incorporating Ayurvedic principles into a holistic wellness routine, you can enhance the effectiveness of other modalities and achieve optimal health outcomes.
- **Eco-Friendly Living:** As sustainability and eco-consciousness become key considerations in modern lifestyles, Ayurveda's emphasis on living in harmony with nature aligns perfectly with the ethos of environmental conservation. Ayurvedic practices encourage eco-friendly habits such as eating seasonally, using natural and organic products, and minimizing waste to promote a healthier planet and a healthier self.

By embracing Ayurveda's principles and incorporating them into our daily lives, we can tap into the ancient wisdom that continues to guide us towards a more balanced, vibrant, and healthy existence.

Chapter 2

The Three Doshas

We've already touched upon the idea of doshas. But you need to know more, right? In this chapter, we delve further into the fundamental building blocks of Ayurvedic philosophy.

According to Ayurveda, each person is made up of a unique combination of three Doshas - Vata, Pitta, and Kapha - which govern our physical, mental, and emotional characteristics. Understanding your dominant Dosha can offer deep insights into your natural tendencies, strengths, and potential imbalances.

Let's jump in!

Understanding Doshas: Vata, Pitta, and Kapha Explained

To appreciate the power of doshas, you need to learn about each one in turn. Let's do that now.

Vata, the Air and Space Energy

Picture a whimsical dancer moving gracefully through the wind. That's Vata, the dosha associated with the elements of air and space. Vata governs movement, creativity, and communication in our bodies and minds. If you have a Vata constitution, you might be quick-witted, adaptable, and bursting with ideas. Your energy is like the wind - unpredictable, changing, and always in motion.

However, when Vata is out of balance, you may experience anxiety, restlessness, and scattered thoughts. It's crucial for Vata types to find grounding practices like meditation, yoga, or regular routines to calm the whirlwind of the mind. Nourishing, warm foods and self-care rituals can also help balance Vata energy and bring stability to your life.

Pitta, the Fire Energy

Now, let's turn up the heat and meet Pitta, the fiery dosha driven by the elements of fire and water. Pitta governs digestion, metabolism, and transformation in our bodies and minds. If you are a Pitta type, you are likely a natural leader with a sharp intellect, strong drive, and a fiery passion for life. Your energy is like a blazing fire - intense, focused, and full of ambition.

But when Pitta is imbalanced, you may experience irritability, perfectionism, and burnout. Cooling practices like swimming, spending time in nature, or enjoying cooling foods can help soothe Pitta's intense flames. Learning to let go of control, practicing relaxation techniques, and maintaining a balanced diet are key to keeping Pitta's energy in check and maintaining harmony within yourself.

Kapha, the Earth, and Water Energy

Lastly, let's take a deep breath and sink into the nurturing embrace of Kapha, the dosha ruled by the elements of earth and water. Kapha governs structure, stability, and endurance in our bodies and minds. If you have a Kapha constitution, you are likely calm, compassionate, and grounded, with a strong sense of loyalty and love for routine. Your energy is like a gentle stream - steady, nurturing, and deeply rooted.

However, when Kapha is out of balance, you may experience lethargy, attachment, and resistance to change. Engaging in stimulating activities, incorporating movement into your daily routine, and enjoying warming spices can help invigorate Kapha energy and bring vitality back into your life. Finding ways to challenge yourself, practicing gratitude, and embracing new experiences are essential for Kapha types to maintain balance and harmony.

Remember, we all have a unique combination of Vata, Pitta, and Kapha energies within us, and achieving balance is a lifelong journey. By understanding the qualities of each dosha and recognizing their effects on your body and mind, you can make informed choices to support your well-being and lead a harmonious life.

Dosha Quiz: How to Determine Your Primary Dosha

Your next question is sure to be about your own primary dosha. Well, look no further! This quiz will help you unravel the mysteries of your primary dosha, Vata, Pitta, or Kapha.

1. What best describes your body frame?

a) Thin, wiry, or slender

b) Medium build, athletic, or muscular

c) Solid, sturdy, or curvy

2. How do you usually respond to stress?

a) I tend to feel anxious, restless, and overwhelmed.

b) I become irritable, impatient, and demanding.

c) I feel lethargic, unmotivated, and withdrawn.

3. What is your skin type?

a) Dry, rough, or may experience skin conditions like eczema

b) Sensitive, prone to redness or inflammation, may have acne

c) Smooth, oily, or well-hydrated

4. When it comes to food, what do you crave the most?

a) Light and crunchy snacks like popcorn or crackers

b) Spicy and tangy flavors like salsa or jalapenos

c) Comforting and heavy meals like pasta or mashed potatoes

5. Which climate do you prefer?

a) Warm and humid weather

b) Hot and dry climate

c) Cool and damp environment

6. How do you handle tasks and projects?

a) I am creative and imaginative, but I may struggle with follow-through.

b) I am organized, driven, and goal-oriented.

c) I am methodical, patient, and prefer routine

7. What is your sleep pattern like?

a) I have difficulty falling asleep and often wake up during the night.

b) I have intense dreams and may wake up feeling hot.

c) I am a deep sleeper and sometimes struggle to wake up in the morning.

8. How do you communicate with others?

a) I am articulate but may ramble or lose track of the conversation.

b) I am assertive, direct, and sometimes critical.

c) I am a good listener and tend to speak slowly and thoughtfully.

9. What physical issues do you experience most frequently?

a) Digestive issues like gas, bloating, or constipation

b) Inflammation, acid reflux, or skin irritations

c) Slow metabolism, weight gain, or sinus congestion

10. How do you unwind and relax?

a) Engaging in creative activities like painting or writing

b) Exercising or doing intense physical activities

c) Taking hot baths, meditating, or spending time in nature

Now, let's discover your dominant dosha based on your responses.

If you answered mostly a's:

Congratulations! You are predominantly Vata! Your mind-body type is characterized by creativity, enthusiasm, and sensitivity. Embrace practices that ground and nurture your Vata nature, such as warm meals, calming activities, and routines.

If you answered mostly b's:

You are predominantly Pitta! Your dosha embodies passion, focus, and intensity. Balance your Pitta tendencies with cooling practices, relaxation techniques, and mindfulness to maintain harmony in body and mind.

If you answered mostly c's:

You are predominantly Kapha! Your dosha exudes stability, compassion, and endurance. Embrace invigorating activities, light foods, and movement to keep your Kapha energy balanced and vibrant.

Remember, Ayurveda is all about finding balance and harmony within yourself. Your dosha may change over time or vary depending on the seasons and circumstances.

Balancing Doshas: The Importance of Maintaining Dosha Balance

We know that the doshas are the three vital energies that govern our physical and mental well-being. These doshas - Vata, Pitta, and Kapha - are derived from the five elements: ether, air, fire, water, and earth. Each dosha has its own unique qualities and functions in our body. Balancing these doshas is key to maintaining good health, vitality, and harmony within ourselves.

Let's start with Vata dosha, which is associated with movement and is composed of ether and air elements. Vata governs all bodily functions related to movement, such as breathing, circulation, and nerve impulses. When Vata is in balance, it promotes creativity, agility, and enthusiasm. However, when Vata is aggravated, it can lead to anxiety, insomnia, and digestive issues. To balance Vata, it's important to follow a routine, stay warm, practice grounding exercises like yoga, and eat warm, nourishing foods.

Next up is Pitta dosha, which is related to metabolism and transformation and is made up of fire and water elements. Pitta controls digestion, metabolism, and hormones. When Pitta is balanced, it enhances intelligence, courage, and passion. On the flip side, an excess of Pitta can manifest as irritability, inflammation, and skin issues. To keep Pitta in check, it's recommended to stay cool, practice relaxation techniques, eat cooling foods, and avoid spicy and greasy foods.

Last but not least, we have Kapha dosha, which embodies structure and stability and is a combination of earth and water elements. Kapha regulates strength, immunity, and lubrication in the body. When Kapha is balanced, it promotes love, compassion, and stability. Yet, when Kapha becomes imbalanced, it can lead to lethargy, weight gain, and respiratory issues. To maintain Kapha equilibrium, it's beneficial to stay active, incorporate stimulating activities, eat light and spicy foods, and avoid heavy, sweet, and dairy-laden meals.

Once you identify your dosha type, you can tailor your lifestyle, diet, and activities to harmonize your doshas.

To maintain dosha balance, Ayurveda emphasizes the importance of following a daily routine, or dinacharya. This routine includes practices like waking up early, scraping the tongue, oil pulling, self-massage with warm oil, and meditation. Establishing a consistent routine helps regulate your biological clock, promotes digestion, and calms the mind.

In addition to a daily routine, diet plays a crucial role in balancing doshas. Ayurveda categorizes foods based on their taste (rasa), energy (virya), and post-digestive effect (vipaka) to determine their effects on doshas. For instance, sweet, sour, and salty tastes pacify Vata, while bitter, astringent, and pungent tastes pacify Kapha.

When it comes to lifestyle habits, incorporating regular exercise, adequate sleep, stress management techniques, and self-care practices are essential for dosha balance. Engage in activities that bring joy and relaxation, such as nature walks, aromatherapy, yoga, or spending time with loved ones.

Remember, listening to your body and being mindful of how you feel physically, emotionally, and mentally is key to maintaining dosha equilibrium. If you notice any signs of dosha imbalance, such as digestive issues, skin problems, mood swings, or fatigue, listen to your body's signals and make the necessary adjustments to restore balance.

Chapter 3

Ayurvedic Diet and Nutrition

Ayurveda has long emphasized the significance of food in maintaining health and promoting overall well-being. According to Ayurvedic principles, food is not just nourishment for the body but also a form of medicine that can prevent diseases, balance energies within the body, and promote longevity.

To help you learn more, let's delve into the fascinating world of Ayurvedic dietary principles and explore how the choices we make in our daily meals can have a profound impact on our health.

In Ayurveda, food is classified based on its taste (rasa), its effect on the body post-digestion (vipaka), and its heating or cooling properties (virya). These classifications help determine the inherent qualities of different foods and how they interact with the body's doshas (basic physiological energies): – Vata, Pitta, and Kapha.

Vata, associated with the elements of air and ether, is characterized by qualities such as being cold, light, dry, and mobile. Pitta, governed by the elements of fire and water, is characterized by qualities such as being hot, sharp, and intense. Kapha, associated with the elements of earth and water, is characterized by qualities such as being heavy, slow, and stable. If this makes little sense right now, don't worry! We're going to talk about food for each dosha in the next section.

In Ayurveda, the concept of Agni (digestive fire) is very important. A strong Agni is essential for proper digestion, assimilation of nutrients, and elimination of waste products. To nourish Agni, it is advised to eat mindfully, chew food thoroughly, and avoid overeating or consuming incompatible food combinations.

Ayurveda also emphasizes the importance of eating according to the seasons and your constitution. For example, during the cold winter months, it is beneficial to favor warm, cooked foods that are grounding and nourishing. On the other hand, during the hot summer months, opting for light, cooling foods can help balance Pitta and prevent overheating.

Continuing with the same idea, Ayurveda considers food not just in terms of its physical properties but also its prana (life force) and its effect on the mind and emotions. Consuming fresh, organic, and locally sourced foods is believed to be more energetically vibrant and supportive of overall health.

One of the key principles of Ayurvedic dietary guidelines is the practice of Sattvic eating, which focuses on pure, wholesome foods that promote clarity, vitality, and balance. Sattvic foods include fresh fruits and vegetables, whole grains, nuts, seeds, and dairy products in moderation. By consuming Sattvic foods, you can cultivate a sense of inner peace and harmony.

Ayurveda also recognizes the concept of food as medicine (Bhavaprakash Nighantu), wherein specific foods are prescribed to treat various imbalances or diseases. For example, turmeric is revered for its anti-inflammatory properties, ginger is used to aid digestion, and ghee is considered a nourishing tonic for the body.

In addition to choosing the right foods, Ayurveda also emphasizes the importance of mindful eating practices. This includes eating in a calm and peaceful environment, free from distractions, savoring each bite, and expressing gratitude for the nourishment provided by the food.

There is also the concept of Aharvidhi Vidhan to consider, which involves guidelines for how to eat to promote optimal digestion and assimilation of nutrients. This includes eating only when hungry, avoiding excessive snacking between meals, and allowing for proper time gaps between meals for digestion to occur efficiently.

Ayurveda also recognizes the individuality of each person and the need for personalized dietary recommendations based on one's unique constitution (Prakriti) and imbalances (Vikriti). By understanding one's doshic makeup and current state of health, you can make informed choices about the foods that will best support your well-being.

As you can see, it's about doing what is right for you and your specific dosha. So, let's talk about the foods you should eat and avoid depending on your main dosha type.

Foods for Each Dosha

We touched upon what types of foods each dosha "likes," but what does that look like in practice? What should you eat versus what you should avoid? Let's learn more.

Vata Dosha

Vata, associated with the elements of air and ether, is characterized by qualities such as being cold, light, dry, and mobile.

What to Eat:

- Warm, nourishing, and grounding foods such as cooked grains, root vegetables, warm soups, stews, and herbal teas.
- Dairy products like warm milk and ghee are beneficial for balancing Vata.
- Sweet, sour, and salty tastes help pacify Vata dosha.
- Nuts, seeds, and oils provide essential fats for the Vata constitution.

What to Avoid:

- Cold, dry, and raw foods can aggravate Vata dosha.
- Bitter, astringent, and pungent tastes should be consumed in moderation.
- Caffeinated beverages and excessive intake of sugar can disturb Vata balance.
- Avoid processed foods and carbonated drinks.

Pitta Dosha

Pitta, governed by the elements of fire and water, is characterized by qualities such as being hot, sharp, and intense.

What to Eat:

- Cooling, and hydrating foods such as cucumber, mint, coconut, and coriander are beneficial for Pitta dosha.
- Sweet, bitter, and astringent tastes help balance the fiery nature of Pitta.
- Vegetables like broccoli, cauliflower, and leafy greens are great choices for Pitta individuals.
- Moderate amounts of grains, legumes, and cooling spices like fennel and coriander can help pacify Pitta dosha.

What to Avoid:

- Spicy, oily, and fried foods can exacerbate Pitta dosha.
- Sour and salty tastes should be consumed in moderation.
- Avoid excessive intake of caffeine and alcohol.
- Limit consumption of red meat and processed foods.

Kapha Dosha

Kapha, associated with the elements of earth and water, is characterized by qualities such as heavy, slow, and stable.

What to Eat:

- Light, dry, and warm foods help balance Kapha dosha. Incorporate plenty of cooked vegetables, grains, and legumes into your diet.
- Pungent, bitter, and astringent tastes help reduce Kapha's heaviness.
- Spices like ginger, black pepper, and turmeric can aid digestion and metabolism in Kapha individuals.
- Fruits like apples, pears, and berries are suitable choices for the Kapha constitution.

What to Avoid:

- Heavy, oily, and sweet foods can worsen Kapha imbalance.
- Dairy products and excess consumption of nuts should be limited.
- Avoid cold and excessively moist foods.
- Minimize your intake of sugary and processed foods.

Remember, Ayurveda emphasizes the importance of listening to your body's unique needs and adjusting your diet accordingly. Experiment with different foods and observe how your body responds to find the optimal balance for your dosha type.

Seasonal Eating: Adjusting Your Diet With The Seasons

According to Ayurveda, each season brings with it a unique energy that influences our bodies, minds, and overall well-being. By aligning our diets with the rhythms of nature, we can tap into the healing power of seasonal foods and support our body's innate ability to thrive.

Let's dive into the magic of seasonal eating through an Ayurvedic lens:

Embracing the Wisdom of Nature

In Ayurveda, it is believed that nature provides us with everything we need to nourish and heal ourselves. By eating foods that are in season, we can harness the vital energies present in fresh, locally sourced produce. In the spring, opt for lighter, cleansing foods like leafy greens, sprouts, and berries to support detoxification and renewal.

As summer rolls around, indulge in juicy fruits, cooling vegetables, and hydrating foods to balance the heat and Pitta dosha. Come fall, embrace hearty root vegetables, warming spices, and nourishing soups to ground Vata energy, and prepare for the winter ahead.

Balancing the Doshas

Ayurveda recognizes three primary doshas – Vata, Pitta, and Kapha – that govern our physical, mental, and emotional well-being. Each season is associated with a different dosha, and adjusting your diet to pacify the dominant dosha can help maintain equilibrium within the body. For example, during the cold, dry Vata season of fall and early winter, opt for foods that are grounding, nourishing, and warming to counterbalance Vata's erratic qualities.

In the fiery Pitta season of summer, focus on cooling, hydrating foods to soothe Pitta's intensity. In the wet, heavy Kapha season of spring, choose light, spicy foods to stimulate digestion and uplift Kapha energy.

Connecting with the Elemental Energies

Ayurveda views the world through the lens of the five elements – earth, water, fire, air, and ether – and believes that these elements influence all aspects of our being, including our dietary needs. Each season is associated with a unique combination of these elements, and by tuning into the elemental energies of nature, we can choose foods that resonate with the current season. For example, the earthy and grounding qualities of root vegetables like sweet potatoes and carrots are perfect for fall, while the fiery and transformative nature of spices like ginger and turmeric is ideal for winter.

By embracing these elemental energies, we can attune ourselves to the natural rhythms of the universe and find greater balance within.

Cultivating Mindful Eating

Seasonal eating is not just about nourishing the body; it is also a practice of mindfulness and gratitude. By savoring the flavors, textures, and aromas of seasonal foods, we can deepen our connection to the earth and the abundance it provides. Take the time to appreciate the vibrant colors of a ripe summer tomato, the earthy sweetness of a winter squash, or the crisp freshness of a spring salad.

Engage all your senses in the act of eating, and allow yourself to be fully present with each bite. In doing so, you not only nourish your body but also feed your soul.

Experimenting with Seasonal Recipes

One of the joys of seasonal eating is the opportunity to get creative in the kitchen and experiment with new flavors and combinations. Try incorporating seasonal ingredients into your favorite recipes or exploring traditional Ayurvedic dishes tailored to the current season. Whip up a batch of hearty lentil soup with winter root vegetables, infuse your summer salads with cooling mint and cilantro, or indulge in a nourishing stew of spring greens and spices.

Let your imagination run wild and allow the seasonal bounty to inspire your culinary creations.

The Art of Meal Planning & General Tips

Meal planning in Ayurveda is not just about what you eat, but also when and how you eat it. By understanding your dosha and incorporating Ayurvedic principles into your meal planning, you can optimize your health and well-being.

Here are some tips to help you get started:

- **Include All Six Tastes:** Ayurveda recognizes six tastes: sweet, sour, salty, bitter, pungent, and astringent. A balanced meal should include all six tastes in order to satisfy your palate and nourish your body. For example, a meal could consist of grains (sweet), lemon (sour), salted vegetables (salty), leafy greens (bitter), ginger (pungent), and beans (astringent).

- **Mindful Eating:** Ayurveda emphasizes the importance of being present while eating. Take the time to sit down and savor your meals without distractions. Chew your food thoroughly to aid digestion and appreciate the flavors and textures of each bite.

- **Create a Routine:** Establishing a regular meal schedule can help regulate your digestion and metabolism. Aim to eat your meals at the same time each day to support your body's natural rhythms.

- **Cook with Love:** In Ayurveda, the energy and intention you put into cooking can impact the quality of your food. When preparing meals, infuse them with love and positive energy to enhance their nourishing effects on your body and mind.

- **Herbs and Spices:** Incorporating Ayurvedic herbs and spices into your cooking can enhance the healing properties of your meals. Turmeric, ginger, cumin, and coriander are just a few examples of spices known for their medicinal benefits.

- **Listen to Your Body:** Pay attention to how your body responds to different foods. Notice any digestive issues, energy levels, or mood changes after eating certain meals. Adjust your diet accordingly to maintain balance and well-being.

- **Plan Ahead:** Taking the time to plan your meals in advance can save you time and stress during the week. Make a shopping list, prep ingredients, and cook in batches to have healthy meals ready when you need them.
- **Stay Hydrated:** Drinking plenty of water throughout the day is essential for proper digestion and detoxification. In Ayurveda, warm water is often recommended to help eliminate toxins and balance the doshas.

By incorporating these Ayurvedic principles into your meal planning, you can create a nourishing and balanced diet that supports your overall health and well-being.

Chapter 4

Daily Routines (Dinacharya)

Dinacharya, a key concept in Ayurveda, refers to daily routines and practices that are believed to promote health and well-being by aligning the body with the natural daily rhythms of the universe. The word "Dinacharya" is derived from Sanskrit, with "Dina" meaning day and "Charya" meaning conduct or care.

In Ayurveda, it is believed that following a consistent dinacharya helps to maintain balance in the body and mind, preventing disease and promoting longevity. The dinacharya practices are tailored to your constitution or dosha.

A typical dinacharya includes practices such as waking up early in the morning before sunrise, practicing gentle yoga or stretching, cleansing the body through practices like tongue scraping and oil pulling, and engaging in meditation or mindfulness exercises. Other important aspects of dinacharya include regular meal times, specific dietary guidelines, and maintaining a bedtime routine to ensure adequate rest and rejuvenation.

Let's delve more into why routine is so important in Ayurveda and how you can create your own.

The Importance of Routine

Imagine a world where your daily habits not only impact your physical health but also influence your mental, emotional, and spiritual well-being. This is the philosophy that Ayurveda is built upon. Ayurveda teaches us that our habits can either nourish or deplete our life force, known as "prana," and that establishing a healthy daily routine is key to achieving balance and harmony within our bodies and minds.

In Ayurveda, the concept of "dinacharya," or daily routine, is emphasized as a fundamental aspect of health maintenance. By following a consistent routine that aligns with your unique mind-body type, or dosha, you can enhance your overall well-being and reduce the risk of imbalances and illness.

One of the core principles of Ayurveda is that each of us is unique, with our own specific constitution and needs. This is why it's essential to tailor your daily routine to suit your own doshic balance. For example, a person with a predominance of the Vata dosha may benefit from grounding practices, such as a warm oil massage before bathing, while someone with a Pitta constitution may thrive on cooling activities like taking a leisurely walk by the water.

One of the key ways in which routine impacts health in Ayurveda is through the concept of "agni," or digestive fire. According to Ayurvedic philosophy, a strong and balanced agni is essential for proper digestion, absorption, and assimilation of nutrients. By establishing healthy eating habits, such as eating regular meals at consistent times, avoiding heavy or processed foods, and taking time to savor and appreciate each bite, you can support your agni and promote optimal digestion.

In addition to diet, Ayurveda places great importance on daily practices that support overall well-being, such as proper sleep, exercise, and stress management. Establishing a regular sleep schedule, engaging in physical activity that aligns with your dosha, and incorporating mindfulness practices like meditation or pranayama can all contribute to a healthier and more balanced life.

Additionally, the mind-body connection is at the heart of Ayurveda, with the understanding that our thoughts, emotions, and beliefs can have a profound impact on our physical health. Incorporating practices that nourish the mind, such as journaling, gratitude exercises, or spending time in nature, can help to cultivate a positive mindset and promote emotional well-being.

By embracing the wisdom of Ayurveda and incorporating its principles into your daily routine, you can create a lifestyle that not only supports your physical health but also nurtures your mind and spirit. Remember, consistency is key when it comes to establishing new habits, so start small and gradually build upon your routine to create a personalized practice that resonates with you.

It's time to embrace the power of routine, prioritize self-care, and watch as your overall well-being blossoms like a beautifully tended garden. Your future self will thank you for it!

Morning Rituals: Starting the Day Right with Ayurvedic Practices

Let's start with the moment you open your eyes. By incorporating Ayurvedic practices into your morning routine, you can set the tone for a day filled with intention, energy, and well-being.

Wake Up with the Sun

In Ayurveda, the hours before sunrise are known as the "Brahma Muhurta," a time of day that is considered most conducive to spiritual practices and mental clarity. By aligning your waking time with the rising sun, you not only synchronize your body's internal clock but also tap into the potent energy of a new day.

As the first rays of sunlight gently kiss your eyelids, take a moment to express gratitude for the gift of another day. Welcome the day with a gentle smile and a heart full of appreciation for the opportunities and experiences that lie ahead.

Practice Abhyanga: Self-Massage with Warm Oil

One of the foundational practices in Ayurveda is Abhyanga, the art of self-massage using warm oil. This nourishing ritual helps to nourish the skin, soothe the nervous system, and promote lymphatic flow. Before stepping into the shower, take a few minutes to massage your body with warm sesame or coconut oil, moving in gentle, circular motions towards the heart.

As you massage your skin, offer loving kindness to yourself, and honor the sacred temple that houses your spirit. Feel the warmth of the oil seep into your pores, bringing a sense of grounding and tranquility to your being.

Cleanse Your Senses with Oil Pulling and Tongue Scraping

After your Abhyanga practice, indulge in the ancient Ayurvedic rituals of oil pulling and tongue scraping to cleanse your senses and promote oral hygiene. Oil pulling involves swishing a tablespoon of coconut or sesame oil in your mouth for 5–10 minutes, helping to remove toxins and bacteria from your oral cavity.

Following oil pulling, gently scrape your tongue with a copper or stainless steel tongue scraper to remove accumulated ama (toxins) and bacteria. This simple practice not only freshens your breath but also stimulates digestion and detoxification pathways in the body.

Hydrate Yourself with Warm Lemon Water

Before indulging in your breakfast, quench your body's thirst with a warm cup of lemon water. Squeeze half a fresh lemon into a cup of warm water and sip mindfully, relishing the invigorating tang of citrus and the soothing warmth of the liquid.

Lemon water not only hydrates the body after a night of fasting but also kickstarts your digestive fire (Agni) and alkalizes your system. Embrace this simple yet powerful ritual as a way to cleanse and rejuvenate your body from the inside out.

Practice Pranayama: Breathwork for Vitality

As you continue to awaken your body and mind, engage in the practice of Pranayama, or yogic breathwork, to cultivate inner vitality and mental clarity. Choose a simple breathing technique such as Nadi Shodhana (alternate nostril breathing) or Bhastrika (bellows breath) to invigorate your prana (life force) and balance your energy channels.

Sit comfortably in a quiet space, close your eyes, and place your hands on your belly. Inhale deeply through your nose, feeling your abdomen expand, then exhale fully, releasing any tension or stagnation from your being. Allow the rhythm of your breath to guide you into a state of presence and centeredness.

Set Intentions through Meditation and Visualization

Before stepping into the demands of the day, take a few moments to connect with your innermost desires and set clear intentions for how you wish to show up in the world. Find a comfortable seated position, close your eyes, and bring your awareness to your heart center.

Through the practice of meditation and visualization, invite feelings of abundance, joy, and purpose. Envision your day unfolding with grace and ease, affirming your worthiness and capability to handle whatever comes your way. Allow this sacred space of stillness to anchor you in the present moment and empower you to navigate the day with mindfulness and intention.

Nourish Your Body with a Sattvic Breakfast

As you conclude your morning rituals, honor your body's needs by nourishing it with a sattvic (pure) breakfast that supports your vitality and well-being. Choose whole, unprocessed foods such as fresh fruits, whole grains, nuts, and seeds to fuel your body with essential nutrients and prana.

Sit down mindfully to enjoy your breakfast, savoring each bite and expressing gratitude for the nourishment that sustains you. Cultivate a sense of reverence for the gifts of the earth and the interconnectedness of all beings as you receive the blessings of your morning meal.

Evening Rituals: Wind-Down Techniques for Better Sleep

As the sun begins to dip below the horizon and the hustle and bustle of the day gradually fade away, it's time to embrace the tranquility of the evening. Ayurveda places great emphasis on the importance of establishing rituals to support the natural rhythms of the body and mind. And truly, there's nothing quite like the feeling of sinking into bed, utterly at peace, and ready to drift off into dreamland.

To kick off your evening wind-down, let's start by setting the scene. Create a peaceful sanctuary in your bedroom by dimming the lights and lighting some soothing candles or incense. Play some gentle music or nature sounds to further enhance the relaxing ambiance.

Let's take a look at some Ayurvedic wind-down techniques to help you ease into a deep and restorative slumber.

Abhyanga (Self-Massage)

Treat yourself to a calming self-massage with warm, aromatic oils like sesame or coconut oil. In Ayurveda, this practice is known as Abhyanga and is believed to promote relaxation, improve circulation, and nourish the skin. As you massage your body in gentle, circular motions, take a few moments to appreciate and connect with your physical self.

Sip on Herbal Tea

Enjoy a cup of soothing herbal tea to help calm your mind and body. Ayurvedic favorites include chamomile, peppermint, or ashwagandha tea, which are known for their calming and relaxing properties. Sipping on a warm cup of tea can be a comforting way to wind down and signal to your body that it's time to relax.

Practice Pranayama

Engage in some gentle breathing exercises, such as Pranayama, to help calm the mind and release any tension or stress from the day.

One popular Pranayama technique is Nadi Shodhana (alternate nostril breathing), which helps balance the energy channels in the body and promotes a sense of peace and relaxation.

Mindful Meditation

Take a few minutes to practice mindful meditation before bedtime. Sit comfortably, close your eyes, and focus on your breath as you let go of any racing thoughts or worries. Allow yourself to be fully present in the moment and acknowledge any sensations or emotions that arise without judgment. This practice can help quiet the mind and prepare you for a restful night's sleep.

Digital Detox

Unplug from electronic devices at least an hour before bedtime to reduce exposure to blue light, which can disrupt your natural sleep-wake cycle. Instead of scrolling through social media or watching TV, opt for activities that promote relaxation, such as reading a book, journaling, or simply enjoying some quiet time with yourself.

Warm Bath

Indulge in a warm bath infused with Epsom salts, lavender essential oil, or rose petals to help relax your muscles and soothe your senses. The combination of warm water and aromatherapy can be incredibly calming and rejuvenating, setting the stage for a blissful night of sleep.

Gratitude Practice

Before drifting off to sleep, take a moment to reflect on the day and express gratitude for the blessings and lessons it has brought. Cultivating a sense of gratitude can shift your focus from worries and stress to a sense of contentment and abundance, creating a positive mindset that can improve the quality of your sleep.

By incorporating these Ayurvedic wind-down techniques into your evening ritual, you can create a peaceful and nurturing bedtime routine that supports your overall well-being and helps you enjoy a restful night's sleep.

Personalizing Your Routine: Adapting Routines to Your Lifestyle and Dosha

Personalizing your routine involves understanding your dosha and adapting your lifestyle practices to bring balance and harmony to your mind, body, and spirit. By aligning your daily habits with your doshic makeup, you can optimize your overall well-being and enhance your natural vitality.

Now, the key to personalizing your routine lies in identifying your dominant dosha and making conscious choices that support its optimal expression. Here are some practical tips for adapting your daily habits to align with your doshic constitution:

Morning Routine

Start your day with a grounding ritual that resonates with your dosha. Vata types may benefit from gentle movements like yoga or tai chi to calm their active minds. Pitta individuals can embrace cooling practices such as meditation or breathing exercises to promote inner tranquility. Kapha personalities may find invigorating activities like brisk walks or dry brushing stimulating.

Dietary Choices

Tailor your diet to pacify your dominant dosha. Vata types can favor warm, nourishing foods like soups, stews, and cooked grains to soothe their delicate digestive systems. Pitta individuals should opt for cooling, hydrating foods such as salads, fresh fruits, and leafy greens to balance their fiery nature. Kapha personalities benefit from light, spicy dishes like stir-fries, lentil soups, and herbal teas to offset their tendency towards sluggishness.

Exercise Regimen

Select exercises that support your doshic constitution. Vata individuals thrive on activities that foster stability and focus, such as gentle yoga, swimming, or Pilates. Pitta types enjoy challenging workouts like running, cycling, or weight training to release excess energy. Kapha personalities find solace in dynamic practices like dance, aerobics, or martial arts to invigorate their sluggish metabolism.

Sleep Routine

Establish a bedtime routine that promotes restful sleep based on your dosha. Vata types benefit from calming activities like reading, journaling, or listening to calming music before bed to unwind their active minds. Pitta individuals should engage in relaxation techniques such as meditation, deep breathing, or progressive muscle relaxation to cool their fiery temperament. Kapha personalities can engage in stimulating practices like self-massage, dry brushing, or light stretching to counterbalance their tendency towards heaviness.

Self-Care Practices

Incorporate personalized self-care rituals into your daily routine to nurture your mind, body, and soul. Vata types may appreciate warm oil massages, aromatherapy, or grounding rituals to foster a sense of stability and comfort. Pitta individuals can benefit from cooling practices like rosewater mists, soothing baths, or mindful breathing exercises to soothe their sensitive nature. Kapha personalities find rejuvenation in invigorating activities like energetic yoga, dry brushing, or herbal steams to awaken their senses.

Remember, personalizing your routine is a journey of self-discovery and self-care. Embrace the uniqueness of your doshic constitution and honor your body's innate wisdom. By adapting your daily habits to support your dosha, you can cultivate balance, harmony, and vitality in all aspects of your life.

Chapter 5

Ayurvedic Detoxification (Panchakarma)

Panchakarma is an ancient Ayurvedic detoxification process that has been revered for centuries as a powerful method to cleanse not just the body but also the mind and spirit.

Panchakarma, derived from Sanskrit words meaning "five actions," is a comprehensive detoxification and rejuvenation protocol that is at the heart of Ayurvedic medicine. The primary goal of Panchakarma is to rid the body of accumulated toxins, or "ama," that are believed to be the root cause of disease and imbalance, according to Ayurvedic principles.

Imagine your body as a temple, a sacred vessel that needs regular maintenance and cleansing to function at its optimal level. In the same way, we declutter our living spaces, Panchakarma aims to declutter our physical and energetic bodies, allowing the natural healing mechanisms of the body to kick into high gear.

Detoxification in Ayurveda goes beyond the physical realm; it encompasses the mind, emotions, and spirit as well. Ayurveda recognizes that we are not just a collection of organs and tissues but a holistic being composed of interconnected layers of existence. The accumulation of toxins, or ama, can manifest as physical ailments, mental fog, emotional imbalances, and spiritual stagnation.

By undergoing Panchakarma or other detox protocols, we allow the body to release deep-seated toxins, rejuvenate cellular function, balance the doshas, and restore harmony to our being. Detoxification in Ayurveda is not about deprivation or harsh cleansing methods but about nurturing the body with healing foods, herbal remedies, self-care practices, and mindful living.

In addition to physical cleansing, detox in Ayurveda aims to reset the mind and emotions, creating space for clarity, peace, and joy to emerge. As toxins are released from the body, stagnant emotions, limiting beliefs, and mental clutter can also be purged, leading to a profound sense of lightness and clarity.

The Benefits of Panchakarma and Detox in Ayurveda

- **Rejuvenation and Vitality:** Panchakarma is like hitting the reset button for your entire being. By removing accumulated toxins and restoring balance to the doshas, you can experience renewed energy, vitality, and a sense of well-being.

- **Enhanced Digestion and Metabolism:** A clean digestive system is key to overall health, according to Ayurveda. Panchakarma helps improve digestive fire (agni), assimilation of nutrients, and elimination of waste, leading to improved metabolism and nutrient absorption.

- **Mental Clarity and Emotional Balance:** As the body detoxifies, the mind also experiences a cleansing process. Many individuals report feeling more mentally alert, emotionally stable, and spiritually connected after undergoing Panchakarma, or detoxification.

- **Stronger Immunity:** A healthy immune system is vital for warding off illnesses and maintaining optimal health. By eliminating toxins and restoring balance to the body, Panchakarma can strengthen the immune system and enhance the body's natural defense mechanisms.

- **Stress Relief and Relaxation:** In our fast-paced modern world, stress has become a common culprit behind many health issues. Panchakarma offers a unique opportunity to unwind, relax, and rejuvenate the body-mind complex, promoting a deep sense of relaxation and peace.

It's important to remember that panchakarma and detoxification are not just about cleansing the physical body; they are about nurturing the entire being on a holistic level. By honoring the interconnectedness of body, mind, and spirit, we can embark on a transformative journey of healing, renewal, and self-discovery.

Types of Panchakarma

There are five main types of Panchakarma therapies, each with its own unique focus and benefits. Let's explore each one in detail.

Vamana (Emesis Therapy)

Vamana is the therapeutic process of induced vomiting, primarily used to expel excess Kapha dosha from the body. This detoxification method is beneficial for those suffering from conditions related to Kapha imbalance, such as respiratory disorders, congestion, allergies, and obesity.

During Vamana, the patient is given a specific medicated drink that induces vomiting, thus eliminating toxins and excess mucus from the body. It is crucial to undergo Vamana under the supervision of a qualified Ayurvedic practitioner to ensure safety and effectiveness.

Virechana (Purgation Therapy)

Virechana involves the use of therapeutic purgation to cleanse the body of excess Pitta dosha and accumulated toxins. This cleansing process is particularly beneficial for individuals with liver disorders, skin conditions, digestive issues, and inflammation.

The patient is administered specific herbal laxatives to facilitate the elimination of waste and toxins from the intestines. Virechana helps to improve digestion, metabolism, and overall liver function, promoting balance and harmony within the body.

Basti (Enema Therapy)

Basti is a powerful therapy that focuses on balancing Vata dosha by eliminating toxins and regulating the digestive system. It involves the administration of herbal decoctions and oils through the rectum to cleanse the colon and nourish the tissues.

Basti is known for its rejuvenating and strengthening effects on the body, making it beneficial for various chronic conditions such as arthritis, constipation, neurological disorders, and reproductive health issues. The therapy helps to lubricate the intestines, remove accumulated waste, and restore balance to the body.

Nasya (Nasal Administration)

Nasya therapy involves the administration of medicated oils or herbal preparations through the nostrils to cleanse and rejuvenate the nasal passages, sinuses, and head. This therapy is useful for conditions related to the upper respiratory system, such as allergies, sinusitis, headaches, and neurological imbalances.

Nasya helps to clear congestion, improve breathing, enhance mental clarity, and promote overall relaxation. It is also beneficial for balancing the doshas in the head region and supporting optimal sensory functions.

Raktamokshana (Bloodletting Therapy)

Raktamokshana is a specialized therapy that involves the removal of impure blood from the body to eliminate toxins and balance the doshas. This ancient practice is beneficial for conditions related to blood disorders, skin diseases, and metabolic imbalances.

Raktamokshana can be performed using various methods, such as leech therapy, venesection, or using specialized tools to draw out stagnated blood. This therapy helps to improve circulation, enhance detoxification, and promote the proper function of vital organs.

Each of the five types of Panchakarma therapies plays a vital role in cleansing, rejuvenating, and restoring balance to the body according to Ayurvedic principles. By undergoing these therapies under the guidance of a knowledgeable practitioner, you can experience profound healing on physical, mental, and emotional levels.

Remember, Ayurveda views each person as a unique combination of doshas, and the Panchakarma therapies can be customized to address individual imbalances and health concerns.

Home Detox Techniques: Simple Practices for Beginners

I'm excited to share with you some simple and effective home detox techniques rooted in Ayurveda that are perfect for beginners.

So, how can you incorporate Ayurvedic detox techniques into your daily routine? Let's start with some simple practices that you can easily do at home:

- **Start Your Day with Warm Lemon Water:** Ayurveda recommends starting your day with a glass of warm water mixed with freshly squeezed lemon juice. This helps to kickstart your digestion, flush out toxins, and alkalize your body.
- **Practice Abhyanga (Self-Massage):** Treat yourself to a rejuvenating self-massage using warm, herbal oils such as sesame or coconut oil. Massage your body in long, gentle strokes before showering to promote relaxation, improve circulation, and release toxins.
- **Try Tongue Scraping:** This simple Ayurvedic practice involves using a tongue scraper to gently remove toxins and bacteria from the surface of your tongue. It not only improves oral hygiene but also enhances digestion and overall detoxification.
- **Enjoy Detoxifying Teas:** Sip on herbal teas such as ginger, turmeric, and dandelion root throughout the day to support detoxification. These teas help to stimulate digestion, support liver function, and reduce inflammation in the body.
- **Practice Mindful Eating:** Ayurveda emphasizes the importance of mindful eating to support digestion and detoxification. Take time to savor your meals, chew your food thoroughly, and avoid distractions while eating. This

simple practice can have a profound impact on your overall well-being.
- **Incorporate Yoga and Pranayama:** Engage in gentle yoga postures and breathing exercises to stimulate your body's natural detoxification processes. Yoga and pranayama (breathwork) help to improve circulation, release tension, and promote the elimination of toxins from the body.
- **Dry Brushing:** Dry brushing is a popular Ayurvedic technique that involves using a dry brush to exfoliate the skin and stimulate the lymphatic system. This practice helps to remove dead skin cells, improve circulation, and support detoxification.
- **Prioritize Sleep:** Adequate rest is essential for detoxification and overall well-being. Aim to get 7-9 hours of quality sleep each night to allow your body to repair, regenerate, and eliminate toxins while you rest.
- **Mindfulness and Meditation:** Incorporate mindfulness practices and meditation into your daily routine to reduce stress, promote mental clarity, and support detoxification at a deeper level. Quieting the mind can have a powerful impact on your body's ability to detoxify.
- **Stay Hydrated:** Hydration is key to supporting your body's detoxification processes. Drink plenty of water throughout the day to flush out toxins, support digestion, and keep your body hydrated and healthy.

As you begin to incorporate these simple Ayurvedic detox techniques into your daily routine, remember to listen to your body and adjust as needed. Consistency is key when it comes to supporting your body's natural detoxification processes, so be patient and gentle with yourself as you embark on this journey to wellness.

When to Seek Professional Help: Understanding Your Limits

Now, let's delve into the importance of knowing when to seek professional assistance during your Panchakarma journey. While Ayurveda advocates self-care and self-awareness, there are certain situations where professional guidance becomes crucial for a safe and effective detoxification process.

One of the key indicators that you may need professional help is if you are experiencing severe or persistent symptoms during Panchakarma. Ayurveda teaches us to listen to our bodies and honor the signals they send us. If you find yourself struggling with intense detox reactions, physical discomfort, or emotional distress that feels overwhelming, it's time to reach out to a qualified Ayurvedic practitioner for support.

Additionally, if you have pre-existing health conditions or are taking medications, it's essential to consult with a professional before beginning Panchakarma. Certain health conditions may require modifications to the traditional detox program, and a knowledgeable practitioner can help tailor the treatment to suit your specific needs and ensure your safety throughout the process.

Moreover, seeking professional help can also be beneficial if you are new to Ayurveda or Panchakarma. A skilled practitioner can provide you with guidance on how to navigate the intricacies of this ancient healing system, offer personalized recommendations based on your unique constitution, and support you in making informed decisions for your well-being.

Now, let's shift our focus to understanding your limits while practicing Panchakarma. While the detoxification process can be incredibly rewarding, it's essential to listen to your body and honor your boundaries to prevent burnout or overwhelm.

Learning to recognize when you've reached your limit can be a valuable skill during Panchakarma. Pay attention to signs of fatigue, emotional strain, or physical discomfort, and don't hesitate to take a step back and rest when needed. Remember, self-care is an integral part of the healing journey, and it's okay to prioritize your well-being by giving yourself the time and space to recharge.

Setting realistic expectations for yourself is another crucial aspect of navigating your limits during Panchakarma. Understand that the detox process may bring up deep-seated emotions, physical challenges, or lifestyle changes that require patience and resilience. By being gentle with yourself and embracing the process with an open heart, you can cultivate a sense of balance and harmony throughout your journey.

In addition, communicating openly with your Ayurvedic practitioner about your goals, concerns, and limitations can help create a supportive environment that honors your individual needs. Together, you can work collaboratively to tailor the Panchakarma experience to align with your comfort level and ensure a positive outcome.

Chapter 6

Ayurvedic Herbs and Supplements

In Ayurveda, herbs play a pivotal role in restoring and maintaining harmony within the body, mind, and spirit. Herbs are seen as potent allies in rebalancing doshas and promoting overall well-being.

One of the key benefits of using herbs in Ayurveda is their natural and holistic approach to healing. Unlike modern medicine, which often focuses on treating symptoms, Ayurvedic herbs target the root cause of imbalances in the body. By addressing underlying issues, herbs help restore equilibrium and support the body's innate ability to heal itself.

Herbs in Ayurveda are carefully selected based on their taste, energy, and post-digestive effect, ensuring that they complement an individual's unique constitution. This personalized approach to herbal medicine highlights the importance of treating each person as an individual with distinct needs and requirements.

Another significant benefit of using herbs in Ayurveda is their gentle yet effective nature. Many Ayurvedic herbs are known for their subtle yet profound effects on the body, offering a gentle and sustainable approach to healing. Unlike harsh chemical medications, which may come with unwanted side effects, Ayurvedic herbs work in harmony with the body, promoting health and vitality without causing harm.

Furthermore, the use of herbs in Ayurveda promotes a sense of connection with nature and the environment. Ayurveda views humans as an integral part of the natural world, and herbs are seen as gifts from Mother Earth to support our well-being. By harnessing the power of plants, Ayurveda encourages a deeper appreciation for the healing properties of the natural world and fosters a sense of harmony with our surroundings.

The diverse range of herbs used in Ayurveda reflects the vast array of healing properties found in nature. From soothing herbs like chamomile and fennel to invigorating herbs like ginger and turmeric, Ayurvedic herbs offer a comprehensive toolkit for addressing a wide range of health concerns. Whether you're seeking to boost immunity, improve digestion, or calm the mind, there's an herb in Ayurveda to support your unique health goals.

One of the most fascinating aspects of Ayurvedic herbs is their ability to work synergistically with one another. In Ayurveda, herbal formulations are often created by combining multiple herbs to enhance their therapeutic effects. This synergistic approach ensures that each herb complements the others, creating a powerful blend that addresses multiple aspects of a health issue.

Ayurvedic herbs are not only used internally but also externally in the form of oils, ointments, and poultices. This holistic approach to herbal medicine acknowledges the importance of treating the body both internally and externally to promote optimal health and well-being. Whether applied topically or ingested, Ayurvedic herbs offer a versatile and comprehensive approach to healing.

Furthermore, Ayurvedic herbs are often used in conjunction with other holistic practices, such as yoga, meditation, and pranayama (breathwork). This integrated approach to wellness recognizes the interconnectedness of the body, mind, and spirit and emphasizes the importance of maintaining balance in all aspects of life. By incorporating herbs into a holistic wellness routine, individuals can enhance their overall health and vitality on multiple levels.

Now that you know why herbs are fantastic to add to your Ayurvedic practice, let's take a look at some of the most commonly used ones.

Common Ayurvedic Herbs

The natural world is huge, so it shouldn't be a surprise that there are countless herbs you can incorporate into your Ayurvedic practice. However, the ten most commonly used ones are:

- Ashwagandha (Withania somnifera)
- Turmeric (Curcuma longa)
- Triphala (a combination of three fruits: Amalaki, Bibhitaki, and Haritaki)
- Tulsi (Ocimum sanctum, also known as Holy Basil)
- Brahmi (Bacopa monnieri)
- Ginger (Zingiber officinale)
- Amla (Emblica officinalis, also known as Indian Gooseberry)
- Neem (Azadirachta indica)
- Guggul (Commiphora wightii)
- Licorice (Glycyrrhiza glabra)

Let's take a detailed look at each one.

Ashwagandha

Ashwagandha, also known as "Indian Winter Cherry" or "Indian Ginseng," is a powerful herb that has been revered in Ayurvedic medicine for thousands of years. Its botanical name, Withania somnifera, reflects its potent rejuvenating and restorative properties.

This herb is believed to embody the characteristics of a warrior: strong, resilient, and adaptable. Just like a warrior, Ashwagandha helps to combat stress, improve vitality, and enhance overall well-being. It is known for its unique ability to balance all three doshas – Vata, Pitta, and Kapha – making it a versatile herb suited for a wide range of individuals.

In Ayurveda, Ashwagandha is classified as a rasayana, which is a category of herbs that promote longevity, vitality, and overall health. It is particularly revered for its adaptogenic properties, which means it helps the body adapt to stress and maintain homeostasis.

One of the key benefits of Ashwagandha is its ability to support the nervous system. In Ayurveda, it is considered a medhya herb, which means it enhances cognitive function and promotes mental clarity. Ashwagandha is known to calm the mind, reduce anxiety, and promote restful sleep, making it an invaluable herb for those dealing with stress and insomnia.

Ashwagandha is also renowned for its rejuvenating effects on the body. It is believed to strengthen the immune system, increase vitality, and improve overall energy levels. This makes it a valuable herb for individuals looking to boost their resilience and endurance.

From a personality standpoint, Ashwagandha can be likened to a wise sage, full of ancient knowledge and profound insights. It imparts a sense of groundedness and stability, helping individuals connect to their inner strength and wisdom. Just like a sage,

Ashwagandha guides individuals on a path towards holistic well-being and balance.

In Ayurveda, Ashwagandha is often recommended for individuals with high Vata imbalances, such as anxiety, restlessness, and insomnia. Its grounding and nourishing properties help to pacify excess Vata and bring about a sense of calm and stability.

Ashwagandha's warming and nourishing qualities make it beneficial for individuals with high Pitta imbalances as well. It helps to soothe inflammation, support the adrenal glands, and promote a sense of coolness and balance in the body.

For those with high Kapha imbalances, Ashwagandha's stimulating and rejuvenating properties can help invigorate the mind and body. It helps to increase energy levels, improve digestion, and uplift the spirits, making it a valuable herb for individuals dealing with lethargy and heaviness.

Incorporating Ashwagandha into your daily routine can bring about a sense of vitality, resilience, and balance. Whether you're looking to combat stress, improve cognitive function, or enhance your overall well-being, this herb has much to offer.

Just like a trusted companion, Ashwagandha guides you on a journey towards optimal health and vitality, supporting you every step of the way. Embrace the wisdom of this ancient herb and experience its transformative effects on your mind, body, and spirit. Ashwagandha truly is a gift from nature, a warrior herb standing strong and resilient, ready to support you in your quest for well-being.

Turmeric

Turmeric, the golden spice of Ayurveda, is truly a gem in the world of holistic health and wellness. Vibrant in color and rich in history, this potent herb has been prized for centuries for its numerous health benefits.

Imagine walking through a bustling market in ancient India, where the aroma of freshly ground spices fills the air. Among the myriad of herbs and spices, turmeric stands out with its bright yellow hue, beckoning you to experience its magical properties. In Ayurveda, turmeric is classified as "kapha-pacifying," helping to balance the earth and water elements in the body. It is known to possess warming energy, promote circulation, and assist in the digestion of heavy foods.

Turmeric is revered for its ability to pacify all three doshas: Vata, Pitta, and Kapha. It is a true all-rounder that can adapt to the unique needs of each individual, making it a versatile herb in Ayurvedic medicine. Turmeric's bitter and pungent taste works to stimulate digestion, cleanse the blood, and support healthy liver function. It is also a powerful anti-inflammatory agent, making it invaluable for those dealing with joint pain and inflammation.

In terms of energetics, turmeric carries the qualities of being light, dry, and heating. It kindles the digestive fire, known as "Agni" in Ayurveda, helping to improve metabolism and support the body's natural detoxification processes. This makes turmeric an essential ingredient in traditional Ayurvedic cooking, where it is used in curries, dals, and medicinal teas.

Beyond its culinary uses, turmeric is also a star player in Ayurvedic skincare and beauty rituals. Its antioxidant and anti-inflammatory properties make it a wonderful remedy for acne, eczema, and other skin conditions. A paste made from turmeric and honey can work wonders for brightening the complexion and promoting healthy, radiant skin.

Turmeric's benefits extend beyond the physical realm, as it is also revered for its mental and spiritual properties. In Ayurveda, turmeric is said to have a purifying effect on the mind, helping to clear away mental fog and promote clarity of thought. Its warm and invigorating energy can uplift the spirits and promote a sense of well-being.

To incorporate turmeric into your daily routine, you can start by adding it to your cooking. A sprinkle of turmeric in soups, stews, and roasted vegetables can enhance both the flavor and health benefits of your meals. You can also enjoy a soothing cup of turmeric tea by steeping freshly grated turmeric in hot water with a dash of honey and lemon.

For those looking to harness the full power of turmeric, Ayurveda offers various formulations and remedies. Turmeric capsules, powders, and oils are widely available and can be used to address specific health concerns. Whether you are looking to support joint health, boost immunity, or improve digestion, turmeric has something to offer for everyone.

Triphala

Triphala is considered one of the most revered herbal formulations in Ayurveda, the ancient Indian system of medicine that focuses on balancing the body, mind, and spirit to achieve optimal health. This powerful combination of three fruits, Amla (Emblica officinalis), Haritaki (Terminalia chebula), and Bibhitaki (Terminalia belerica), has been used for centuries to promote overall well-being and longevity.

Picture Triphala as a dynamic trio of Ayurvedic superheroes, each fruit bringing its own unique strengths to the table. Amla, also known as Indian gooseberry, is a powerhouse of vitamin C and antioxidants. It rejuvenates the body and enhances immunity, like a resilient shield protecting you from illnesses. Haritaki, the gentle cleanser, supports digestive health and detoxification, ensuring that your internal systems run smoothly like a well-oiled machine. Finally, Bibhitaki, the balancer, promotes respiratory health and helps to maintain equilibrium in the body, mind, and spirit, akin to a wise counselor keeping everything in harmony.

Triphala, with its holistic approach, addresses a wide range of health issues and is known for its gentle yet effective nature. It supports healthy digestion, relieves constipation, and detoxifies the body, making it a cornerstone for good gastrointestinal health. Think of it as a gentle broom sweeping away toxins and debris, leaving your digestive system clean and rejuvenated.

But Triphala's benefits don't stop there. It also nourishes the eyes, hair, and skin, promoting a radiant appearance from within. It's like a beauty elixir that works on enhancing your outer glow by nourishing your inner vitality. Triphala's antioxidant properties help to combat free radicals, which are often the culprit behind premature aging and various health issues.

Furthermore, Triphala has a unique ability to support weight management by balancing the three Doshas – Vata, Pitta, and Kapha – in the body. It aids in metabolism, digestion, and elimination, promoting a healthy weight and overall well-being.

Triphala doesn't believe in crash diets or quick fixes; it's all about sustainable and balanced health that lasts a lifetime.

When it comes to mental well-being, Triphala shines as a rejuvenator for the mind. It helps to alleviate stress, improve cognitive function, and enhance clarity and focus. Imagine having a calm and focused mind, free from the chaos and clutter of everyday life, thanks to the balancing effects of Triphala.

Tulsi

Tulsi, also known as Holy Basil, is a beloved herb in Ayurveda, celebrated for its numerous healing properties and sacred significance. With a personality as vibrant and invigorating as its aroma, Tulsi is often referred to as the "Queen of Herbs" due to its exceptional adaptogenic qualities.

In Ayurveda, Tulsi is classified as a sattvic herb, known for its ability to balance all three doshas (Vata, Pitta, and Kapha). With its bitter and pungent taste, Tulsi helps pacify Kapha dosha, while its warming qualities aid in soothing Vata imbalance. Additionally, its cooling properties make it beneficial for Pitta dosha, making it a versatile herb for promoting overall well-being.

Tulsi is rich in essential oils, vitamins, and minerals, making it a potent herb for boosting the immune system and improving resilience to stress. Its adaptogenic properties help the body adapt to physical, emotional, and environmental stressors, promoting a sense of balance and harmony.

When it comes to personality, Tulsi is known for its nurturing and protective nature. Just like a caring mother, it offers support and strength during challenging times, helping individuals navigate through life's ups and downs with grace and resilience. Tulsi exudes a sense of calm and serenity, providing a sanctuary of peace amidst life's chaos.

Tulsi is often used in Ayurvedic medicine to treat a wide range of health conditions. It is considered a potent rasayana, or rejuvenating herb, that helps promote longevity and vitality. Tulsi is known for its antimicrobial properties, making it effective in treating respiratory infections, coughs, and colds. Its antiinflammatory properties help reduce inflammation in the body, making it a valuable herb for managing conditions like arthritis and inflammatory bowel diseases.

As a powerful antioxidant, Tulsi helps protect the body from damaging free radicals, reducing the risk of chronic diseases and premature aging. Its detoxifying properties support liver function, aiding in the elimination of toxins from the body. Tulsi is also known for its beneficial effects on the nervous system, helping improve cognitive function, memory, and mental clarity.

In Ayurveda, Tulsi is not just a medicinal herb but also a spiritual ally. It is revered for its purifying and calming influence on the mind and spirit. Tulsi is often used in rituals and ceremonies to enhance spiritual awareness and connection with the divine. Its subtle yet profound energy helps create a sacred space for meditation and inner reflection.

Brahmi

Nestled in the lush greenery of the Indian subcontinent, Brahmi, also known as Bacopa monnieri, has long been celebrated as a powerful adaptogen and cognitive enhancer in Ayurvedic tradition.

In Ayurveda, Brahmi is revered for its ability to pacify all three doshas - Vata, Pitta, and Kapha, making it a versatile herb suitable for almost everyone. Its cooling and grounding qualities soothe fiery Pitta imbalances, while its nourishing essence calms restless Vata energies. At the same time, it gently balances the heavy qualities of Kapha, bringing a sense of lightness and clarity to the mind and body.

Brahmi is particularly cherished for its impact on the intellect and mental function. Known as a Medhya Rasayana in Ayurveda, it is believed to enhance cognitive abilities, memory, and overall brain health. Imagine Brahmi as a wise sage whispering ancient secrets to your mind, enhancing your learning and comprehension with each passing day.

The herb's profound effects on the mind extend to its ability to calm the nervous system and promote mental clarity. In a world filled with distractions and stress, Brahmi acts as a soothing balm, helping you find inner peace and focus amidst the chaos. It gently uplifts the mood, easing anxiety and promoting a sense of tranquility that lingers like a sweet melody in your soul.

But Brahmi's benefits do not stop at the mind. Its rejuvenating properties also extend to the physical body, nourishing the tissues and supporting overall vitality. Imagine your body as a temple, with Brahmi as the gentle caretaker, tending to every cell and organ with love and devotion.

As you welcome Brahmi into your wellness routine, you may notice an increase in energy, stamina, and resilience. Like a gentle breeze that revitalizes the spirit, Brahmi infuses your being with a newfound sense of vitality and strength, enabling you to navigate life's challenges with grace and poise.

In Ayurvedic terms, Brahmi is said to enhance Ojas, the subtle essence of vitality and immunity. By bolstering your body's natural defenses, Brahmi acts as a shield against environmental stressors and imbalances, helping you maintain optimal health and well-being throughout the year.

So, as you sip on a cup of Brahmi tea or add a few drops of its herbal extract to your daily routine, remember the wisdom and grace of this extraordinary herb. Let Brahmi be your guiding light in the journey towards balance and harmony, a steadfast companion on the path to radiant health and vibrant vitality.

Ginger

Ginger, known as "shunthi" in Sanskrit, has been a beloved herb in Ayurvedic medicine for centuries, appreciated for its warming properties and ability to balance the body's doshas – Vata, Pitta, and Kapha. This knobby rhizome, with its unique blend of flavors, holds a special place in Ayurveda as a versatile herb that can be used in cooking, teas, and medicinal remedies. Just like a fiery personality, ginger leaves a lasting impression wherever it goes.

In Ayurveda, ginger is particularly respected for its digestive properties. It enhances the digestive fire, or "agni," aiding in the proper digestion and assimilation of food. A cup of warm ginger tea after meals can help soothe any lingering digestive discomfort, promoting a sense of lightness and balance in the stomach. It's like a warm hug for your belly after a hearty meal!

From an Ayurvedic perspective, ginger is known to pacify Vata and Kapha doshas while potentially aggravating Pitta when consumed in excess. This makes it a wonderful herb for balancing the cold and damp qualities of winter or calming an anxious mind, all while offering a spicy kick of flavor to awaken the senses. Like a trustworthy friend, Ginger is always there to provide comfort and support when needed.

In addition to its digestive benefits, ginger is also revered for its anti-inflammatory properties. This makes it a popular choice in Ayurvedic treatments for conditions like arthritis and muscle pain. Its warming nature helps to improve circulation and reduce inflammation, providing relief to those with achy joints and muscles. Ginger's ability to ignite a gentle fire within the body can help melt away tension and stiffness, leaving you feeling rejuvenated and invigorated.

Furthermore, ginger is celebrated for its immune-boosting qualities. Rich in antioxidants and antimicrobial compounds, ginger can help strengthen the body's defense mechanisms against pathogens and infections. A soothing ginger and honey concoction is often used in Ayurveda to alleviate cold and flu symptoms, offering natural relief that tickles the taste buds and warms the soul.

The versatility of ginger extends beyond medicinal uses, as it can also be incorporated into daily cooking to enhance both the flavor and health benefits of a dish. Whether grated, sliced, or juiced, ginger adds a zesty touch to curries, stir-fries, soups, and desserts, infusing each bite with its spicy-sweet essence.

Amla

Meet Amla, the ancient Indian superfruit known for its incredible health benefits and powerful impact on overall well-being. Amla, also known as Indian Gooseberry, has been revered in Ayurveda for thousands of years as a symbol of good health, longevity, and vitality.

With its sour and bitter taste, Amla contains a high concentration of Vitamin C, making it one of the richest natural sources of this essential nutrient. This powerful antioxidant helps boost the immune system, promote healthy skin, and support the body in fighting off illness and disease. Amla is also a potent source of bioflavonoids, which work synergistically with Vitamin C to enhance its effects and provide a wide range of health benefits.

In Ayurveda, Amla is considered a "rasayana" herb, which means it is believed to promote longevity, rejuvenation, and overall vitality. This makes Amla an essential component of many Ayurvedic formulations and remedies aimed at restoring balance to the body and mind.

Amla is known for its ability to support digestion and enhance nutrient absorption. It helps balance the digestive fire, known as "agni" in Ayurveda, which is essential for proper digestion and metabolism. Amla's bitter and sour taste stimulates digestive enzymes and promotes the breakdown of food, helping to prevent indigestion, bloating, and other digestive issues.

Not only does Amla support digestion, but it also acts as a natural detoxifier for the body. It helps cleanse the liver and kidneys, promoting the elimination of toxins and waste products from the body. This detoxifying action helps improve overall health and well-being, leaving you feeling lighter, more energetic and rejuvenated.

Amla is also known for its anti-inflammatory properties, making it an excellent remedy for inflammatory conditions such as arthritis, joint pain, and skin disorders. Its cooling and soothing nature helps reduce inflammation and provide relief from pain and discomfort.

But Amla's benefits extend beyond just physical health; it is also known for its impact on mental and emotional well-being. In Ayurveda, Amla is considered a "medhya" herb, which means it is believed to support cognitive function, memory, and concentration. Its nourishing qualities help calm the mind, reduce stress and anxiety, and promote mental clarity and focus.

Amla is truly a versatile superfruit that can be consumed in various forms: fresh, dried, powdered, or as a juice. It can be incorporated into your diet in countless ways, from adding it to smoothies and salads to brewing it as a tea or tonic. However, you choose to enjoy Amla, rest assured that you are nourishing your body, mind, and spirit with this ancient Ayurvedic gem.

Neem

Neem, also known as Azadirachta indica, is hailed as the "village pharmacy" in India for its wide array of health benefits. This evergreen tree is native to the Indian subcontinent and has been revered for centuries for its medicinal qualities. Neem is considered a symbol of good health and protection, earning it the nickname "the divine tree."

One of the key characteristics of Neem is its bitter taste, which is a reflection of its powerful purifying properties. In Ayurveda, this bitter taste is associated with reducing excess Kapha and Pitta doshas, making Neem an excellent herb for balancing these doshas in the body. Its cleansing and detoxifying effects make it a popular choice for promoting healthy skin, supporting liver function, and aiding digestion.

Neem is a powerhouse of active compounds such as nimbin, nimbidin, and nimbidol, which contribute to its antimicrobial, antifungal, and anti-inflammatory properties. These compounds work together to combat a wide range of health issues, from skin infections and acne to digestive disorders and immune system support.

As the ultimate skin savior, Neem is known for its ability to cleanse, moisturize, and rejuvenate the skin. Its antibacterial and antifungal properties make it a popular ingredient in skincare products for treating acne, eczema, and other skin conditions. Neem oil, derived from the seeds of the Neem tree, is a potent remedy for promoting healthy skin and hair, thanks to its nourishing and protective effects.

In addition to its skincare benefits, Neem is also a versatile herb for promoting overall well-being. It is commonly used in Ayurvedic remedies for supporting healthy blood sugar levels, boosting immunity, and even as a natural insect repellent. Neem leaves are often consumed as a tea or added to dishes for their detoxifying and immune-boosting effects.

Neem's influence extends beyond physical health to spiritual and mental well-being. This herb is believed to have a purifying and protective energy that wards off negative influences and promotes spiritual growth. Adding Neem to your daily routine can help create a sense of balance and harmony within the body, mind, and spirit.

Neem, with its bitter taste and potent properties, may not be the most popular herb in the world of Ayurveda, but its benefits are truly remarkable. From skin care to immune support, this versatile herb has a lot to offer for those seeking natural remedies for their health and well-being.

Guggul

Guggul is a resin-like no other, revered in the realms of Ayurveda for its potent healing properties and age-old wisdom. Picture a tree standing tall and strong in the mystical lands of India, its resin oozing out like liquid gold, holding within it the secrets of wellness and vitality.

In the ancient texts of Ayurveda, guggul shines as a superstar remedy, known for its ability to balance all three doshas - Vata, Pitta, and Kapha. It's like a harmonious orchestra conductor, bringing your body and mind back into perfect rhythm. A true all-rounder, guggul is beloved for its versatile nature, effectively addressing a myriad of health concerns.

When it comes to Ayurvedic energetics, guggul's taste profile is pungent, bitter, and astringent, with a warming potency that kindles your digestive fire. As it journeys through your system, it penetrates deeply, detoxifying and purifying at a cellular level. Guggul's post-digestive effect is sweet, leaving a soothing touch as it replenishes and nurtures your tissues.

Guggul's primary action lies in its profound ability to support healthy cholesterol levels and promote cardiovascular wellness. It's like a loyal guardian, standing sentinel against the buildup of plaque and ensuring your heart beats harmoniously. But Guggul doesn't stop there - oh no! This benevolent resin is also known for its anti-inflammatory prowess and soothing joints and muscles, making movement a joy once more.

As we delve deeper into guggul's realm, we uncover its talent for kindling the digestive flames, aiding in metabolism and weight management. It's like a whisper from the ancient sages, guiding you towards balance and vitality. Guggul's purifying nature extends to the liver, supporting its detoxification functions and promoting radiant skin from within.

But wait, there's more! Guggul's influence on the respiratory system is nothing short of magical. Like a breath of fresh air on a misty morning, it clears congestion, eases breathing, and uplifts your spirits. It's the gentle hand that guides you towards clarity and lightness, one inhalation at a time.

And let's not forget Guggul's impact on the mind. This resin holds a special place in Ayurvedic tradition for its ability to pacify the mind, calm the nerves, and uplift the spirit. It's like a wise old friend, offering solace in times of turbulence and clarity in moments of confusion.

Licorice

Licorice, also known as "Yashtimadhu" in Ayurvedic texts, is a herb with a rich history of medicinal use in various cultures. In Ayurveda, Licorice is classified as a "Rasayana" herb, which means it is renowned for its rejuvenating properties. This herb holds a special place in Ayurvedic pharmacology for its ability to balance all three doshas: Vata, Pitta, and Kapha. Licorice is particularly beneficial for Pitta dosha imbalances, as it helps to cool and soothe excess heat in the body.

One of the key characteristics of Licorice is its sweet taste, which is attributed to the compound glycyrrhizin. This natural sweetness makes Licorice a delightful addition to herbal formulations, balancing out the bitter and pungent tastes of other herbs. The sweet taste of Licorice also has a nourishing and grounding effect on the body and mind, making it a wonderful choice for promoting overall well-being.

Licorice is revered for its adaptogenic properties, which means it helps the body adapt to stress and maintain a state of homeostasis. This makes Licorice a valuable herb for supporting the body during times of physical or emotional stress. From supporting the adrenal glands to promoting healthy digestion, Licorice works holistically to keep the body in balance.

When it comes to digestion, Licorice is a true superstar. This herb is known for its ability to soothe the digestive tract, relieve gastrointestinal discomfort, and support healthy bowel movements. Licorice can help alleviate symptoms of indigestion, bloating, and heartburn, making it a go-to remedy for maintaining gut health.

Licorice also boasts powerful antioxidant properties, helping to protect the body from oxidative stress and free radical damage. By neutralizing harmful molecules in the body, Licorice promotes cellular health and overall vitality. This herb is a true ally in the fight against premature aging and disease, keeping you feeling vibrant and youthful from the inside out.

In addition to its physical benefits, Licorice has a calming effect on the mind and emotions. This herb is traditionally used in Ayurveda to promote mental clarity, emotional balance, and a sense of inner peace. Licorice can help reduce feelings of stress and anxiety, bringing a sense of calm and tranquility to the mind.

Licorice is a versatile herb that can be enjoyed in various forms, including teas, powders, and syrups. Whether you sip on a cup of Licorice tea to soothe a sore throat or incorporate Licorice powder into your cooking for digestive support, this herb is easy to incorporate into your daily routine.

Making Herbal Preparations: Teas, Tinctures, and Powders

Making herbal preparations in Ayurveda is as delightful as it is beneficial for both the body and the soul. From teas to tinctures and powders, there's a wide array of methods to harness the power of nature's pharmacy.

Let's start with the basics: teas. Herbal teas are not only a soothing and fragrant way to enjoy the benefits of herbs, but they also provide a gentle way to introduce the healing properties of herbs into your daily routine. To make a calming and balancing herbal tea, try this recipe:

Soothing Balance Tea
Ingredients:
- 1 tsp dried chamomile flowers
- 1 tsp dried lavender flowers
- 1 tsp dried rose petals
- 1 tsp dried lemon balm
- 2 cups of water

Instructions:
6. Boil the water in a saucepan.

7. Add the dried herbs to the boiling water.
8. Cover and let steep for 10–15 minutes.
9. Strain the herbs and enjoy your soothing balance tea.

Next up, tinctures. Tinctures are concentrated liquid extracts of herbs that preserve their medicinal properties. They are easy to make and convenient to take. Try this recipe for an energizing and immune-boosting tincture:

Immune Boost Tincture

Ingredients:

- 1 part echinacea root
- 1 part astragalus root
- 1 part ginger root
- Vodka or brandy

Instructions:

- Chop the roots into small pieces.
- Place the herbs in a glass jar and cover with the alcohol.
- Shake the jar daily and let it infuse for 4-6 weeks.
- Strain the tincture and store it in a dark glass bottle.
- Take 1-2 droppers full daily to boost your immune system.

Lastly, let's talk about powders. Herbal powders are versatile and can be easily incorporated into smoothies, teas, or capsules. They are a convenient way to consume a potent dose of herbs. Here is a recipe for a grounding and nourishing herbal powder:

Nourishing Ashwagandha Powder

Ingredients:

- 1/2 cup ashwagandha root powder
- 1/4 cup cinnamon powder
- 1/4 cup cardamom powder

Instructions:

1. Mix all the powders together in a bowl.
2. Store the powder in an airtight container.
3. Add a teaspoon of the powder to your morning smoothie or warm milk for a nourishing boost.

In Ayurveda, every herb has specific healing properties that can be utilized to restore balance and harmony to the body. Experiment with different herbs and preparations to find what works best for you. Remember, herbal preparations are not only meant to heal the body but also to nourish the spirit. Embrace the process of creating these herbal remedies as a form of self-care and self-love.

Now, how about a couple more recipes to add to your herbal repertoire?

Digestive Tea Blend

Ingredients:

- 1 tsp fennel seeds
- 1 tsp coriander seeds
- 1 tsp cumin seeds
- 2 cups of water

Instructions:

1. Toast the seeds in a dry pan until fragrant.
2. Crush the seeds slightly to release their aroma.
3. Boil the water and add the seeds.
4. Let steep for 10 minutes, strain, and enjoy after meals for better digestion.

Calming Lavender Tincture

Ingredients:

- 1 part dried lavender flowers
- Vodka or brandy

Instructions:

- Place the dried lavender flowers in a glass jar.
- Cover with alcohol and let it infuse for 4-6 weeks.
- Strain the tincture and store it in a dark glass bottle.
- Take a dropper full before bed for a restful night's sleep.

Remember to have fun, be creative, and let the healing power of herbs guide you on your journey to wellness.

Safety and Dosage: Guidelines for Using Herbs Responsibly

When it comes to dosage, the golden rule in Ayurveda is moderation. It is always advisable to start with a lower dose and gradually increase it as needed, allowing your body to adjust and respond to the herb's effects. Consulting with a qualified Ayurvedic practitioner can provide valuable insights into the appropriate dosage for your specific condition and constitution, ensuring a safe and harmonious healing journey.

In addition to dosage, the quality and purity of the herbs you use play a crucial role in their safety and efficacy. Opt for organic, sustainably sourced herbs from reputable suppliers, and avoid herbs that are contaminated with pesticides, heavy metals, or other harmful substances. Ayurveda emphasizes the importance of honoring the integrity of nature and choosing products that are in harmony with the environment and our well-being.

As with any form of medicine, it is essential to be mindful of potential interactions between herbs and other medications you may be taking. Some herbs can interfere with the effectiveness of certain drugs or exacerbate underlying health conditions, so it is advisable to inform your healthcare provider about your herbal regimen to ensure compatibility and safety.

To enhance the absorption and effectiveness of herbs, Ayurveda offers various preparation methods, such as decoctions, powders, and oils. Each method has its own unique benefits and can be tailored to suit your preferences and needs. Experimenting with different preparations can add a delightful dimension to your herbal journey and enhance the therapeutic effects of the herbs you choose.

In the vast and enchanting realm of Ayurveda, safety, and dosage are paramount considerations that guide us in harnessing the healing power of herbs. By approaching herbs with respect, wisdom, and an open heart, we can unlock their full potential and embark on a transformative path towards well-being and balance.

Chapter 7

Ayurvedic Bodywork and Self-Care

Imagine you are surrounded by the soothing scent of essential oils, soft music playing in the background, and warm herbal oils being gently massaged into your skin. This is the magic of Ayurvedic bodywork, where every touch is intentional and every movement is designed to restore balance to your unique constitution, or dosha.

But Ayurvedic self-care is not just about the treatments you receive from a practitioner; it's also about the practices you incorporate into your daily routine to maintain that sense of balance and well-being. From self-massage with nourishing oils to practicing mindfulness and meditation, Ayurvedic self-care empowers you to take charge of your health and wellness in a holistic way.

In this chapter, we'll explore methods to ensure you're getting all the self-care you need in your Ayurvedic endeavors.

Abhyanga (Self-Massage)

Abhyanga, the ancient practice of self-massage in Ayurveda, is a luxurious and nurturing ritual that offers a host of physical, mental, and emotional benefits. This beautiful practice involves lovingly anointing the body with warm oil, allowing it to penetrate deep into the skin and tissues, and then gently massaging the body to promote relaxation, balance, and overall well-being.

Let's start by exploring the many benefits of abhyanga. First and foremost, abhyanga helps to nourish and moisturize the skin, leaving it soft, supple, and radiant. The warm oil used in abhyanga also helps to improve circulation, boosting the flow of nutrients and oxygen throughout the body. This can help to reduce muscle tension, alleviate aches and pains, and promote overall relaxation. In addition, abhyanga is believed to support the lymphatic system, helping to detoxify the body and boost the immune system.

On a mental and emotional level, abhyanga is a deeply grounding and soothing practice. The act of massaging the body with warm oil can help to calm the mind, reduce stress and anxiety, and promote a sense of inner peace. The rhythmic motions of the massage can help to release emotional tension stored in the body, allowing you to feel more balanced and centered. In Ayurveda, it is believed that abhyanga helps to balance the doshas, or the unique elemental energies within each individual, leading to improved overall health and well-being.

Now, let's dive into some techniques for performing an abhyanga self-massage ritual. To begin, choose a high-quality oil that is appropriate for your dosha or current imbalances. Warm the oil slightly by placing the bottle in a bowl of warm water or by using a gentle heating method. Start by standing on a towel or mat in a warm room, as you want to be comfortable and relaxed during the massage.

Begin by applying a small amount of oil to your scalp, massaging it into the roots of your hair using circular motions. Then, move on to your face and ears, using gentle upward strokes to nourish and rejuvenate the delicate skin. Next, massage your neck and shoulders, using long, soothing strokes to release tension and stress. Move down to your arms and hands, paying special attention to the joints and muscles that may hold tension.

As you move to your chest and abdomen, use gentle circular motions to promote digestion and release emotional tension stored in the solar plexus area. Continue down to your legs and feet, massaging each muscle and joint with care and attention. Take your time with each part of your body, allowing the warm oil and loving touch to penetrate deeply and nourish your entire being.

After you have completed the massage, take a warm bath or shower to further enhance the benefits of the oil. Allow the water to cleanse and rejuvenate your body, leaving you feeling refreshed and renewed. Pat your skin dry with a soft towel, taking a few moments to bask in the glow of your self-care ritual.

Remember, abhyanga is a practice of self-love and self-care, so be gentle and kind to yourself throughout the process. Allow yourself to fully experience the nurturing touch of the oil and the healing power of your own hands. You deserve this time to reconnect with your body, mind, and spirit and to honor the ancient wisdom of Ayurveda.

Shirodhara: Oil Pouring Therapy for Stress Relief

Are you feeling overwhelmed by the hustle and bustle of daily life? Are stress and anxiety creeping in, making it difficult to find your inner calm? Well, fear not, because Shirodhara will have you feeling like you're floating on cloud nine in no time!

Shirodhara, derived from the Sanskrit words "Shiro" (head) and "Dhara" (flow), is a traditional Ayurvedic therapy that involves the continuous and gentle pouring of warm herbal oil over the forehead and scalp. This deeply relaxing treatment is not just about pampering yourself; it's a holistic approach to healing and rejuvenation that can help alleviate stress, anxiety, insomnia, and a myriad of other health issues.

Picture this: you're lying down on a comfortable massage table, soft music playing in the background, as a skilled therapist begins to pour a stream of warm, herb-infused oil onto your forehead in a rhythmic motion. The oil flows gently over your scalp, creating a sensation of pure bliss as it penetrates deep into your nervous system, soothing your mind and calming your senses.

One of the key principles of Ayurveda is the belief that our physical, mental, and emotional well-being are interconnected. When stress and tension build up in our bodies, it can manifest in a variety of ways, from headaches and muscle stiffness to digestive issues and insomnia. Shirodhara works by balancing the subtle energies within the body, promoting relaxation, and enhancing the body's natural healing processes.

The benefits of Shirodhara extend far beyond just stress relief. This therapeutic practice is known to improve mental clarity, enhance concentration, and promote a sense of inner peace and well-being. By calming the mind and soothing the nervous system, Shirodhara can also help improve sleep quality, boost immunity, and promote overall vitality and longevity.

But what sets Shirodhara apart from other relaxation techniques is its ability to induce a state of deep meditation and promote a profound sense of inner transformation. As the warm oil cascades over your forehead, it can help quiet the chatter of the mind, creating a space for introspection and self-discovery. Many people who have experienced Shirodhara report feeling a deep sense of clarity, insight, and emotional release during the treatment.

Of course, it's not possible to perform Shirodhara on yourself, but you could perform it on someone else. Here's how:

- **Set the scene:** Create a peaceful and calming atmosphere in the room where you will be performing Shirodhara. Dim the lights, play soft instrumental music, and light some aromatic candles or incense to enhance the experience.
- **Choose the right oil:** Select a high-quality, warm oil such as sesame, coconut, or almond oil for your Shirodhara treatment. Warm the oil gently in a double boiler or a bowl placed in hot water until it reaches a comfortable temperature.
- **Position the recipient:** Have the person receiving the treatment lie down on a comfortable surface with their head supported by a small pillow. Place a towel or plastic sheet under their head to catch any excess oil.
- **Begin the pour:** Using a special vessel called a Shirodhara pot or a simple container with a small hole in the bottom, start pouring the warm oil in a steady stream over the center of the

person's forehead, just above the eyebrows. Adjust the flow of oil to a gentle and consistent stream.

- **Relax and rejuvenate:** Encourage the recipient to close their eyes, take deep breaths, and surrender to the soothing sensation of the warm oil cascading over their forehead. Let the oil flow for 20–30 minutes, allowing them to drift into a state of deep relaxation.

- **End with a scalp massage:** After the Shirodhara session, gently massage the scalp and neck to help further relax the muscles and promote circulation. Allow the recipient to rest for a few minutes before they slowly rise from the treatment.

Marma Therapy: The Art of Energy Point Massage

Marma massage, also known as energy point massage, is a traditional Indian healing technique that focuses on stimulating specific points in the body to promote physical, emotional, and spiritual well-being. These energy points, known as Marma points, are believed to be junctures where two or more types of tissue meet, such as muscles, veins, ligaments, or bones, and are considered vital energy centers within the body.

The origins of Marma massage date back thousands of years to ancient Indian healing traditions, where it was used as a form of medicine to restore balance and the flow of energy within the body. Marma points are believed to be closely connected to the body's energy channels, or nadis, through which prana, or life force, flows. By stimulating these points through massage, practitioners aim to remove blockages, improve energy flow, and restore harmony to the body and mind.

To perform Marma massage, it is important to have a clear understanding of the location and significance of the Marma points on the body. There are said to be 107 major Marma points, with each point having its own unique properties and effects on the body. Some Marma points are considered more vital than others and require special care and attention when massaging.

Before beginning a Marma massage session, it is essential to create a peaceful and calming environment to help the recipient relax and fully benefit from the treatment. Soft lighting, soothing music, and the use of essential oils can enhance the overall experience and promote a sense of tranquility. It is also important to establish a connection with the recipient and ensure open communication throughout the massage session.

To perform Marma massage, start by applying a small amount of warm oil to the hands to create a smooth and lubricated surface for massaging. Begin by gently massaging the recipient's body with long, smooth strokes to help relax the muscles and prepare the body for the more targeted Marma point stimulation.

Once the recipient is relaxed, gently palpate the Marma points using light pressure and circular motions to awaken the energy centers. Focus on each Marma point individually, paying attention to any areas of tenderness or sensitivity. Use your intuition and expertise to determine the appropriate amount of pressure and duration for each point based on the recipient's needs and comfort level.

As you stimulate the Marma points, encourage the recipient to take slow, deep breaths to help facilitate the flow of energy throughout the body. Pay attention to the recipient's reactions and adjust your technique accordingly to ensure a comfortable and effective massage experience.

Incorporating different massage techniques such as kneading, tapping, and vibration can help enhance the effects of Marma massage and promote relaxation, stress relief, and overall well-being. Be mindful of the recipient's feedback and adapt your approach to address any areas of tension or discomfort.

Throughout the massage session, maintain a sense of presence and mindfulness to create a sacred space for healing and rejuvenation. Express genuine care and compassion for the recipient and convey positive energy through your touch and intention.

After completing the Marma massage, allow the recipient time to rest and integrate the experience. Offer a warm cup of herbal tea or water to help hydrate and ground the body. Encourage the recipient to reflect on their experience and notice any changes or sensations that arise following the treatment.

Integrating Self-Care Practices

Ayurveda is not just a system of medicine; it's a way of life that promotes holistic well-being. Within that, self-care is vital.

Daily self-care routines in Ayurveda focus on setting a harmonious rhythm for your day, starting with a morning routine called Dinacharya. This routine is tailored to balance your dosha. We already mentioned a few morning routines you can try within this, but let's quickly refresh your memory:

- **Tongue scraping:** Your tongue accumulates toxins overnight, and tongue scraping helps remove these toxins for better oral hygiene and digestion.
- **Oil pulling:** Swishing coconut or sesame oil in your mouth for a few minutes helps detoxify and freshen your breath.
- **Dry brushing:** Use a natural bristle brush to stimulate circulation and exfoliate dead skin cells, promoting healthy skin.
- **Abhyanga:** Self-massage with warm oil, such as sesame or almond oil, nourishes the skin, calms the mind, and improves circulation.
- **Pranayama:** Breathing exercises like alternate nostril breathing help balance energy flow and calm the mind.
- **Meditation:** Take a few minutes to center yourself and set intentions for the day ahead.

These practices help ground and prepare you for the day ahead, creating a foundation for overall well-being. Throughout the day, mindful eating practices, staying hydrated, and taking short breaks for stretching or deep breathing can further support your self-care journey.

Weekly self-care routines in Ayurveda often involve deeper rejuvenation and detoxification. Here are some examples of weekly self-care practices you can incorporate:

- **Abhyanga:** Regular self-massage with warm oil not only nourishes the skin but also supports relaxation and stress relief.
- **Soothing baths:** Adding calming essential oils like lavender or eucalyptus to your bath can help unwind and release tension.
- **Detox rituals:** Ayurvedic detox practices, such as Panchakarma, can be done seasonally to purify the body and reset your system.
- **Yoga practice:** Engaging in regular yoga practice helps balance the doshas, improves flexibility, and enhances overall well-being.
- **Nature connection:** Spending time in nature, whether it's a walk in the park or forest bathing, can recharge your energies and promote inner harmony.

Get creative with your routines - listen to uplifting music while doing your self-massage, add some humor to your meditation practice, or involve friends in a group yoga session. The key is to make self-care a pleasurable and rewarding experience that resonates with your unique personality and preferences.

Remember, self-care in Ayurveda is not a one-size-fits-all approach. It's about tuning into your body, mind, and spirit, and tailoring your practices to suit your individual needs and doshic balance. By incorporating daily and weekly self-care rituals into your routine, you'll not only enhance your overall well-being but also cultivate a deeper connection with yourself and the world around you.

Chapter 8

Mind-Body Connection

Ayurveda places great emphasis on the mind-body connection. Mental health is considered essential for maintaining balance in the body. The mind is seen as the central point where all experiences, emotions, and thoughts converge.

According to Ayurvedic principles, the mind is composed of three Gunas, or qualities: Sattva (purity, harmony), Rajas (activity, energy), and Tamas (inertia, darkness). When these Gunas are in balance, the mind is clear, focused, and stable, leading to good mental health.

However, when the mind is disturbed or imbalanced, it can lead to a disruption of the Doshas – Vata, Pitta, and Kapha). Imbalance in the Doshas can manifest as physical ailments ranging from digestive issues to chronic diseases. This highlights the intricate relationship between mental and physical health in Ayurveda.

Ayurveda views mental health holistically, considering not just the symptoms but also the root cause of any imbalance. In Ayurvedic philosophy, each individual has a unique mind-body constitution known as Prakriti, which determines their predisposition to certain mental and physical imbalances. By understanding your Prakriti, Ayurveda offers personalized recommendations for maintaining mental well-being and preventing disease.

One of the key principles in Ayurveda is the concept of Ahara (diet) and Vihara (lifestyle) as essential factors in maintaining mental health. A diet that is suitable for one's Prakriti can help balance the Doshas and promote a healthy mind. Regular exercise, meditation, and relaxation techniques are also recommended to calm the mind, reduce stress, and enhance mental clarity.

Ayurveda recognizes the mind as a powerful healer and prescribes various mental practices to maintain mental health. These practices include meditation, Pranayama (breath control), and Yoga, which are believed to have a profound impact on the mind-body system. Meditation, in particular, is considered a powerful tool for calming the mind, increasing self-awareness, and promoting emotional well-being.

Ayurveda also recognizes the influence of external factors on mental health. The environment in which we live, the people we interact with, and the activities we engage in all have an impact on our mental well-being. According to Ayurveda, creating a supportive and nurturing environment is essential for maintaining mental health. This includes surrounding oneself with positive influences, engaging in activities that bring joy and fulfillment, and cultivating meaningful relationships.

Emotional health is another aspect of mental well-being that Ayurveda places great importance on. In Ayurveda, emotions are seen as subtle energies that can influence the Doshas and, consequently, our physical health. Suppressing emotions or experiencing prolonged emotional disturbance can lead to imbalances in the Doshas and result in various health problems.

Ayurveda offers a holistic approach to mental health, addressing not just the symptoms but also the underlying causes of mental imbalances. By recognizing the interconnectedness of the mind and body, Ayurveda provides a comprehensive framework for maintaining mental well-being and preventing disease. Through a combination of diet, lifestyle modifications, mental practices, and emotional healing, Ayurveda empowers you to take charge of your mental health and lead a balanced and fulfilling life.

Meditation and Mindfulness: Techniques For Calming the Mind

At the heart of Ayurveda lies the art of mindfulness—the practice of being fully present in the here and now. In a world filled with distractions and busyness, cultivating mindfulness is like tending to the garden of your soul. It allows you to embrace each moment with awareness and intention, leading to a deep sense of contentment and inner clarity.

Meditation, the sacred art of inner contemplation, is also a powerful tool in Ayurveda for quieting the mind and nurturing the spirit. Through meditation, we learn to transcend the chatter of our thoughts and connect with the vast, silent space within us, the source of pure consciousness and infinite wisdom.

Now, let us explore some techniques and exercises to awaken your inner light and cultivate mindfulness and meditation in your daily life:

Body Scan Meditation

- Lie down in a quiet, peaceful space and close your eyes.
- Start at your toes and gradually move your awareness up through your body, noticing any sensations or areas of tension.
- As you scan each body part, gently release any tightness or discomfort, inviting relaxation and ease.

This body scan meditation promotes deep relaxation and a profound sense of connection to your physical self.

Mantra Meditation

- Choose a sacred mantra or affirmation that resonates with your heart.
- Sit in a comfortable position, close your eyes, and repeat the mantra silently or aloud.
- Let the vibration of the sacred words cleanse your mind and uplift your spirit.

- Dive deep into the ocean of your inner being, where pure love and wisdom reside.

Mindful Eating

- Before eating, take a moment to express gratitude for the nourishment before you.
- Chew each bite slowly and savor the flavors and textures.
- Be fully present with each morsel, noticing how it nourishes your body and delights your senses.

Mindful eating not only promotes digestive health but also deepens your connection to the abundance of life.

Nature Walk Meditation

- Go on a walk through a local park or natural setting, observing the intricate details of the world around you.
- Feel the earth beneath your feet, listen to the songs of birds, and inhale the fragrant scents of the forest.
- Let nature's serenity guide you into a state of profound peace and harmony.

Pranayama: Breathing Techniques for Energy and Balance

Pranayama, a Sanskrit word meaning "extension of the breath" or "extension of life force," is a key aspect of Ayurveda. The breath is seen as the vital link between the body, mind, and spirit. By controlling the breath through specific techniques, you can enhance the flow of prana, or life force, throughout your body, leading to improved health and vitality.

Now, let's delve into some breathing techniques that can help you harness the energy and balance that Pranayama has to offer:

Nadi Shodhana (Alternate Nostril Breathing)

This technique involves breathing through one nostril at a time while closing off the other nostril with your thumb. Start by inhaling through one nostril, then exhaling through the other, and continue switching back and forth.

Nadi Shodhana is known to balance the left and right hemispheres of the brain, bringing a sense of calmness and mental clarity.

Kapalabhati (Skull Shining Breath)

This dynamic breathing technique involves quick, forceful exhalations followed by passive inhalations. Kapalabhati is believed to cleanse the mind and body, increase oxygen flow, and boost energy levels.

Imagine each exhalation as a way to release any stagnant energy within you, allowing for a renewed sense of vitality.

Ujjayi (Victorious Breath)

Ujjayi breath involves breathing in and out through the nose with a slight constriction in the back of the throat, creating a soft, ocean-like sound. This technique is not only calming but also helps to build internal heat and focus the mind.

Imagine the sound of the ocean waves as you inhale and exhale, inviting a sense of peace and tranquility.

Bhramari (Bee Breath)

Bhramari involves making a humming sound while exhaling, creating a vibration that resonates throughout the body. This technique is excellent for relieving stress and anxiety and promoting deep relaxation.

Picture yourself surrounded by the gentle buzzing of bees, allowing yourself to let go of any tension and find inner peace.

Sitali (Cooling Breath)

Sitali involves rolling the tongue into a tube-like shape and inhaling through the mouth, then exhaling through the nose. This breath is cooling and soothing, making it ideal for calming the mind and reducing body heat.

Visualize a refreshing breeze flowing through your body as you practice Sitali, bringing a sense of rejuvenation and balance.

By incorporating these breathing techniques into your daily routine, you can tap into the immense benefits of Pranayama in Ayurveda. Remember, the key is to practice mindfulness and intention, allowing yourself to connect deeply with your breath and inner self.

Managing Stress and Emotions: Ayurvedic Approaches to Mental Well-being

Managing stress and emotions using Ayurvedic principles is like embarking on a journey to discover the inner harmony and peace that reside within you. Ayurveda offers a unique perspective on mental well-being by emphasizing the connection between mind, body, and spirit.

Imagine yourself as a beautiful flower swaying gently in the breeze, rooted deeply in the rich soil of your Ayurvedic wisdom. Just as flowers need sunlight, water, and care to bloom, you too can nurture your mental well-being through the practices and principles of Ayurveda.

In Ayurveda, managing stress and emotions starts with understanding your dosha. By identifying your dominant dosha, you can tailor your mental well-being practices to achieve balance and harmony.

Let's take a closer look at each dosha and the Ayurvedic approaches to managing stress and emotions:

- **Vata:** To manage stress and emotions as a Vata type, focus on grounding practices such as meditation, gentle yoga, and warm, nourishing foods. Cultivate a sense of routine and stability to calm your busy mind and soothe your spirit.
- **Pitta:** To support your mental well-being as a Pitta type, practice cooling and calming activities like swimming, spending time in nature, and engaging in creative expression. Avoid situations that trigger your competitiveness, and learn to let go of control to find inner peace.
- **Kapha:** To maintain mental well-being as a Kapha type, engage in energizing activities like hiking, dancing, and practicing invigorating pranayama (breathwork). Cultivate a sense of lightness and playfulness to uplift your spirit and dispel any stagnant energy.

In addition to understanding your dosha, Ayurveda offers a variety of holistic practices to support your mental well-being:

- **Abhyanga:** Take time each day to massage your limbs in gentle, circular motions, allowing the healing properties of the oils to penetrate your skin and calm your nervous system.
- **Pranayama:** Practice deep, mindful breathing exercises such as Nadi Shodhana (alternate nostril breathing) or Bhramari (humming bee breath) to clear your mind, balance your energy, and promote relaxation.
- **Sattvic Diet:** Ayurveda emphasizes the importance of eating sattvic foods - fresh, organic, and minimally processed to nourish your body and mind. Include a variety of fruits, vegetables, whole grains, and healthy fats in your diet to maintain mental clarity, digestive health, and emotional balance.
- **Mindfulness and Meditation:** Cultivate mindfulness through practices such as meditation, yoga, or simply taking moments throughout the day to pause, breathe, and connect with the

present moment. By being fully present and aware, you can cultivate inner peace and resilience in the face of stress and emotional challenges.

- **Nature Connection:** Spending time in nature is a powerful way to rejuvenate your mind, body, and spirit. Take walks in the forest, sit by a tranquil lake, or simply bask in the warmth of the sun to reconnect with the natural rhythms of life and find inner tranquility.

Chapter 9

An Ayurvedic Approach to Exercise

We know that in Ayurveda, keeping the body in balance is of utmost importance, and exercise plays a key role in achieving and maintaining that balance. When you move your body through exercise, you're not only strengthening your muscles and improving your cardiovascular health, but you're also boosting your metabolism, improving digestion, and helping to release toxins from your system.

From an Ayurvedic perspective, engaging in the right type and amount of exercise can help bring all three doshas back into harmony. For example, if you're feeling sluggish and heavy, invigorating activities like brisk walking or yoga can help stimulate your energy and uplift your mood. On the other hand, if you're feeling anxious or overheated, cooling exercises like swimming or gentle stretching can help calm your mind and soothe your body.

So, whether you're into yoga, dancing, hiking, or even just going for a leisurely stroll in nature, remember that each movement you make is a step towards better health and well-being in the eyes of Ayurveda.

Exercise and Doshas: Finding the Right Type of Exercise for Your Dosha

When it comes to choosing the right type of exercise for your dosha, Ayurveda offers insightful guidance tailored to individual needs. Let's explore how you can align your workout routine with your dosha to optimize your health and vitality.

Vata Dosha

If your constitution is predominantly Vata, characterized by qualities of air and space, you may benefit from grounding, nurturing, and calming exercises. Vata types are prone to being light, quick-witted, and creative but can also experience tendencies towards anxiety and instability.

To balance Vata dosha, opt for exercises that provide stability and grounding, such as yoga, Tai Chi, or gentle strength training. These activities can help calm the restless energy of Vata and promote a sense of centeredness and focus. Engaging in regular, rhythmic movements can also support Vata types in establishing a sense of routine and stability.

Pitta Dosha

If you have a dominant Pitta dosha embodies qualities of fire and water, exhibiting traits of ambition, intensity, and sharp intellect. Pitta types are prone to heat-related imbalances, such as inflammation and irritability, and can benefit from cooling and soothing forms of exercise.

For Pitta dosha, activities that promote balance, relaxation, and a sense of flow are ideal. Swimming, cycling, or Pilates are excellent choices for Pitta types, as they offer a combination of physical challenge and mental focus without excessive intensity. These workouts can help Pitta individuals channel their competitive drive in healthy ways and prevent overheating or burnout.

Kapha Dosha

Kapha dosha, embodying the qualities of earth and water, is characterized by stability, endurance, and nurturing tendencies. Kapha types often have strong, sturdy physiques but can struggle with sluggishness, lethargy, and weight gain if imbalanced.

To balance Kapha dosha, opt for energizing, invigorating exercises that promote movement and circulation. High-intensity interval training (HIIT), dancing, or hiking are excellent choices for Kapha types, as they help stimulate metabolism, build strength, and uplift the spirits. These dynamic workouts can help Kapha individuals combat stagnation and enhance their vitality and motivation.

While aligning your exercise routine with your dosha can be beneficial, it's important to remember that we're all unique, and a holistic approach to health considers individual variations beyond doshic influences. Listen to your body's cues, observe how different types of exercise make you feel, and adjust your workout regimen accordingly.

Incorporating mindfulness practices such as deep breathing, meditation, or self-reflection can also enhance the benefits of exercise and support overall doshic balance. Remember to stay hydrated, eat nourishing foods aligned with your dosha, and prioritize rest and recovery to complement your physical activities.

Yoga and Ayurveda: The Synergy Between Yoga and Ayurvedic Practices

Yoga and Ayurveda are two ancient practices that have been intertwined for centuries, offering a synergistic approach to health and wellness.

Yoga, originating from ancient India, is a practice that combines physical postures (asanas), breathing techniques (pranayama), meditation, and philosophy to promote overall well-being.

The synergy between Yoga and Ayurveda lies in their shared emphasis on self-awareness, balance, and harmony. Both practices recognize the interconnectedness of the body, mind, and spirit, viewing health as a holistic experience that encompasses all aspects of one's being.

We know that in Ayurveda, each person is believed to possess a unique mind-body constitution, known as doshas, which influence their physical and emotional tendencies. Similarly, Yoga recognizes the importance of individualized practices, encouraging us to listen to our bodies and honor our personal limits.

Yoga Asanas for Each Dosha

- **Vata Dosha:** Grounding poses such as Warrior I, Tree Pose, and Child's Pose help to calm an overactive Vata energy, reducing anxiety and improving focus.
- **Pitta Dosha:** Cooling poses like the Extended Triangle Pose, Forward Fold, and Cobra Pose are beneficial for balancing Pitta dosha, releasing tension, and promoting relaxation.
- **Kapha Dosha:** Invigorating poses such as Bridge Pose, Half Moon Pose, and Camel Pose can stimulate Kapha energy, boosting metabolism and uplifting mood.

Ayurvedic Self-Massage (Abhyanga)

Before or after your Yoga practice, indulge in a nourishing self-massage using warm sesame or coconut oil. This Ayurvedic practice helps to promote circulation, relax the muscles, and balance the doshas, leaving you feeling rejuvenated and centered.

Meditation and Mindfulness

Conclude your practice with a few minutes of meditation or mindfulness to cultivate inner peace, clarity, and spiritual connection. Focus on your breath, observe your thoughts without judgment, and cultivate a sense of gratitude for the present moment.

As you explore the connection between Yoga and Ayurveda, remember to approach your practice with curiosity, compassion, and a sense of playfulness. Allow yourself to experiment with different techniques, listen to your body's needs, and honor your unique journey towards holistic well-being.

By integrating the wisdom of Yoga and Ayurveda into your daily life, you can create a harmonious balance between body, mind, and spirit, nurturing optimal health and vitality.

Creating an Exercise Routine: Tips for a Balanced and Sustainable Practice

When it comes to designing an exercise routine that aligns with Ayurvedic principles, there are a few key factors to consider to ensure that you are nurturing yourself in a holistic way.

We've already covered the importance of identifying your dominant dosha and choosing exercises that align with it.

It is also important to consider the time of day when you choose to exercise, as Ayurveda places great emphasis on the cyclic nature of the body's energies. According to Ayurvedic principles, the best time to engage in physical activity is during the Kapha time of day, which is from 6 am to 10 am. This is when your energy and strength are naturally at their peak, making it easier to enjoy your workout and reap its benefits.

In addition to choosing the right type of exercise and the optimal time of day, it is essential to listen to your body and practice mindfulness during your workouts. Pay attention to how your body responds to different movements and adjust your routine accordingly. If you feel fatigued or experience pain, it may be a sign that you need to dial back the intensity or switch to a different form of exercise.

Another key aspect of creating a balanced and sustainable exercise routine in Ayurveda is incorporating self-care practices to support your body's recovery and rejuvenation. This could include activities like Abhyanga (self-massage with warm oil), Shirodhara (oil pouring on the forehead), or Pranayama (breathwork) to help calm the mind and nurture your body after a workout.

Lastly, remember that consistency is key when it comes to maintaining a healthy exercise routine. Instead of pushing yourself to the limit with sporadic intense workouts, aim for regular, moderate exercise that you enjoy and can sustain in the long run. This will not only help you stay motivated but also prevent burnout and injury. Remember, you don't have to join the gym and go every single day; you simply need to find a routine that you enjoy and that brings you benefits.

Recovery and Rest: Importance of Rest in Maintaining Health

Rest and recovery are fundamental aspects of Ayurveda. Maintaining a balance between activity and rest is considered essential for overall well-being and optimal health. Just as a plant needs time to rest and rejuvenate to flourish, so too do our bodies and minds require periods of rest to replenish and restore their vital energies.

At the heart of Ayurvedic philosophy lies the concept of balance, known as "Sattva." This balance encompasses not only our physical state but also our mental and emotional well-being. Proper rest and recovery play a pivotal role in maintaining this delicate equilibrium. When we push ourselves beyond our limits, ignoring the signs of fatigue and burnout, we disrupt the natural rhythm of our bodies and minds, setting the stage for imbalances and dis-ease.

So, how can you ensure that you prioritize rest and recovery in your daily life, in alignment with Ayurvedic principles? Here are some tips to help you infuse your routine with a little rest:

- **Listen to your body:** Your body is a wise and intuitive guide, always communicating its needs to you. Pay attention to signals of fatigue, such as low energy, irritability, or difficulty concentrating. When your body whispers, "I need rest," listen attentively and honor its request.
- **Establish a bedtime routine:** Ayurveda emphasizes the importance of aligning our daily routine with the natural rhythms of the day. Set a regular bedtime and create a calming bedtime ritual to signal to your body that it's time to wind down. This could include activities like gentle stretching,

reading a book, or practicing relaxation techniques like meditation or deep breathing.

- **Unplug and unwind:** In our hyper-connected world, it's easy to be constantly plugged into technology, and bombarded by notifications and stimuli. Make a conscious effort to unplug at least an hour before bedtime to allow your mind to unwind and prepare for restful sleep.
- **Nourish your body with restorative practices:** Ayurveda offers a treasure trove of restorative practices to replenish your energy reserves. Try incorporating practices like Abhyanga (self-massage with warm oil), Shirodhara (pouring warm oil on the forehead), or Nidra Yoga (yogic sleep) into your routine to promote deep relaxation and rejuvenation.
- **Simplify your schedule:** In the pursuit of productivity and achievement, we often overload our schedules with commitments and activities. Simplify your schedule by prioritizing your tasks, learning to say no when necessary, and creating space for rest and leisure. Remember, productivity is not just about doing more; it's about doing what truly matters.
- **Connect with nature:** Spending time in nature is a potent elixir for the body and soul. Take a leisurely stroll in a park, breathe in the fresh air, or simply sit and soak in the sights and sounds of your natural surroundings. Nature has a calming and grounding effect, helping you disconnect from the chaos of everyday life and reconnect with your inner peace.
- **Practice mindfulness:** Mindfulness is the art of being fully present in the moment, without judgment or distraction. Cultivate mindfulness in your daily activities, whether it's eating a meal, washing dishes, or going for a walk. By immersing yourself in the present moment, you can experience a sense of calm and relaxation that transcends external stressors.
- **Seek professional guidance:** If you're struggling to prioritize rest and recovery or experiencing chronic fatigue, consider seeking guidance from an Ayurvedic practitioner or holistic

health coach. They can provide personalized recommendations tailored to your unique constitution and health needs, helping you navigate the path to optimal well-being.

In the end, rest and recovery are not luxuries but vital components of a balanced and vibrant life. By honoring the wisdom of Ayurveda and embracing the art of rest, you can cultivate a deeper sense of harmony, vitality, and joy in your journey towards holistic wellness.

Chapter 10

Ayurveda and Disease Prevention

Ayurveda is like that wise old friend who always reminds you to take care of yourself before things go haywire. Imagine a world where you could avoid getting sick by simply aligning your lifestyle with the rhythms of nature. That's what Ayurveda is all about.

Preventative health in Ayurveda starts with understanding your own doshic constitution and making choices that support it. By following a lifestyle that aligns with your dominant dosha, you can maintain balance and ward off illness before it even stands a chance. For example, if you are predominantly Vata, focusing on grounding activities, warm, nourishing foods, and regular routines can help keep your mind and body in equilibrium.

But it's not just about what you eat or how you move your body – Ayurveda also emphasizes the importance of mental and emotional well-being in preventing illness. Stress, anxiety, and negative emotions can disrupt the doshic balance and weaken your immune system, making you more susceptible to disease. That's why practices like meditation, yoga, and pranayama (breathwork) are vital components of an Ayurvedic lifestyle, helping to calm the mind, reduce stress, and promote overall well-being.

Another key aspect of preventative health in Ayurveda is the concept of seasonal routines. Just like nature goes through its own cycles, our bodies also respond to the changing seasons. By adapting our diet, exercise, and self-care practices according to the time of year, we can support our body's natural ability to stay healthy and resilient. For example, in the cold winter months, focusing on warming foods and staying hydrated can help balance the Vata dosha and prevent common winter ailments like colds and flu.

Ayurveda also places a strong emphasis on daily routines, known as dinacharya, which help to establish a sense of structure and stability in your life. From waking up with the sun to practicing oil pulling and tongue scraping, these simple yet powerful rituals can have a profound impact on your overall health and well-being. By incorporating these practices into your daily routine, you create a solid foundation for preventative health and set yourself up for long-term wellness.

In addition to lifestyle practices, Ayurveda also offers a wide range of herbal remedies, dietary supplements, and therapies to support the body's natural healing abilities and prevent illness. From rejuvenating tonics like Ashwagandha and Triphala to detoxifying treatments like Panchakarma, Ayurveda provides a holistic approach to health that addresses the root cause of imbalances rather than just masking symptoms.

But perhaps the most powerful aspect of Ayurveda's preventative health approach is its emphasis on self-awareness and self-care. By tuning into your body's signals and heeding its wisdom, you can make informed choices that support your health and well-being. Whether it's taking time to rest when you feel tired, nourishing yourself with wholesome foods, or engaging in practices that bring you joy and relaxation, Ayurveda teaches us to listen to our bodies and take proactive steps to prevent illness before it takes hold.

So, the next time you feel tempted to push through fatigue, ignore stress or indulge in unhealthy habits, remember the wisdom of Ayurveda that true health is not just the absence of disease but a vibrant state of balance and harmony that comes from taking care of yourself on all levels.

Strengthening Immunity: Ayurvedic Practices for a Robust Immune System

Ayurveda views immunity as the body's ability to defend against disease-causing agents and maintain balance. According to Ayurvedic principles, a robust immune system is closely linked to the balance of the three doshas and the optimal functioning of the body's digestive fire, or Agni.

Agni in Ayurveda refers to the digestive fire or digestive power within the body. It is responsible for the digestion, absorption, and assimilation of food, as well as the transformation of food into energy. A balanced Agni is essential for overall health and well-being, according to Ayurvedic principles.

If Agni is weak or imbalanced, it can lead to various health issues, such as indigestion, bloating, and decreased immunity. Ayurveda focuses on maintaining and strengthening Agni through proper diet, lifestyle practices, and herbal remedies to support optimal digestion and overall health.

When the doshas are in harmony and Agni is strong, the body is better equipped to fight off pathogens and maintain health.

Ayurvedic Practices to Strengthen Immunity

- **Balance Your Doshas:** To enhance immunity, it's essential to balance the doshas through diet, lifestyle, and herbal remedies. Determine your unique doshic constitution and incorporate foods and practices that support equilibrium. For example, Vata types may benefit from warming and grounding foods; Pitta individuals can focus on cooling and soothing choices; and Kapha individuals should opt for light and stimulating options.
- **Support Digestive Fire:** Ayurveda places great importance on maintaining a healthy digestive system for strong immunity. To strengthen Agni, consume warm and cooked foods, avoid overeating, and incorporate digestive spices like ginger, cumin, and turmeric into your meals. Additionally, practicing mindful

eating and avoiding processed foods can aid in improving digestion and the assimilation of nutrients.

- **Herbal Support:** Ayurveda offers a plethora of herbs known for their immune-boosting properties. Some popular choices include Ashwagandha, Tulsi (Holy Basil), Amalaki (Indian Gooseberry), and Triphala. These herbs not only strengthen the immune system but also promote overall well-being and vitality. Incorporate these herbs into your daily routine through teas, supplements, or Ayurvedic formulations.
- **Daily Routine:** Establishing a daily routine, or Dinacharya, is crucial for maintaining balance and supporting immunity. Wake up early, practice self-care rituals like oil massage (Abhyanga) and tongue scraping, engage in regular exercise or yoga and prioritize restorative sleep. Consistency in daily habits plays a significant role in enhancing overall health and immunity.
- **Stress Management:** Chronic stress can weaken the immune system and disrupt the body's natural defenses. Ayurveda emphasizes the importance of managing stress through practices like meditation, pranayama (breathwork), and mindfulness. Incorporate stress-relieving techniques into your routine to promote emotional well-being and immunity.
- **Detoxification:** Toxins, or Ama, accumulate in the body due to poor digestion and lifestyle choices, compromising immunity. Ayurveda recommends periodic detoxification practices, such as Panchakarma therapy, to eliminate Ama and rejuvenate the body. Consult with an Ayurvedic practitioner to determine the most suitable detox plan for your individual needs.
- **Seasonal Adaptation:** Ayurveda recognizes the influence of seasonal changes on health and immunity. Adjust your diet and lifestyle habits according to the seasons to align with nature's rhythms and prevent imbalances. For example, favor warm and nourishing foods in the winter and light and hydrating foods in the summer to support your immune system during different seasons.

- **Hydration and Nourishment:** Stay hydrated and nourished to support your immune system. Drink warm water throughout the day and consume hydrating foods like soups, stews, and herbal teas. Opt for organic, fresh, and seasonal produce to provide your body with essential nutrients and antioxidants.

Start by assessing your current lifestyle habits and identifying areas where you can introduce Ayurvedic principles. Remember, consistency is key when it comes to reaping the benefits of these time-honored practices.

You could also create a personalized wellness plan incorporating Ayurvedic dietary recommendations, herbal supplements, stress-relief techniques, and daily rituals. If it helps, consult with an Ayurvedic practitioner for tailored guidance and support in implementing these practices effectively.

Understanding Disease in Ayurveda: Causes and Progression of Diseases

In Ayurveda, the onset of disease is seen as a gradual process that begins with the accumulation of toxins and imbalances in the body. These imbalances can be caused by a variety of factors, including poor diet, lack of exercise, stress, and environmental toxins.

Let's imagine a scenario where someone follows an unhealthy diet that is high in processed foods, sugar, and fats. Over time, this person's digestive system becomes compromised, leading to a buildup of toxins and impurities in the body. As a result, their Pitta dosha becomes out of balance, causing inflammation, indigestion, and skin problems.

If left unaddressed, this imbalance could eventually lead to the progression of more serious diseases, such as diabetes, heart disease, or autoimmune disorders. Ayurveda teaches us that by understanding the root causes of these imbalances and making changes to our lifestyle and habits, we can prevent the progression of disease and promote overall health and well-being.

By paying attention to the early signs of imbalance in the body, such as fatigue, digestive issues, or skin problems, we can address these issues before they progress into more serious health problems. Ayurveda teaches us to listen to our bodies, trust our intuition, and make choices that support our unique constitution and doshic balance.

Let's explore some of the diseases and conditions that Ayurveda commonly addresses:

- **Digestive Disorders:** Ayurveda places great emphasis on digestion, considering it a cornerstone of health. Conditions like indigestion, bloating, Irritable Bowel Syndrome (IBS), and acid reflux are often attributed to imbalances in the digestive fire, known as Agni. Ayurvedic treatments aim to strengthen Agni through dietary modifications, herbal remedies, and lifestyle changes.
- **Stress and Anxiety:** In our fast-paced modern world, stress and anxiety have become all too common. Ayurveda views these conditions as imbalances in the nervous system and mental well-being. Practices such as meditation, yoga, and Ayurvedic herbs like Ashwagandha are recommended to calm the mind and restore balance.
- **Skin Disorders:** Conditions like eczema, psoriasis, and acne are often associated with imbalances in the Pitta dosha, which governs digestion and metabolism. Ayurvedic treatments focus on reducing inflammation, purifying the blood, and promoting skin health through a proper diet, herbal remedies, and detoxification therapies.
- **Respiratory Issues:** Asthma, bronchitis, and allergies can be linked to imbalances in the Kapha dosha, which governs mucous and fluid balance in the body. Ayurvedic treatments aim to clear excess mucous, strengthen the respiratory system,

and boost immunity through herbal formulas, steam therapy, and breathing exercises.

- **Joint Pain and Arthritis:** Conditions like osteoarthritis and rheumatoid arthritis are often attributed to imbalances in the Vata dosha, which governs movement and nerve impulses. Ayurvedic treatments focus on reducing inflammation, lubricating joints, and improving circulation through diet, lifestyle adjustments, and herbal remedies like turmeric and ginger.
- **Hormonal Imbalance:** Disorders like PCOS, endometriosis, and thyroid imbalances are often related to disruptions in hormonal levels. Ayurveda addresses these imbalances by focusing on diet, stress management, and herbal supplements to support hormonal equilibrium and overall well-being.
- **Heart Health:** Ayurveda recognizes the importance of maintaining a healthy heart to promote longevity and vitality. Conditions like high blood pressure, cholesterol imbalances, and heart disease are approached through diet, lifestyle changes, and herbal remedies that support heart health and circulation.

As you can see, Ayurveda offers a comprehensive approach to treating a wide range of diseases and conditions by addressing the root causes of imbalances in the body and mind. By restoring harmony to the doshas through personalized treatments and lifestyle modifications, Ayurveda aims to not only alleviate symptoms but also promote long-lasting health and wellness.

Common Ailments and Remedies: Ayurvedic Solutions for Everyday Issues.

To show you just how useful and flexible Ayurveda is, let's explore common ailments that we all face in our everyday lives and discover some Ayurvedic remedies to help alleviate these issues.

- **Digestive Issues:** One of the most common complaints we hear about is digestive issues. From bloating and indigestion to constipation and gas, our digestive system can get a bit out of whack sometimes. One Ayurvedic remedy for improving digestion is to drink a warm glass of water with freshly squeezed lemon juice first thing in the morning. This helps kick-start your digestive system and detoxify your body.
- **Stress and Anxiety:** In today's fast-paced world, stress and anxiety seem to be constant companions for many of us. Ayurveda recommends incorporating daily meditation and mindfulness practices to help calm the mind and reduce stress levels. Additionally, drinking calming herbal teas like chamomile or ashwagandha can also help alleviate anxiety symptoms.
- **Common Cold and Flu:** During the colder months, it's not uncommon to come down with a cold or the flu. Ayurveda suggests boosting your immune system with the use of spices like turmeric, ginger, and garlic in your cooking. You can also try steam inhalation with eucalyptus oil to help clear out congestion and ease breathing.
- **Insomnia:** For those nights when sleep just won't come, Ayurveda offers various remedies to promote a restful night's sleep. Try drinking a warm cup of golden milk (milk mixed with turmeric and other spices) before bedtime to help relax your body and mind. You can also practice gentle yoga poses or try a soothing lavender essential oil diffuser to create a calming atmosphere.
- **Headaches:** Whether it's tension headaches from stress or migraines triggered by various factors, Ayurveda has some solutions to offer. Rubbing a few drops of peppermint oil on your temples can help alleviate headache symptoms. Massaging your scalp with warm sesame oil can also help relax tense muscles and improve circulation.
- **Skin Issues:** From acne and eczema to dry skin and wrinkles, our skin can sometimes be a source of frustration. Ayurveda

recommends incorporating a daily skincare routine using natural ingredients like neem, turmeric, and aloe vera to address various skin concerns. Drinking plenty of water and consuming foods rich in antioxidants can also help promote healthy, glowing skin.

- **Menstrual Cramps:** For those days when menstrual cramps make it hard to function, Ayurveda offers some remedies to ease the pain. Drinking warm herbal teas like ginger or cinnamon can help soothe cramps and improve blood circulation. Applying a warm compress to your lower abdomen or practicing gentle yoga poses can also provide relief.
- **Allergies:** Seasonal allergies can be a real nuisance for many people. Ayurveda suggests incorporating immune-boosting foods like honey, turmeric, and local raw honey into your diet to help reduce allergy symptoms. Using a neti pot with saline solution can also help clear out nasal passages and relieve congestion.

By incorporating these Ayurvedic remedies into your daily routine, you can help support your body's natural healing processes and achieve overall well-being.

Chapter 11

Ayurveda Across the Lifespan

The wisdom of Ayurveda can enrich and support every stage of life with its time-tested principles. From infancy to old age, Ayurveda offers a treasure trove of knowledge to enhance well-being and vitality.

Imagine each chapter of life as a unique canvas, waiting to be painted with the vibrant colors of Ayurvedic practices. Just as a skilled artist brings depth and beauty to a masterpiece, Ayurveda guides us to harmonize our body, mind, and spirit in perfect alignment with the rhythms of nature.

Ayurvedic Practices for Different Life Stages: Childhood, Adulthood, and Old Age

Let's take a look at some Ayurvedic practices for different life stages: childhood, adulthood, and old age, with a little actionable advice thrown in for good measure.

Childhood: Planting the Seeds for Health and Well-being

In the tender years of childhood, the foundation for lifelong health is laid. Ayurveda emphasizes the importance of balance and nurturing during this critical stage.

Here are some Ayurvedic practices for promoting well-being in children:

- **Balanced Nutrition:** Understanding your child's dosha can help tailor their diet to maintain balance. Aim for a diet rich in whole foods, organic fruits, vegetables, and grains to nourish their growing bodies.
- **Daily Routine:** Establishing a daily routine for children creates a sense of stability and promotes good health. Encourage regular meal times, and proper sleep, and balance their activities with play and rest. Incorporate fun activities like yoga and meditation to foster mindfulness and a connection to their inner selves.
- **Herbal Support:** Herbal remedies can be beneficial for children to support their immune system, digestion, and overall well-being. Consult with an Ayurvedic practitioner to choose safe and effective herbs for your child's specific needs.
- **Emotional Well-being:** Emotional health is paramount in childhood development. Encourage open communication, provide a loving and nurturing environment, and teach them coping mechanisms such as deep breathing exercises or journaling to deal with stress and emotions.

Adulthood: Nurturing the Fire of Life

As we transition into adulthood, the focus shifts to balancing responsibilities, careers, relationships, and self-care. Ayurvedic principles offer guidance on maintaining vitality and harmony during this stage:

- **Diet and Digestion:** The digestive fire, Agni, plays a crucial role in overall health. Incorporate warm, cooked foods, spices like ginger and turmeric, and herbal teas to support digestion. Avoid processed foods, excessive caffeine, and alcohol, which can dampen Agni.
- **Stress Management:** The demands of adulthood can lead to increased stress levels. Practice mindfulness, meditation, and yoga to manage stress effectively. Engage in grounding activities like spending time in nature, listening to soothing music, or indulging in self-care rituals to nurture your mind and body.
- **Physical Activity:** Regular exercise is vital for maintaining physical health and balancing doshas. Choose activities that align with your body type and preferences, whether it's yoga, strength training, or dancing. Listen to your body's cues and adjust your routine accordingly.
- **Sleep Hygiene:** Quality sleep is essential for rejuvenation and overall well-being. Establish a calming bedtime routine, create a peaceful sleep environment, and wind down with relaxing activities before bed. Aim for 7-9 hours of restful sleep each night to support optimal health.

Old Age: Embracing Wisdom and Grace

In the golden years of old age, Ayurveda emphasizes the importance of preserving vitality, wisdom, and adaptability. Here are some actionable practices to promote wellness in old age:

- **Mind-Body Connection:** Maintain a strong connection between mind and body through practices such as meditation, pranayama (breathwork), and gentle yoga. These practices can help enhance mental clarity, emotional balance, and physical agility.
- **Nutritious Diet:** As we age, our nutritional needs may change. Focus on nourishing, easily digestible foods such as cooked vegetables, whole grains, and plant-based proteins. Include herbs and spices like ashwagandha, turmeric, and tulsi to support vitality and immunity.
- **Joint Health:** Joint stiffness and mobility issues are common in old age. Incorporate gentle exercises, such as Tai Chi or water aerobics, to maintain joint flexibility and strength. Consider Ayurvedic remedies like massage with warm oils or herbal supplements for joint support.
- **Community and Connection:** Stay socially engaged and maintain relationships with loved ones to foster a sense of belonging and purpose. Participate in community activities, volunteer work, or pursue hobbies and interests that bring joy and fulfillment.

As you can see, Ayurveda offers a holistic approach to health and well-being that transcends age boundaries. By incorporating Ayurvedic practices tailored to each life stage, you can cultivate balance, vitality, and harmony in body, mind, and spirit. Remember, wellness is a journey, and embracing the wisdom of Ayurveda can guide you towards a life of thriving in every season.

Pregnancy and Postpartum Care: Special Considerations for Mothers

In Ayurveda, pregnancy is viewed as a sacred time when the mother's body undergoes significant changes to nurture and support the growing life within her. It's essential to focus on balancing the doshas, especially Vata, during this delicate period. The good news is that Ayurveda has plenty of help for mothers and mothers-to-be.

To support the mother's health during pregnancy, Ayurveda recommends a nourishing diet rich in warm, cooked foods that are easy to digest. Incorporating foods like ghee, cooked vegetables, grains, and herbal teas can help to maintain balance and provide essential nutrients for both mother and baby.

Ayurvedic practitioners also recommend gentle forms of exercise, such as prenatal yoga and daily walks, to keep the body strong and flexible. Rest and relaxation are equally important, as stress can have a negative impact on the mother's and baby's well-being.

After childbirth, the mother enters the postpartum period, where her body undergoes a process of recovery and rejuvenation. Ayurveda places great emphasis on postpartum care to support the mother in restoring her strength and vitality.

One of the key practices in postpartum care is the use of Ayurvedic oils for self-massage, known as Abhyanga. This gentle massage helps to nourish the skin, improve circulation, and promote relaxation. Warm oil infused with herbs like ashwagandha and bala can be particularly beneficial for new mothers.

Ayurvedic dietary recommendations during the postpartum period focus on warming, nourishing foods that are easy to digest. Foods like Kitchari, a traditional Ayurvedic dish made with rice, mung beans, and warming spices, are often recommended to support the mother's recovery and promote healing.

Emotional and Spiritual Support

Ayurveda recognizes the importance of emotional and spiritual well-being during pregnancy and postpartum. Practices like meditation, pranayama (breathing exercises), and mindfulness can help mothers cultivate mental clarity, emotional balance, and spiritual connection during this transformative time.

It's essential for mothers to prioritize self-care and seek support from loved ones, healthcare providers, and Ayurvedic practitioners. Creating a nurturing and supportive environment can greatly enhance the mother's experience and promote a smooth transition into motherhood.

Aging Gracefully: Ayurvedic Strategies for Healthy Aging

Unfortunately, old age is something that comes to us all. Nobody has found the fountain of youth yet! So, while aging is a natural process that we all go through, how we age is within our control.

In Ayurveda, there are time-tested strategies for aging gracefully and maintaining optimal health and vitality. Let's explore how you can incorporate Ayurvedic principles into your life to support healthy aging.

First and foremost, Ayurveda emphasizes the importance of balance in all aspects of life – physical, mental, and emotional. As we age, it becomes even more crucial to pay attention to maintaining this balance to support our overall well-being. By understanding your dosha and incorporating foods that are suitable for your constitution, you can support healthy aging and prevent imbalances.

For example, if you have a Vata constitution, which is associated with qualities such as dryness and coldness, you may benefit from incorporating warm, nourishing foods like cooked grains, root vegetables, and warming spices into your diet. On the other hand, if you have a Pitta constitution, characterized by qualities like heat and intensity, you may benefit from cooling foods like fresh fruits, vegetables, and herbs. By aligning your diet with your dosha, you can support your body's natural balance and promote healthy aging.

In addition to diet, Ayurveda emphasizes the importance of regular physical activity to maintain strength, flexibility, and vitality as we age. Practices like yoga and meditation are highly recommended for supporting overall well-being and promoting longevity. Yoga not only helps to strengthen the body but also calms the mind and reduces stress, which is crucial for healthy aging. Even simple practices like walking in nature or gentle stretching exercises can have profound benefits for your physical and mental health.

Furthermore, Ayurveda places great importance on the concept of Ojas. In Ayurveda, Ojas refers to the vital essence of the body, which governs immunity, strength, and overall vitality. It is considered the foundation of good health and well-being.

Ojas is said to be the final byproduct of digestion and is responsible for nourishing all the tissues of the body. It is also believed to be the subtle essence of all bodily tissues and provides resilience against disease. Maintaining and nourishing Ojas is essential for optimal health, according to Ayurvedic principles.

So, as we age, it's essential to nourish and support our Ojas to maintain optimal health and vitality. One way to do this is by incorporating adaptogenic herbs like Ashwagandha, Shatavari, and Tulsi into your routine. These herbs are known for their rejuvenating and immune-boosting properties and can help support your body's resilience to stress and illness.

Another key aspect of aging gracefully in Ayurveda is maintaining a healthy digestive system. According to Ayurveda, strong digestion is the cornerstone of good health, and poor digestion can lead to a variety of health issues as we age. To support your digestion, it's essential to eat mindfully, chew your food thoroughly, and avoid overeating. Additionally, incorporating digestive spices like ginger, cumin, and fennel into your meals can help stimulate digestion and prevent digestive issues.

In Ayurveda, daily routines, or Dinacharya are highly recommended for promoting health and longevity. Establishing a daily routine that includes practices like oil pulling, self-massage with warm oil, and meditation can help balance your doshas, calm your mind, and support healthy aging. Oil pulling, in particular, is a traditional Ayurvedic practice that involves swishing oil in your mouth to improve oral health, support detoxification, and promote overall well-being.

Furthermore, Ayurveda emphasizes the importance of rest and relaxation for healthy aging. Getting an adequate amount of quality sleep is crucial for rejuvenating the body and mind, supporting immune function, and maintaining optimal health. In Ayurveda, it is recommended to go to bed early and wake up with the sunrise to align with the body's natural rhythms. Creating a calming bedtime routine, such as sipping herbal tea, practicing relaxation techniques, or reading a book, can help promote restful sleep and support healthy aging.

Lastly, maintaining strong social connections and a sense of purpose are essential aspects of aging gracefully in Ayurveda. Building meaningful relationships, engaging in activities that bring you joy, and cultivating a sense of gratitude can have a profound impact on your overall well-being as you age. Connecting with loved ones, volunteering in your community, or pursuing hobbies and interests that light you up can help you stay vibrant and engaged in life.

Adapting Practices Over Time: How to Evolve Your Routine With Age

As we journey through life, our bodies and needs change, and it's important to adapt our Ayurvedic practices to suit our evolving selves. Let's take a look at how to evolve your Ayurvedic routine with age so you can continue to support your health and vitality at every stage of life.

In your 20s: Lay the Foundation

Your 20s are a time of youthful energy and vitality, but it's also a crucial period for establishing healthy habits that will support you in the years to come. In Ayurveda, this is the Kapha stage of life, where energy and growth are at their peak. It's important to focus on establishing a daily routine that nurtures your mind, body, and spirit.

Start your day with a gentle yoga practice or meditation to center yourself and set a positive tone for the day ahead. Incorporate plenty of fresh, seasonal fruits and vegetables into your diet to provide your body with essential nutrients and support digestion. Stay hydrated by drinking plenty of water and herbal teas throughout the day.

As you navigate the demands of work, relationships, and social life, be mindful of your stress levels and make time for self-care activities that help you relax and recharge. This can be as simple as taking a leisurely walk in nature, indulging in a warm bath with calming essential oils or practicing deep breathing exercises to calm the mind.

In your 30s: Focus on Balance

In your 30s, you may find yourself juggling the responsibilities of a career, family, and personal growth. This is the Pitta stage of life in Ayurveda, characterized by focus, ambition, and drive. It's important to focus on maintaining balance in all areas of your life to prevent burnout and support your overall well-being.

Make self-care a priority by carving out time each day for activities that help you relax and recharge. This could be a restorative yoga practice, a leisurely walk in the park, or a relaxing cup of herbal tea before bed. Pay attention to your diet and make sure to include foods that support digestion and help manage stress, such as whole grains, leafy greens, and calming herbal teas.

Incorporate Ayurvedic practices such as self-massage with warm oil (abhyanga) to nourish your skin, calm your nervous system, and promote relaxation. Practice mindfulness and be present in the moment, whether you're enjoying a meal with loved ones, taking a walk in nature, or simply sitting quietly and observing your thoughts.

In your 40s: Embrace Change

As you enter your 40s, you may notice shifts in your body and energy levels that require adjustments to your Ayurvedic routine. This is the Vata stage of life, characterized by movement, change, and creativity. It's important to embrace these changes and adapt your practices to suit your evolving needs.

Focus on incorporating grounding practices into your daily routine, such as yoga poses that help you feel centered and rooted or meditation techniques that help calm a busy mind. Pay attention to your diet and include nourishing, warming foods that support digestion and help balance Vata energy, such as soups, stews, and cooked grains.

Prioritize self-care activities that help you feel grounded and connected to yourself, such as spending time in nature, journaling, or practicing deep breathing exercises. Make time for regular exercise that helps you stay active and energized, whether it's a daily walk, a yoga class, or a dance session in your living room.

In your 50s and beyond: Cultivate Wisdom

As you move into your 50s and beyond, you have the opportunity to cultivate wisdom and embrace the fullness of life experience. This is a time to reflect on your journey, honor your body's needs, and embrace practices that support your health and vitality as you age gracefully.

Focus on gentle, restorative practices that nourish your body and spirit, such as restorative yoga, gentle stretching, or meditation. Pay attention to your diet and include foods that support digestion and nourish your body, such as warm soups, cooked vegetables, and herbal teas.

Prioritize self-care activities that help you feel grounded and present, such as spending time with loved ones, engaging in creative pursuits, or practicing gratitude. Embrace Ayurvedic practices such as self-massage with warm oil (abhyanga) to support circulation, nourish your skin, and promote relaxation.

Chapter 12

Integrating Ayurveda into Modern Life

Despite its ancient roots, Ayurveda can easily be integrated into our fast-paced modern lives.

As we navigate the hustle and bustle of modern life, Ayurveda serves as a gentle guide, nudging us towards a more intentional and mindful approach to living. Whether it's through simple daily practices, nourishing food choices, or personalized self-care rituals, Ayurveda empowers us to create a life that is deeply rooted in our own unique rhythms and needs.

Challenges and Solutions: Common Obstacles in Adopting Ayurveda and How to Overcome Them

Despite its long-standing history and proven effectiveness, Ayurveda faces several challenges in gaining mainstream acceptance and adoption. Let's take a closer look at some of the common obstacles and how we can tackle them head-on.

Common Challenges in Adopting Ayurveda

- **Lack of Awareness and Understanding:** Many people are unfamiliar with Ayurveda and its principles, leading to misconceptions and a reluctance to explore its benefits. For example, some individuals may dismiss Ayurveda as pseudoscience due to a lack of understanding about its holistic approach to healing.
- **Limited Access to Qualified Practitioners:** Finding experienced and well-trained Ayurvedic practitioners can be challenging, especially in certain regions where Ayurveda is

not as prevalent. In rural areas or countries where Ayurveda is not widely practiced, individuals may struggle to access reputable practitioners for guidance and treatment.

- **Integration with Modern Medicine:** Many individuals are hesitant to embrace Ayurveda as a standalone treatment due to concerns about its compatibility with modern medical practices. Some doctors may discourage patients from incorporating Ayurvedic remedies alongside conventional treatments, leading to confusion and hesitation.
- **Perception of Ayurveda as Time-Consuming:** The holistic nature of Ayurveda, which emphasizes personalized treatments and lifestyle modifications, may be perceived as requiring significant time and commitment. For example, busy people may struggle to incorporate Ayurvedic practices into their daily routines, viewing it as an additional burden.

Now we know the potential issues, how can we overcome them? Luckily, there are plenty of ways.

Creative Solutions to Overcome Challenges

- **Education and Awareness Campaigns:** Engage in educational initiatives to raise awareness about Ayurveda's benefits and debunk myths surrounding the practice. Host workshops, seminars, and online webinars to provide accessible information to a wider audience.
- **Training and Certification Programs:** Establish training programs for aspiring Ayurvedic practitioners to ensure a steady supply of qualified professionals. Encourage universities and healthcare institutions to offer courses on Ayurveda to increase the expertise and availability of practitioners.
- **Collaboration with Modern Medicine:** Foster partnerships between Ayurvedic and allopathic healthcare providers to create integrated treatment plans for patients. Conduct research studies to validate the efficacy of Ayurvedic practices and build credibility within the medical community.

- **Personalized Ayurvedic Consultations:** Offer online consultations and telehealth services to make Ayurvedic guidance more accessible to individuals with limited access to practitioners. Provide tailored treatment plans and lifestyle recommendations based on each individual's unique constitution and health goals.

By implementing these creative solutions, we can address the challenges hindering the widespread adoption of Ayurveda and pave the way for a more integrated and holistic approach to healthcare.

Combining Ayurveda with Other Health Practices: Finding a Balance with Modern Medicine

In a world where health trends come and go, the timeless wisdom of Ayurveda has stood the test of time, offering holistic and natural solutions to maintain wellness. Combining Ayurveda with modern medicine presents a dynamic approach that harnesses the strengths of both systems to address the complexities of health in the 21st century. It might seem complicated, but it can be done!

The Synergy Between Ayurveda and Modern Medicine

Ayurveda, with its emphasis on balancing mind, body, and spirit, can complement the disease-centric focus of modern medicine by addressing root causes and promoting overall well-being. Then, modern medicine, with its advanced diagnostics and treatments, can provide immediate relief for acute conditions, while Ayurveda focuses on preventive strategies and lifestyle modifications.

For example, a patient with diabetes may benefit from the combination of Ayurvedic dietary recommendations and herbs to regulate blood sugar levels, along with modern medications and monitoring for optimal control. Additionally, yoga and meditation can be incorporated as part of the treatment plan to reduce stress and improve overall health outcomes.

Finding a Balance in Treatment Approaches

Collaborative healthcare teams consisting of Ayurvedic practitioners, modern medicine doctors, nutritionists, and mental health professionals can offer a comprehensive approach to patient care. However, open communication and mutual respect between practitioners of different modalities are key to ensuring a seamless integration of treatments.

Incorporating Ayurvedic Practices in Modern Healthcare Settings

Integrative medicine clinics that offer a range of services from Ayurveda, acupuncture, naturopathy, and modern medicine are gaining popularity as patients seek holistic approaches to health. Wellness retreats and spas that incorporate Ayurvedic principles alongside modern amenities provide a relaxing environment for individuals to rejuvenate and restore balance.

Benefits of Combining Ayurveda with Other Health Practices

There are several benefits of choosing to combine the ancient wisdom of Ayurveda with modern health practices, including:

- **Individualized care:** Ayurveda's focus on understanding each person's unique constitution can enhance personalized treatment plans in conjunction with modern medical interventions.
- **Holistic approach:** By addressing physical, mental, and emotional aspects of health, the integration of Ayurveda with modern medicine can lead to comprehensive healing and improved overall well-being.

But, of course, it doesn't come without its challenges. A lack of standardization and regulation in the Ayurvedic industry can lead to discrepancies in treatment approaches. Seeking qualified and certified practitioners can help ensure quality care. Of course, bridging the gap in knowledge and understanding between

Ayurveda and modern medicine through collaborative research and continuing education programs can foster a cohesive approach to healthcare too.

In the end, embracing the strengths of both systems and finding a harmonious balance means we can embark on a journey towards optimal health and wellness that is as unique as we are. Remember, a blend of ancient wisdom and contemporary advancements can pave the way for a healthier and happier you!

Community and Resources: Finding Support and Further Learning

If you've read this far and you're keen to deepen your understanding of Ayurveda and connect with like-minded individuals who share your passion for holistic wellness, you're in luck! Ayurveda is not just a system of medicine; it's a way of life that thrives on community and resources to support its practitioners in their wellness journey.

Importance of Community in Ayurveda

Community plays a vital role in Ayurveda as it provides a supportive environment for individuals to learn, grow, and share their experiences.

Here are some key reasons why community is essential in Ayurveda:

- **Sharing Knowledge and Experiences:** The beauty of Ayurveda lies in its ancient wisdom passed down through generations. By being part of a community of Ayurvedic practitioners and enthusiasts, you can exchange valuable knowledge, tips, and experiences to enhance your understanding of Ayurveda.
- **Accountability and Motivation:** It's easy to veer off track when embarking on a new wellness journey. Being part of a supportive community can help you stay accountable and

motivated to follow through with your Ayurvedic practices and lifestyle changes.

- **Emotional Support:** Wellness is not just about physical health; it encompasses mental and emotional well-being as well. Being part of a community allows you to receive emotional support, share your struggles, and celebrate your successes with like-minded individuals.

- **Networking Opportunities:** In the world of Ayurveda, networking is key to expanding your knowledge and growing your practice. By connecting with other practitioners, teachers, and enthusiasts, you open doors to new opportunities for learning and collaboration.

Key Resources for Further Learning in Ayurveda

Now that you understand the importance of community in Ayurveda, let's dive into some key resources that can help you further your learning and connect with like-minded individuals:

- **Ayurvedic Institutes and Schools:** Joining an Ayurvedic institute or school is a great way to immerse yourself in the teachings of Ayurveda. These institutions offer courses, workshops, and training programs led by experienced practitioners and educators.

- **Online Communities and Forums:** In this digital age, online communities and forums provide a convenient platform for connecting with Ayurvedic enthusiasts from around the world. Platforms like Reddit, Facebook groups, and dedicated Ayurveda forums offer a space to ask questions, share resources, and engage in discussions on various Ayurvedic topics.

- **Ayurvedic Retreats and Workshops:** Retreats and workshops offer a unique opportunity to deepen your understanding of Ayurveda in a retreat-style setting. These immersive experiences often include lectures, hands-on workshops, yoga sessions, and Ayurvedic treatments, providing a holistic approach to learning.

- **Ayurvedic Practitioners and Mentors:** Building a relationship with an experienced Ayurvedic practitioner or mentor can provide invaluable guidance and support on your Ayurvedic journey. Look for practitioners who resonate with you and offer mentorship programs or one-on-one consultations.
- **Ayurvedic Books and Publications:** Reading books authored by renowned Ayurvedic experts is a great way to expand your knowledge and explore different perspectives within the field. Some must-read books include "The Complete Book of Ayurvedic Home Remedies" by Vasant Lad and "Ayurveda: The Science of Self-Healing" by Dr. Vasant Lad.

Practical Tips for Finding Support in Ayurveda

Now that you're equipped with knowledge about the importance of community in Ayurveda and key resources for further learning, here are some practical tips for finding the support you need to thrive in your Ayurvedic lifestyle:

- **Attend Ayurvedic Events and Gatherings:** Keep an eye out for Ayurvedic events, workshops, and gatherings in your local community or online. These events offer an opportunity to meet like-minded individuals, learn from experts, and connect with practitioners in your area.
- **Join Online Ayurvedic Groups:** Explore online Ayurvedic groups and communities on social media platforms and forums. Engage in discussions, ask questions, and share your experiences to foster connections with fellow Ayurvedic enthusiasts.
- **Seek Out Local Ayurvedic Practitioners:** Research Ayurvedic practitioners in your area and reach out to them for guidance and support. Many practitioners offer consultations, workshops, and classes that can help you deepen your understanding of Ayurveda and receive personalized recommendations.
- **Start Your Own Ayurvedic Study Group:** Take the initiative to start a study group with friends, family, or colleagues

who are interested in Ayurveda. Meet regularly to discuss Ayurvedic concepts, share resources, and support each other on your wellness journey.
- **Invest in Continued Education:** Consider enrolling in advanced courses, workshops, or retreats to further your education in Ayurveda. Investing in continued education not only expands your knowledge but also provides an opportunity to connect with experts and practitioners in the field.
- **Practice Self-Care and Mindfulness:** Remember that self-care and mindfulness are essential components of Ayurveda. Prioritize practices such as meditation, yoga, healthy eating, and adequate rest to support your overall well-being and stay grounded in your Ayurvedic lifestyle.

Remember, the journey to optimal health is not meant to be taken alone, so embrace the power of community and resources in Ayurveda to enrich your wellness experience!

Personal Stories and Testimonials

It always helps to read real-life stories to give extra weight to the effectiveness of something. When it comes to Ayurveda, there are plenty of real-life experiences to back it up. There are five personal stories and testimonials showcasing the wonderful impact of Ayurveda.

Sarah's Journey to Wellness

Meet Sarah, a busy professional juggling work and family life. Stressed and exhausted, she turned to Ayurveda for balance. Through personalized consultations and dietary changes, Sarah learned to listen to her body. With the help of meditation and herbal supplements, she reclaimed her energy and peace of mind.

Now, Sarah starts her day with yoga and a warm cup of herbal tea, feeling vibrant and centered.

John's Transformation Through Ayurvedic Diet

John struggled with digestive issues for years. Traditional medicine offered little relief until he discovered Ayurveda. By incorporating digestive spices, like ginger and turmeric, into his meals and following his body's natural rhythms, John found great comfort and healing.

Today, he enthusiastically shares his love for Ayurvedic cooking, inspiring friends and family to embrace the power of food as medicine.

Mia's Ayurvedic Skincare Success

Mia, a skincare enthusiast, battled with stubborn acne for years. Frustrated with chemical-laden products, she sought an alternative in Ayurveda. With the guidance of an Ayurvedic practitioner, Mia adopted a holistic skincare routine using natural ingredients like neem and aloe vera.

Over time, her skin cleared up, revealing a radiant glow. Now, Mia swears by Ayurvedic beauty rituals and encourages others to embrace their natural beauty.

Miguel's Mind-Body Harmony with Ayurvedic Practices

Miguel, a fitness enthusiast, found himself mentally drained despite his rigorous workout routine. Desiring a deeper connection between mind and body, he turned to Ayurveda for guidance. By incorporating daily self-care practices such as oil pulling, tongue scraping, and Abhyanga massage, Miguel experienced a profound shift in his overall well-being.

Today, he exudes vitality and balance, becoming a living testament to the transformative power of Ayurveda.

Lily's Ayurvedic Pregnancy Journey

Lily, a soon-to-be mother, embraced Ayurveda during her pregnancy for a holistic approach to health. Through mindful eating, gentle yoga, and Ayurvedic herbs, she navigated each trimester with grace and ease.

With the support of an Ayurvedic practitioner, Lily experienced a smooth delivery and postpartum recovery. Now, she cherishes the bond she's formed with her baby, grateful for the nourishing principles of Ayurveda that guided her throughout this miraculous journey.

Each of these stories exemplifies the diverse ways in which Ayurveda can positively impact individuals' lives, from enhancing physical wellness to fostering emotional balance.

Through these personal anecdotes, we witness the transformative power of Ayurveda in bringing harmony to mind, body, and spirit. It truly is a holistic approach to well-being that resonates with the essence of who we are.

Conclusion

Now that we're at the end of this book, how are you feeling about introducing Ayurveda into your life? This centuries-old wisdom guides us towards a harmonious balance of mind, body, and spirit. Incorporating its key aspects and practices into your life could be a real game-changer.

But of course, first, you need to be sure that you understand everything about it. That's what this book aims to do. So, before we say goodbye, let's recap the key points we've explored and offer some uplifting words of encouragement for the transformative journey that lies ahead.

Ayurveda, known as the "Science of Life," emphasizes the interconnectedness of all aspects of our being. It recognizes that each individual is unique and requires a personalized approach to achieve optimal well-being. The fundamental principles of Ayurveda revolve around the three doshas, Vata, Pitta, and Kapha, which govern different bodily functions and characteristics. Understanding your dominant dosha can help you tailor your lifestyle, diet, and wellness practices to restore balance and vitality.

We have delved into the importance of maintaining a daily routine, or Dinacharya, to align ourselves with the natural rhythms of the day and nurture our bodies with self-care rituals. The concept of Ritucharya highlights the significance of adapting our lifestyle according to the changing seasons to stay in tune with nature.

Ayurveda places great emphasis on the role of diet and nutrition in maintaining good health. By incorporating wholesome and seasonal foods that are suitable for your dosha, you can support your body's innate healing wisdom and prevent imbalances. Alongside dietary choices, Ayurveda promotes the use of herbs, spices, and lifestyle practices such as yoga, meditation, and pranayama to create holistic wellness.

Embarking on a journey towards holistic well-being through Ayurveda can be both exciting and challenging. As you explore the world of Ayurvedic principles and practices, remember to approach this path with compassion, curiosity, and an open heart. It's not about striving for perfection but rather about cultivating awareness and making small, sustainable changes that resonate with your unique constitution.

There will be moments of doubt and setbacks along the way, but remember that each step you take towards embracing Ayurveda in your life is a step towards greater balance and vitality. Allow yourself the grace to learn and grow, recognizing that transformation is a gradual process that unfolds at its own pace. Be patient with yourself and trust in the innate intelligence of your body to guide you towards optimal health and well-being.

Surround yourself with a supportive community of like-minded individuals who share your passion for Ayurveda. Seek out teachers, practitioners, and resources that inspire and empower you on your journey. Share your experiences, ask questions, and celebrate your successes, no matter how small they may seem. Remember that you are not alone on this path, and there is a vast network of individuals who are walking alongside you, cheering you on every step of the way.

As you navigate the intricate pathways of Ayurveda, allow yourself to embrace the ebb and flow of life's rhythms with grace and resilience. Stay attuned to your body's signals, listen to its whispers of wisdom, and honor the innate intelligence that resides within you. Let go of the need for external validation or comparison, and instead, cultivate a deep sense of self-awareness and self-love that forms the foundation of your well-being.

In closing, may this journey into the heart of Ayurveda be a catalyst for profound transformation and self-discovery. May you weave the ancient wisdom of Ayurveda into the fabric of your daily life, creating a tapestry of health, harmony, and happiness. Trust in the power of Ayurveda to illuminate your path and guide you towards a life of balance, vitality, and fulfillment. Remember, the journey is not about reaching a destination but about embracing the beauty of the process and the growth that unfolds along the way.

With a heart full of gratitude and a spirit of adventure, step forward into the vibrant world of Ayurveda, knowing that you are embarking on a journey of self-discovery and healing that has the potential to transform your life in ways you never imagined. Embrace this ancient wisdom with an open mind and a willing spirit, and watch as the sacred teachings of Ayurveda unfurl before you, revealing the profound beauty and power of living in harmony with nature and your true self.

May your journey be filled with light, love, and boundless possibilities.

References

Admin. (2024, January 8). *Ayurveda: A Brief Introduction and guide.* Ayurveda. https://ayurveda.com/ayurveda-a-brief-introduction-and-guide/

Banyan Botanicals. (2024, May 1). *Ayurvedic Diet Library | Recipes, Food Combining, Dosha-Specific Foods.* https://www.banyanbotanicals.com/pages/ayurvedic-diet

Clinic, C. (2024, July 2). *What is Ayurveda and does it work?* Cleveland Clinic. https://health.clevelandclinic.org/what-is-ayurveda

Cpt, K. D. M. R. (2023, September 19). *What are the Ayurveda doshas? Vata, Kapha, and Pitta explained.* Healthline. https://www.healthline.com/nutrition/vata-dosha-pitta-dosha-kapha-dosha

Gudritz, L. (2019, August 13). *What happened when I tried the Ayurvedic diet for a week.* Healthline. https://www.healthline.com/health/food-nutrition/i-tried-the-ayurvedic-diet

Jain, R. (2024, February 19). Ayurveda 101: What are the 3 doshas and how to identify yours. *Arhanta Yoga Ashrams.* https://www.arhantayoga.org/blog/what-is-ayurveda-and-its-principles/?utm_source=google&utm_campaign=19237825864&utm_content=&utm_medium=&gad_source=1&gbraid=0AAAAADiB6OrbS_SXjkiCaUhVaOdCaE0CCd&gclid=EAIaIQobChMIqr7LxeCmhwMVLpGDBx2A4whLEAAYAyAAEgIUI_D_BwE

Migala, J. (2024, July 9). *What is the Ayurvedic diet? Ayurvedic cooking for beginners.* EverydayHealth.com. https://www.everydayhealth.com/diet-nutrition/ayurvedic-diet/guide/

Principles of Ayurveda. (2023, May 25). Everest Ayurveda. https://www.everest-ayurveda.com/principles-ayurveda

Pukka. (2020, December 9). *Ayurvedic Dosha | Understand your Dosha Type & Real-Life Examples | Pukka Herbs UK.* Pukka Herbs. https://www.pukkaherbs.com/uk/en/wellbeing-articles/understanding-the-dosha

Rd, R. a. M. (2023, November 14). *What is the Ayurvedic diet? benefits, downsides, and more.* Healthline. https://www.healthline.com/nutrition/ayurvedic-diet

The healing benefits of Ayurvedic massage. (n.d.). https://www.ayurvedacollege.net/blogs/the-healing-benefits-of-ayurvedic-massage

Vishram, A. (2023, October 26). *Ayurvedic Massage: A Complete guide — spa Theory*. Spa Theory. https://www.spatheory.com/spa-theory-wellness-beauty-blog/ayurvedic-massage#:~:text=Ayurvedic%20Massage%20offers%20a%20range,and%20spirit%2C%20promoting%20overall%20wellness.

What are the main fundamental principles of Ayurveda? (n.d.). https://www.mamcbhopal.com/what-are-the-main-fundamental-principles-of-ayurveda.php#:~:text=The%20fundamental%20principles%20of%20Ayurveda,Kapha%20(water%20and%20earth).

Wikipedia contributors. (2024, July 2). *Ayurveda*. Wikipedia. https://en.wikipedia.org/wiki/Ayurveda

Worth, T. (2023, November 23). *Ayurveda: Does it really work?* WebMD. https://www.webmd.com/balance/ayurvedic-treatments

THE VAGUS NERVE UNLOCKING THE BODY'S SUPERHIGHWAY

A Journey into Healing, Wellness, and Mind-Body Harmony

MONIKA DANIEL

Chapter 1

Introduction to the Vagus Nerve

Welcome to the fascinating world of the vagus nerve, the unsung hero of our nervous system. In this chapter, we're going to delve deep into the intricate workings of this remarkable nerve, shedding light on its crucial role in regulating various bodily functions and influencing our overall health and well-being.

The vagus nerve, also known as the "wandering nerve," is like the ultimate multitasker, overseeing a wide range of functions such as heart rate, digestion, and even mood. It's basically the behind-the-scenes superstar keeping everything in check without asking for much recognition.

As we journey through the complexities of the vagus nerve, you'll discover how it acts as a powerful communication pathway between the brain and the body, playing a key role in the intricate dance of signals that keep us in balance. From its impact on our stress response to its connection to inflammation and immune function, the vagus nerve truly embodies the saying, "mind over matter."

An Overview of the Nervous System

Before we can really explore the vagus nerve and its uses, we need to go a little deeper. That means we need to explore the nervous system in more detail.

The nervous system is a fascinating and intricate network that serves as the command center of the human body. It is responsible for controlling everything from basic reflexes to complex cognitive functions. Let's take a closer look at this amazing system that allows us to move, think, feel, and experience the world around us.

At the core of the nervous system is the brain, which acts as the control center. It processes information received from the body's sensory organs and sends out signals to direct the body's responses. The brain is divided into different regions, each responsible for specific functions such as motor control, language processing, memory, and emotions.

Connected to the brain is the spinal cord, which runs down the length of the back and serves as a communication highway between the brain and the rest of the body. The spinal cord is responsible for transmitting sensory information from the body to the brain and carrying motor signals from the brain to the muscles.

The nervous system is divided into two main parts: the central nervous system (CNS) and the peripheral nervous system (PNS). The CNS consists of the brain and spinal cord, while the PNS includes all the nerves that branch out from the CNS to reach every part of the body.

Within the PNS, there are two subdivisions: the somatic nervous system and the autonomic nervous system. The somatic nervous system is responsible for voluntary movements and sensory information, while the autonomic nervous system controls involuntary processes such as heart rate, digestion, and breathing.

One of the key components of the nervous system is the neuron, which is a specialized cell that transmits electrical and chemical signals. Neurons communicate with each other through a structure called a synapse, where neurotransmitters are released to carry signals across the small gap between neurons.

The nervous system also includes supporting cells called glial cells, which provide structural support for neurons, insulate them, and help with their nutrition. Glial cells play a crucial role in maintaining the overall health and function of the nervous system.

In addition to neurons and glial cells, the nervous system also includes specialized cells called sensory receptors, which detect various stimuli such as light, sound, touch, and temperature. These receptors convert sensory input into electrical signals that can be processed by the brain.

The nervous system is constantly receiving and processing information from the environment to help us respond to changes and maintain homeostasis. It coordinates voluntary movements, regulates essential bodily functions, and enables us to experience sensations and emotions.

It's truly amazing to think about how the nervous system works seamlessly to keep us alive and functioning every day. From the simplest reflex actions to the most complex thoughts and behaviors, the nervous system is at the heart of everything we do.

The vagus nerve plays a crucial role in our complex nervous system. As the longest cranial nerve, it meanders its way from the brainstem through the neck and thorax, all the way down to the abdomen, forming a vital bridge of communication between the brain and various organs.

The Discovery and Significance of the Vagus Nerve

The vagus nerve was first discovered by a talented anatomist named Francis Glisson in the 17th century. Glisson's curiosity led him to uncover what would later be recognized as one of the most significant nerves in the body.

The vagus nerve, also known as the 10th cranial nerve, is a long and wandering nerve that starts at the base of the brain and branches out like a complex network, reaching various parts of the body, including the heart, lungs, stomach, and intestines. Its name "vagus" is derived from the Latin word meaning "wandering," aptly describing its meandering path throughout the body.

Introduction to the Vagus Nerve

The significance of the vagus nerve lies in its role as the primary component of the parasympathetic nervous system, the part of the autonomic nervous system responsible for regulating rest and digest functions. This nerve acts as a superhighway for communication between the brain and the body, relaying crucial information and controlling essential bodily functions.

One of the most remarkable features of the vagus nerve is its bidirectional communication system. Not only does it transmit signals from the brain to the body, but it also sends feedback from the body to the brain. This constant dialogue between the two ensures that our bodily functions are finely tuned and regulated, maintaining a delicate balance necessary for our overall well-being.

Research into the vagus nerve has revealed its profound impact on various aspects of human health. Studies have shown that stimulating the vagus nerve can have therapeutic effects on conditions such as epilepsy, depression, and even inflammatory disorders. This has led to the development of innovative treatments such as vagus nerve stimulation therapy, which holds promise for improving the lives of many individuals suffering from these conditions.

Furthermore, the vagus nerve plays a crucial role in the body's stress response system. When activated, it helps to modulate the body's fight-or-flight response, promoting a sense of calm and relaxation. This is why activities such as deep breathing, meditation, and yoga, which stimulate the vagus nerve, are often recommended for stress relief and overall well-being.

The vagus nerve's influence extends beyond physical health and into the realm of emotional well-being. It is often referred to as the "wanderer of emotions," as it is intricately linked to our feelings and mood regulation. By understanding the connection between the vagus nerve and emotional health, we can explore new avenues for promoting mental wellness and resilience.

In addition to its role in health and well-being, the vagus nerve also holds intriguing implications for the field of neuroscience.

Scientists continue to unravel the mysteries of this complex nerve, seeking to understand its intricate pathways and how they influence our thoughts, behaviors, and perceptions. The vagus nerve serves as a gateway to unlocking the secrets of the mind-body connection, bridging the gap between our physical and emotional experiences.

How to Harness the Power of the Vagus Nerve

Exploring the wonders of the vagus nerve is like peeking into the intricate machinery that powers our body and mind. This mighty nerve serves as the communication highway between your brain and various organs, impacting everything from digestion to mood. By delving deeper into the world of the vagus nerve, you can unlock a treasure trove of knowledge that may potentially revolutionize your understanding of health and well-being.

Learning more about the vagus nerve can be likened to embarking on a thrilling journey of self-discovery. It's like uncovering a hidden superpower within yourself—one that holds the key to regulating stress, improving digestion, enhancing your immune system, and even fostering a greater sense of calm and relaxation.

In essence, understanding the vagus nerve can provide you with a deeper appreciation of the remarkable interconnectedness of your body and mind. So, why not take a step further into this fascinating realm and empower yourself with valuable insights that could truly enrich your life? The vagus nerve beckons, inviting you to discover its secrets and embrace the potential for greater well-being.

Let's embark on this enlightening adventure together!

Chapter 2

Anatomy and Functions of the Vagus Nerve

The vagus nerve, also known as the 10th cranial nerve, is a fascinating and crucial component of the human nervous system. Stretching from the brainstem to the abdomen, this nerve plays a vital role in regulating numerous bodily functions, from heart rate and digestion to speech and breathing.

Let's delve into the intricate anatomy of the vagus nerve to better understand its structure and functions.

Starting at the brainstem, the vagus nerve emerges from the medulla oblongata and travels down towards the neck, serving as the longest and most complex of the cranial nerves. It is a mixed nerve, meaning it contains both sensory and motor fibers that transmit signals in two directions. The vagus nerve branches out extensively, forming connections with various organs and tissues throughout the body, making it a key player in the parasympathetic nervous system.

As the vagus nerve descends into the neck, it gives off several branches that innervate structures such as the larynx and pharynx, playing a crucial role in speech, swallowing, and vocalization. These branches also provide sensory feedback, allowing us to perceive sensations such as taste and touch in the throat and oral cavity.

Moving further down into the chest cavity, the vagus nerve continues its journey, branching out to innervate the heart and lungs. Through its connections with the cardiac plexus, the vagus nerve helps regulate heart rate and cardiac function, playing a vital role in maintaining cardiovascular homeostasis. Additionally, the nerve fibers that extend to the lungs contribute to the control of respiration, ensuring proper oxygen exchange and carbon dioxide elimination.

Descending into the abdomen, the vagus nerve forms connections with various organs of the gastrointestinal tract, including the stomach, liver, pancreas, and intestines. These connections are crucial for the regulation of digestion and nutrient absorption. The vagus nerve stimulates the release of digestive enzymes and controls processes such as peristalsis, which aids in the movement of food through the gastrointestinal tract.

Within the abdomen, the vagus nerve also plays a role in the gut-brain axis, facilitating communication between the digestive system and the central nervous system. This bidirectional communication is essential for regulating appetite, food intake, and the gut microbiome. Dysfunction of the vagus nerve can lead to digestive disorders such as gastroparesis, a condition characterized by delayed stomach emptying.

The vagus nerve also interacts with the autonomic nervous system, helping to maintain overall physiological balance in the body. As a major component of the parasympathetic nervous system, the vagus nerve counteracts the "fight or flight" response of the sympathetic nervous system, promoting rest, relaxation, and digestion. This delicate balance between the two branches of the autonomic nervous system is crucial for overall health and wellbeing.

In addition to its role in regulating physiological functions, the vagus nerve also plays a role in modulating emotional responses and stress. Known as the "wandering nerve," the vagus nerve has connections to various brain regions involved in emotional regulation, such as the amygdala and prefrontal cortex. Stimulation of the vagus nerve, through practices like deep breathing or meditation, can help promote relaxation and reduce stress.

Overall, the vagus nerve is a remarkable structure that exemplifies the intricate interconnectedness of the human body. Its far-reaching connections and multifaceted functions highlight the importance of this nerve in maintaining homeostasis and overall well-being. Understanding the detailed anatomy of the vagus nerve can shed light on its essential role in regulating vital bodily functions and supporting holistic health.

Primary Functions in the Body

The vagus nerve plays a crucial role in the body by connecting the brain to various organs and systems, helping to regulate important functions that keep us alive and well. Let's dive into the fascinating world of the vagus nerve and explore its primary functions in detail.

One of the key functions of the vagus nerve is its role in the parasympathetic nervous system, which is responsible for the body's rest and digest response. When activated, the vagus nerve promotes relaxation, slows down the heart rate, and enhances digestion by stimulating the release of gastric juices and enzymes. This helps the body to conserve energy and focus on processes like digestion and healing.

Furthermore, the vagus nerve plays a vital role in regulating the cardiovascular system. By innervating the heart, the vagus nerve helps to control heart rate and blood pressure, maintaining optimal cardiovascular function. When you take a deep breath and feel your heart rate slow down, you can thank the vagus nerve for its calming influence on the heart.

The vagus nerve is also involved in the communication between the gut and the brain, known as the gut-brain axis. This bi-directional connection allows the brain to influence gut function and vice versa. The vagus nerve transmits signals related to appetite, satiety, and digestion, playing a crucial role in the regulation of food intake and metabolism. It also helps to modulate emotions and mood through its connection with the brain, highlighting the intricate link between gut and brain health.

Another important function of the vagus nerve is its role in inflammation regulation. Through its anti-inflammatory effects, the vagus nerve helps to dampen the body's inflammatory response, reducing the risk of chronic inflammation and associated health conditions. This neuroimmune communication highlights the vagus nerve's ability to modulate the immune system and maintain immune balance within the body.

Furthermore, the vagus nerve is involved in the regulation of respiratory function. By innervating the muscles involved in breathing, the vagus nerve helps to control the rate and depth of respiration, ensuring proper oxygen exchange in the body. This function is essential for maintaining respiratory efficiency and overall health.

In addition to its physiological functions, the vagus nerve also plays a role in social engagement and emotional regulation. Known as the "social nerve," the vagus nerve is involved in facial expressions, vocalization, and eye contact, all of which are essential for social interactions and communication. The vagus nerve also helps to regulate emotional responses by modulating the release of neurotransmitters involved in mood regulation, such as serotonin and dopamine.

Overall, the vagus nerve is a multifaceted and essential component of the nervous system, with diverse functions that impact nearly every aspect of our health and well-being. From regulating the cardiovascular system and digestion to modulating inflammation and emotional responses, the vagus nerve plays a pivotal role in maintaining balance and harmony within the body.

As we continue to uncover the intricate connections between the vagus nerve and various bodily functions, we gain a deeper appreciation for the complexity and sophistication of our internal systems. The more we understand and support the functions of the vagus nerve, the better equipped we are to optimize our health and vitality.

What is Vagal Tone?

Throughout this book, you'll hear us referring to something called 'vagal tone.' So, before we delve in, let's define what it is.

Vagal tone is like the body's very own built-in chill pill. It's all about that vagus nerve, the longest cranial nerve in the body, which plays a key role in helping us stay calm, cool, and collected. Think of it as the conductor of the relaxation orchestra within us.

When our vagal tone is high, it's like having a soothing symphony playing in the background, keeping stress at bay and promoting a sense of well-being. On the flip side, a low vagal tone can make us feel more frazzled and on edge. So, it's no wonder that nurturing and boosting our vagal tone is a hot topic in the world of wellness and self-care.

In a nutshell, vagal tone is all about keeping our mind and body in harmony, like a peaceful duet that helps us navigate the ups and downs of life with grace and composure.

The Benefits of Working With the Vagus Nerve

Engaging with the vagus nerve can have a variety of benefits for your physical and mental health. Here's a detailed look:

- **Heart Health:** Stimulation of the vagus nerve can help to reduce heart rate and blood pressure, making it beneficial for heart health.
- **Digestive Efficiency:** It also positively influences the digestive system by improving gastric motility, which helps the body process and absorb nutrients effectively and ease various digestive disorders.
- **Reduced Inflammation:** By activating the vagus nerve, it's possible to reduce the levels of cytokines, which are inflammatory molecules, leading to decreased inflammation in the body.

- **Immunity Boost:** Enhanced vagal tone can lead to a better-functioning immune system, allowing the body to more effectively fight off infections and heal after injury.
- **Stress Reduction:** Regular engagement of the vagus nerve helps in the reduction of stress by controlling the body's relaxation response.
- **Anxiety and Depression:** Techniques that stimulate the vagus nerve have been shown to decrease symptoms of anxiety and depression due to their role in releasing mood-regulating neurotransmitters.
- **Better Sleep:** As it helps manage the body's relaxation response, it can also contribute to better sleep patterns and quality.
- **Increased Resilience:** Improved vagal tone can increase overall psychological and emotional resilience, helping to better manage emotional challenges.
- **Mind-Body Connection:** Working with the vagus nerve enhances the mind-body connection, aiding in greater awareness and presence.
- **Longevity:** There is some evidence suggesting that improved vagal tone is associated with greater longevity due to its positive effect on various body organs and systems.

When the Vagus Nerve Isn't Functioning Well ...

While the vagus nerve significantly contributes to well-functioning bodily systems, its impairment can lead to a cascade of health issues. Dysfunction in the vagus nerve can be typically linked to what's termed 'vagal tone'. A high vagal tone implies that the body can relax faster after stress - the desirable state. On the flip side, a low vagal tone is often associated with chronic stress, inflammation, and mood imbalances, among other issues.

Digestive Dilemmas:

Poor vagus nerve function can wreak havoc on the gut. It often presents as sluggish digestion, constipation, or gastroparesis—a condition where the stomach cannot empty properly. On the opposite spectrum, erratic signals can lead to cramps and irritable bowel syndrome. Consequently, if the maestro isn't cueing the orchestra properly, the symphony of digestion plays out of tune.

Cardiovascular Concerns:

In the cardiovascular realm, if the vagus nerve is underperforming, its capacity to control the heart rate is compromised. This inefficiency can heighten the risk of irregular heart rhythms and potentially increase stress on the heart. Moreover, it may affect blood pressure regulation, complicating cardiovascular health further.

Emotional Turbulence:

Mental health might take a hit as well if the vagal tone is low. Individuals might have a harder time managing stress, experience mood swings, or struggle with anxiety and depression. The calming influence the vagus nerve typically exerts fades, often leaving feelings of high tension in its absence.

Boosting Vagus Nerve Function

Given its significant impact, nurturing the health of the vagus nerve should be a prime focus for those looking toward holistic wellness.

Some ways to engage and stimulate this nerve include deep and slow breathing exercises, which promote relaxation and help to enhance vagal tone. Regular physical activity, another stimulant, naturally boosts the nerve's function while improving mood and digestion. Additionally, adopting tactics such as yoga and meditation has shown promising results in stress management and maintaining a good vagal tone. These are all things we're going to talk about in much more detail as we move through this book.

Put simply, the vagus nerve's role in sustaining good health cannot be overstated. It intricately connects multiple organs and systems, ensuring the body works not just as separate units but as a coherent, integrated ensemble.

Like a conductor leading an orchestra without drawing attention to itself, the vagus nerve supports and regulates key body functions quietly yet powerfully. To maintain this silent conductor in prime condition, embracing practices that support nerve health and reduce stress can be profoundly beneficial. Ultimately, a well-tuned vagus nerve sets the stage for a healthy, harmonious life—across both the physical and emotional realms.

What is the State of Your Vagus Nerve?

To help you understand how well your vagus nerve is functioning, let's try a quiz.

How would you describe your stress levels on a daily basis?

a) Low, I rarely feel stressed.

b) Moderate, I have some stressful moments but can manage them.

c) High, I often feel overwhelmed and stressed.

Do you experience any digestive issues, such as bloating, constipation, or diarrhea?

a) Rarely or never

b) Occasionally

c) Frequently

How well do you handle changes in temperature, such as going from a warm room to a cold room?

a) I adapt well without any issues.

b) I notice the change, but it doesn't affect me significantly.

c) I struggle to adjust and feel uncomfortable.

What is your sleep quality like?

a) I typically sleep well and wake up feeling rested.

b) I have trouble falling asleep or staying asleep occasionally.

c) I frequently have difficulty sleeping and wake up feeling tired.

How often do you practice relaxation techniques such as deep breathing, meditation, or yoga?

a) Daily

b) Occasionally

c) Rarely or never

Scoring:

- For every (a) answer, give yourself 1 point.

- For every (b) answer, give yourself 2 points.

- For every (c) answer, give yourself 3 points.

Interpretation:

- **5-8 points:** Your vagus nerve appears to be functioning well; keep up the good work maintaining your overall well-being!
- **9-12 points:** Your vagus nerve may be experiencing some challenges; consider incorporating more relaxation techniques and stress management strategies into your daily routine.
- **13-15 points:** Your vagus nerve could benefit from some extra care and attention. It's important to prioritize relaxation, stress reduction, and digestive health to support its function.

Remember, this quiz is just a fun way to gauge potential areas for improvement in your overall health and well-being. For any concerns about your vagus nerve or overall health, it's always best to consult with a healthcare professional.

Chapter 3

The Vagus Nerve and the Autonomic Nervous System

Because the nervous system is a complicated deal, let's dig even deeper than before. To truly understand the vagus nerve, we need to know about the autonomic nervous system in particular.

The autonomic nervous system is like the behind-the-scenes crew of your body, constantly working to keep things running smoothly without you even having to think about it. It's responsible for regulating all the automatic processes in your body, such as heart rate, digestion, breathing, and even bladder control.

Now, the autonomic nervous system has two main branches: the sympathetic nervous system and the parasympathetic nervous system. Think of them as the yin and yang of your body's internal control center.

The sympathetic nervous system is like your body's gas pedal. It kicks into gear in times of stress or danger, preparing you for fight or flight by increasing your heart rate, dilating your pupils, and releasing adrenaline to give you that extra boost of energy. It's like your body's own superhero, ready to jump into action when needed.

On the other hand, the parasympathetic nervous system is like your body's brake pedal. It helps you relax and rest after a stressful situation, slowing down your heart rate, constricting your pupils, and promoting digestion. It's like the calming voice in your head, telling you everything is going to be okay.

These two branches work together in a delicate balance, constantly adjusting and adapting to keep your body functioning properly. It's like a perfectly choreographed dance, with each branch taking the lead when needed and stepping back when not.

Now, here's where things get really interesting. Sometimes, the autonomic nervous system can get out of whack, causing problems like anxiety, high blood pressure, or digestive issues. This is where techniques like deep breathing, meditation, and exercise can help bring the system back into balance.

So, the next time you feel your heart racing or your stomach churning, remember that it's all thanks to your amazing autonomic nervous system working hard behind the scenes to keep you healthy and thriving.

In conclusion, the autonomic nervous system is like the unsung hero of your body, silently working to maintain harmony and balance in all your automatic bodily functions. It's a truly remarkable system that deserves recognition for all the hard work it does to keep you alive and well.

The Role of the Vagus Nerve in the Parasympathetic System

We know that the vagus nerve is the longest cranial nerve in the human body, extending from the brainstem all the way down to the abdomen, and it carries a plethora of essential information between the brain and various organs.

One of the most remarkable aspects of the vagus nerve is its bidirectional communication system. It not only transmits signals from the brain to the organs, but it also receives feedback from these organs, providing a continuous loop of information that helps maintain homeostasis within the body. This two-way communication allows the vagus nerve to finely tune the parasympathetic response as needed, adjusting heart rate, digestion, and other autonomic functions in response to different internal and external stimuli.

The vagus nerve is aptly named after the Latin word "vagus," meaning wandering, reflecting its extensive reach and ability to influence a wide array of bodily functions. It interacts with various organs, including the heart, lungs, liver, and intestines, exerting its influence through both the motor and sensory fibers it contains. By releasing acetylcholine, a neurotransmitter that promotes relaxation and restorative processes, the vagus nerve helps to counterbalance the sympathetic nervous system's fight-or-flight response, promoting a state of rest and digest.

One of the vagus nerve's primary functions is to lower heart rate and blood pressure during times of relaxation. This helps conserve energy and promote efficient digestion by diverting blood flow to the digestive organs. Additionally, the vagus nerve stimulates the release of digestive enzymes and promotes the peristaltic movement of the intestines, aiding in the absorption of nutrients and the elimination of waste.

But the role of the vagus nerve doesn't stop at digestion and heart rate regulation. It also plays a crucial role in modulating inflammation and immune responses. Through its anti-inflammatory effects, the vagus nerve helps regulate the body's response to stress and injury, promoting healing and reducing the risk of chronic inflammatory conditions. This neuro-immune communication highlights the intricate link between the nervous and immune systems, with the vagus nerve serving as a key mediator of this cross-talk.

Furthermore, the vagus nerve is closely involved in regulating mood and emotional responses. Its connections to various brain regions, including the amygdala and prefrontal cortex, enable it to influence emotional processing and stress responses. By dampening the body's stress response and promoting feelings of calm and relaxation, the vagus nerve contributes to emotional well-being and resilience in the face of life's challenges.

In addition to its role in physiological functions, the vagus nerve has been a subject of interest in the field of bioelectronic medicine. Researchers have explored the potential of vagus nerve stimulation as a therapeutic intervention for a variety of conditions, including epilepsy, depression, and inflammatory disorders. By modulating the activity of the vagus nerve through electrical stimulation, clinicians aim to restore balance to the autonomic nervous system and alleviate symptoms associated with these conditions.

Achieving Balance Between the Sympathetic and Parasympathetic Systems

Achieving the balance between the sympathetic and parasympathetic nervous systems is crucial for maintaining overall well-being and optimal functioning. These two systems work together to regulate our body's responses to stress and relaxation, with the sympathetic system responsible for the "fight or flight" response and the parasympathetic system for the "rest and digest" response. Finding harmony between these two systems is key to living a healthy and balanced life.

Let's start by diving into the sympathetic nervous system, often referred to as our body's "gas pedal." When we perceive a threat or are faced with a stressful situation, the sympathetic system kicks into gear, releasing adrenaline and triggering a cascade of physiological responses designed to help us either fight the threat or run away from it. Our heart rate increases, our breathing becomes faster and shallower, and our muscles tense up in preparation for action.

While the sympathetic system is essential for our survival, chronic activation can lead to negative health consequences, including increased risk of heart disease, anxiety, and weakened immune function. This is where the parasympathetic nervous system, our body's "brake pedal," comes into play. This system helps counterbalance the effects of stress by promoting relaxation, aiding digestion, and restoring our body to a state of calm.

Achieving balance between these two systems requires a multi-faceted approach that addresses both physical and mental aspects of well-being. Here are some strategies to help you find harmony between your sympathetic and parasympathetic systems:

- **Mindfulness practices:** Mindfulness techniques, such as meditation, deep breathing, and body scans, can help activate the parasympathetic system and promote feelings of relaxation and calm. Taking a few minutes each day to engage in mindfulness practices can help reduce stress levels and improve overall well-being.
- **Physical activity:** Regular exercise is a powerful tool for achieving balance between the sympathetic and parasympathetic systems. Exercise helps to release pent-up energy and tension while also promoting relaxation and reducing cortisol levels. Find a physical activity that you enjoy, whether it's yoga, jogging, or dancing, and make it a regular part of your routine.
- **Healthy eating habits:** Eating a balanced diet rich in whole foods, fruits, vegetables, and lean proteins can support the functioning of both the sympathetic and parasympathetic systems. Avoiding excessive caffeine and sugar can help prevent spikes in cortisol levels and promote a more stable mood and energy throughout the day.
- **Quality sleep:** Getting enough restful sleep is essential for maintaining a healthy balance between the sympathetic and parasympathetic systems. Aim for 7-9 hours of sleep each night and establish a bedtime routine that promotes relaxation, such as reading a book, taking a warm bath, or practicing gentle yoga poses.
- **Stress management techniques**: Finding healthy ways to cope with stress can help prevent chronic activation of the sympathetic nervous system. Try incorporating stress-reducing activities into your daily routine, such as spending time in nature, journaling, or connecting with loved ones.
- **Self-care practices:** Taking time for yourself and engaging in activities that bring you joy and relaxation can help nurture

your parasympathetic system. Whether it's enjoying a bubble bath, practicing a hobby, or going for a leisurely walk, prioritize self-care to support your overall well-being.

By implementing these strategies and prioritizing balance between the sympathetic and parasympathetic systems, you can cultivate a sense of harmony in your mind and body. Remember that achieving balance is an ongoing process that requires self-awareness, patience, and dedication. By taking small steps each day towards promoting relaxation and reducing stress, you can create a life that is healthy, vibrant, and grounded in tranquility.

From this point on, let's start looking at how the vagus nerve can help with various issues and what you can do to help the process along. Let's start with improving mental health.

Chapter 4

The Vagus Nerve and Mental Health

In this chapter, we will delve into the intricate web of connections between the vagus nerve and mental health, unraveling the mysteries behind its profound influence on our well-being.

Through its bidirectional communication with the brain, the vagus nerve acts as a conduit for signals that impact our mood, cognition, and behavior. From calming our fight-or-flight response to fostering feelings of connection and empathy, this enigmatic nerve holds the key to understanding the mind-body connection like never before.

Influence on Mood and Emotional Regulation

As the 10th cranial nerve, the vagus nerve is a key player in our body's ability to regulate emotions and mood. It plays a significant role in the communication between the brain and the body, promoting a sense of well-being and emotional stability.

One of the vagus nerve's primary roles is in regulating the parasympathetic nervous system, which is responsible for the body's rest-and-digest response. When activated, the vagus nerve helps to calm the body by slowing down heart rate, relaxing muscles, and stimulating the release of feel-good hormones like oxytocin and dopamine. This activation is crucial for reducing stress and promoting relaxation, which is essential for maintaining a healthy emotional balance.

Research has shown that individuals with a strong vagal tone, meaning their vagus nerve is functioning optimally, tend to have better emotional regulation and resilience to stress. A higher vagal tone is associated with improved mood, greater emotional stability, and increased overall well-being. On the other hand, low vagal tone has been linked to conditions such as depression, anxiety, and mood disorders.

One of the ways the vagus nerve influences mood and emotional regulation is through its connection to the brain's limbic system, which is responsible for processing emotions. The vagus nerve sends signals to the amygdala, the brain's fear center, to help regulate the intensity of emotional responses. By modulating the activity of the amygdala, the vagus nerve helps us navigate through challenging situations without becoming overwhelmed by fear or anxiety.

Moreover, the vagus nerve plays a crucial role in the body's stress response system. When we encounter stressful situations, the vagus nerve helps to regulate the release of cortisol, the stress hormone. By promoting relaxation and calming the body's stress response, the vagus nerve helps to prevent the negative effects of chronic stress on mood and emotional well-being.

Furthermore, the vagus nerve influences the production of neurotransmitters such as serotonin and GABA, which are essential for regulating mood and emotions. Serotonin, often referred to as the "happiness hormone," is involved in mood regulation, while GABA is a calming neurotransmitter that helps to reduce anxiety and promote relaxation. The vagus nerve plays a role in the synthesis and release of these neurotransmitters, contributing to emotional balance and mental well-being.

In addition to its direct influence on emotional regulation, the vagus nerve also plays a role in social bonding and connection. Oxytocin, often referred to as the "love hormone," is released in response to positive social interactions such as hugging or connecting with loved ones. The vagus nerve helps to stimulate the release of oxytocin, promoting feelings of trust, bonding, and emotional connection.

Practices that stimulate and strengthen the vagus nerve can be beneficial for enhancing mood and emotional regulation. Mindfulness meditation, deep breathing exercises, yoga, and acupuncture are all techniques that have been shown to activate the vagus nerve and improve vagal tone. These practices help to promote relaxation, reduce stress, and enhance emotional well-being by supporting the optimal functioning of the vagus nerve.

Moreover, physical activity has been found to be beneficial for vagal tone and emotional regulation. Regular exercise helps to stimulate the vagus nerve, promoting relaxation and reducing stress levels. Activities such as walking, running, and swimming can all help to enhance vagal tone and improve mood by supporting the body's natural stress response system.

The diet also plays a role in supporting the vagus nerve and emotional well-being. Consuming a diet rich in omega-3 fatty acids, antioxidants, and fiber can help to reduce inflammation in the body, which can impact vagal tone. Foods such as fatty fish, nuts, seeds, fruits, and vegetables can all support the health of the vagus nerve and contribute to better mood and emotional regulation.

Connection to Anxiety, Depression, and Stress

First off, picture the vagus nerve as a major highway that runs from the brainstem down to the abdomen, touching various major organs along the way. It plays a key role in the parasympathetic nervous system, which is responsible for the body's rest and digest responses. When stimulated, the vagus nerve acts like a calming agent, helping to regulate heart rate, digestion, and even mood.

Anxiety, that feeling of unease or worry, can be linked to an overactive vagus nerve. When the vagus nerve is in hyperdrive, it can lead to an imbalance in the body's stress response system. This can result in heightened feelings of anxiety as the body struggles to modulate its stress levels. People experiencing chronic anxiety may have an overly sensitive vagus nerve, which can exacerbate their symptoms.

On the flip side, depression, a mood disorder characterized by persistent feelings of sadness and hopelessness, can also be influenced by the vagus nerve. Studies have shown that individuals with depression often have reduced vagal tone, meaning their vagus nerve isn't functioning as effectively in regulating mood and emotions. This can contribute to a sense of emotional dysregulation and make it harder for individuals to bounce back from negative experiences.

Now, let's talk about stress, that all-too-familiar feeling of being overwhelmed by life's demands. The vagus nerve serves as a key player in the body's stress response system, helping to signal when it's time to relax and unwind. However, chronic stress can lead to vagal tone imbalance, affecting the nerve's ability to properly regulate stress levels. This can create a vicious cycle where heightened stress levels further impact the vagus nerve, perpetuating feelings of anxiety and depression.

Overall, the vagus nerve plays a crucial role in our emotional well-being, with strong connections to anxiety, depression, and stress. By understanding how this nerve operates and incorporating practices that support its function, you can take proactive steps towards promoting a healthier mind and body. Remember, your vagus nerve is a powerful ally in the battle against negative emotions; treat it well, and it will reward you with a greater sense of calm and resilience.

How to Use the Vagus Nerve to Improve Mental Health

In recent years, researchers and healthcare professionals have been exploring how stimulating and nurturing the vagus nerve can have a positive impact on mental health. By understanding how the vagus nerve works and incorporating specific techniques into your daily routine, you can potentially improve your overall mental well-being.

One of the key ways to work with the vagus nerve to enhance mental health is through techniques that focus on stimulating the nerve's functioning. These techniques can range from simple breathing exercises to more advanced biofeedback methods.

Let's delve into some actionable strategies that you can incorporate into your daily routine to tap into the power of the vagus nerve for better mental health.

Deep Breathing Exercises:

One of the most effective ways to stimulate the vagus nerve is through deep breathing exercises. By taking slow, deep breaths, you can activate the parasympathetic nervous system, which is responsible for promoting relaxation and reducing stress.

Start by finding a quiet and comfortable place to sit or lie down. Inhale deeply through your nose for a count of four, hold your breath for a moment, and then exhale slowly through your mouth for a count of six. Repeat this process several times, focusing on the sensation of your breath entering and leaving your body. This simple yet powerful technique can help calm your mind and body, promoting a sense of inner peace and well-being.

Cold Exposure

Another effective way to stimulate the vagus nerve is through cold exposure. Cold showers or immersing yourself in cold water can activate the body's "fight or flight" response, triggering the vagus nerve to kick in and help regulate your autonomic nervous system. Start by gradually exposing yourself to cold temperatures, whether through cold showers, ice baths, or simply splashing cold water on your face.

The shock of cold can stimulate the vagus nerve and promote a sense of alertness and mental clarity. Over time, regular cold exposure can potentially improve your resilience to stress and enhance your mental health.

Yoga and Meditation

Practices like yoga and meditation have been shown to have a positive impact on mental health by calming the mind and body and promoting relaxation. Certain yoga poses and meditation techniques specifically target the vagus nerve, helping to regulate the heart rate and promote a sense of tranquility. Incorporate yoga poses like Fish Pose, Cobra Pose, and Lion's Breath into your practice to stimulate the vagus nerve and promote relaxation.

Fish Pose:

- Start by lying flat on your back on the yoga mat with your legs extended and your arms resting by your sides.
- Bring your hands palms down underneath your hips, with your elbows tucked in close to your body.
- Press your forearms and elbows into the mat as you inhale and gently arch your back, lifting your chest and upper body off the mat.
- Rest the top of your head lightly on the mat, allowing your neck to gently arch back.
- Keep your legs and feet active by pressing them into the mat.
- Hold the pose for 5-10 breaths, breathing deeply and focusing on opening the heart center.
- To come out of the pose, gently release the head back to the mat and lower your chest back down.
- Remove your hands from under your hips and rest in Corpse Pose (Savasana) for a few breaths to relax and integrate the pose.

Remember to listen to your body and only go as far into the pose as feels comfortable for you.

Cobra Pose:

- Start by lying flat on your stomach on your mat, with your legs straight and your feet hip-width apart. Place your palms on the mat under your shoulders, with your elbows close to your torso.
- Inhale deeply and press the tops of your feet, thighs, and pelvis into the mat while keeping your pubic bone grounded.
- On your next inhale, slowly begin to straighten your arms, lifting your chest off the mat. Keep your elbows slightly bent, and draw your shoulder blades together and down your back.
- Ensure that your gaze is forward, your neck is in line with your spine, and your chin is slightly tucked.
- Take deep breaths as you hold the pose, feeling a gentle stretch in your back and abdomen. Avoid putting too much pressure on your hands; use the strength of your back muscles to lift yourself.
- To come out of the pose, exhale slowly and lower your chest back down to the mat, releasing any tension in your body.
- Repeat the Cobra Pose a few times, focusing on your breath and maintaining proper alignment. Listen to your body and adjust the pose as needed to suit your comfort level.

Remember to warm up your body before attempting any yoga poses, and always listen to your body to prevent injury.

Lion's Breath:

- Find a comfortable seated position on your mat. You can sit cross-legged or on your knees, whichever is more comfortable for you.
- Place your hands on your knees or thighs, palms facing down.
- Take a deep inhale through your nose, filling your lungs with air. Feel your belly rise as you breathe in.

- As you exhale, open your mouth wide, stick out your tongue, and exhale forcefully, making a "ha" sound. Imagine you are trying to fog up a mirror with your breath.
- While exhaling, also gaze towards the space between your eyebrows (your third eye) or up towards the ceiling, if that feels comfortable for you.
- As you exhale, try to release any tension in your face, jaw, shoulders, and throat. Let go of any stress or negative energy with each Lion's Breath.
- Repeat this breathing exercise 3-5 times, or as many times as you feel comfortable.
- After completing the Lion's Breath, take a moment to notice how you feel. You may feel more relaxed, energized, or centered.

Remember to listen to your body and only practice Lion's Breath as much as feels comfortable for you.

Additionally, mindfulness meditation, focusing on the present moment, and observing your thoughts without judgment can help activate the vagus nerve and reduce symptoms of anxiety and depression.

Social Connections

The vagus nerve is also closely linked to social connections and human bonding. Engaging in meaningful and positive social interactions can help stimulate the vagus nerve and promote emotional well-being. Make an effort to nurture your relationships with friends, family, and loved ones, whether through face-to-face conversations, phone calls, or virtual meet-ups.

Connecting with others can help increase feelings of safety and trust, activating the vagus nerve's "rest and digest" response and promoting a sense of calm and contentment.

Laughter and Play

Laughter has been shown to have a profound impact on mental health, releasing endorphins and reducing stress levels. Engaging in activities that bring joy and laughter, such as watching a funny movie, playing with pets, or engaging in playful interactions, can help stimulate the vagus nerve and enhance your mood.

Try incorporating more moments of laughter and playfulness into your daily routine to boost your mental well-being and activate the vagus nerve's relaxation response.

Chapter 5

The Vagus Nerve and Physical Health

We know that the vagus nerve, a crucial part of the parasympathetic nervous system, plays a significant role in regulating various bodily functions such as heart rate, digestion, and inflammation. In recent years, researchers have uncovered the profound impact that stimulating the vagus nerve can have on improving overall health.

Whether you are seeking relief from chronic pain, looking to boost your immune system, or simply hoping to enhance your overall well-being, harnessing the power of the vagus nerve can offer a wealth of benefits.

Impact on Cardiovascular Health

The vagus nerve has two main branches, the left vagus nerve and the right vagus nerve, which innervate different regions of the body. The right vagus nerve primarily influences the sinoatrial (SA) node, while the left vagus nerve predominantly affects the atrioventricular (AV) node. These two branches work together to regulate heart rate, blood pressure, and heart rhythm, among other cardiovascular functions.

One of the key ways in which the vagus nerve can help improve cardiovascular health is through its role in regulating heart rate. The vagus nerve acts as a brake on the heart, slowing down the heart rate when the body is at rest or under low stress. This parasympathetic activity helps maintain healthy heart rate variability, which is a strong indicator of cardiovascular health. Individuals with higher heart rate variability are often more resilient to stress and have a lower risk of developing cardiovascular disease.

In addition to regulating heart rate, the vagus nerve also plays a crucial role in controlling blood pressure. When the body is under stress or in a fight-or-flight response, the sympathetic nervous system is activated, causing an increase in heart rate and blood pressure. The vagus nerve, through its parasympathetic activity, helps counteract this response by promoting relaxation and lowering blood pressure. By activating the vagus nerve through various techniques, such as deep breathing exercises or biofeedback, individuals can help maintain healthy blood pressure levels and reduce the risk of hypertension.

Moreover, the vagus nerve is involved in the regulation of heart rhythm, particularly through its modulation of the SA and AV nodes. By influencing the electrical signals that control the heart's contractions, the vagus nerve helps maintain a regular and coordinated heart rhythm. When the vagus nerve is functioning optimally, the risk of arrhythmias, such as atrial fibrillation, is reduced. Studies have shown that enhancing vagal tone, or the strength of vagus nerve activity, can help prevent the occurrence of various heart rhythm disorders.

Another fascinating aspect of the vagus nerve is its role in reducing inflammation throughout the body. Chronic inflammation is a known risk factor for cardiovascular disease, as it can damage blood vessels and promote the development of atherosclerosis. The vagus nerve exerts anti-inflammatory effects through its release of neurotransmitters, such as acetylcholine, which inhibits the production of pro-inflammatory cytokines. By activating the vagus nerve, either through methods like meditation or vagus nerve stimulation, individuals can help mitigate inflammation and protect their cardiovascular health.

Furthermore, the vagus nerve is involved in the regulation of the gastrointestinal system, which has a direct impact on cardiovascular health. The gut-brain axis, a complex communication network between the brain and the digestive system, is partially mediated by the vagus nerve. A healthy gut microbiome, influenced by vagal activity, can produce beneficial metabolites that reduce cardiovascular risk factors, such as cholesterol levels and blood sugar regulation. By promoting gut health through diet and lifestyle choices that support vagal function, individuals can positively impact their cardiovascular health.

In recent years, research has highlighted the potential therapeutic applications of vagus nerve stimulation for improving cardiovascular health. Vagus nerve stimulation involves the targeted delivery of electrical impulses to the vagus nerve, which can modulate its activity and influence various physiological processes. Clinical studies have shown promising results in using vagus nerve stimulation to treat heart failure, hypertension, and other cardiovascular conditions, demonstrating the therapeutic potential of harnessing the power of this nerve.

Role in Digestion and Gut Health

The vagus nerve plays a crucial role in the digestive process by regulating key functions such as swallowing, digestion, and nutrient absorption. When we consume food, sensory information is relayed to the brain via the vagus nerve, which then signals the release of digestive enzymes and hormones to facilitate proper digestion.

One of the most significant ways in which the vagus nerve impacts digestive health is through its role in the "rest and digest" response of the parasympathetic nervous system. When the body is in a state of relaxation, the vagus nerve stimulates the release of digestive juices in the stomach, enhances intestinal motility, and promotes nutrient absorption. This ensures that our bodies can efficiently break down food and extract essential nutrients to support overall health.

Furthermore, the vagus nerve communicates with the enteric nervous system, sometimes referred to as the "second brain," which is a complex network of neurons found in the gastrointestinal tract. This intricate communication network helps regulate gut motility, the secretion of digestive enzymes, and the maintenance of a healthy gut microbiome.

Gut-Brain Axis and the Vagus Nerve

The connection between the gut and the brain, often referred to as the gut-brain axis, is a bidirectional communication network that involves the vagus nerve as a central player. Research has shown that the vagus nerve plays a crucial role in transmitting signals between the gut and the brain, influencing various aspects of health, including mood, cognition, and immune function.

In recent years, there has been growing interest in the impact of the gut-brain axis on overall well-being, with studies highlighting the role of the vagus nerve in regulating gut health and influencing mental health conditions such as anxiety and depression. By maintaining a healthy gut environment through proper digestion and nutrient absorption, the vagus nerve can help support optimal brain function and emotional well-being.

Vagus Nerve Stimulation and Gut Health

In addition to its natural functions, the vagus nerve can also be stimulated artificially through techniques such as vagus nerve stimulation (VNS). VNS is a therapeutic approach that involves sending electrical impulses to the vagus nerve to treat various conditions, including epilepsy, depression, and inflammatory disorders.

Recent research has also explored the potential benefits of vagus nerve stimulation for promoting gut health and alleviating digestive disorders such as irritable bowel syndrome (IBS) and inflammatory bowel disease (IBD). By modulating the activity of the vagus nerve, researchers believe that VNS may help regulate gut inflammation, restore gut motility, and rebalance the gut microbiome, thereby improving overall digestive health.

Lifestyle Factors and Vagus Nerve Function

While the vagus nerve plays a significant role in digestive health, its function can be influenced by various lifestyle factors. Practices such as deep breathing, meditation, and yoga have been shown to stimulate the vagus nerve and promote relaxation, which can in turn enhance digestion and gut function.

Furthermore, maintaining a healthy diet rich in fiber, probiotics, and prebiotics can support a thriving gut microbiome and optimize vagus nerve function. By nourishing the gut with a diverse array of nutrients, you can help ensure that the vagus nerve and the enteric nervous system work synergistically to support optimal digestive health.

Effects on Immune Response and Inflammation

The vagus nerve plays a significant role in regulating various bodily functions, including digestion, heart rate, and even our immune response.

One of the key ways in which the vagus nerve influences the immune response is through a process known as the "cholinergic anti-inflammatory pathway." When the body encounters a threat, such as an infection or injury, immune cells release pro-inflammatory molecules to help combat the invader. However, excessive inflammation can lead to tissue damage and contribute to the development of chronic conditions like autoimmune diseases.

Here's where the vagus nerve steps in as a powerful mediator of inflammation. By releasing acetylcholine, a neurotransmitter that activates the cholinergic anti-inflammatory pathway, the vagus nerve can dampen the immune response and help maintain balance in the inflammatory process. This mechanism acts as a feedback loop, preventing excessive inflammation and promoting tissue repair once the threat has been neutralized.

Research has shown that stimulating the vagus nerve, either through techniques like deep breathing, meditation, or devices such as vagus nerve stimulators, can have profound effects on the immune response. By activating the cholinergic anti-inflammatory pathway, these interventions can help reduce inflammation, improve immune function, and support overall well-being.

Furthermore, the vagus nerve's influence on inflammation goes beyond just the immune system. It also plays a role in regulating the gut-brain axis – the bidirectional communication between the gut and the brain. This communication pathway is essential for maintaining gut health and influencing mood, cognition, and even immune function.

In addition to its anti-inflammatory effects, the vagus nerve can modulate the release of stress hormones like cortisol, which can impact immune function. Chronic stress can dysregulate the immune response, leading to increased inflammation and vulnerability to infections. By activating the vagus nerve through relaxation techniques or other interventions, we can help mitigate the detrimental effects of stress on the immune system.

It's important to note that individual differences in vagal tone—the strength of the vagus nerve's influence on bodily functions – can impact how effectively the immune response is regulated. Factors like genetics, lifestyle, and environmental influences can all play a role in determining vagal tone and, consequently, immune function.

Overall, the vagus nerve's effects on immune response and inflammation highlight the intricate interplay between the nervous system, the immune system, and overall health. By understanding and leveraging the power of the vagus nerve, we can support our immune system, reduce inflammation, and promote greater well-being.

On the other hand, if this important nerve isn't functioning well, it can have a significant impact on inflammation and the immune system.

When the vagus nerve isn't working properly, this regulation can be disrupted, leading to an overactive inflammatory response. This can contribute to various health issues, such as chronic inflammation, which in turn can weaken the immune system's ability to fight off infections and diseases.

So, it's safe to say that keeping our vagus nerve in tip-top shape is key to maintaining a well-balanced immune system and preventing inflammation from going haywire.

Vagus Nerve Strategies to Improve Physical Health

When it comes to optimizing physical health, tapping into the power of the vagus nerve can be a game-changer. By incorporating specific practices and lifestyle habits that activate the vagus nerve, you can significantly boost your physical health.

In our last section, we talked about yoga, deep breathing, and cold exposure, and these are things that can help with physical health too. However, there are a few extra strategies to add to your list.

So, here are actionable strategies to harness the potential of the vagus nerve for better overall well-being:

Regular Exercise

Engage in regular physical activity to support optimal vagal tone and overall physical health. Aim for a combination of cardiovascular exercise, strength training, and flexibility exercises to keep your body strong and resilient. Exercise has been shown to increase heart rate variability, an indicator of vagal tone.

Consider incorporating activities like yoga, Pilates, or tai chi into your workout routine. These mind-body practices are not only great for physical fitness but also help promote relaxation and activate the vagus nerve. Find a form of exercise that you enjoy and make it a regular part of your routine.

Proper Nutrition

Fuel your body with a balanced diet rich in nutrients that support vagal function and overall physical health. Include foods high in omega-3 fatty acids, such as fatty fish, flaxseeds, and walnuts, which can help reduce inflammation and support brain health, including vagal tone.

Make sure to stay hydrated throughout the day by drinking an adequate amount of water. Dehydration can negatively impact vagal function and overall energy levels. Aim to drink at least 8–10 glasses of water daily to keep your body hydrated and functioning optimally.

Mindful Eating

Practice mindful eating to support digestion and activate the vagus nerve's role in the gut-brain connection. Take the time to savor each bite, chew your food slowly, and pay attention to your body's hunger and fullness cues. Mindful eating can help reduce stress and promote optimal digestion.

Consider incorporating foods that are known to support gut health, such as fermented foods like yogurt, kefir, and kimchi. These foods contain probiotics that can help maintain a healthy balance of gut bacteria, which is essential for vagal function and overall digestive health.

Quality Sleep

Prioritize getting an adequate amount of quality sleep each night to support vagal tone and overall physical recovery. Create a bedtime routine that helps signal to your body that it's time to wind down, such as dimming the lights, disconnecting from screens, and practicing relaxation techniques like deep breathing or gentle stretching.

Aim for 7-9 hours of quality sleep per night to allow your body to repair and rejuvenate. Poor sleep can negatively impact vagal function and contribute to various health issues, so make sleep a priority for optimal physical health.

By implementing these actionable strategies and incorporating vagus nerve-stimulating practices into your daily routine, you can harness the power of this vital nerve to enhance your physical health and overall well-being.

Remember that consistency is key, so start small and gradually incorporate these habits into your lifestyle to reap the full benefits. Prioritize self-care, listen to your body, and enjoy the journey to improved physical health through the activation of the vagus nerve.

Chapter 6

The Vagus Nerve and Chronic Illness

What's next? Well, in this chapter, we will delve into the intricate web of connections between the vagus nerve and chronic illnesses.

Recent research has shed light on the link between the vagus nerve and chronic illnesses such as autoimmune disorders, depression, and even gastrointestinal issues. By understanding the mechanisms through which the vagus nerve impacts these conditions, we gain valuable insight into potential therapeutic interventions and lifestyle changes that can make a tangible difference in our health outcomes.

By understanding all of this, you can start to make changes that may bring you relief from troublesome symptoms.

Connection to Chronic Pain and Fibromyalgia

Did you know that the vagus nerve also has a significant impact on chronic pain conditions like fibromyalgia?

Chronic pain is a complex and debilitating condition that affects millions of people worldwide. Fibromyalgia, in particular, is a chronic pain disorder characterized by widespread musculoskeletal pain, fatigue, and tenderness in specific areas of the body. While the exact cause of fibromyalgia is still unknown, researchers have identified a strong link between the vagus nerve and the development of chronic pain conditions.

One of the key ways in which the vagus nerve influences chronic pain is through its role in regulating inflammation. We know that inflammation is the body's natural response to injury or illness, but when it becomes chronic, it can contribute to the development of pain and other symptoms associated with conditions like fibromyalgia. The vagus nerve helps to modulate inflammation by releasing neurotransmitters like acetylcholine, which have anti-inflammatory effects.

Additionally, the vagus nerve is involved in the body's stress response system, known as the HPA axis. Chronic stress can trigger inflammation and exacerbate pain symptoms in conditions like fibromyalgia. The vagus nerve plays a crucial role in regulating the body's stress response by influencing the release of cortisol, a hormone involved in the body's response to stress. When the vagus nerve is not functioning properly, it can lead to dysregulation of the HPA axis, contributing to the development of chronic pain conditions.

Furthermore, the vagus nerve is also connected to the brain's limbic system, which is responsible for processing emotions and sensations. Dysfunction in the vagus nerve can disrupt the communication between the brain and the body, leading to alterations in pain perception and sensory processing. This can contribute to the development of hypersensitivity to pain in conditions like fibromyalgia.

Research has shown that individuals with fibromyalgia often have decreased vagal tone, which refers to the strength and efficiency of the signals sent by the vagus nerve. Low vagal tone has been associated with increased inflammation, heightened stress responses, and alterations in pain processing, all of which can contribute to the development and maintenance of chronic pain conditions.

By understanding the connection between the vagus nerve and chronic pain, we can explore new avenues for managing and treating these complex conditions. Through lifestyle modifications, mind-body practices, and targeted interventions, we can improve vagal tone, reduce inflammation, and alleviate pain symptoms, leading to a better quality of life.

The Vagus Nerve's Role in Autoimmune Diseases

The vagus nerve plays a fascinating and increasingly appreciated role in autoimmune diseases. We know that one of its key functions is to regulate the body's inflammatory response, which is crucial to maintaining immune balance. In recent years, researchers have discovered that the vagus nerve can act as a powerful modulator of the immune system, impacting the development and progression of autoimmune diseases.

Autoimmune diseases occur when the body's immune system mistakenly attacks its own tissues and organs, leading to chronic inflammation and tissue damage. Conditions such as rheumatoid arthritis, lupus, Crohn's disease, and multiple sclerosis are just a few examples of autoimmune diseases that can have debilitating effects on individuals. The intricate interplay between the immune system and the vagus nerve has provided new insights into the mechanisms underlying these conditions.

The vagus nerve exerts its influence on the immune system through a process known as the cholinergic anti-inflammatory pathway. This pathway involves the release of acetylcholine, a neurotransmitter that activates receptors on immune cells, leading to the suppression of pro-inflammatory cytokines and the promotion of anti-inflammatory responses. By dampening the immune response in this manner, the vagus nerve helps to prevent excessive inflammation and tissue damage. However, in the context of autoimmune diseases, dysregulation of this pathway can result in unchecked inflammation and immune dysregulation.

Research has shown that dysfunction of the vagus nerve and the cholinergic anti-inflammatory pathway can contribute to the development and progression of autoimmune diseases. For example, in rheumatoid arthritis, a chronic inflammatory condition affecting the joints, impaired vagus nerve function has been implicated in promoting joint inflammation and tissue destruction. Studies have demonstrated that stimulating the vagus nerve through techniques such as vagus nerve stimulation (VNS) or bioelectronic devices can potentially reduce inflammation and alleviate symptoms in rheumatoid arthritis patients.

Similarly, in systemic lupus erythematosus (SLE), an autoimmune disease characterized by widespread inflammation and organ damage, abnormalities in vagus nerve signaling have been observed. Dysfunctional vagus nerve activity may exacerbate the inflammatory response in SLE, contributing to disease flares and tissue damage. By targeting the vagus nerve with therapeutic interventions, such as VNS or pharmacological agents that enhance vagal tone, researchers aim to modulate the immune response and improve outcomes for individuals with SLE.

Crohn's disease, a chronic inflammatory bowel disorder, also showcases the intricate relationship between the vagus nerve and autoimmune diseases. Dysfunction of the vagus nerve can disrupt the balance between pro-inflammatory and anti-inflammatory signaling in the gut, leading to intestinal inflammation and symptoms characteristic of Crohn's disease. Therapeutic strategies aimed at restoring vagus nerve function in Crohn's disease patients may hold promise for attenuating inflammation and improving gastrointestinal health.

Multiple sclerosis (MS), a progressive autoimmune disorder affecting the central nervous system, highlights the role of the vagus nerve in modulating neuroinflammation. Studies have revealed that vagus nerve stimulation can reduce inflammatory responses in the brain and spinal cord in animal models of MS, suggesting a potential therapeutic approach for managing disease progression in MS patients. By harnessing the anti-inflammatory properties of the vagus nerve, researchers are exploring novel treatment strategies for autoimmune conditions that impact the nervous system.

In addition to its direct effects on immune function, the vagus nerve is also implicated in the regulation of the gut-brain axis, a bidirectional communication system between the gastrointestinal tract and the brain. The gut microbiota, which plays a crucial role in immune regulation and inflammation, can influence vagal signaling and immune responses. Dysbiosis, or an imbalance in the gut microbiota, has been associated with autoimmune diseases and may impact vagus nerve function. Strategies to modulate the gut microbiota, such as probiotics and dietary interventions, could potentially enhance vagal tone and mitigate inflammation in autoimmune conditions.

By understanding and harnessing the mechanisms by which the vagus nerve regulates immune responses, researchers are paving the way for innovative therapeutic approaches to manage autoimmune diseases. From rheumatoid arthritis to lupus, Crohn's disease to multiple sclerosis, the vagus nerve's role in autoimmune diseases offers new avenues for intervention and hope for individuals living with these challenging conditions.

As research continues to unravel the complexities of this dynamic interplay, the potential for targeted therapies that harness the power of the vagus nerve to modulate immune responses and mitigate inflammation is increasingly promising.

Vagal Nerve Stimulation as a Treatment Option

Vagus nerve stimulation (VNS) has garnered increasing interest in the medical field for its potential therapeutic benefits in treating various conditions such as fibromyalgia, chronic pain, and autoimmune diseases. By modulating the activity of the vagus nerve through stimulation, it is believed that people suffering from these conditions may experience relief and improvement in their symptoms.

However, it's important to remember that you shouldn't make any changes to your lifestyle or medication routine without speaking to your doctor first. Always check in with your medical team to ensure that you're getting the very best treatment for your condition. Everyone is different, and there is no one-size-fits-all approach here.

Understanding Vagus Nerve Stimulation (VNS)

Before delving into the specific benefits of VNS for fibromyalgia, chronic pain, and autoimmune diseases, it's important to understand how this therapy works.

Vagus nerve stimulation involves sending electrical impulses to the vagus nerve, which then communicates with the brain and various organs to regulate functions such as heart rate, digestion, inflammation, and pain perception. By modulating the activity of the vagus nerve, VNS can influence the body's response to stress, inflammation, and pain.

VNS for Fibromyalgia

Fibromyalgia is a chronic condition characterized by widespread musculoskeletal pain, fatigue, and heightened sensitivity to pain. Research suggests that VNS may be beneficial for individuals with fibromyalgia by modulating pain signals and reducing inflammation. By stimulating the vagus nerve, VNS can help regulate the body's pain response and potentially alleviate the symptoms associated with fibromyalgia.

Actionable Advice for Fibromyalgia and VNS

- **Consult with a healthcare provider:** Before considering VNS as a treatment option for fibromyalgia, it is important to consult with a healthcare provider who can assess your condition and determine if VNS is appropriate for you.
- **Explore non-invasive VNS devices:** There are non-invasive VNS devices available that can be used at home to stimulate the vagus nerve. These devices may provide a convenient and safe option for individuals seeking to incorporate VNS into their fibromyalgia management.

- **Combine VNS with other therapies:** VNS can be used in conjunction with other therapies such as medication, physical therapy, and lifestyle modifications to enhance the overall management of fibromyalgia symptoms.

VNS for Chronic Pain

Chronic pain is a complex condition that can have a profound impact on a person's quality of life. VNS has shown promise in providing relief for individuals suffering from chronic pain by modulating pain signals and reducing inflammation. By targeting the vagus nerve, VNS can help regulate the body's pain response and potentially alleviate chronic pain symptoms.

Actionable Advice for Chronic Pain and VNS

- **Consider VNS as an adjunct therapy:** Individuals with chronic pain may benefit from incorporating VNS as an adjunct therapy to their existing pain management plan. Consult with a healthcare provider to determine if VNS is a suitable option for your specific condition.
- **Practice self-care techniques:** In addition to VNS therapy, incorporating self-care techniques such as relaxation exercises, mindfulness, and gentle physical activity can help manage chronic pain and improve overall well-being.
- **Monitor and track progress:** Keep track of your symptoms and pain levels while undergoing VNS therapy to assess its effectiveness in managing chronic pain. Share this information with your healthcare provider for personalized care.

VNS for Autoimmune Diseases

Autoimmune diseases are characterized by the body's immune system attacking its tissues, leading to inflammation and tissue damage. VNS has emerged as a potential treatment option for autoimmune diseases by modulating the immune response and reducing inflammation.

By targeting the vagus nerve, VNS may help regulate the immune system and alleviate symptoms associated with autoimmune diseases.

Actionable Advice for Autoimmune Diseases and VNS

- **Consult with a specialist:** If you have been diagnosed with an autoimmune disease and are considering VNS therapy, consult with a specialist in both neurology and immunology to determine the best course of treatment for your specific condition.
- **Adopt an anti-inflammatory diet:** In conjunction with VNS therapy, adopting an anti-inflammatory diet rich in fruits, vegetables, and omega-3 fatty acids may help manage the symptoms of autoimmune diseases and support overall health.
- **Prioritize stress management:** Chronic stress can exacerbate the symptoms of autoimmune diseases. Incorporate stress-reducing activities such as meditation, yoga, or deep breathing exercises to complement VNS therapy and support your immune system.

Overall, vagus nerve stimulation shows promise as a novel therapy for conditions such as fibromyalgia, chronic pain, and autoimmune diseases by modulating pain signals, inflammation, and the immune response. By understanding the potential benefits of VNS and incorporating actionable advice into your treatment plan, you can explore this innovative therapy as part of your journey towards improved health and well-being. Remember, always consult with a healthcare provider before starting any new treatment regimen to ensure it is safe and appropriate for your individual needs.

Chapter 7

Vagus Nerve Stimulation Techniques

We've given some advice for each particular issue so far, but in this chapter, let's really delve into how you can stimulate the vagus nerve and get the best out of the approach you're taking. It's all very well and good to tell you to go out and speak to people, be sociable, breathe deeply, and do some yoga, but how?

That's what we're going to answer in this chapter.

We're about to get practical, so buckle up!

Overview of Vagus Nerve Stimulation (VNS)

We touched up on Vagus Nerve Stimulation earlier, but let's delve right into the details.

Vagus nerve stimulation, also known as VNS, is a fascinating therapeutic approach that involves the use of a device to provide electrical stimulation to the vagus nerve, an essential part of the nervous system responsible for controlling many bodily functions. Let's dive into the intricate workings of this remarkable treatment method.

The vagus nerve is the longest cranial nerve in the body, running from the brainstem through the neck and branching out to various organs in the chest and abdomen. It plays a crucial role in regulating key bodily processes such as heart rate, digestion, and inflammation. By targeting this important nerve with electrical stimulation, VNS can modulate the communication between the brain and the body, leading to a range of potential therapeutic benefits.

So, how does vagus nerve stimulation work on a technical level? The process begins with the implantation of a small device – typically a generator – under the skin in the chest area. This generator is connected to a lead that is carefully placed around the vagus nerve, usually on the left side of the neck. Once in position, the device is programmed to deliver electrical impulses to the nerve at regular intervals determined by a healthcare provider.

These electrical impulses travel along the vagus nerve to the brainstem, where they influence the activity of various brain regions involved in regulating mood, behavior, and autonomic functions. By modulating the neural signals passing through the vagus nerve, VNS can have a profound impact on conditions such as epilepsy, depression, and chronic pain.

One of the key mechanisms by which vagus nerve stimulation exerts its effects is through the activation of the locus coeruleus, a brain region involved in the release of neurotransmitters such as norepinephrine. This activation can lead to changes in brain activity that help regulate mood and emotional responses, providing relief for individuals with depression or anxiety disorders.

In addition to its effects on the brain, VNS can also influence the activity of the autonomic nervous system, which controls involuntary functions such as heart rate and digestion. By modulating the parasympathetic branch of the autonomic nervous system, vagus nerve stimulation can help regulate heart rate variability, reduce inflammation, and improve overall well-being.

Interestingly, VNS has been shown to have anti-inflammatory effects, which may contribute to its therapeutic benefits in conditions such as rheumatoid arthritis and inflammatory bowel disease. By dampening the body's inflammatory response, VNS can help alleviate symptoms and improve the quality of life for individuals with these chronic conditions.

Another fascinating aspect of vagus nerve stimulation is its potential to enhance memory and cognitive function. Research has shown that VNS can improve learning and memory in both animal models and human studies, suggesting that this therapeutic approach may have applications in the treatment of cognitive disorders such as Alzheimer's disease.

Overall, vagus nerve stimulation offers a promising avenue for treating a variety of neurological and psychiatric conditions by harnessing the body's own neural pathways. By targeting the vagus nerve with controlled electrical impulses, this innovative therapy can modulate brain activity, regulate autonomic functions, and reduce inflammation, leading to improved health and well-being for individuals in need.

Non-invasive Techniques to Stimulate the Vagus Nerve

Stimulating the vagus nerve through non-invasive techniques can have profound effects on both physical and mental well-being. If a more invasive option doesn't call out to you, there are some non-invasive options to try. Let's explore various methods to stimulate the vagus nerve without the need for invasive procedures.

Deep Breathing Techniques

Deep breathing is a simple yet powerful way to stimulate the vagus nerve. By taking slow, deep breaths, you can activate the parasympathetic nervous system and promote relaxation.

Here are two exercises you can try:

Diaphragmatic Breathing

- Find a comfortable position, either sitting or lying down.
- Place one hand on your chest and the other on your abdomen.
- Inhale deeply through your nose, focusing on expanding your abdomen as you breathe in.
- Exhale slowly through your mouth, feeling your abdomen contract.
- Repeat this deep breathing pattern for a few minutes, focusing on the rise and fall of your diaphragm.

Alternate Nostril Breathing

- Sit comfortably with your spine straight.
- Place your left hand on your left knee, palm facing up.
- Use your right thumb to close off your right nostril, and inhale deeply through your left nostril.
- Close off your left nostril with your right ring finger and exhale through your right nostril.
- Keeping your left nostril closed, inhale through your right nostril.
- Close off your right nostril and exhale through your left nostril.
- Continue this alternate breathing pattern for several minutes, focusing on the rhythm of your breath and the sensation of air passing through each nostril.

These exercises can help activate the parasympathetic nervous system through deep, mindful breathing, which in turn can stimulate the vagus nerve and promote relaxation and overall well-being.

Cold Exposure

Exposing your body to cold temperatures, such as cold showers or swimming in cold water, can stimulate the vagus nerve. The shock of cold triggers the body's fight or flight response, leading to vagus nerve activation.

Cold Water Face Immersion Technique

- Fill a basin with cold water.
- Take a deep breath and submerge your face in the cold water for about 30 seconds to 1 minute.
- Focus on your breathing and try to remain calm while you feel the cold sensation on your face.
- After the time is up, slowly lift your face out of the water and take a few deep breaths.
- Repeat this exercise a few times, gradually increasing the duration of immersion.

Cold Shower Therapy

- Start by taking your regular warm shower.
- Gradually turn the water temperature to cold, starting from your feet and moving upwards to your head.
- Stay under the cold water for about 1-3 minutes while focusing on your breath and trying to relax.
- Feel the sensation of the cold water on your skin and try to embrace it rather than resist it.
- After the cold exposure, switch back to warm water to help your body gradually warm up.
- Practice this cold shower therapy regularly to help stimulate your vagus nerve and improve your overall well-being.

Meditation and Mindfulness

Practicing meditation and mindfulness can help calm the mind and stimulate the vagus nerve. Mindful breathing exercises and body scans can enhance vagal tone and promote relaxation. Dedicate 10-15 minutes each day to meditation or mindfulness practice. Focus on your breath, and sensations in your body, and bring awareness to the present moment.

Loving-Kindness Meditation

- Begin by finding a quiet and peaceful space to sit comfortably.
- Close your eyes and take a few deep breaths to center yourself.
- Repeat the following phrases silently or aloud:
    - "May I be happy?
    - May I be healthy?
    - May I be safe?
    - May I live with ease?"
- Visualize a sphere of warm, loving energy surrounding you as you send these wishes to yourself.
- Next, imagine someone you care about deeply (a loved one, friend, or pet) and direct the same phrases towards them.
- Extend this practice to include all beings, sending out feelings of compassion and kindness to everyone in the world.

This meditation helps stimulate the vagus nerve by fostering a sense of connection, empathy, and positivity, which are all beneficial for overall well-being.

Gratitude Meditation

- Find a quiet and comfortable space where you can sit or lie down in a relaxed position.
- Close your eyes and take a few deep breaths, inhaling slowly through your nose and exhaling through your mouth.

- Bring your attention to your breath. Notice the sensation of the air entering your nostrils, filling your lungs, and exhaling out.
- Now, shift your focus to your heart center. Visualize a warm, soothing light radiating from this area, spreading throughout your body.
- As you continue to breathe deeply and slowly, imagine sending gratitude and compassion to yourself and those around you.
- Now, gently place one hand on your chest and the other hand on your stomach. Feel the gentle rise and fall of your breath with each inhalation and exhalation.
- Next, bring your awareness to your throat and the area around it. Take a moment to swallow and notice the sensation in this area.
- Slowly begin to hum or chant a soothing sound, feeling the vibrations in your throat and chest. This gentle vocalization can help stimulate the vagus nerve.
- As you hum, visualize the vibrations traveling down your body, connecting with the vagus nerve and promoting relaxation and calmness.
- Take a few more deep breaths and then slowly open your eyes. Sit quietly for a moment, noticing how you feel after the meditation.

Singing and Chanting

Engaging in singing or chanting activities can stimulate the vagus nerve through the vibrations produced by vocal cords. Singing has been shown to increase heart rate variability, an indicator of vagal tone.

It can be as simple as singing along to your favorite songs, joining a choir or singing group, or practicing chanting mantras for a few minutes each day to stimulate the vagus nerve.

Humming Meditation

- Sit or stand comfortably with your back straight and relaxed.
- Take a few deep breaths to center yourself.
- Start humming, creating a soft, low-toned sound.
- Focus on the vibration in your chest and throat as you continue to hum.
- Imagine the sound traveling down your throat and vibrating through your body.
- Slowly increase the volume and intensity of your humming.
- Feel the vibration expanding throughout your body, resonating with your vagus nerve.
- Continue humming for a few minutes, allowing yourself to relax and let go of any tension.
- After a few minutes, gradually decrease the volume of your humming until it fades away.
- Take a moment to sit quietly and notice any changes in how you feel.

Vowel Chanting

- Find a comfortable seated position with your back straight and shoulders relaxed.
- Take a deep breath and exhale slowly to release any tension in your body.

- Begin chanting the vowel sounds: "A, E, I, O, U" in a continuous loop.
- Focus on each sound as it vibrates through your throat, chest, and abdomen.
- Feel the resonance of each vowel sound stimulating your vagus nerve.
- Experiment with varying the pitch and intensity of your chanting to find what feels most soothing.
- Allow the sounds to flow naturally, without forcing or straining.
- Continue chanting for a few minutes, allowing the vibrations to reverberate through your body.
- Gradually slow down the chanting until you come to a peaceful stop.
- Take a moment to sit in silence and notice any sensations or relaxation in your body and mind.

These exercises are designed to help you connect with and stimulate your vagus nerve through the power of sound and vibration.

Laughter Therapy

Laughter is a natural way to stimulate the vagus nerve and promote relaxation. The act of laughing triggers the release of endorphins and activates the parasympathetic nervous system.

It's simple too. Just incorporate laughter into your daily routine by watching comedies, sharing jokes with friends, or engaging in laughter yoga sessions. Or you can try these fun exercises:

Funny Faces

Have the participants make exaggerated and silly facial expressions for a minute or two. Encourage them to really go for it and make the most ridiculous faces they can think of. This exercise not only promotes laughter but also stimulates the muscles in the face, which can in turn stimulate the vagus nerve.

Story Time Laughter

Have the group sit in a circle and start telling a story, but with a twist - every time a certain word is mentioned (e.g. "banana"), everyone has to burst into laughter, no matter what. This unexpected laughter can activate the vagus nerve and help to create a fun and positive atmosphere. Rotate the word throughout the story to keep the laughter going.

Acupuncture

Acupuncture is an ancient Chinese medical practice that involves inserting thin needles into specific points on the body to promote healing and balance. According to traditional Chinese medicine (TCM) principles, acupuncture helps restore the flow of Qi (pronounced "chee"), the vital energy that flows through the body along meridian pathways.

From a modern perspective, acupuncture has gained popularity as a complementary therapy for managing various health conditions, including pain, anxiety, and digestion issues. The mechanism of action behind acupuncture's effectiveness is still a topic of research, but several theories have emerged to explain its benefits.

One of the proposed mechanisms of acupuncture is its ability to stimulate the release of endorphins, the body's natural painkillers. When the needles are inserted into specific acupuncture points, they trigger the release of endorphins, serotonin, and other neurotransmitters that help alleviate pain and improve mood.

Another theory suggests that acupuncture may modulate the body's nervous system, specifically the autonomic nervous system (ANS). The ANS comprises the sympathetic nervous system (fight or flight response) and the parasympathetic nervous system (rest and digest response). By stimulating certain acupuncture points, acupuncturists can help rebalance the ANS, promoting relaxation and stress reduction.

Now, let's dive into how acupuncture can help stimulate the vagus nerve.

Several acupuncture points along the body's meridians are believed to influence the vagus nerve indirectly. By targeting these points, acupuncturists can help regulate the activity of the vagus nerve, promoting a state of relaxation and reducing inflammation.

One of the key ways acupuncture stimulates the vagus nerve is through the activation of sensory fibers in the skin. When the acupuncture needles are inserted into specific points, they send signals to the brain, triggering a cascade of responses that ultimately lead to vagus nerve activation.

Research has shown that acupuncture can enhance vagal tone, which refers to the activity of the vagus nerve. Improved vagal tone is associated with better heart rate variability, indicating a healthier balance between the sympathetic and parasympathetic branches of the autonomic nervous system.

In addition to enhancing vagal tone, acupuncture has been found to reduce inflammation in the body. Chronic inflammation is linked to a range of health conditions, including autoimmune disorders, cardiovascular disease, and Alzheimer's disease. By stimulating the vagus nerve, acupuncture can help dampen the inflammatory response, promoting overall health and well-being.

Furthermore, acupuncture has been shown to promote the release of neurotransmitters like acetylcholine, which plays a key role in vagus nerve function. Acetylcholine is a neurotransmitter that helps regulate heart rate, digestion, and other autonomic functions. By boosting acetylcholine levels, acupuncture can support vagus nerve activity and improve overall nervous system function.

Overall, acupuncture offers a holistic approach to health and wellness by addressing the body's natural healing mechanisms. By stimulating the vagus nerve and modulating the autonomic nervous system, acupuncture can help improve various health conditions and promote a state of balance and well-being.

Medical Devices and Surgical Options

In recent years, there has been growing interest in the use of medical devices and surgical options to specifically target and enhance the function of the vagus nerve. While these shouldn't be your first port of call, let's talk about them to give you a fully-rounded impression of the vagus nerve and what you can do to simulate it.

Medical Devices for Vagus Nerve Stimulation

Vagus Nerve Stimulation (VNS) Therapy

We've already talked about this popular type of therapy, but let's sum it up here as it fits into this section very nicely.

Vagus Nerve Stimulation (VNS) therapy is a well-established treatment method for epilepsy and depression. It involves the implantation of a small device that delivers electrical impulses to the vagus nerve, helping to regulate abnormal brain activity and neurotransmitter levels. VNS therapy has been shown to be effective in reducing seizure frequency in epilepsy patients and improving mood in patients with treatment-resistant depression.

Transcutaneous Vagus Nerve Stimulation (tVNS)

Transcutaneous Vagus Nerve Stimulation (tVNS) is a non-invasive form of vagus nerve stimulation that involves applying electrical stimulation to the skin overlying the vagus nerve.

This method is used to modulate autonomic nervous system activity and has shown promise in treating conditions such as chronic pain, depression, and anxiety. tVNS devices are portable and can be used at home, making them a convenient option for patients seeking ongoing vagus nerve stimulation therapy.

Auricular Vagus Nerve Stimulation (aVNS)

Auricular Vagus Nerve Stimulation (aVNS) involves stimulating the vagus nerve through the ear using specialized devices. By targeting specific areas of the ear that are connected to the vagus nerve, aVNS can modulate autonomic nervous system function and promote relaxation and stress reduction.

This form of vagus nerve stimulation has been studied for its potential benefits in treating conditions such as PTSD, insomnia, and inflammatory disorders.

Implantable Vagus Nerve Stimulation Devices

Implantable vagus nerve stimulation devices are surgically implanted under the skin and provide continuous electrical stimulation to the vagus nerve. These devices are typically used in the treatment of epilepsy, depression, and chronic pain.

Implantable VNS devices have adjustable settings that allow healthcare providers to tailor the stimulation parameters to each individual patient's needs.

Surgical Options for Vagus Nerve Stimulation

Vagus Nerve Decompression

Vagus nerve decompression is a surgical procedure that involves relieving compression or irritation of the vagus nerve. This can be caused by surrounding structures, such as blood vessels or tumors, putting pressure on the nerve.

By decompressing the vagus nerve, surgeons can alleviate symptoms such as chronic cough, voice hoarseness, and swallowing difficulties.

Vagus Nerve Truncation

Vagus nerve truncation is a surgical procedure that involves cutting a portion of the vagus nerve to disrupt abnormal signaling patterns. This method is sometimes used in the treatment of severe cases of epilepsy or treatment-resistant depression where other therapies have been ineffective.

Vagus nerve truncation is a last-resort option and is only considered when all other treatment options have been exhausted.

Vagus Nerve Stimulation for Obesity

In recent years, vagus nerve stimulation has been explored as a potential treatment for obesity. Surgical options such as laparoscopic implantation of vagus nerve stimulators have been studied for their ability to reduce appetite and promote weight loss. These devices deliver electrical impulses to the vagus nerve, leading to decreased food intake and improved metabolism.

While still considered experimental, vagus nerve stimulation for obesity shows promise as a novel approach to combating this widespread health issue.

Vagus Nerve Stimulation for Inflammatory Disorders

Vagus nerve stimulation has also shown potential as a treatment for inflammatory disorders such as rheumatoid arthritis and inflammatory bowel disease. By modulating the activity of the vagus nerve, researchers believe that it may be possible to dampen the body's inflammatory response and reduce symptoms of these chronic conditions.

Surgical options for vagus nerve stimulation in inflammatory disorders are still in the early stages of research but hold promise for the future of immune-modulating therapies.

Medical devices and surgical options for stimulating and improving vagus nerve function offer a range of innovative approaches to treating a variety of health conditions. From vagus nerve stimulation therapy for epilepsy and depression to surgical interventions for obesity and inflammatory disorders, there are numerous possibilities for harnessing the power of the vagus nerve to enhance overall well-being.

As research continues to advance in this field, the development of more targeted and effective treatments for vagus nerve dysfunction holds promise for improving the quality of life for many patients in the future.

Chapter 8

The Mind-Body Connection

The mind-body connection is a fascinating and complex relationship. Let's dig deeper.

Our minds and bodies are not separate entities, but rather intricately intertwined, working in harmony to shape our experiences and perceptions of the world around us. The mind-body connection is a powerful force that influences every aspect of our lives, from our thoughts and emotions to our physical health and vitality.

As we delve deeper into the complexities of this connection, we begin to unravel the mysteries of how our thoughts and feelings can impact our physical health, and vice versa. The mind has the remarkable ability to influence the body's response to stress, leading to a cascade of physiological changes that can either enhance or detract from our well-being.

Chronic stress has been shown to have a profound impact on both our mental and physical health, leading to a host of conditions ranging from anxiety and depression to heart disease and chronic pain. By understanding how stress affects the body on a biological level, we can begin to take proactive steps to reduce its impact and promote overall well-being.

Exploring the mind-body connection also opens up a world of possibilities for enhancing our health and happiness through practices such as mindfulness, meditation, and yoga. These ancient practices have been shown to have profound effects on both the mind and body, promoting relaxation, stress reduction, and overall well-being.

In delving into the mind-body connection, we also explore the fascinating field of psychoneuroimmunology, which examines the intricate interplay between the mind, the nervous system, and the immune system. This emerging field of study sheds light on how our thoughts and emotions can influence our immune response, highlighting the powerful role that our mental state plays in shaping our physical health.

How the Vagus Nerve Mediates the Mind-Body Connection

The vagus nerve plays a crucial role in the parasympathetic nervous system, which is responsible for regulating many bodily functions at rest and during relaxation. But what makes the vagus nerve truly intriguing is its ability to bridge the gap between the mind and body, orchestrating a complex network of communication that influences our overall well-being.

One of the key ways in which the vagus nerve impacts the mind-body connection is through its role in the body's stress response. When we experience stress, whether it be physical or emotional, the sympathetic nervous system is activated, leading to the familiar "fight or flight" response. However, the vagus nerve acts as a counterbalance to this stress response by initiating the body's relaxation response through its parasympathetic function. This helps bring our bodies back to a state of equilibrium after the stress has passed, promoting relaxation and reducing the impact of chronic stress on our health.

Furthermore, the vagus nerve is intricately linked to our emotional well-being. Research has shown that the vagus nerve plays a significant role in regulating our mood and emotional responses. When the vagus nerve is functioning optimally, it can help modulate our emotions, promote feelings of calmness, and increase our resilience to emotional challenges. This connection between the vagus nerve and our emotional state highlights the important role it plays in the mind-body relationship.

Moreover, the vagus nerve is also involved in the gut-brain axis, the bidirectional communication pathway between the gut and the brain. As it innervates many of the organs in the abdomen, including the stomach and intestines, the vagus nerve plays a crucial role in regulating digestion and influencing our gut health. Interestingly, emerging research suggests that the health of the gut microbiome, which is the community of microorganisms living in our digestive system, can impact the function of the vagus nerve and, in turn, influence our mood and cognitive function. This further underscores the intricate interplay between the vagus nerve, our gut health, and our overall well-being.

In addition to its role in stress regulation, emotional well-being, and gut health, the vagus nerve is also involved in promoting restorative sleep. Adequate sleep is essential for our physical and mental health, and the vagus nerve contributes to the regulation of our sleep-wake cycle. By promoting relaxation and reducing stress, the vagus nerve helps prepare our bodies for restful sleep, allowing us to recharge and rejuvenate both our mind and body.

There's more! The vagus nerve has been implicated in the body's inflammatory response. Inflammation is a natural process that helps the body fight off infections and heal from injuries. However, chronic inflammation has been linked to a variety of health issues, including autoimmune diseases, heart disease, and mood disorders. The vagus nerve plays a crucial role in regulating inflammation by communicating with the immune system and exerting anti-inflammatory effects. This connection highlights the vital role of the vagus nerve in maintaining a balanced immune response and protecting our overall health.

So, as we can see, the vagus nerve serves as a vital link between the mind and body, orchestrating a symphony of communication that influences our overall health and well-being. From regulating our stress response and emotional state to promoting gut health and restorative sleep, the vagus nerve plays a multifaceted role in maintaining the delicate balance between mind and body.

Practice to Enhance Vagal Tone

We've covered a few practices to help stimulate the vagus nerve, but what about affecting your vagal tone in general? Some of this overlaps, but there are many different exercises you can try within each practice. So, if you've heard some in the last section, let's give you even more exercises that can focus on vagal tone in particular and not just general stimulation.

The key thing to remember is that you need to practice these regularly. The more you practice, the more effect you'll have on your vagal tone over the long term.

First, remember that enhancing vagal tone is like giving your body's natural relaxation system a tune-up. A healthy vagus nerve promotes better digestion, reduced inflammation, lower stress levels, improved mood, and overall well-being.

Here are some practices to help boost your vagal tone:

Deep Breathing for Vagal Tone

We know that slow, deep breathing stimulates the vagus nerve and activates the relaxation response. Here are two advanced deep breathing techniques that focus on improving vagal tone in particular.

Resonant Frequency Breathing

This technique involves finding your individual resonant breathing frequency, which is typically around 5-7 breaths per minute.

- Sit or lie down comfortably, and take slow, deep breaths in and out through the nose.
- Gradually decrease the length of each breath cycle while maintaining a smooth and even rhythm.
- Use a timer or a breathing app to help maintain consistency and gradually increase the duration of the practice over time.

Resonant-frequency breathing has been shown to increase heart rate variability and improve vagal tone.

Extended Exhalation Breathing

This technique involves extending the exhale phase of your breathing cycle to stimulate the parasympathetic nervous system and enhance vagal tone.

- Start by inhaling deeply and slowly through the nose for a count of 4, then exhale even more slowly and completely through the mouth for a count of 8.
- Focus on completely emptying the lungs and engaging the diaphragm to push out every last bit of air.
- Repeat this pattern for several minutes, gradually increasing the length of the exhalation as you become more comfortable with the practice.

Extended-exhalation breathing can help reduce stress and anxiety while promoting relaxation and vagal tone improvement.

Yoga and Tai Chi

These mind-body practices promote relaxation, mindfulness, and gentle movement, all of which can stimulate the vagus nerve.

Here are four particularly useful yoga poses, followed by two Tai Chi exercises.

Bridge Pose (Setu Bandhasana)

This pose helps stimulate the vagus nerve by opening the chest and throat area, which can help regulate heart rate and blood pressure.

To do the bridge pose, also known as Setu Bandhasana in yoga, you can follow these steps:

- Lie on your back with your knees bent and your feet flat on the floor, hip-width apart.
- Press your feet into the floor as you lift your hips up toward the ceiling.
- Interlace your fingers underneath your back and press your arms into the ground for support.
- Make sure your thighs are parallel to each other and your knees are directly above your ankles.
- Keep your neck and head relaxed on the mat.
- Hold the pose for a few breaths, then slowly lower your hips back down to the starting position.

Supported Shoulderstand (Salamba Sarvangasana)

This inversion pose can improve vagal tone by promoting relaxation and reducing stress. It also helps to calm the nervous system and improve circulation.

Here's a step-by-step guide on how to do the supported Shoulderstand pose:

- Start by laying down on your back with your arms by your sides, palms facing down.
- Bend your knees and bring your feet up towards your buttocks.

- Press your hands into the floor and lift your legs up towards the ceiling, using your core strength.
- Continue to lift your legs until they are perpendicular to the floor.
- Support your lower back with your hands, keeping your elbows close to your body.
- Slowly walk your hands down your back towards your shoulder blades, lifting your hips higher as you do so.
- Find a comfortable position with your hands supporting your lower back and your legs extended straight up towards the ceiling.
- Keep your neck and head in a neutral position, with your gaze towards your toes.
- Hold the pose for 5–10 breaths, breathing deeply and maintaining a steady foundation with your hands supporting your back.
- To come out of the pose, slowly release your hands from your back and gently roll down one vertebra at a time until your legs are back on the floor.

Legs Up the Wall Pose (Viparita Karani)

This gentle inversion pose can help stimulate the vagus nerve and improve circulation. It also promotes relaxation and reduces anxiety, which can have a positive impact on vagal tone.

Here's how to do the pose:

- Find a clear wall space: Locate a wall with enough space for you to lie down comfortably with your legs extended.
- Sit close to the wall: Sit sideways next to the wall with your hip touching it.
- Lie down on your back: Slowly lower your back to the ground while extending your legs up the wall. Your hips should be touching the wall, and your legs should be straight up.

- Adjust your position: Scoot your hips closer to the wall if you need to until you feel comfortable. Your body should be in an L-shape, with your legs supported by the wall and your torso resting on the ground.
- Relax and breathe: Close your eyes, relax your arms by your sides, and focus on your breath. Stay in this pose for 5–15 minutes, breathing deeply and allowing your body to relax.
- Release the pose: To come out of the pose, gently bend your knees towards your chest, roll onto one side, and slowly sit up.

Reclining Bound Angle Pose (Supta Baddha Konasana)

This restorative pose opens the chest and abdomen, helping to stimulate the vagus nerve. It also promotes relaxation and deep breathing, which can improve vagal tone and overall well-being.

Here is how you can do the Reclining Bound Angle Pose (Supta Baddha Konasana):

- Begin by sitting on the floor with your legs extended in front of you.
- Bend your knees and bring the soles of your feet together, letting your knees fall out to the sides.
- Slowly lean back, supporting yourself with your hands as you lower your back to the floor. You can use a pillow or yoga block under your back for support if needed.
- Allow your arms to relax by your sides, palms facing up.
- Close your eyes and focus on your breath, allowing your body to relax and sink deeper into the pose.
- Stay in this pose for 5–10 minutes, breathing deeply and feeling the opening in your hips and groin area.
- When you are ready to come out of the pose, gently bring your knees together and roll to one side before slowly coming up to a seated position.

Remember to listen to your body and only go as far into the pose as feels comfortable for you.

Here are two Tai Chi exercises that can help improve vagal tone:

Breathing Exercise with Tai Chi Movement

- Start by standing in a relaxed posture with your feet shoulder-width apart and your knees slightly bent.
- Take a few deep breaths to center yourself.
- Begin a simple Tai Chi movement, such as "Cloud Hands."
- Keep your back straight, shoulders relaxed, and arms at your sides.
- Begin by shifting your weight to your right leg while simultaneously turning your upper body to the right.
- Lift your left hand up to shoulder height with your palm facing down, and extend your right hand downwards with your palm facing up.
- Slowly shift your weight to your left leg as you bring your right hand up to shoulder height with your palm facing down and extend your left hand downwards with your palm facing up. Your body should now be facing the left side.
- Continue this fluid motion of shifting your weight from side to side while moving your hands in a circular motion. Imagine that you are gently pushing clouds away as you move gracefully from one side to the other.
- As you practice, focus on your breathing and try to synchronize your movements with each inhale and exhale. Remember to keep your movements smooth and controlled, maintaining a sense of calm and relaxation throughout.
- Repeat the Cloud Hands movement for several minutes, allowing your body to flow naturally with the gentle rhythm of the exercise.

Meditative Standing Exercise

- Stand in a comfortable and stable position with your feet rooted to the ground.

- Close your eyes and focus on your breath, allowing it to become slow and deep.
- Imagine a sense of calm and relaxation spreading throughout your body as you continue breathing deeply.
- Engage in gentle swaying or rocking movements, mimicking the flow of energy within your body.

This meditative standing practice can help activate the vagus nerve and promote a state of relaxation and well-being.

Meditation

Mindfulness meditation has been shown to increase vagal tone. Take a few minutes each day to sit quietly, focus on your breath, and cultivate a sense of calm and awareness. This can have a profound impact on your vagal tone over time.

Here are two advanced meditation techniques that are ideal for vagal tone improvement.

Humming Meditation

- Sit comfortably in a quiet space.
- Close your eyes and take a few deep breaths to center yourself. Begin to lightly hum a simple, soothing melody.
- Focus on the vibration of the humming in your throat and chest.
- As you continue to hum, bring your awareness to the sensations in your body and any emotions that may arise.
- The vibrations from the humming can help stimulate the vagus nerve, which in turn can enhance the vagal tone.
- Practice this meditation for at least 10–15 minutes daily for optimal benefits.

Gut-Brain Connection Meditation

- Find a quiet and comfortable place to sit or lie down.
- Close your eyes and bring your awareness to your gut area.
- Visualize a warm, healing light radiating from your gut and spreading throughout your body.
- As you focus on this light, imagine it communicating with your brain, establishing a harmonious connection between your gut and brain.

This visualization practice can help enhance the communication between the gut and brain, which is closely tied to the vagus nerve and can positively impact the vagal tone. Practice this meditation regularly to strengthen the gut-brain connection and improve overall well-being.

Cold Exposure

We know that cold showers or immersion in cold water can activate the vagus nerve, but advanced techniques done regularly can increase vagal tone. Start slowly and build up your tolerance over time. Even splashing cold water on your face can have a similar effect.

Ice Pack on the Neck

Place a cold ice pack on the back of your neck for 3-5 minutes. The vagus nerve runs close to the surface in this area, and the cold temperature can help stimulate and tone the nerve.

Immersion in Cold Water

If you have access to a cold body of water, like a pool or natural body of water, consider immersing yourself for a short period of time. Start with shorter durations and gradually increase as your body adjusts. The cold water immersion can trigger the body's "dive reflex," activating the vagus nerve and improving its tone.

Remember to start slowly and gradually build up your tolerance to cold exposure exercises to avoid any negative effects. Over time, these exercises can help improve vagal tone and contribute to overall health and well-being.

Heart Rate Variability Biofeedback

This technique involves monitoring your heart rate variability, which is influenced by your vagal tone. By practicing coherence techniques through biofeedback devices, you can train your body to regulate stress responses and improve vagal tone.

Heart Rate Variability (HRV) is a measure of the variation in time intervals between heartbeats, reflecting the dynamic interplay between the sympathetic (fight-or-flight) and parasympathetic (rest-and-digest) branches of the autonomic nervous system. A high HRV indicates a healthy autonomic nervous system, adaptive stress response, and better overall health, whereas a low HRV may be indicative of stress, poor health, or decreased vagal tone.

So, how does it work?

HRV biofeedback involves monitoring and controlling heart rate variability patterns through real-time feedback mechanisms. By using specialized biofeedback devices or apps that measure HRV, individuals can learn to regulate their breathing and heart rate to improve vagal tone and achieve a state of coherence characterized by synchronized physiological rhythms and enhanced well-being.

Practicing HRV Biofeedback

- Find a quiet and comfortable place to sit or lie down.
- Begin by focusing on your breath, taking slow and deep breaths in through your nose and out through your mouth.
- Use a biofeedback device or app to monitor your heart rate variability in real-time.
- Adjust your breathing pattern to increase the variability between heartbeats, aiming for a smooth and coherent rhythm.
- Visualize positive emotions or experiences to enhance the coherence of your heart rate variability patterns.
- Practice HRV biofeedback regularly for at least 10–20 minutes a day to improve vagal tone and overall well-being.

Intermittent Fasting

Intermittent fasting (IF) has gained immense popularity in recent years as a dietary strategy that involves cycling between periods of eating and fasting. This approach is not just about weight loss; it has been touted for its potential health benefits, including improving vagal tone.

Intermittent fasting is not a diet in the traditional sense but rather a pattern of eating that alternates between periods of eating and fasting. Unlike traditional diets that focus on what to eat, intermittent fasting is more about when to eat. It does not specify which foods to eat but emphasizes the timing of meals.

There are several different methods of intermittent fasting, with the most common ones being time-restricted feeding, alternate-day fasting, and the 5:2 diet.

- **Time-Restricted Feeding (TRF):** Time-restricted feeding involves limiting your daily eating window to a specific number of hours, typically between 6 to 8 hours. The remaining hours of the day are considered the fasting period. For example, if you choose an 8-hour eating window from 12 pm to 8 pm, you would fast for the remaining 16 hours.

- **Alternate-Day Fasting:** This method involves alternating between days of regular eating and days of fasting. On fasting days, individuals may consume very few calories or nothing at all, while on non-fasting days, they eat normally.

- **5:2 Diet:** The 5:2 diet involves eating normally for five days of the week and restricting calorie intake to around 500-600 calories on two non-consecutive days. This approach allows for flexibility in choosing the fasting days.

Each of these methods has its own benefits and challenges, and individuals may choose the one that best fits their lifestyle and preferences.

Improving Vagal Tone through Intermittent Fasting

Intermittent fasting has been shown to positively influence vagal tone through several mechanisms:

- **Reduced Inflammation:** Fasting has been found to reduce inflammation in the body, which can have a direct impact on vagal tone. Chronic inflammation can impair vagal function, so by decreasing inflammation through fasting, vagal tone can be improved.
- **Enhanced Autophagy:** Autophagy is a process in which the body breaks down and recycles damaged cells and proteins. Fasting promotes autophagy, which not only helps in cellular repair but also supports vagal tone by maintaining the health of nerve cells.
- **Improved Gut Health:** The gut-brain axis plays a significant role in vagal tone, as the vagus nerve communicates bidirectionally between the gut and the brain. Intermittent fasting has been shown to promote a healthy gut microbiome, which in turn can positively influence vagal tone.
- **Decreased Oxidative Stress:** Fasting induces a state of mild stress in the body, leading to the activation of various cellular repair mechanisms. By reducing oxidative stress, intermittent fasting can support overall nerve health, including vagal tone.
- **Better Blood Sugar Regulation:** Intermittent fasting can help regulate blood sugar levels by improving insulin sensitivity. Stable blood sugar levels are essential for maintaining vagal tone, as fluctuations in glucose levels can impact nerve function.

By incorporating intermittent fasting into your lifestyle, you may experience improvements in vagal tone, which can have a ripple effect on overall health and well-being.

Remember to consult with a healthcare provider or nutritionist before making any significant changes to your diet, especially if you have underlying health conditions.

Gargling

Believe it or not, gargling with warm salt water can also help improve vagal tone, which is essential for maintaining a healthy nervous system and overall well-being.

Here are two exercises you can do to improve vagal tone through gargling:

Salt Water Gargle

- Mix a teaspoon of salt in a glass of warm water.
- Take a sip of the solution and tilt your head back slightly.
- Gargle the water in your mouth for about 30 seconds before spitting it out.
- Repeat this a few times to stimulate the vagus nerve and promote relaxation.

Sing or Hum While Gargling

Another effective way to enhance vagal tone through gargling is to incorporate singing or humming. After doing a salt water gargle, try singing a simple tune or humming a melody while keeping the water in your mouth. The vibrations created by vocalization, combined with the act of gargling, can further stimulate the vagus nerve.

Remember, consistency is key when it comes to enhancing vagal tone. Incorporate these practices into your daily routine, listen to your body, and be patient with yourself as you work towards improving your overall well-being through increased vagal tone. Your body and mind will thank you for it!

The Importance of Emotional and Psychological Health

Emotional and psychological health are essential components of overall well-being. All too often, we focus simply on physical health, but these elements are just as vital. After all, they are the pillars upon which we build our resilience, cope with challenges, and navigate life's ups and downs.

Let's dig a bit deeper to understand the profound significance of emotional and psychological health and explore why nurturing these aspects of ourselves is crucial for a fulfilling and balanced life.

To start, let's consider the interconnected nature of emotional and psychological health. Emotional health pertains to our ability to recognize, express, and manage our feelings in a healthy way. It involves being self-aware, understanding our emotions, and effectively coping with stress. On the other hand, psychological health encompasses our cognitive and emotional well-being, including our thoughts, beliefs, and attitudes. It involves finding meaning in life, building healthy relationships, and maintaining a positive outlook.

Together, emotional and psychological health shape our mental resilience and influence how we perceive and interact with the world around us. When these aspects are nurtured and prioritized, we are better equipped to handle life's challenges, bounce back from setbacks, and cultivate a sense of inner peace.

It is important to recognize the impact of emotional and psychological health on our physical well-being. Research has shown that chronic stress, anxiety, and other negative emotions can contribute to a range of physical health issues, such as cardiovascular disease, a weakened immune system, and digestive problems. By taking care of our emotional and psychological well-being, we can reduce the risk of developing such health issues and promote overall wellness.

Moreover, emotional and psychological health plays a significant role in our relationships with others. When we are in tune with our emotions and have a strong sense of self-awareness, we are better able to communicate effectively, empathize with others, and establish healthy boundaries. This, in turn, fosters deeper connections, enhances interpersonal relationships, and promotes a sense of belonging and community.

Cultivating emotional and psychological health also leads to improved decision-making and problem-solving abilities. When we are emotionally balanced and mentally clear, we are better equipped to think rationally, consider different perspectives, and make sound choices. This not only benefits our personal lives but also our professional endeavors, as we become more effective leaders, collaborators, and innovators.

One of the key aspects of nurturing emotional and psychological health is practicing self-care. This involves engaging in activities that promote relaxation, self-reflection, and emotional release. Whether it's meditating, journaling, exercising, or spending time in nature, taking time for oneself is crucial for maintaining a healthy emotional and psychological state.

Another essential component of emotional and psychological health is seeking support when needed. It's important to remember that asking for help is a sign of strength, not weakness. Whether it's talking to a trusted friend, seeking guidance from a therapist, or joining a support group, reaching out to others can provide valuable insight, perspective, and comfort during challenging times.

In addition to self-care and seeking support, developing emotional intelligence is paramount for nurturing emotional and psychological health. Emotional intelligence involves recognizing, understanding, and managing our own emotions, as well as being attuned to the emotions of others. By honing our emotional intelligence skills, we can enhance our self-awareness, interpersonal relationships, and overall well-being.

Furthermore, practicing mindfulness is a powerful tool for promoting emotional and psychological health. Mindfulness involves being present at the moment without judgment or distraction and observing one's thoughts and feelings with awareness. By incorporating mindfulness practices into our daily routines, such as mindful breathing, meditation, or body scans, we can cultivate a sense of calm, clarity, and inner peace.

If you're feeling like your emotional or psychological health is taking a hit, it's important to take action and seek support. Remember, it's absolutely okay not to be okay sometimes. Working on your vagal tone is one thing to do, but here are some other steps you can take. You'll find that a lot of them overlap with vagal nerve stimulation, which shows just how easy this practice is to incorporate into your daily life.

- **Reach out to someone:** Whether it's a friend, family member, or mental health professional, sharing how you're feeling can be incredibly relieving.
- **Practice self-care:** Allocate time for activities that bring you joy and relaxation. This could be anything from going for a walk in nature, reading a book, or treating yourself to a nice meal.
- **Get moving:** Exercise is a wonderful way of boosting your mood and clearing your mind. Even a short walk or some gentle stretching can make a difference.
- **Explore mindfulness techniques:** Meditation, deep breathing exercises, or even just taking a moment to focus on the present can help calm your racing thoughts.
- **Consider professional help:** If you find that your emotional struggles persist, seek out a therapist or counselor who can provide invaluable support and guidance.

Remember, it's okay to not have all the answers right away. Allow yourself the time and space to navigate your emotions and be kind to yourself along the way. You're not alone in this journey towards better emotional well-being.

Chapter 9

Diet, Nutrition, and the Vagus Nerve

Imagine the vagus nerve as a superhighway of communication between the gut and the brain, influencing everything from digestion to mood. But did you know that the foods we consume can actually influence the health and activity of this vital nerve? It's like giving your vagus nerve a daily dose of nourishment and care through the foods on your plate.

Throughout this chapter, we will explore the impact of various nutrients, vitamins, and dietary choices on optimizing vagus nerve function. From probiotic-rich foods that promote gut health to anti-inflammatory nutrients that calm the nervous system, we'll uncover the keys to supporting a healthy vagal tone through mindful eating habits.

Get ready to empower yourself with practical insights and tips that can enhance both your physical well-being and mental health. It's time to feed your brain and gut with knowledge that nourishes from within.

The Impact of Diet on Vagal Tone

One of the factors that can influence vagal tone is diet. The foods we eat can either support or hinder the function of the vagus nerve, ultimately affecting our overall well-being. By making conscious choices about what we put into our bodies, we can positively impact our vagal tone and promote better health.

A Good Diet and Vagal Tone

A nutrient-dense diet rich in fruits, vegetables, whole grains, lean proteins, and healthy fats can have a positive impact on vagal tone. These foods provide essential nutrients that support the health of the vagus nerve and the parasympathetic nervous system. Here are some key components of a good diet that can help improve vagal tone:

- **Omega-3 Fatty Acids:** Foods rich in omega-3 fatty acids, such as fatty fish (salmon, mackerel, and sardines), flaxseeds, chia seeds, and walnuts, have anti-inflammatory properties that support vagal tone. Omega-3 fatty acids have been shown to reduce inflammation and improve heart rate variability, which is a marker of vagal tone.
- **Fiber-Rich Foods:** Fiber is essential for gut health, and a healthy gut is crucial for optimal vagal tone. Foods high in fiber, such as fruits, vegetables, legumes, and whole grains, support the growth of beneficial gut bacteria, which play a role in regulating the parasympathetic nervous system.
- **Antioxidant-Rich Foods:** Antioxidants help protect cells from damage caused by free radicals and oxidative stress, which can impact vagal tone. Foods like berries, dark leafy greens, nuts, seeds, and green tea are rich in antioxidants and can support overall nerve health.
- **Probiotic-Rich Foods:** Probiotics are beneficial bacteria that support gut health and play a role in regulating the vagus nerve. Fermented foods like yogurt, kefir, kimchi, sauerkraut, and kombucha can help maintain a healthy balance of gut bacteria and support vagal tone.
- **Balanced Macronutrients:** A diet that includes a balance of carbohydrates, proteins, and fats provides the body with the energy and nutrients it needs to function optimally. Maintaining stable blood sugar levels through balanced meals can help support vagal tone and overall nervous system health.

- **Adequate Hydration:** Staying hydrated is essential for overall health, including optimal nervous system function. Dehydration can affect nerve signaling, including the vagus nerve. Drinking an adequate amount of water throughout the day can support a healthy vagal tone.

Incorporating these dietary components into your daily eating habits can help support a healthy vagal tone and overall well-being. Remember, a good diet is not just about what you eat but also how you eat. Eating mindfully, chewing your food thoroughly, and enjoying meals in a relaxed environment can further support optimal vagal tone.

A Bad Diet and Vagal Tone

On the flip side, a poor diet high in processed foods, refined sugars, unhealthy fats, and artificial additives can have a negative impact on vagal tone. These dietary factors can contribute to inflammation, oxidative stress, and gut dysbiosis, all of which can disrupt the functioning of the vagus nerve and the parasympathetic nervous system. Here's how a bad diet can affect vagal tone:

- **Inflammatory Foods:** Processed foods, sugary treats, refined grains, and unhealthy fats can promote inflammation in the body, including the nervous system. Chronic inflammation can impair vagal tone and disrupt the balance of the autonomic nervous system, leading to dysregulation of bodily functions.
- **Sugar and High-Glycemic Foods:** Consuming excessive amounts of sugar and high-glycemic foods can spike blood sugar levels, leading to insulin resistance and metabolic dysfunction. Poor blood sugar control can impact nerve health and vagal tone, affecting the body's ability to relax and recover.
- **Artificial Additives:** Artificial sweeteners, preservatives, colorings, and flavorings found in processed foods can have negative effects on gut health and overall nerve function. These additives may disrupt the gut microbiome, leading to dysbiosis and compromising vagal tone.

- **Lack of Nutrient-Dense Foods:** A diet lacking in essential nutrients like omega-3 fatty acids, antioxidants, vitamins, and minerals can deprive the body of the building blocks needed for optimal nerve function. Without proper nourishment, the vagus nerve may not function at its best, affecting the parasympathetic tone.
- **Excessive Caffeine and Alcohol:** While moderate consumption of caffeine and alcohol may not have significant negative effects on vagal tone, excessive intake can disrupt the balance of the autonomic nervous system. Both stimulants can interfere with sleep, stress levels, and overall nervous system function.

If your current diet includes a lot of processed foods, sugary snacks, and unhealthy fats, it may be beneficial to make gradual changes towards a more nutrient-dense, whole foods-based diet. By reducing your intake of inflammatory and processed foods and focusing on whole, natural foods, you can support your vagal tone and overall nervous system function.

Put simply, the connection between diet and vagal tone highlights the importance of nourishing your body with wholesome, nutrient-rich foods that support optimal nerve function. Remember, small changes in your eating habits can have a big impact on your health, so choose foods that support a healthy vagal tone and a balanced autonomic nervous system.

Good vs. Bad Eating Habits

It's not only about what you eat but also how you eat it. By adopting good eating habits and avoiding bad ones, we can positively influence our vagal tone and experience improved health and vitality.

Let's delve into some factors that can affect vagal tone through our eating habits:

Good Eating Habits

- **Mindful Eating:** One of the best habits you can cultivate is mindful eating. Being present and focused during meals can help signal to your body that it's time to rest and digest. Slow down, savor each bite, and pay attention to your body's hunger and fullness cues.
- **Balanced Meals:** Eating a well-balanced diet rich in nutrients is essential for supporting overall health, including vagal tone. Ensure your meals contain a good mix of protein, healthy fats, complex carbohydrates, vitamins, and minerals to provide your body with the fuel it needs to function optimally.
- **Probiotic-Rich Foods:** Including probiotic-rich foods in your diet can benefit gut health, which is closely linked to vagal tone. Fermented foods like yogurt, kimchi, sauerkraut, and kefir can help maintain a healthy balance of gut bacteria, promoting a better vagal tone.
- **Hydration:** We've said it once; we'll say it again. Staying adequately hydrated is key for supporting your body's overall functioning, including the vagus nerve. Aim to drink plenty of water throughout the day to keep your body properly hydrated and maintain optimal vagal tone.
- **Regular Meal Times:** Establishing regular meal times can help regulate your body's internal clock and promote a sense of routine. Consistency in when you eat can support healthy digestion and signal to your body that it's time for nourishment and rest.

Bad Eating Habits

- **Overeating:** Consuming large portions of food in one sitting can put stress on your digestive system and may negatively impact your vagal tone. Overeating can lead to discomfort, bloating, and sluggishness, affecting the body's ability to efficiently process nutrients.

- **Excessive Caffeine:** While a moderate amount of caffeine can provide a temporary energy boost, consuming too much caffeine can overstimulate the nervous system and potentially affect vagal tone. Be mindful of your caffeine intake and consider opting for decaffeinated options or herbal teas.
- **Skipping Meals:** Irregular meal patterns, such as skipping meals or going for long periods without eating, can disrupt the body's natural rhythms and impact vagal tone. Consistent meal times signal to your body that it's time for nourishment and can support healthy digestion. However, there is some suggestion that intermittent fasting may actually help the vagus nerve. This is something you need to balance carefully and understand before you try it. Overall, regular meals are generally the better option.
- **High Sugar Intake:** Diets high in refined sugars and sugary beverages can lead to blood sugar spikes and crashes, affecting energy levels and potentially impacting vagal tone. Opt for natural sources of sweetness, like fruits, to satisfy your sweet tooth without compromising your health.
- **Eating Late at Night:** Consuming heavy meals late at night can disrupt your body's natural sleep-wake cycle and digestive processes. Late-night eating may lead to indigestion, reflux, and discomfort, potentially affecting your vagal tone and overall well-being.

By incorporating good eating habits and minimizing bad ones, you can support a healthy vagal tone and promote overall wellness. Remember that every small change you make towards a healthier diet and lifestyle can have a significant impact on your body's ability to function optimally. Stay mindful, stay balanced, and nourish yourself with foods that support your well-being.

How Crash Diets and Binge Eating Affect the Vagus Nerve

Yo-yo dieting, unsustainable dieting, crash dieting, and binge eating can have a significant impact on the vagus nerve, which plays a crucial role in regulating various bodily functions. Unfortunately, we live in a society that encourages us to follow diets and try to fit into a so-called "acceptable" body type.

Put simply, you should forget about all of that, but to help you, let's look at how these unhealthy eating patterns can negatively affect the vagus nerve and, consequently, overall well-being:

Yo-yo Dieting

Yo-yo dieting, also known as weight cycling, involves repeatedly losing and gaining weight through cycles of restrictive eating and subsequent overeating. This pattern of fluctuating weight can lead to chronic inflammation, which can impact the vagus nerve's function. Inflammation in the body can disrupt communication between the brain and the gut, affecting satiety signals and potentially leading to dysregulation of appetite and metabolism.

Unsustainable Dieting

Unsustainable dieting practices, such as extreme calorie restriction or following fad diets that lack essential nutrients, can deprive the body of the fuel it needs to function optimally. Inadequate intake of nutrients can compromise the health of the vagus nerve, which relies on a balance of vitamins and minerals for proper functioning.

Nutrient deficiencies can impair neurotransmitter production and signal transmission along the vagus nerve, impacting digestion, heart rate, and mood regulation.

Crash Dieting

Crash diets, characterized by rapid and drastic weight loss achieved through severely reduced calorie intake, can trigger stress responses in the body. Stress activates the sympathetic nervous system, which counteracts the parasympathetic activities controlled by the vagus nerve.

Prolonged stress from crash dieting can lead to chronic dysregulation of the vagus nerve, disrupting digestive processes and contributing to symptoms like bloating, constipation, and acid reflux.

Binge Eating

Binge eating episodes involve consuming large quantities of food in a short period, often accompanied by feelings of guilt and loss of control. The rapid influx of calories and macronutrients during binge eating can overload the digestive system and trigger inflammation, which can impair vagus nerve function.

Chronic binge eating may disrupt the brain-gut axis, weakening the connection between the central nervous system and the gastrointestinal tract, leading to irregular appetite regulation and emotional eating patterns.

These detrimental effects on the vagus nerve can manifest in various symptoms, such as digestive issues (e.g., bloating, abdominal pain, constipation), irregular heart rate, mood disturbances, and disruptions in hunger cues and fullness signals. Long-term damage to the vagus nerve resulting from yo-yo dieting, unsustainable dieting, crash dieting, and binge eating can impact overall health and well-being.

It is essential to prioritize sustainable and balanced eating habits that nourish the body and support vagus nerve health. Incorporating nutrient-dense foods, practicing mindful eating, and establishing a healthy relationship with food can promote proper vagus nerve function and overall wellness. Remember, consistency and moderation are key to fostering a harmonious connection between the brain, gut, and vagus nerve.

Chapter 10

Lifestyle Changes for Vagus Nerve Health

In the fast-paced world we live in, prioritizing our health and well-being can often take a backseat to our busy schedules. But what if we told you that making a few simple lifestyle changes could have a significant impact on one of the key players in our body's nervous system - the vagus nerve?

While altering ingrained habits may not always be a walk in the park, rest assured that it is indeed possible with some mindful effort and dedication. In this chapter, we'll explore how taking steps to support and nurture your vagus nerve through lifestyle modifications can lead to profound benefits for your overall health and well-being.

Stress Management Techniques

Stress is an insidious force that can wreak havoc on both our mental and physical well-being, yet its effects are often underestimated or dismissed. From its detrimental impact on our immune system to its role in the development of chronic conditions like heart disease and diabetes, stress is a silent but potent adversary that demands our attention and understanding.

Why is stress bad for you? The answer lies in the intricate interplay between our minds and bodies. When we experience stress, our bodies kick into high gear, initiating the "fight or flight" response that has been essential for human survival throughout evolution. This response, orchestrated by the sympathetic nervous system, floods our bodies with adrenaline and cortisol, preparing us to confront or flee from perceived threats. While this response can be life-saving in short bursts, chronic stress leads to a perpetual state of activation that takes a toll on our health.

The mechanisms behind why stress is bad for us are manifold. Firstly, prolonged exposure to stress hormones like cortisol can impair the functioning of our immune system, making us more susceptible to infections and illnesses. Additionally, chronic stress can contribute to the development of inflammation throughout the body, a key driver of various diseases including arthritis, asthma, and even cancer.

Moreover, stress has a profound impact on our cardiovascular system, increasing the risk of hypertension, heart disease, and stroke. The constant barrage of stress hormones can elevate blood pressure, promote the buildup of plaque in the arteries, and disrupt the balance of cholesterol in our bloodstream. Over time, these changes can have grave consequences for our heart health and overall well-being.

But why does stress happen in the first place? Our modern lifestyles, with their relentless pace and pressures, can be a breeding ground for stress. Whether it's looming deadlines at work, financial worries, relationship conflicts, or health concerns, the sources of stress are endless and ubiquitous. Our brains, wired to detect and respond to threats, interpret these stressors as dangers to be dealt with, triggering the body's stress response.

Within the body, chronic stress sets off a cascade of physiological changes that can have far-reaching effects on our health. The hypothalamic-pituitary-adrenal (HPA) axis, a crucial component of our stress response system, becomes dysregulated with chronic stress. The hypothalamus in the brain signals the pituitary gland to release adrenocorticotropic hormone (ACTH), which in turn prompts the adrenal glands to release cortisol. These chronically elevated cortisol levels can disrupt various bodily functions, from immune regulation to metabolism.

One fascinating aspect of the stress response is the role of the vagus nerve, a key player in the body's parasympathetic nervous system.

The vagus nerve plays a crucial role in regulating our body's relaxation response. When we are stressed, the vagus nerve can become compromised, leading to a reduced ability to counteract the activation of the sympathetic nervous system.

The vagus nerve is instrumental in modulating inflammation, with its branches reaching various organs, including the heart, lungs, and digestive system. When the vagus nerve is functioning optimally, it helps to keep inflammation in check and promotes a state of calm and balance in the body. However, chronic stress can dampen vagal tone, increasing the risk of inflammation and its associated health issues.

In addition to its role in inflammation, the vagus nerve is also involved in the regulation of heart rate, digestion, and mood. A strong vagal tone is associated with a slower heart rate, better digestion, and improved emotional resilience. By contrast, a weakened vagal tone resulting from chronic stress can lead to heart rhythm abnormalities, gastrointestinal disturbances, and an increased susceptibility to mood disorders like anxiety and depression.

That leads us nicely to how to manage stress.

Stress management is essential for maintaining our mental and physical well-being in today's fast-paced world. Here are some practical and proven strategies to help you combat stress:

Deep Breathing Exercises

One of the simplest yet most effective stress management techniques is deep breathing. By focusing on your breath and taking slow, deep breaths, you can activate your body's relaxation response, reducing anxiety and slowing down your heart rate.

We've already given you several deep breathing exercises throughout this book so far, and any of those will work to help you reduce stress. The key is consistency.

Progressive Muscle Relaxation

This technique involves tensing and then releasing each muscle group in your body, starting from your toes and working your way up to your head. By consciously relaxing your muscles, you can release physical tension and promote a sense of calmness.

Here's how to do it:

Progressive muscle relaxation is a wonderful technique to help reduce stress and promote relaxation in the body. Here is a step-by-step guide on how to do progressive muscle relaxation:

- Find a quiet and comfortable place to sit or lie down.
- Close your eyes and take a few deep breaths to relax your mind and body.
- Start by focusing on your feet. Tense the muscles in your toes and feet for about 5-10 seconds, then slowly release the tension and let your muscles relax. Pay attention to the sensation of relaxation in your feet.
- Move your focus to your calves and thighs. Tighten these muscles for 5-10 seconds, then release and feel the tension melting away.
- Continue this process, moving up your body. Tense and relax your stomach, chest, back, arms, shoulders, neck, and face, one by one.
- As you tense each muscle group, try to focus on the difference between tension and relaxation. Notice how different it feels when the muscles are relaxed.
- Remember to breathe deeply and slowly throughout the exercise.
- Once you have completed tensing and relaxing all your muscle groups, take a few moments to enjoy the overall feeling of relaxation in your body.
- Open your eyes when you are ready and take a moment to appreciate the sense of calmness and relaxation you have created.

Progressive muscle relaxation can be a very effective technique when practiced regularly. It can help you release physical tension, reduce stress levels, and improve overall well-being.

Mindfulness Meditation

We've talked about mindfulness and meditation separately, but when they come together, they work wonderfully to combat stress. Mindfulness meditation helps you stay present in the moment and become aware of your thoughts and feelings without judgment. By practicing mindfulness regularly, you can cultivate a greater sense of inner peace and reduce stress levels.

Here's an exercise to try:

Sure! Here is a simple walking mindfulness meditation exercise you can try:

- Find a quiet and peaceful place to walk where you won't be disturbed.
- Start by standing still and taking a few deep breaths to center yourself and bring your attention to the present moment.
- Begin walking slowly and mindfully, paying full attention to each step you take. Feel the sensation of your feet touching the ground, the muscles moving in your legs, and the rhythm of your breath.
- Notice the sights, sounds, and smells around you without getting caught up in them. Simply observe them as they come and go.
- If your mind starts to wander, gently bring your focus back to the physical sensations of walking. You can also use a simple mantra or affirmation to help anchor your attention, such as "I am present in this moment" or "I walk with awareness."
- Continue walking mindfully for as long as you like, allowing yourself to fully immerse in the experience of each step and being present in the moment.
- When you're ready to end the meditation, gradually slow down your pace and come to a stop. Take a moment to feel gratitude for this time you've given yourself to be mindful and present.

Physical Exercise

Engaging in regular physical exercise is not only beneficial for your physical health but also for your mental well-being. Exercise releases endorphins, the body's natural stress relievers, and helps you reduce anxiety and improve your mood.

You don't have to join the gym if that's not something that appeals to you. Going for a walk or a jog can be just as effective; even swimming does the trick. The key is making sure it's something you enjoy, while also doing it consistently.

Yoga

Yoga combines physical postures, breathing techniques, and meditation to help you achieve a sense of balance and relaxation. Practicing yoga regularly can help you improve flexibility, reduce muscle tension, and calm your mind.

Here is a great yoga routine for stress relief:

Of course! Here's a simple yoga routine that you can do to help relieve stress:

- Start in a seated position with your legs crossed. Take a few deep breaths to center yourself.
- **Begin with Cat-Cow pose:** Inhale as you arch your back and look up (Cow pose), then exhale as you round your back and tuck your chin to your chest (Cat pose). Repeat this flow for a few breaths.
- **Move into Child's pose:** Sit back on your heels, extend your arms forward, and rest your forehead on the mat. Hold this pose for a few breaths, focusing on releasing tension in your back and shoulders.
- **Transition into Downward Facing Dog:** Lift your hips up and back, pressing your hands and feet into the mat. Pedal your feet to stretch out the calves and hamstrings.
- **Flow through a few rounds of Sun Salutation:** Start in Mountain pose, then reach up to the sky in Upward Salute, fold forward into Forward Fold, step back into Plank pose, lower down into Chaturanga, flow into Upward Facing Dog, and finally push back into Downward Facing Dog. Repeat this sequence a few times, moving with your breath.
- **End with Corpse pose:** Lie flat on your back, arms by your sides, palms facing up. Close your eyes and focus on deep, slow breaths. Stay in this pose for at least 5-10 minutes, allowing your body to fully relax.

Remember to listen to your body and modify any poses as needed.

Journaling

Writing down your thoughts and emotions can be a powerful way to process stress and gain perspective on challenging situations. Keeping a journal allows you to express yourself freely and identify patterns in your behavior that may be contributing to your stress.

Here are some tips for effective journaling:

- Set aside dedicated time for journaling each day. Consistency is key to reaping the benefits of stress relief through journaling.
- Find a quiet and comfortable space to write in where you can focus without distractions.
- Start by jotting down your thoughts and feelings uncensored. Don't worry about grammar or structure at first; just let your emotions flow onto the paper.
- Reflect on what triggers your stress and write about it. This can help you identify patterns and gain insights into what is causing your stress.
- Write down positive affirmations, gratitude lists, or things that bring you joy. Shifting your focus to positive thoughts can help reduce stress and improve your mood.
- Use journal prompts to spark inspiration and reflection. There are plenty of resources online with prompts specifically designed for stress relief.
- Consider incorporating mindfulness techniques into your journaling practice, such as deep breathing exercises or body scans, to help you stay present and grounded.
- Don't be too hard on yourself if you miss a day of journaling. Just pick up where you left off and continue to make it a habit.
- Experiment with different journaling formats, such as bullet journaling, art journaling, or gratitude journals, to find what works best for you.
- Remember, journaling is a personal practice, so allow yourself the freedom to explore and express yourself in a way that feels most comfortable and beneficial to you.

Healthy Eating

Eating a balanced diet rich in whole foods, fruits, and vegetables can support your body's ability to cope with stress. Avoiding excessive caffeine, sugar, and processed foods can help regulate your mood and energy levels.

Here are some foods you should pack into your daily diet for stress management:

- Berries such as blueberries, strawberries, and raspberries are rich in antioxidants that can help combat stress.
- Fatty fish like salmon, mackerel, and sardines are high in omega-3 fatty acids, which have been shown to reduce anxiety and stress.
- Nuts and seeds, such as almonds, walnuts, flaxseeds, and chia seeds, are good sources of healthy fats and magnesium, which can help reduce stress.
- Dark chocolate in moderation can help lower cortisol levels and reduce the effects of stress on the body.
- Green leafy vegetables like spinach, kale, and Swiss chard are high in magnesium, which can help relax the muscles and calm the nervous system.
- Whole grains such as quinoa, brown rice, and oats can help stabilize blood sugar levels and keep you feeling full and energized, reducing stress.
- Herbal teas like chamomile, peppermint, and lavender can have calming effects on the body and help reduce stress and anxiety.
- Avocados are packed with healthy fats and potassium, which can help lower blood pressure and reduce the effects of stress.
- Citrus fruits like oranges, lemons, and grapefruits are rich in vitamin C, which can help boost the immune system and combat stress.

- Fermented foods like yogurt, kefir, and sauerkraut contain probiotics that can support a healthy gut, which is linked to reduced stress and anxiety levels.

Incorporating these foods into your diet can help manage stress and improve your overall well-being.

Social Support

Connecting with friends, family, or support groups can provide a valuable outlet for sharing your feelings and receiving emotional support.

Talking to someone you trust about your stressors can help you feel understood and less alone.

Time Management

Effective time management can help you reduce stress by prioritizing tasks, setting realistic goals, and avoiding procrastination. Creating a daily or weekly schedule can help you stay organized and in control of your responsibilities.

Here are some useful time-management techniques:

- **Prioritize tasks:** Make a to-do list and prioritize your tasks based on urgency and importance. Focus on completing high-priority tasks first before moving on to less important ones.
- **Set specific goals:** Set clear, achievable goals for your day, week, or month. This will give you a sense of direction and purpose, helping you stay motivated and focused.
- **Break tasks into smaller steps:** Large tasks can feel overwhelming, so break them down into smaller, more manageable steps. This will help you make progress and avoid procrastination.
- **Use a calendar or planner:** Keep track of your appointments, deadlines, and important dates using a calendar or planner. This will help you stay organized and ensure that you don't forget anything important.
- **Eliminate distractions:** Identify your biggest distractions and find ways to minimize or eliminate them. This could include turning off notifications, setting specific work hours, or working in a quiet environment.
- **Delegate tasks:** If possible, delegate tasks to others to free up your time for more important or high-priority activities. Delegating can help you be more efficient and make better use of your resources.
- **Learn to say no:** It's important to set boundaries and learn to say no to tasks or commitments that do not align with your goals or priorities. This will help you avoid overcommitting and feeling overwhelmed.

- **Pomodoro Technique:** The Pomodoro Technique is a time management method developed by Francesco Cirillo in the late 1980s. It involves breaking your work into intervals, traditionally 25 minutes in length, separated by short breaks. Here's how it typically works:
- Choose a task you want to work on.
- Set a timer for 25 minutes (this is called a "Pomodoro").
- Work on the task until the timer rings.
- Take a short break (around 5 minutes).
- Repeat this process: after four Pomodoros, take a longer break (around 15–30 minutes).
- **Eat the Frog Technique:** This technique is based on the concept of tackling your most challenging or unpleasant task first thing in the morning; essentially, "eating the frog" means completing the task you want to procrastinate on the most. The idea is that once you've completed the hardest task, the rest of your day will feel easier and more productive. By facing the most difficult task head-on, you can prevent it from weighing on you throughout the day and potentially delaying other tasks.

Setting Boundaries

Learning to say no and setting boundaries in your personal and professional life is essential for reducing stress. By establishing clear limits and honoring your own needs, you can prevent burnout and overwhelm.

Here's how you do it:

- **Identify your limits:** Take some time to reflect on what makes you feel uncomfortable, stressed, or unhappy in your relationships. This will help you define your boundaries more clearly.
- **Communicate assertively:** Clearly and respectfully communicate your boundaries to others. Use "I" statements to express your needs and wants. For example, "I feel overwhelmed when I am asked to work overtime every day. I need to limit my working hours."
- **Be consistent:** Once you've set your boundaries, stick to them. Consistency is key to establishing and maintaining healthy boundaries.
- **Practice self-care:** Setting boundaries also means taking care of yourself. Make time for self-care activities that nurture your physical, emotional, and mental well-being.
- **Seek support:** If you're finding it challenging to set or maintain boundaries, consider seeking support from a counselor, therapist, or trusted friend. They can provide guidance and encouragement as you navigate this process.

Remember, setting boundaries is a skill that takes practice. Be patient with yourself and trust that you deserve to have your boundaries respected.

Self-Care Practices

No, it is not selfish to focus on yourself and enjoy self-care. It's a necessity that we all need to learn to do more of.

Engaging in regular self-care activities such as reading a book, taking a bubble bath, or practicing a hobby you enjoy can help you relax and recharge. Making time for yourself is essential for maintaining a healthy balance in your life.

Incorporating these stress management techniques into your daily routine can help you build resilience and cope with stress more effectively. Remember to be patient with yourself and experiment with different strategies to find what works best for you. By taking proactive steps to manage your stress, you can improve your overall well-being and quality of life.

The Importance of Sleep and Relaxation

In today's fast-paced world, prioritizing sleep and relaxation may often take a backseat to the demands of daily life. However, the benefits of a good night's rest and regular relaxation practices cannot be overstated when it comes to maintaining overall health and well-being. From improved cognitive function to a strengthened immune system, quality sleep and relaxation are essential pillars of a healthy lifestyle.

Sleep isn't lazy or a time to do just nothing; it is a crucial physiological process that allows our bodies and minds to recharge and repair. Adequate sleep is essential for optimal physical, mental, and emotional functioning. Research has shown that a lack of sleep can have a detrimental impact on various aspects of health, including cognitive function, mood regulation, immune function, and metabolic health.

When you're sleep-deprived, nothing good comes of it. In fact, even one night of poor sleep can leave you in a sleep debt you badly need to pay back.

One of the key reasons why sleep is so important for good health is its role in cognitive function. During sleep, the brain consolidates memories, processes information, and rejuvenates neural pathways. Inadequate sleep can impair concentration, memory, and decision-making skills, ultimately hindering our ability to perform daily tasks effectively.

On top of that, sleep plays a critical role in supporting overall immune function. A well-rested body is better equipped to fight off infections and illnesses, as sleep helps regulate the immune response and promotes the production of cytokines, which are crucial in fighting off inflammation and infection.

Furthermore, sleep is closely linked to metabolic health. Chronic sleep deprivation has been associated with an increased risk of obesity, diabetes, and cardiovascular disease. Poor sleep can disrupt hormone regulation, leading to imbalances in appetite-regulating hormones such as leptin and ghrelin, which can contribute to weight gain and metabolic dysfunction.

It's not just sleep that's so important; but general relaxation too.

Incorporating relaxation practices into our daily routine is essential for managing stress and promoting overall well-being. Chronic stress can have a profound impact on our physical and mental health, contributing to a range of health issues such as high blood pressure, anxiety, depression, and insomnia.

Relaxation techniques such as deep breathing, meditation, yoga, and tai chi can help lower stress levels, reduce anxiety, and promote a sense of calm and balance. By activating the body's relaxation response, these practices can counteract the harmful effects of chronic stress, leading to improved mental clarity, emotional stability, and physical health.

Tips for Good Sleep Hygiene

Developing good sleep hygiene practices is essential for ensuring restful and restorative sleep. Here are some tips to help improve the quality of your sleep:

- **Establish a Regular Sleep Schedule:** Try to go to bed and wake up at the same time every day, even on weekends. Consistency helps regulate your body's internal clock, making it easier to fall asleep and wake up naturally.
- **Create a Relaxing Bedtime Routine:** Engage in calming activities before bed, such as reading, taking a warm bath, or practicing relaxation techniques. Avoid stimulating activities like watching TV or using electronic devices, as the blue light emitted can disrupt your body's natural sleep-wake cycle.
- **Create a Comfortable Sleep Environment:** Make sure your bedroom is cool, dark, and quiet to create an ideal sleep environment. Invest in a comfortable mattress and pillows that support a good night's rest. In fact, when was the last time you changed your pillows? Perhaps it's time.
- **Limit Caffeine and Alcohol Intake:** Avoid consuming caffeine and alcohol close to bedtime, as they can interfere with your ability to fall asleep and stay asleep.
- **Exercise Regularly:** Regular physical activity can help improve sleep quality and overall health. Aim for at least 30 minutes of moderate exercise most days of the week, but avoid vigorous exercise close to bedtime.
- **Manage Stress:** Incorporate relaxation techniques into your daily routine to help manage stress and promote relaxation. Deep breathing exercises, meditation, and mindfulness can help calm the mind and prepare the body for restful sleep.

Remember, prioritizing sleep and relaxation is essential for achieving optimal health and well-being. Quality sleep is not a luxury but a fundamental need that supports physical, mental, and emotional health. It's vital.

Exercise and its Effects on the Vagus Nerve

Exercise is a powerful tool that can have profound effects on the vagus nerve, impacting our overall well-being in ways we might not even realize. When we engage in physical activity, we are not just working our muscles and cardiovascular system; we are also influencing the intricate network of the vagus nerve and the autonomic nervous system as a whole.

One of the key ways in which exercise affects the vagus nerve is through its ability to increase heart rate variability (HRV). HRV is a measure of the variation in time intervals between heartbeats, which reflects the balance between the sympathetic and parasympathetic branches of the autonomic nervous system. The vagus nerve plays a crucial role in this balance, as it is responsible for activating the parasympathetic response that helps to calm the body and reduce stress.

Regular exercise has been shown to increase HRV, indicating a stronger parasympathetic tone and better overall autonomic nervous system function. This can lead to improved stress resilience, better emotional regulation, and enhanced recovery from physical and mental exertion. In other words, exercise can help us stay calm under pressure and bounce back more quickly from life's challenges.

Furthermore, exercise has been found to stimulate the release of neurotransmitters such as acetylcholine and norepinephrine, which play important roles in regulating the activity of the vagus nerve. These neurotransmitters can enhance the connection between the brain and the body, promoting better communication and coordination between different systems. This improved neural efficiency can result in greater physical performance, faster reaction times, and enhanced cognitive function.

So, what are some good exercises to do in order to reap these benefits for the vagus nerve? Here are a few examples:

- **Yoga:** Yoga combines physical postures, breathwork, and mindfulness practices that can help stimulate the vagus nerve and promote relaxation. Poses such as Child's Pose, Bridge Pose, and Legs-Up-the-Wall are particularly effective for activating the parasympathetic response.
- **Cardiovascular exercise:** Activities such as running, cycling, swimming, and dancing can elevate heart rate variability and improve overall autonomic function. Aim for moderate-intensity exercise for at least 30 minutes most days of the week.
- **Strength training:** Resistance training not only builds muscle strength but also enhances neural connections and coordination. Exercises like squats, deadlifts, push-ups, and rows can engage the vagus nerve and improve overall nervous system health.
- **Mind-body practices:** Activities like tai chi, qigong, and Pilates combine movement with mindfulness and breath awareness, creating a holistic approach to improving vagal tone and overall well-being.

The recommended amount of exercise per week for adults is at least 150 minutes of moderate-intensity aerobic activity, such as brisk walking or cycling, or 75 minutes of vigorous-intensity aerobic activity, such as running or swimming. It's also beneficial to include muscle-strengthening activities on two or more days per week. Remember, it's important to find activities you enjoy to make exercise a sustainable and enjoyable part of your lifestyle.

Incorporating a variety of exercises into your routine can help to keep the vagus nerve healthy and functioning optimally. Remember to listen to your body, pay attention to how you feel during and after exercise, and adjust your routine as needed to support your overall health and well-being. So, lace up those running shoes, roll out your yoga mat, or grab those dumbbells - your vagus nerve will thank you!

Chapter 11

Case Studies and Personal Stories

It's all very well and good reading about why the vagus nerve is important and how stimulating it leads to overall health and well-being. But you want to hear and see results, right? That means you want to hear some real-life stories of people who made it work for them.

So, before we move on to our last chapter, let's quickly give you exactly what you want.

Case Study 1: Sarah's Journey to Inner Harmony

Meet Sarah, a vibrant soul who had long struggled with anxiety and digestive issues. After extensive research, she embarked on a journey to improve her vagal tone through a combination of yoga, deep breathing exercises, and cold water immersion.

By regularly engaging in these practices, Sarah noticed a significant reduction in her anxiety levels and a remarkable improvement in her digestion. She describes the sensation of calm washing over her, like a soothing wave emanating from deep within.

Through her journey, Sarah learned the invaluable lesson that true healing begins from within, and that by nurturing her vagus nerve, she could cultivate a profound sense of inner harmony.

Case Study 2: David's Resilience Revolution

David, a former elite athlete, faced a challenging transition into retirement, grappling with feelings of purposelessness and depression. Determined to reclaim his vitality, he delved into the world of vagus nerve stimulation, exploring techniques such as sound therapy, meditation, and heart rate variability training.

Through consistent practice, David experienced a remarkable shift in his emotional well-being, finding newfound resilience and a sense of purpose in life. He describes the sensation of his heart rhythm aligning with the rhythm of the universe, a powerful reminder of the interconnectedness of all living beings.

For David, the journey of enhancing his vagal tone became a transformative revolution, empowering him to navigate life's ups and downs with grace and strength.

Case Study 3: Maria's Metamorphosis Through Breathwork

Maria, a busy professional juggling multiple responsibilities, found herself constantly battling stress and fatigue. Seeking a holistic approach to wellness, she delved into the practice of breathwork, a powerful tool for stimulating the vagus nerve and promoting relaxation.

Through rhythmic breathing exercises and guided meditation, Maria discovered a profound sense of mental clarity and rejuvenation. She describes the sensation of her breath becoming a conduit for inner peace, harmonizing her mind and body in a symphony of healing.

Through her journey, Maria learned the profound impact of conscious breathing on her overall well-being, awakening to the transformative potential of the mind-body connection.

Case Study 4: Mark's Mindful Mastery of Stress

Mark, a high-powered executive navigating the pressures of corporate life, found himself plagued by chronic stress and burnout. Seeking a sustainable solution to his mental health struggles, he delved into the practice of mindfulness, gradually honing his ability to cultivate present-moment awareness and inner calm.

Through mindfulness meditation, somatic experiencing, and Qi Gong practices, Mark experienced a profound shift in his stress response, learning to navigate life's challenges with equanimity and resilience. He describes the sensation of his body becoming a sanctuary of stillness, a refuge from the chaos of the external world.

For Mark, the journey of mastering his mind through vagus nerve stimulation became a powerful lesson in the art of self-care and self-mastery.

Case Study 5: Sarah and David's Sacred Connection

Sarah and David, two kindred spirits united by their shared passion for holistic healing, embarked on a transformative journey together, exploring the depths of vagus nerve stimulation and its profound impact on their lives.

Through a fusion of practices such as partner yoga, heartfelt conversations, and therapeutic touch, Sarah and David cultivated a deep sense of connection and empathy, nourishing their vagal wellness and strengthening their bond. They describe the sensation of their energies intertwining, creating a sacred space of healing and love that radiated outwards, uplifting those around them.

For Sarah and David, the journey of shared vagal exploration became a testament to the transformative power of human connection and the ripple effect of wellness in fostering a more compassionate world.

Through the power of holistic practices, conscious awareness, and a deep commitment to self-care, these people unlocked a treasure trove of healing potential within themselves, paving the way for a life of profound well-being and vitality. May their stories serve as a beacon of hope and inspiration for all who seek to embark on their own journey of vagal exploration, reminding us that the path to true healing begins by listening to the whispers of our own wandering nerves.

Chapter 12

Future Directions and Conclusion

As we reach the end of our journey into the vagus nerve, let's look to the future.

What might we be able to use vagal nerve stimulation for as the years tick by? What areas do researchers see promise in?

Let's delve deeper.

While traditionally associated with regulating essential bodily functions like heart rate and digestion, recent research has uncovered a wealth of potential applications for vagal nerve stimulation (VNS) that extend far beyond its original scope.

As we delve into the realm of emerging research, it becomes increasingly evident that the vagus nerve holds the key to unlocking a myriad of therapeutic possibilities. Let's explore some of the cutting-edge studies and potential future uses of VNS that are shaping the landscape of modern medicine.

Mood Disorders and Depression

One of the most promising areas of research involving VNS is its potential to treat mood disorders such as depression. Studies have shown that stimulating the vagus nerve can have a profound effect on mood regulation by influencing the release of neurotransmitters like serotonin and norepinephrine.

This has led to the development of VNS as a therapy for treatment-resistant depression, offering hope for those who have not responded to traditional antidepressant medications.

In the future, we may see VNS used more widely as a non-invasive and effective treatment for various mood disorders, providing patients with a new avenue for managing their mental health.

Chronic Pain Management

Chronic pain is a complex condition that can significantly impact a person's quality of life. VNS has emerged as a promising alternative for managing chronic pain by modulating pain perception pathways in the brain.

Research suggests that stimulating the vagus nerve can reduce the intensity of pain signals and provide long-lasting relief for individuals suffering from conditions such as fibromyalgia, neuropathic pain, and migraines.

With further advancements in VNS technology and research, we can anticipate more personalized and targeted approaches to managing chronic pain, offering patients a safe and effective alternative to traditional pain management strategies.

Inflammatory Disorders

Inflammation is a common denominator in a wide range of health conditions, from autoimmune diseases to metabolic disorders. VNS has shown great potential for modulating the body's inflammatory response by inhibiting the release of pro-inflammatory cytokines and promoting anti-inflammatory pathways.

This has sparked interest in using VNS as a therapy for conditions like rheumatoid arthritis, inflammatory bowel disease, and even metabolic syndrome.

As researchers continue to unravel the intricate mechanisms behind VNS's anti-inflammatory effects, we may witness the development of novel therapies that target inflammation at its core, offering new hope for patients grappling with chronic inflammatory disorders.

Cognitive Enhancement and Memory

The idea of enhancing cognitive function and memory through VNS may seem like something out of a science fiction novel, but recent research has shown that stimulating the vagus nerve can indeed have profound effects on cognitive processing and memory consolidation.

By improving communication between different brain regions and enhancing neuroplasticity, VNS holds promise as a potential therapy for enhancing cognitive performance in both healthy individuals and those with cognitive impairments.

In the future, we could see VNS being explored as a tool for enhancing memory retention, boosting learning capabilities, and even slowing down cognitive decline in conditions like Alzheimer's disease.

Cardiovascular Health

Given the vagus nerve's integral role in regulating heart rate and cardiovascular function, it comes as no surprise that VNS has been investigated as a potential therapy for enhancing cardiovascular health. By modulating the autonomic nervous system, VNS can help regulate blood pressure, heart rate variability, and overall cardiac function, making it a promising adjunctive treatment for conditions like hypertension, heart failure, and arrhythmias.

As researchers delve deeper into the cardiovascular benefits of VNS, we may witness the emergence of innovative therapies that target specific aspects of cardiovascular health, offering patients a holistic approach to managing their heart health.

In conclusion, the future of vagal nerve stimulation is brimming with possibilities, each holding the potential to transform the landscape of modern medicine. From treating mood disorders and chronic pain to managing inflammatory conditions and enhancing cognitive function, VNS offers a versatile and promising platform for addressing a wide array of health challenges.

As researchers continue to push the boundaries of knowledge and innovation, we can look forward to a future where vagal nerve stimulation plays a prominent role in revolutionizing healthcare and improving the lives of countless individuals worldwide. The journey towards unlocking the full potential of VNS may be ongoing, but with each new discovery and breakthrough, we move one step closer to a future where the healing power of the vagus nerve knows no bounds.

Resources for Further Learning

Understanding the functions and potential benefits of optimizing vagal tone has become an area of growing interest in the wellness and medical communities. If you're looking to delve deeper into the world of the vagus nerve, there are numerous resources available to expand knowledge, find support, and connect with like-minded individuals.

Books on the Vagus Nerve

One of the best ways to deepen your understanding of the vagus nerve is through books written by experts in the field. Several notable books provide valuable insights into the science behind the vagus nerve, as well as practical tips for harnessing its power.

- **"The Polyvagal Theory: Neurophysiological Foundations of Emotions, Attachment, Communication, and Self-Regulation" by Stephen Porges:** This seminal work explores the polyvagal theory, a groundbreaking concept that illuminates the role of the vagus nerve in our emotional and social lives.
- **"Accessing the Healing Power of the Vagus Nerve: Self-Help Exercises for Anxiety, Depression, Trauma, and Autism" by Stanley Rosenberg:** In this practical guide, Rosenberg offers a wealth of exercises and techniques for improving vagal tone and promoting overall well-being.
- **"The Body Keeps the Score: Brain, Mind, and Body in the Healing of Trauma" by Bessel van der Kolk:** While not solely focused on the vagus nerve, this book delves into the profound impact of trauma on the body and mind, emphasizing the role of the vagus nerve in the healing process.

Online Resources

The internet is a treasure trove of information on the vagus nerve, with numerous websites, podcasts, and online communities dedicated to exploring its intricacies. Here are some online resources that can help you further your learning journey:

- **Vagus Nerve Hub (vagusnervehub.com):** This comprehensive website offers articles, interviews, and resources on the vagus nerve, covering topics such as vagal tone, vagus nerve stimulation, and polyvagal theory.
- **"The Vagus Nerve: An Owner's Manual" Podcast:** Hosted by a team of experts in psychology and neuroscience, this podcast delves into the fascinating world of the vagus nerve, offering insights and practical tips for enhancing vagal tone.
- **Social Media Groups:** Platforms such as Facebook and Reddit host communities of individuals interested in the vagus nerve and related topics. Joining these groups can provide opportunities to connect with like-minded individuals, share experiences, and learn from others' perspectives.

Workshops and Courses

For those seeking a more hands-on approach to learning about the vagus nerve, attending workshops or enrolling in courses can offer valuable opportunities for in-depth exploration.

Many wellness centers, yoga studios, and health clinics offer workshops focused on vagal health and regulation. Additionally, several online platforms host courses taught by experts in the field. Here are a few options to consider:

- **The Vagus Nerve Workshop at The Breathing Project:** This workshop offers practical exercises and techniques for activating and toning the vagus nerve through breathwork, movement, and mindfulness practices.
- **"Healing Trauma: A Brief Mindful Pause" Course on Insight Timer:** Led by a trauma-informed mindfulness teacher, this course explores the connection between trauma, the nervous system, and the vagus nerve, offering practices for healing and regulation.

- **Online Vagus Nerve Retreats:** Some wellness retreat centers offer virtual retreats focused on vagal health and well-being. These retreats typically include workshops, guided meditations, and discussions led by experts in the field.

Medical Professionals and Therapists

If you're looking for personalized guidance and support in exploring the vagus nerve, seeking out medical professionals and therapists with expertise in this area can be beneficial.

Integrative medicine practitioners, functional medicine doctors, and therapists specializing in trauma-informed care may offer insights and techniques for enhancing vagal tone and overall well-being.

Conclusion

Congratulations! You've reached the end of this book and clearly demonstrated your keenness to learn more about the vagus nerve and harness its tremendous potential.

In conclusion, the vagus nerve is a fascinating and powerful pathway in our bodies that connects our brain to almost every organ. Throughout this book, we've delved into the intricate functions of the vagus nerve, understanding how it influences our emotional well-being, immune response, digestion, heart health, and more. We've explored the ways in which vagal tone can be enhanced through various stimulation techniques, leading to improved overall health and well-being.

As we wrap up our journey through the wonders of the vagus nerve, it's important to acknowledge the incredible potential that lies within each of us to optimize our vagal tone. By incorporating simple yet effective practices such as deep breathing exercises, meditation, yoga, mindfulness, social connections, laughter, cold exposure, and physical activity into our daily routines, we can actively stimulate and strengthen our vagus nerve.

Imagine a life where stress and anxiety no longer hold you captive, where your immune system is robust and resilient, where your digestion is smooth and efficient, and where your heart beats in harmony with your emotions. This is the reality that awaits those who choose to prioritize their vagal tone and take proactive steps towards enhancing it.

So, dear reader, I encourage you to embark on this journey of self-discovery and empowerment. Start by incorporating one simple vagal stimulation technique into your daily routine today. Whether it's practicing a few minutes of deep belly breathing in the morning, engaging in a heartwarming conversation with a loved one, or immersing yourself in the healing power of nature, every small step you take towards improving your vagal tone matters.

And remember, progress is not about perfection. It's about consistency and commitment to your own well-being. Be gentle with yourself, celebrate your victories no matter how small, and trust in the wisdom of your body to guide you towards greater health and vitality.

As you continue on your journey towards better vagal tone and overall wellness, I leave you with this empowering thought: you have the power to influence the health of your vagus nerve and, in doing so, transform your life for the better. Embrace the potential that lies within you, nurture your vagus nerve with care and intention, and watch as a newfound sense of balance, resilience, and joy blossoms within you.

May your journey be filled with moments of healing, growth, and transformation. May your vagus nerve be a beacon of light, guiding you toward a life of vitality and well-being. May you always remember that the power to heal is within you.

References

Bolster your brain by stimulating the vagus nerve. (n.d.). Cedars-Sinai. https://www.cedars-sinai.org/blog/stimulating-the-vagus-nerve.html

Burton, N. (2022, November 7). *4 Meditations to stimulate the vagus nerve.* DailyOM.com. https://www.dailyom.com/journal/meditations-to-stimulate-the-vagus-nerve/

Clinic, C. (2024, June 27). *5 ways to stimulate your vagus nerve.* Cleveland Clinic. https://health.clevelandclinic.org/vagus-nerve-stimulation

Gonzalez, A. (2024, May 2). *A 12-Minute breathing practice to activate your vagus nerve.* Mindful. https://www.mindful.org/a-12-minute-breathing-practice-to-activate-your-vagus-nerve/

Hersh, E. (2024, March 27). *12 healthy sleep hygiene tips.* Healthline. https://www.healthline.com/health/sleep-hygiene

Hoehl, S., & Bertenthal, B. I. (2021). An interactionist perspective on the development of coordinated social attention. *Advances in Child Development and Behavior*, 1–41. https://doi.org/10.1016/bs.acdb.2021.05.001

Kate. (2024, May 10). *6 Vagus nerve Exercises to boost your Well-being – free online yoga video.* YogaUOnline. https://yogauonline.com/yoga-practice-teaching-tips/yoga-practice-tips/6-ways-to-stimulate-your-vagus-nerve-with-yoga-and-breathing/

Kenny, B. J., & Bordoni, B. (2022, November 7). *Neuroanatomy, cranial nerve 10 (Vagus nerve).* StatPearls - NCBI Bookshelf. https://www.ncbi.nlm.nih.gov/books/NBK537171/

Neff, M. A. (2023, September 8). *Improve vagal tone.* Insights of a Neurodivergent Clinician. https://neurodivergentinsights.com/blog/how-to-improve-vagal-tone

Practicing deep breathing for better physical and mental health. | OneStep Digital Physical Therapy. (n.d.). https://www.onestep.co/resources-blog/deep-breathing-better-physical-mental-health#:~:text=The%20relationship%20between%20breathing%20and,of%20stress%20hormones%20like%20cortisol.

Professional, C. C. M. (n.d.). *Vagus nerve.* Cleveland Clinic. https://my.clevelandclinic.org/health/body/22279-vagus-nerve

Robinson, L., & Smith, M., MA. (2024, May 14). Stress Management: Techniques & Strategies to Deal with Stress. *HelpGuide.org.* https://www.helpguide.org/articles/stress/stress-management.htm

Ruscio, M., DC, & Ruscio, M., DC. (2024, May 9). *What is vagal tone and how to improve yours - Dr. Michael Ruscio, DC.* Dr. Michael Ruscio, DC. https://drruscio.com/vagal-tone/

Segal, D. (2022, October 6). *Vagus nerve: What to know.* WebMD. https://www.webmd.com/brain/vagus-nerve-what-to-know

Seladi-Schulman, J., PhD. (2023, February 14). *What is the Vagus Nerve?* Healthline. https://www.healthline.com/human-body-maps/vagus-nerve

Stress management - Mayo Clinic. (2023, October 26). https://www.mayoclinic.org/tests-procedures/stress-management/about/pac-20384898#:~:text=Stress%20management%20approaches%20include%3A,your%20emotional%20awareness%20and%20reactions.

Suni, E., & Suni, E. (2024, March 4). *Mastering Sleep Hygiene: Your path to quality sleep.* Sleep Foundation. https://www.sleepfoundation.org/sleep-hygiene

The Editors of Encyclopaedia Britannica. (2024, June 20). *Vagus nerve | Definition, Function, & Facts.* Encyclopedia Britannica. https://www.britannica.com/science/vagus-nerve

Vagal tone: a physiologic marker of stress vulnerability. (1992, September 1). PubMed. https://pubmed.ncbi.nlm.nih.gov/1513615/

Wikipedia contributors. (2024a, July 1). *Vagus nerve.* Wikipedia. https://en.wikipedia.org/wiki/Vagus_nerve

Wikipedia contributors. (2024b, July 13). *Vagal tone.* Wikipedia. https://en.wikipedia.org/wiki/Vagal_tone#:~:text=Vagal%20tone%20is%20activity%20of,several%20body%20compartments%20at%20rest.

MEDITATION FOR BEGINNERS

A Simple Guide to Finding Peace, Focus, and Clarity in Everyday Life

Monika Daniel

Chapter 1

Introduction to Meditation

As we wade through the chaos of the 21st century, with its constant pings and endless to-dos, the ancient practice of meditation offers a little relief from the storm. Imagine it as your personal pause button—a way to step away from the hustle, just for a little while, and reconnect with the calm, clear person you know is in there somewhere.

See meditation not as some spiritual ritual but more like grabbing a coffee with a friend—the friend, in this case, being your own mind. It's a meet-up where you get to catch up, sort things out, and leave feeling refreshed and ready to face the crowd again.

Now, if you're picturing someone sitting cross-legged, eyes closed, fingertips touching, and a look of serenity so profound it's almost irritating, you're not wrong—but there's so much more to it! Meditation can be dynamic and diverse, just like the people who practice it. From the gentle mindfulness of breathing exercises to the focused intensity of guided visualizations, meditation is really about grounding yourself in the present moment. And the best part? It's accessible to anyone, anywhere—no fancy equipment or special pants required.

Just you, a few minutes, and an open mind. Ready to dive in?

What is Meditation?

To break it down, meditation is the art of finding stillness amidst our bustling lives. A practice as ancient as the hills but as fresh as a modern-day wellness trend, meditation is the unsung hero for millions seeking solace, clarity, and a pinch of enlightenment. Let's dive into understanding what it is, where it came from, and how it's peppered with traditions from around the globe.

So, what exactly is meditation? Picture this: There's a serene lake, still and unmoving, perfectly reflecting the clear blue sky above. Meditation, my friends, is your mind becoming that lake – calm, reflective, undisturbed by the ripples of daily life. More formally, it's a practice where we can use techniques like mindfulness or focusing the mind on a particular object, thought, or activity to achieve a mentally clear and emotionally calm state.

This practice isn't new; it's like the vintage wine of spiritual disciplines.

Buddhism

Ancient India is one of meditation's oldest homes. It's around 500 BCE, and Siddhartha Gautama (you might know him as the Buddha) is about to play a huge role in popularizing meditation. After his enlightenment under the Bodhi tree, meditative practices became central to Buddhism. The Buddha taught various techniques, primarily as a means to cultivate the mind, understand the nature of reality, and, let's not forget, alleviate suffering through the realization of impermanence, suffering, and non-self.

Hinduism

Meanwhile, in other corners of ancient India, Hinduism was developing its own range of meditation practices. The earliest mentions are found in the Vedas, religious texts that date back as far as 1500 BCE. Meditation in Hinduism is often tied to the pursuit of moksha, or liberation from the cycle of life and death. Picture ancient Rishis and ascetics sitting in tranquil forest retreats, exploring consciousness and reaching for the ultimate spiritual cop-out from the endless cycle of rebirths.

Taois`m

Let's zoom over to ancient China, where Laozi, an old sage with a penchant for profound mysticism, founded Taoism around the 6th century BCE. Meditation in Taoism is about aligning with the fundamental nature of reality, or the Tao. Think of it as the universe's watermark on everything, and Taoists meditate to get in sync with this cosmic flow.

Other cultures

And it's not just an Eastern party! Meditation also appeared in other world cultures. The Sufis in Islam practiced forms of contemplative walking or the spinning you see in whirling dervishes, which is a form of active meditation. Jewish Kabbalists practiced forms of contemplation that could certainly give some meditative techniques a run for their money.

As centuries rolled by, these various practices cross-pollinated through trade, conquest, and spiritual tourism, spreading and evolving into the rich global tapestry of meditation we see today.

Fast forward to modern times – meditation has taken the world by storm. No longer cloistered in the mountains with mystical sages, it's now practiced in corporate boardrooms, taught in schools, and featured in hundreds of smartphone apps. Whether it's reducing stress, improving concentration, or simply finding a moment of peace while waiting for your coffee, meditation has something to offer to everyone.

And what a vibrant array of styles we have today. From mindfulness meditation, Vipassana, to Transcendental Meditation, and even moving meditations like Tai Chi and Qigong, there's a flavor to match every personality. Whether you're the quiet contemplator or the active meditator, the world of meditation is your oyster.

Why Meditate?

Let's embark on this mental journey by exploring the fantastic perks of pressing pause and diving deep into our thoughts with meditation.

Stress Reduction

First on our list, and perhaps the most sought-after ticket in today's high-speed world, is stress reduction. Techniques such as mindfulness and transcendental meditation have been shown in numerous studies to significantly reduce stress. During meditation, your body decreases the production of stress markers like cortisol, letting you enjoy a state of rest deeper than the relaxing phases of sleep.

Focus

If your mind often races like a hyper hare, meditation can be the tortoise that steadies the pace. Regular meditation enhances your ability to concentrate and maintain attention. A fascinating study published in the journal Psychological Science showed that participants who engaged in just a few weeks of meditation training improved their scores on the cognitive rigor of the GRE exam. That's right—meditating might even make you a test-taking titan!

Emotional Equilibrium

Riding the rollercoaster of emotions can be exhilarating yet exhausting. Meditation is like having a skilled conductor guiding this ride, helping to balance those intense emotional ups and downs. Through practices like loving-kindness meditation or mindfulness, you learn to observe your emotions without judgment, gaining an incredible toolkit for emotional regulation.

Studies in the world of neuroscience talk about the prefrontal cortex's role in meditators—this brain region sparks up, helping you manage emotions more easily.

Improved Well-being

Now, let's turn the spotlight to overall well-being—your general happiness and satisfaction with life. By reducing stress, improving your mood, and enhancing self-awareness, meditation contributes to an enriched life experience. Regular meditators often report feelings of enhanced self-actualization—basically, becoming the best version of themselves.

A long-term study suggested that those who meditate regularly may even alter their brain's physical structure, specifically areas responsible for processing self-awareness and perspective. That's right, meditation not only feels good, but it also literally builds a better brain!

Common Myths About Meditation

Let's face it, meditation often gets wrapped in a cloak of mystical phrases, enigmatic fables, and, yes, a fair share of myths. Now and then, these misunderstandings drift around, obscuring the real essence of meditation. Let's take a look at some of the most common myths and understand if there is any truth behind them.

Myth #1: Meditation Means Emptying Your Mind Completely

Ah, the old "mind vacuum" myth! The idea here is that to meditate correctly, you must completely clear your mind of thoughts. Imagine that—absolute mental silence, as if someone turned off your brain's incessant radio. Sounds a bit dull, doesn't it? And frankly, nearly impossible.

Meditation isn't about banishing every little thought into the void of nothingness. It's about becoming aware of your thoughts, not wrestling them into submission. When you meditate, you're training to observe these thoughts as they flutter by like leaves on a stream, not attaching to them or getting swept away by their current.

Myth #2: Meditation Is Solely a Religious Practice

This one's half true. While meditation does hold significant places in various religious practices like Buddhism and Hinduism, its benefits are not confined to the walls of temples or spirituality.

Meditation is a tool—a brain gym if you will. It's about mental fitness. People from all walks of life, backgrounds, and belief systems can practice meditation for its benefits, which include reduced stress, improved concentration, and an overall better quality of life. Think of it as universal as jogging; you don't have to be an Olympic sprinter to go for a run.

Myth #3: It Takes Hours of Meditation to Get Any Benefit

Who has hours to spare these days? Between balancing work, family, friends, and the latest binge-worthy streaming series, finding extensive periods to sit in silence seems daunting. This myth can often discourage beginners who barely have time to finish their coffee while it's still warm!

In honesty, quality trumps quantity. Research suggests that even just a few minutes of meditation each day can make a significant difference in how you deal with daily stresses and strains. Think of it as a daily dose of mental multivitamins – even small amounts are beneficial to your health.

Myth #4: You Must Sit in Lotus Position to Meditate

Picture meditation, and you probably imagine someone sitting with legs interlocked, back absurdly straight, on a picturesque clifftop at sunrise. While that does make for a fabulous Instagram photo, it's not the only way to go about it.

Comfort is key in meditation. You can meditate while sitting in a chair, lying down, standing, or even walking. The vital part is not the position but maintaining a good posture and finding a state where you can remain alert and relaxed.

Myth #5: Good Meditators Do Not Have Thoughts During Meditation

If the aim of meditation was to have a blank mind, then every time you got distracted, you'd be failing, right? This could make meditation feel like just another arena for competition or self-criticism.

Meditation is not a battlefield of the mind. Having thoughts during meditation is perfectly normal. It's what you do when you realize you're engrossed in thought that counts. Gently guiding your attention back to your breath or chosen point of focus is where the magic happens. Each return is like a mental rep, strengthening the mind's ability to focus and stay present.

Setting the Foundation

Let's begin by acknowledging a simple truth: meditation isn't a one-and-done deal. It's more like brushing your teeth or, for those of you who've bravely ventured into the world of plant ownership, watering your fussy ficus. It requires regular attention and a gentle hand.

Consistency in meditation is about making this practice a staple in the fabric of your daily life. It's the act of returning to the meditation cushion, chair, or even the park bench, day after day, no matter the emotional weather forecast. This could mean meditating for five minutes daily or a longer session a few times a week. The key is regularity, not duration. Think of it as setting up a coffee date with your mind, where showing up on time, every time, is more important than how long you stay.

And what about patience? This is the soft melody that plays in the background, reminding you that it's perfectly okay not to be a Zen master from the get-go—or ever, for that matter. Meditation is not about achieving some lofty state of enlightenment by Tuesday; it's about being present. When thoughts wander and distractions arise—as they invariably will—patience whispers, "It's okay. Let's return to the breath." It's about celebrating the small victories, like noticing when your mind has wandered off to plan dinner during a mindfulness session.

End of Chapter Exercise

Let's start with a short, guided breathing meditation designed to help you find a moment of peace and clarity in your day. Whether you're completely new to meditation or just need a quick reset, this practice is a perfect way to center yourself.

- Find a comfortable seat in a quiet space where you won't be disturbed. You can sit on a chair with your feet flat on the floor or on a cushion with your legs crossed. Allow your hands to rest gently on your knees or in your lap, and when you're ready, softly close your eyes.
- Let's start by taking a deep breath through your nose, filling your lungs completely. Feel the air move into your nostrils, down into your lungs, and notice your chest and belly expand. Hold this breath for a moment.
- Now, slowly exhale through your mouth. As you release the air, imagine letting go of any stress or tension you've been holding onto. Feel your muscles relax and your mind clear.
- Again, inhale slowly and deeply through your nose, observing the sensation of air filling your body and revitalizing every cell. Pause gently at the top of the breath.
- Then exhale slowly, letting the breath flow out naturally, feeling a sense of release and relaxation deepen with each breath out.
- Continue this pattern—a slow deep inhale, a pause, and a relaxingly slow exhale. With each breath, allow yourself to become more relaxed and present.
- As you settle deeper into this exercise, if your mind begins to wander, gently notice without judgment and bring your focus back to your breathing. Return to the sensation of the air coming in through your nose, filling you with life, and leaving gently through your mouth, carrying away tension.

- Spend a few more cycles of breath in this mindful state, focusing on the rhythm and feeling lighter and more relaxed with each round.
- Now, as this short meditation comes to a close, take one final deep breath in, feeling grateful for the moment you've taken for yourself. Exhale slowly and start to bring your awareness back to the room.
- Gently wiggle your fingers and toes. When you're ready, open your eyes, maybe give a small stretch, and carry this sense of calm and clarity into the rest of your day.

Chapter 2

Preparing for Meditation

The first step in meditation practice is preparation. Imagine meditation as your personal retreat, a quiet corner of your world where you can let go of the hustle and bustle and just breathe. You see, breathing is not just about keeping us alive; in meditation, it becomes an art form, a gentle rhythm guiding us deeper into serenity. Before you dive into this serene pool, let's chat about how you can create the perfect ambiance that whispers, "Relax, you're home."

Think of yourself as the director of your own peaceful play, where every element matters—from the lighting to the props (yes, those cushions and mats are more than mere accessories!). Each detail will play a role in crafting an environment that supports not just your body but also your mood.

Let's unleash some of that inner tranquility by setting up a space that feels like a warm, welcoming hug. Whether you're a seasoned meditator or a curious newcomer, getting the setup just right can make all the difference. So, fluff up those pillows, set the scene with soothing tones, and let's prepare to quiet the mind with the finesse of a maestro tuning an orchestra before the grand symphony—the symphony of your peaceful meditation.

Choosing the Right Space

When it comes to setting up the perfect meditation space in your home, think of it as creating a tiny sanctuary where stress dares not tread. It's a little nook where the hustle and bustle of daily life fades into the background, leaving a serene oasis for you to retreat into. Not just any corner will do, though; selecting and setting up this space is as important as the meditation itself.

Let's explore how to select and craft this calming cocoon—from choosing the right spot to making it as comfortable and personal as your favorite sweater.

Choosing the Right Spot

First things first, location is key. You'll want a peaceful spot that's as far from household traffic (and noise) as possible. If you live in a bustling household, this might take some scouting. Look for a corner that isn't a common thoroughfare for family members or roommates. Even a walk-in closet can double as a Zen den if space is at a premium!

Preferably, natural light should be part of your chosen location, ideally with a view of something calming, like your garden or a quiet street. Windows can work wonders for connecting you to the calming energies of the outdoors. However, avoid settings where you can be easily distracted by what's happening outside. Remember, the goal is calmness and focus.

Crafting a Quiet Environment

Once you've picked your spot, let's soundproof it—not with construction-grade material, but by ensuring it's as shielded from noise as possible. This could mean moving your meditation times to the quieter parts of the day or using soothing background noises, like a sound machine that plays gentle waves or rustling leaves, to drown out the discord from outside.

It's also worth considering the acoustics of your space. Soft furnishings can help muffle sounds—think plush rugs, cushions, or drapes. These not only aid in noise reduction but also enhance the comfort factor.

Comfort Is Key

Speaking of comfort, your seated posture is paramount in meditation. Choose a cushion or chair that supports your sitting style, be it cross-legged or in a more relaxed pose. Your back should be straight yet relaxed, with your knees at or below hip level to avoid strain. The perfect meditation cushion or chair is like a good friend—supportive yet unobtrusive.

Add a few blankets or a shawl to your space, especially if you get chilly easily. Being physically comfortable means you won't be distracted by bodily discomfort, allowing deeper meditation.

Clutter-Free, Mind-Free

A cluttered space is a cluttered mind. This old adage is particularly true in the context of creating a meditation space. Start by keeping your space tidy and free of unnecessary items. This doesn't mean it has to be Spartan; just keep out distractions and keep it orderly. Maybe introduce elements that evoke a sense of tranquility— an indoor plant, a small sculpture, a wall hanging of calming landscapes, or a simple vase of fresh flowers.

Organizing your space also means considering the flow of energy, or chi, as promoted in Feng Shui. Keeping the energy of the room vibrant yet peaceful can involve positioning your seat so that you face the door (but aren't in direct line with it), which subconsciously promotes a sense of safety and openness.

Personal Touches

This is your personal retreat, so infuse it with bits that matter to you. Maybe light a scented candle or incense that brings back happy memories or calms your spirit. Use a meditation app or playlist if you prefer guided sessions, and perhaps keep a journal nearby to jot down thoughts or insights that arise during your practice.

Color can also play a significant role in setting the mood. Earth tones or soft pastels can be particularly soothing and help maintain a sense of grounding. However, choose whatever hues soothe your soul—it's your sanctuary, after all.

Routine and Ritual

Finally, make visiting your meditation space a ritual. Routine helps establish habits. Maybe place a mat rolled up at the corner, waiting for you, enticing you to unroll it and start your session. Or place a bookmark in a meditation book or deck of inspirational cards ready to inspire you.

Meditating at the same time every day can also help reinforce this new routine. The consistency will help make meditation feel as natural as breathing—something you do without much forethought but which sustains you throughout the day.

Creating a designated meditation space in your home is not just about physical location; it's about carving out a mental space too. By carefully choosing and setting up your area, you can build a sanctuary that not only beckons you to come and meditate but profoundly enhances the quality of your practice. Enjoy setting up this sacred space, knowing it's a place where you can pause, breathe, and reconnect with yourself. Each time you enter, leave the world behind and embrace the stillness—it's all yours.

The Ideal Time to Meditate

Now, you might be wondering, "When is the best time to meditate?" Let's explore the benefits of morning versus evening meditation, helping you figure out the perfect time to drop a tranquil anchor into your day.

Morning Meditation: Starting on the Right Foot

There's something magical about the world in the morning. The sun stretches its rays across the sky, and there's an unspoken promise of new possibilities. It's the perfect backdrop for a morning meditation session.

Morning meditation is like setting the tone for a symphony but for your day. It's about grounding yourself before the emails flood in and your to-do list starts buzzing with reminders. Taking this time helps align your mood and set a calm, focused tone for the hours ahead.

Additionally, morning is when your mind is, arguably, at its freshest and least cluttered. Meditating during this time can boost your clarity and focus, making it easier to tackle complex tasks later on with a greater level of productivity and creativity.

By meditating in the morning, you're essentially putting on mental armor to face the day's challenges and stresses. Think of it as a preemptive strike against stress!

Evening Meditation: Unwinding the Day

As the day winds down, the curtain falls, and the audience of your thoughts applauds for an encore, evening meditation enters as a gentle director, guiding them to a graceful exit.

After a long day, meditation can be your personal mental masseuse. Evening sessions work wonders in dissipating the stress and tension that build up over the day. It's like giving your mind a cozy blanket and some warm cocoa to unwind.

Engaging in meditation before bedtime can significantly improve the quality of your sleep. It's like soothing music that gently lulls the busy brain, guiding it toward a restful, deep sleep. Rather than letting your thoughts play hopscotch, you clear the playground and prepare for a peaceful slumber.

Additionally, evening sessions are great for reflective meditation. It's a time to look back at the day, learn from experiences, and cultivate a sense of gratitude. This reflective practice enriches personal growth and emotional understanding.

Incorporating Meditation Into Your Daily Routine

Knowing the benefits is one thing, but weaving meditation into the fabric of your daily life? That's where the magic truly happens. Here's how to make meditation a delightful habit rather than a chore.

It's a good idea to make meditation a ritual. So, attach your meditation to a daily task. Perhaps meditate right after brushing your teeth in the morning or immediately after you shut down your laptop in the evening. By piggybacking it onto established habits, meditation becomes a natural part of your routine.

If the thought of sitting quietly for 30 minutes straight sends shivers down your spine, worry not! Start with just a few minutes. Even a brief pause can be powerful. Gradually, as you get more comfortable, you can increase the duration.

Posture and Comfort

When you meditate, it's important to maintain a comfortable posture to avoid physical distractions, aches, and pains. After all, how can you explore the inner cosmos if you're thinking about that crick in your neck?

Let's talk posture, the unsung hero of a fruitful meditation practice.

Seated Meditation: The Classic

The image that pops into most minds when you say "meditation"—a serene figure, legs folded, eyes closed, a picture of peace. This is your classic seated meditation. It comes in several flavors:

- **Lotus Position:** A favorite but an ambitious start for many, this involves sitting cross-legged with each foot on the opposite thigh. It's the double black diamond of meditation poses—rewarding but challenging!
- **Half-Lotus:** A tad easier, where just one foot rests on the opposite thigh. Kind of like the lotus, but it's keeping its options open.
- **Burmese Position:** Both feet rest flat on the floor. No legs over legs; a truly diplomatic choice for the thighs and knees.

In all these options, the back does its best impression of a mountain—upright and majestic. The hands can chill lightly on the knees or be placed gently in the lap. This posture keeps you awake and alert! You're not just sitting; you're an emperor or empress of your castle of calm.

But let's be real, not everyone is ready to create a pretzel with their legs. If your hips scream when you attempt it, pull over a meditation bench or a chair. The goal here isn't to reenact a Yoga Journal cover but to find a position where you can forget your body and focus on your breath.

Lying Down: Meditation in Repose

The lying-down meditation is also known as the "savasana" in yoga. It's simple: lie flat on your back, let your legs and arms relax completely, and close your eyes. Imagine you're a starfish soaking in the sun on a warm beach, or a pancake perfectly flat on a griddle—pick your analogy. Use a pillow under your knees or head if you like. Comfort is king here.

But a word of caution—while it's the ultimate in relaxation, it's also the sneakiest trap for a quick snooze. If you find yourself snoring, it might be time to reconsider the seated pose. However, for those who find sitting painful, this can be a serene alternative.

Walking Meditation: Who Says You Can't Move?

Yes, walking can be meditative too! Who said you had to be still to meditate? In walking meditation, each step is a mindful adventure. Find a quiet path, perhaps in your garden, a park, or even a tranquil corridor in your home. Now, slow down. Imagine you're exploring the moon's surface, low gravity and all.

The trick here is to synchronize your breath with your steps. Breathe in; take a step; breathe out; another step. Feel the soul (pun intended) of your feet; each touch, roll, and lift off the ground. This type of meditation is perfect for those who don't like sitting too long or those who find the rhythm in repetition soothing.

Finding What Works: The Comfort Quotient

The golden rule across all these postures? Comfort. If you're too aware of your body, you'll be wrestling your own limbs instead of bathing in tranquility. Each session might feel different, so it's perfectly fine to switch things up. You might be a lotus one day and a starfish the next. That's the beauty of it!

And remember, while the posture is important, it's not the essence of meditation. The heart of this practice is the mind. The postures are just vehicles, designed to help you journey inward with ease.

Breathing Basics

Breathing, something we do about 20,000 times a day without a second thought, is monumentally powerful when done with intention. It's the bridge between the conscious and the unconscious, the body and the mind. In the context of meditation, breath acts as your personal tour guide, helping you navigate inner landscapes without getting lost in thought-cloud forests.

In meditation, the gold standard for breathing is natural, steady, and quiet. Imagine you're trying to soothe a timid fawn lying right beside you. That's the gentleness you're aiming for.

Diaphragmatic Breathing

Also known as belly breathing, this technique involves breathing deep into your belly rather than shallow breaths in your chest. Picture your abdomen as a balloon; inhale and watch it effortlessly expand, then exhale and let it softly deflate. It's a simple yet profound way to fuel your meditation.

- Sit comfortably or lie down.
- Place one hand on your chest and the other on your belly.
- Breathe in slowly through your nose, ensuring your diaphragm inflates enough to stretch your lungs.
- Slowly exhale through pursed lips, engaging your belly.

This technique can be a game changer, especially if everyday stress has trained your body into restrictive, shallow breathing.

The 4-7-8 Method

This is the relaxation whisperer of breathing techniques, designed to decrease anxiety and promote calmness. It's almost like a breathing lullaby for your busy brain.

- Breathe in quietly through your nose for 4 seconds.
- Hold your breath for 7 seconds (no, don't turn blue on me, just a calm hold!).
- Exhale completely through your mouth, making a whooshing sound, for 8 seconds.
- Repeat this cycle four times. By the time you're done, your body should feel like it's melting into a state of blissful pudding!

Alternate Nostril Breathing

This technique is a bit quirky, but it's fantastic for harmonizing the left and right hemispheres of the brain, resulting in a delightful state of mental clarity and calm.

- Sit in a comfortable position with your back straight.
- Place your right thumb over your right nostril and inhale deeply through the left nostril.
- Now, switch! Cover your left nostril with your right ring finger, and exhale through the right nostril.
- Inhale through the right nostril, switch, and exhale through the left.

You might be wondering, why all this focus on breathing? Can't we just sit and not think? If only it were that simple! Your breath influences the autonomic nervous system, which handles the things you don't usually need to think about (like heart rate and digestion). Proper breathing helps shift from the fight-or-flight response to relax-and-renew mode, reducing stress and allowing a more meditative state.

Moreover, think of each breath as a mini-break for your thoughts. It's a cue for your brain to pause the endless chatter and enjoy a moment of stillness. As you breathe in calmness and breathe out tension, you almost trick your mind into a state of tranquility.

Incorporating mindful breathing into your meditation isn't about achieving perfection. It's about embracing patience and persistence, getting better one breath at a time. Like any good relationship, it involves understanding, practice, and most importantly, breathing space.

End of Chapter Exercise

Here's a simple and relaxing breathing exercise to help you become more aware of your breath and establish a connection with your breathing. This can be very soothing and is a perfect little break for any part of your day!

- Sit comfortably in a quiet space where you won't be disturbed. You can choose to sit on a chair with your feet flat on the ground or on the floor in a cross-legged position. If you prefer, you can also lie down. Keep your back straight to allow for easy breathing.
- Gently close your eyes. This helps reduce visual distractions and allows you to focus more on your breath and how your body feels.
- Take a moment to notice your natural breath without trying to change it. Feel the air entering through your nostrils, the rise and fall of your chest, or the movement in your belly.
- Start to count as you inhale, silently saying to yourself "one," and as you exhale, count "two." Continue this pattern, only counting to two. This helps maintain focus on your breath without overcomplicating the process.
- Gradually, allow your breaths to become deeper and fuller. Inhale slowly, filling your lungs completely, and then exhale slowly. Try to make your inhale and exhale even in length. An easy pattern could be inhaling for a count of four and exhaling for a count of four.

Preparing for Meditation

- As you continue to breathe deeply, focus on areas of your body that may feel tense. Imagining that each exhale helps release tension from these areas can be very effective.
- After about 5-10 minutes, or however long you feel comfortable, let go of the deep breathing and allow your breath to return to its natural rhythm. Notice if you feel different compared to when you started.
- As you finish your session, gently wiggle your fingers and toes, and when you're ready, open your eyes. Take a moment before getting up to reflect on any changes in your body or mind.

Chapter 3

Mindfulness Meditation

You might have heard about mindfulness. It's a buzz word at the moment, and for good reason. Mindfulness is about being fully present, embracing the now without judgment, and, frankly, giving your bustling mind a well-deserved break.

In this chapter, we'll explore the gentle art of mindfulness meditation, which is somewhat like learning to dance gracefully with your own thoughts and feelings. You'll discover how to develop an attitude of awareness and acceptance that can dramatically transform how you experience everyday life.

What is Mindfulness?

At its core, mindfulness is the practice of being fully present and engaged at the moment, aware of your thoughts and feelings without distraction or judgment. Imagine sitting on a park bench observing the world. You're not trying to change the pace of the walkers or control the direction of the breeze; instead, you're simply noticing and experiencing what is happening right now.

Mindfulness is built on a foundation of self-awareness and acceptance. Here's a quick breakdown:

- **Awareness:** This is all about tuning in. Like turning up the volume on your favorite song, it's about really listening to your thoughts, feelings, bodily sensations, and the environment around you.
- **Non-judgment:** Imagine you miss a bus, and instead of tumbling into a spiral of self-criticism or regret ("Oh, if only

I'd skipped that second cup of coffee!"), you simply observe the event as it is. Non-judgment encourages us to view our experiences without labeling them as good or bad.

- **Living in the moment:** Whether it's savoring a piece of chocolate or soaking in a sunset, mindfulness calls for immersing ourselves fully in the activities of the present moment. It's about not dwelling on past pizzas or future doughnuts!

- **Acceptance:** It means seeing things for what they are. When you drop an ice cream cone, instead of getting caught up in frustration, acceptance lets you recognize the accident just as it is, and perhaps even chuckle at the splat pattern.

History and Evolution of Mindfulness Meditation

Though the mindfulness of today has dressed itself up in secular and scientific clothing, its roots stretch deeply into ancient traditions, particularly within Buddhism. Over 2,500 years ago in the Eastern world, mindfulness was developed as a way to cultivate understanding, wisdom, and enlightenment. It all began with the teachings of the Buddha who proposed mindfulness meditation as a part of the path to awakening.

Fast forward to more recent centuries, and mindfulness found its scenic route to the Western world through various channels. It wasn't until the 20th century that it began to gain traction in a secular context, a movement many attribute to a rather groovy molecular biologist, Jon Kabat-Zinn. In the late 1970s, Kabat-Zinn founded the Mindfulness-Based Stress Reduction (MBSR) program at the University of Massachusetts Medical School. His method pulled mindfulness out of its exclusively religious confines and dressed it up in scientific rigor and accessibility. Thanks to his work, mindfulness has wedged itself into the windows of modern psychotherapy, business management, and even education.

From adorning the walls of therapy offices to being the star at Google's headquarters for boosting employee productivity, mindfulness has become a hip trend. It's taught in schools to help students manage stress and bulldoze through distractions. It's even in our apps and smartphones, nudging us to breathe deeply or observe our thoughts.

Mindfulness Today: A Cultural Phenomenon

Today, mindfulness has a spot at virtually every table, from corporate boardrooms to your local community center. Studies have shown that mindfulness can reduce stress, improve attention, boost creativity, and even strengthen relationships.

Ultimately, mindfulness isn't about getting somewhere else—it's about being exactly where you are, but better. It's about opening your eyes to the colorful details of your daily routine, embracing the chaos of life, and maybe even enjoying that chaos a little more.

How Mindfulness Meditation Works

Let's start with the audience in your mind: your thoughts. In mindfulness meditation, one becomes a gentle observer of these thoughts. It's almost like sitting by a river and watching leaves float by—except, in this case, the leaves are your thoughts, emotions, and sensations.

The key here is not to get wet! I mean, don't plunge into the river chasing after every leaf; observe them from the tranquil riverbank. Here's how you can practice this:

- **Find a Comfy Spot:** Sit or lie down in a quiet place. Comfort is key here—no need to twist yourself into a pretzel unless, of course, you find pretzels particularly comfortable.
- **The Welcoming Committee:** As thoughts pop up, welcome them like old friends. Say a mental "Hello" to your thoughts, and acknowledge their presence, but don't invite them in for tea. This is where you practice detachment gently. Recognize each thought, and then let it float away.
- **Repeat and Be Kind:** Some thoughts are stickier than old gum on a shoe—they keep coming back. Whenever you

catch yourself getting involved with a thought, gently guide your attention back to observing. And remember, be kind to yourself in the process.

The Role of the Breath

The breath in mindfulness meditation isn't just about keeping you alive; it's your anchor. Think of it as the home base in a lively game of tag—you can always return to it when things get too hectic.

Breathing in mindfulness is about observing the breath as it is: the cool air entering through your nostrils, your chest rising and falling, and the warmer air flowing out. This observance anchors you to the present moment and helps declutter the mind. Here's how to buddy up with your breath:

- **Natural Breath:** Begin by just noticing your breath without trying to change it. It's like getting to know a new friend—you wouldn't force them to be someone they're not!
- **Counting Breaths:** If your mind tends to run a marathon, count your breaths. It's like setting a mental pedometer; it gives the mind a gentle focus. One breath in and out is "one," up to ten, and then start back at one.
- **Full Awareness:** Place a hand on your belly and feel it rise and fall with each breath. This full-body engagement can help deepen your focus and connection with the breath.

The Art of Being Present

Now, 'being present' might sound ridiculously simple, but it's surprising how many of us don't manage it. In the end, it's actually about tuning into the now. It's about letting go of the rewind button (past) and the fast-forward button (future) and just hitting 'play' on today.

How can you cultivate this magical ability? Let's explore:

- **Engage Your Senses:** Notice the world around you. What do you see? What can you hear? Maybe it's the distant sound of traffic or the chirping of a bird. Maybe it's the feel of the air on

your skin or the subtle aromas of your environment. Engaging your senses pulls you back into the now.
- **Mindful Actions:** Whether you're brushing your teeth, eating lunch, or walking to the mailbox, turn these everyday actions into mindful exercises. Notice each step, each bite, each stroke. It's amazing how much more alive peanut butter tastes when you're fully present with it!
- **Patience and Practice:** Like any good habit, being present takes practice. The more you do it, the easier it becomes. Your mind will wander off—guaranteed—but with gentle and consistent guidance, it'll start enjoying the view from the present moment more and more.

Mindfulness Meditation isn't about achieving some superhuman state or emptying the mind entirely. It's about training yourself to live more fully, deeply, and vividly in the present. So, breathe, observe, and be gentle with yourself. The beauty of being fully present is that there's nothing to chase after—you're already here, and what a wonderful place to be.

Benefits of Mindfulness Meditation

When you bring mindfulness into your life, it's like turning on a mental dimmer switch that softens those harsh lights of daily hustle and illuminates your inner world with a gentle glow. Let's explore how this serene practice can be a game-changer for your everyday life.

Enhancing Self-Awareness

Have you ever found yourself gobbling down a bag of chips and then suddenly realizing it was empty, and you barely tasted a single bite? Mindfulness meditation is like the friend who gently taps on your shoulder and says, "Hey, let's pay attention." By training your mind to observe your actions, thoughts, and feelings without judgment, mindfulness boosts your self-awareness.

This enhanced self-awareness is akin to getting to know yourself on a first-name basis. It helps you become more attuned to your emotional triggers and habitual reactions, offering you a chance to greet them with a polite nod rather than letting them steer your day. This familiarity with your inner experiences serves as a foundation for personal growth.

Reducing Stress

In the non-stop carousel of daily obligations, stress can often ride along, uninvited. Mindfulness meditation drops into this whirlwind like a calm breeze, sometimes so subtle yet incredibly refreshing. By focusing on the present moment—whether it's your breath, the sensations in your body, or the sounds around you — mindfulness acts as a pause button to your body's stress responses.

Think of it as a mental gym where you exercise slowing down and breathing, not just sweating it out on the treadmill of life. Regular practice diminishes the prevalence of stress hormones like cortisol, akin to taking weights off your shoulders one by one. You will likely find yourself handling stressful situations with more grace and gumption rather than folding under pressure.

Improving Mental Clarity

Ever feel like your brain has too many tabs open? Mindfulness meditation helps in decluttering this mental maze. With each practice, it's as if you're tidying up, organizing thoughts in neatly labeled folders, and closing unnecessary mental tabs. The result is a clearer, more focused mind that can navigate through information and make decisions more efficiently.

This mental decluttering is particularly advantageous in our information-saturated age. With clearer cognition, you're better equipped to tackle complex tasks and creative challenges. It's like upgrading your brain's operating system to handle multitasking and heavy applications more effectively, giving you an edge both personally and professionally.

Applications of Mindfulness in Everyday Life

Now, how do we weave this thread of mindfulness into the fabric of daily living? Mindfulness isn't just confined to meditation cushions; it can tag along with you like a cheerful companion throughout your day.

- **Mindful Eating:** Instead of mindlessly munching away while glued to screens, try engaging fully with the experience of eating. Notice the colors, smell the aromas, taste each flavor, and chew deliberately. It turns every meal into a sensory journey, making eating a more delightful and satisfying experience.
- **Mindful Listening:** Whether in meetings, conversations with loved ones or even listening to music, fully immerse yourself in the sounds and meanings. This not only enhances your relationships and communication but also allows you to enjoy the layers and nuances of sounds, possibly discovering new favorite melodies or meanings in conversations.
- **Mindful Walking:** Turn a simple walk, whether to the mailbox or a stroll in the park, into a refreshing practice. Feel each foot connect with the ground, observe your surroundings with fresh eyes, and breathe in the fresh air. It's a mini-vacation in the midst of a busy day.
- **Mindful Breaks:** In between tasks, instead of diving into your phone, take a few mindful breaths or stretch. It refreshes your mind, making you more ready and rejuvenated for the next task.

Embracing mindfulness meditation doesn't mean you need to change your entire lifestyle; it's about enhancing everyday experiences, adding depth, and reducing the white noise that often leaves us feeling frazzled. By adopting even a few of these practices into your regular routine, you'll notice that life seems a bit more colorful, less stressful, and overwhelmingly more manageable.

End of Chapter Exercise

This simple, 10-minute exercise is designed to help you focus on your breath and bodily sensations, anchoring you in the present moment. Here's how to start:

- Choose a quiet place where you won't be disturbed. This could be a corner of your room, a comfortable chair, or a spot in a local park.
- Set a timer for 10 minutes. This will help you relax without worrying about the time.
- Sit in a comfortable position with your back straight but not stiff. You can sit on a chair with your feet flat on the floor, on a cushion, or on the floor in a cross-legged position. Place your hands comfortably in your lap.
- Gently close your eyes to help bring your attention inward. If you're more comfortable with it, you can also maintain a soft gaze on a fixed point in front of you.
- Begin by taking a few deep breaths—inhaling through your nose and exhaling through your mouth. Then, allow your breathing to return to a natural rhythm. Focus on the sensation of the air entering and leaving your nostrils, or the rise and fall of your chest or abdomen.
- Expand your attention to notice the sensations in your body. Feel the weight of your body on the chair or floor. Observe the texture of your clothing against your skin, the temperature of the air, and any sounds that might be around you.
- It's natural for your mind to wander. Each time you notice your mind drifting to thoughts, feelings, or sounds, acknowledge them without judgment and gently redirect your focus back to your breath or bodily sensations.
- Spend a few minutes moving your awareness to different parts of your body. Notice any tension or discomfort, warmth or coolness, tingling, or numbness. Don't judge or try to change what you feel; just observe.

- Bring your focus back to your breathing. Spend the last few minutes of your meditation simply observing the natural rhythm of your breath. Feel each inhale as an opportunity to absorb freshness and each exhale as a moment to release tension.
- When your timer ends, do not rush to open your eyes or move. Take a moment to notice the stillness of your meditation. Slowly bring some gentle movements to your fingers and toes. Open your eyes softly and gradually orient yourself to your surroundings.
- Take a minute to reflect on your experience. Notice any changes in your mood or bodily sensations.

Chapter 4

Focused Attention Meditation

Focused attention meditation is like having a superpower. It's the art of honing in on one single element—be it your breath, a mantra, or even a pesky fly buzzing around your room—and sticking with it like glue, despite the hustle and bustle around. This technique isn't just about sharpening your concentration skills; it's more like training your brain to become a Zen master amid chaos.

In this chapter, let's delve deeper into focused attention meditation and understand it fully.

The Why and How of Focused Attention Meditation

The primary purpose of focused attention meditation is to cultivate a heightened state of alertness and awareness. It's about training the mind to not just observe thoughts but to pin them down, one at a time, like butterflies in a collection, examining them without judgment before letting them fly away.

This practice serves multiple purposes. Firstly, it can significantly reduce stress, because, let's face it, juggling a thousand thoughts at once can feel like trying to herd cats. By focusing on one thing, the mind gets a break from the chaos, like a mini-vacation in the middle of your day.

Moreover, practicing this type of meditation regularly improves concentration, sharpens memory, and enhances overall mental resilience. It's like doing push-ups for your brain; over time, you build mental muscle that helps you focus better, remember the details like where you put your keys, and stay cool, calm, and collected when life throws curveballs.

Focused Attention vs. Open Awareness: The Friendly Rivals

While focused attention meditation is like having a laser beam for a brain, open awareness meditation is more like a panoramic view. Open awareness, or open monitoring meditation, invites practitioners to notice everything around them without reacting or attaching to any particular thing. Imagine being in a bustling café, soaking up every sight, sound, and smell without zoning in on any specific conversation, melody, or aroma. That's open awareness for you—broad, inclusive, and a bit of an overachiever in sensory perception.

Here's where they differ: focused attention is all about exclusion, while open awareness is about inclusion. Focused attention asks you to focus intensely on one subject, almost in a monogamous kind of way, while open awareness is more of a social butterfly, fluttering around, greeting every thought, feeling, and sensation with a friendly nod.

Choosing between focused attention and open awareness could be likened to choosing between tea and coffee—they both have their perks, and it really boils down to personal taste or what you need more in your life at the moment. If you find yourself easily distracted, constantly losing your train of thought halfway through a sentence, focused attention might be the brew for you. It's great for tightening up those loose bolts in your attention span.

On the other hand, if you're the type whose mind feels perpetually clouded with fog, where you're not even sure what you're thinking, open awareness might just clear the sky for you. It can help in becoming more aware of your mental patterns and behavior, thus fostering a deeper understanding of yourself.

Starting Your Journey

To get started with focused attention meditation, all you need is a quiet spot and something to focus on. It could be as simple as following the rhythm of your breath—the inhale, the pause, the exhale—or a repeated mantra that resonates with you. The key is to keep coming back to your focus point every time you notice your mind has wandered off to plan dinner or replay an awkward conversation.

The beauty of this practice lies in its simplicity and the fact that you can do it anywhere, anytime. Whether you're on a crowded subway or enjoying a quiet morning by the window, five minutes of focused attention can reset your mind and boost your brainpower for the day ahead.

Choosing a Focus Point

Choosing a focal point for attention-focused meditation is like picking a dance partner for the slowest, calmest dance you'll ever perform. The options are plentiful, ranging from the subtle rhythm of your breath to the steadfast glow of a candle flame, each with its own unique flair. Let's explore the various objects you might choose and their unexpected charms.

Breath

Your breath is the most obvious choice. After all, it's like the old friend who's always there, unassuming yet vital. Focusing on your breath is a classic for good reason. It's always accessible, it's rhythmic, and it mirrors your emotional landscape—speeding up when you're agitated and slowing down when you're calm. It's perfect for beginners, but it's also deep enough for the seasoned meditator who wants simplicity.

Candle Flame

There's something mesmerizing about fire, isn't there? A candle flame provides a visual point of focus that is as poetic as it is practical. It's ideal for those who find beauty in the flicker and prefer a visual anchor. Just you and the little dance of light, keeping each other company. Plus, it's a great option if you find closing your eyes less comforting.

Mantra

A mantra is a phrase or a sound that's repeated during meditation. It could be traditional, like "Om," or something personally meaningful, such as "Peace" or "I am calm." Mantras are especially groovy for those who love the sound or find silent meditation daunting. The repetition of a mantra can be incredibly soothing and can help tame a wild mind wandering off to yesterday's dinner choices.

Body Scans

Not quite ready to pick just one spot? A body scan involves shifting your focus through different parts of the body. It's a thorough choice, sort of like a check-in with each member of your corporeal team. "How's it going, toes? What's the news, knees?" It's wonderfully grounding and can be a big relief if you've been all up in your head.

Nature Sounds

For lovers of the outdoors trapped indoors, nature sounds can be a beautiful focus. Whether it's the sound of waves, wind rustling through leaves, or a babbling brook, focusing on these sounds can be expansively calming and bring a sense of peace.

How to Choose the Right Focus for Your Practice

Choosing the right focal point in meditation is a bit like dating; you might have to meet a few contenders to find your match. Here are some pointers to help you pinpoint your perfect meditative partner:

- **Consider Your Personality:** Are you a visual person? Maybe the candle flame or a visual image will capture your attention best. Love music or the sound of voices? A mantra or nature

sounds might be your thing. If you are a tactile person, focusing on breath sensations or a tactile object could be it.
- **Think About Your Needs:** What's driving you to meditation? Seeking relaxation, perhaps the gentle pattern of your breath or a soft mantra could help. Looking for healing? A body scan could help reconnect and nurture. If your mind usually runs at NASCAR speed, a tactile focus like holding a small object might help rein it in.
- **Experiment:** You know yourself best, but sometimes you surprise yourself. Give different methods a try. Spend a few sessions with each to really see how you feel about them. It's okay to switch it up until something just clicks.
- **Accessibility:** Consider what's easy to incorporate into your everyday routine. The breath is super travel-friendly, but if a candle suits you better, find ways to make it easier to use on a regular basis.

Maintaining Focus

Maintaining focus during focused attention meditation can sometimes feel like trying to keep a puppy on a leash in a park full of squirrels. Exciting, right? But, just like training our furry friends, the key is consistency, patience, and a gentle approach. Whether you're a seasoned meditator or a curious newcomer, learning to handle distractions and gently guide your attention back to your focus point is crucial in reaping the full benefits of this practice.

The first thing to note is that distractions are inevitable. They come in all shapes and sizes - from a noisy lawnmower next door to a sudden itch on your nose or an unwelcome thought about your to-do list. Recognizing that distractions are a normal part of meditation is the first step to managing them effectively.

- **Acknowledge, Don't Judge:** When you notice a distraction, acknowledge it without judgment. Imagine naming it gently, perhaps saying inwardly, "Ah, there's a thought," or "Hello, Mr.

Itch," and then letting it pass by without engaging further. This helps in reducing the impact distractions have on your focus.

- **Choose Your Battles:** Sometimes, trying to block out a persistent noise or ignore a major distraction can be more distracting! If something continually pulls your attention away, briefly give it your attention, note its presence, and then deliberately return your focus to your meditation. You might visualize putting the distraction in a bubble and watching it float away.
- **Use the Goldilocks Rule:** Not too tight, not too loose. If you grip your focus too tightly, you'll get frustrated. Too loosely, and your mind will wander off on a tangent. Aim for a relaxed but attentive state. Think of it like holding a hummingbird in your hand—too tight, and you squish it; too loose, and it flies away.

Gently Bringing Attention Back

This perhaps is the most delicate part of the practice. It's about cultivating a gracious return to your focus point.

- **The Art of the Bounce Back:** Visualize your attention as a boomerang. Whenever it strays, it always comes back to you. By practicing the return, you're not just refocusing but strengthening the 'attention muscles' of your brain.
- **Develop a 'Back to Breath' Mantra:** Whenever you find your thoughts wandering, silently say to yourself, "back to breath," or "return to focus." This simple phrase can serve as a gentle reminder that brings your attention back without self-criticism.
- **Mindful Reminding:** Forget beating yourself up when your mind wanders—treat it as a reminder of your intention to meditate. Each return is a victory, not a defeat.

Being harsh or getting frustrated with yourself can turn the practice into a chore, something that feels punishing instead of calming. Remember, meditation is a break for your mind, akin

Focused Attention Meditation

to softly pressing the reset button, not forcefully rebooting the system.

By approaching each return to focus with kindness and patience, you transform the practice into a nurturing space, teaching yourself how to remain calm and kind under stress as well.

Additionally, the beauty of focused attention meditation lies not just in individual sessions but in the cumulative effect over time. Regular practice trains your mind to return to a state of focus more easily in daily life. It's like building a mental resilience that allows you to stay more present and less reactive, whether you're stuck in traffic or facing a stressful work deadline.

In essence, focused attention meditation is about delighting in the details—the texture of your breath, the subtlety of silence, or the mantra's rhythmic cadence. It's about building an intimate space with your own consciousness, where every returned focus feels like coming home.

By sincerely engaging with these techniques—acknowledging distractions without judgment, gently corralling your wandering mind back to your focal point, and continuing this nurturing cycle—you cultivate a sanctified space for your psyche. Over time, your meditation sessions become like second nature, a peaceful retreat from the chaos, whispering gentle reminders of the power of persistence and the serenity of self-discipline.

End of Chapter Exercise

This exercise will utilize a candle flame as the object of focus, but feel free to adapt it to a mantra or another visual object if preferred. You'll need:

- A quiet, comfortable place to sit where you won't be disturbed
- A candle and something to light it with
- Optional: timer to signal when your session ends.

- Set up your candle on a stable surface at eye level where you can gaze at it comfortably without straining your neck. Light the candle. Sit down in a comfortable position, ideally cross-legged on the floor or on a chair with your feet flat on the ground.
- Close your eyes gently. Take a deep breath in, hold it for a moment, then exhale slowly. Repeat this deep breathing three times to signal to your body that it's time to relax.
- Open your eyes and gently fix your gaze on the candle flame. Focus on the base of the flame, where it meets the wick. Try to keep your body still and your breathing natural.
- Continue to gaze at the flame. Your mind may wander, which is natural. Each time you notice your thoughts drifting, gently acknowledge them and then redirect your focus back to the candle flame.
- Maintain a relaxed breathing pattern. If it helps, silently count your breaths – inhale, one, exhale, two, and so on, up to ten, then start back at one. This can assist in sustaining your concentration.
- Slowly shift your focus from the flame to the surrounding area. Take a few deep breaths. When you feel ready, gently close your eyes once again.
- Reflect on the experience. Acknowledge how your mind feels. Do you feel more focused, or perhaps more relaxed?
- Blow out the candle carefully. Sit for a moment to appreciate the stillness. Stretch if you need to, and gradually get up when you're ready.

Chapter 5

Loving-Kindness Meditation (Metta)

In this chapter, let's talk about one of the most heartwarming practices in the world of meditation: loving-kindness meditation, also known as Metta meditation. This journey isn't just about chilling out; it's about opening up—your heart, your mind, and maybe even your world.

So, let's dive in with some good vibes and discover why loving-kindness meditation is your new best friend for fostering compassion and positivity!

What is Loving-Kindness Meditation?

Imagine combining the warmth of a cozy blanket with the soothing vibes of your favorite chill-out track. That's pretty much the essence of loving-kindness meditation. It's a traditional practice designed to cultivate an attitude of love and kindness toward everything, even your grumpy neighbor or that challenging coworker.

In technical terms, loving-kindness meditation is all about developing unconditional, inclusive love—a love with wisdom. You're not just sending good vibes to those you feel comfortable with, but extending them out to all living beings, irrespective of their relation to you.

Picture this: instead of brewing over a conflict or holding onto bitterness, you train your mind to wish well, to hope for happiness, and to visualize peace for others and yourself. Sound revolutionary? That's because it is!

Origins and Principles of Metta Meditation

The roots of loving kindness Meditation lie deep within the Buddhist tradition; specifically, it comes from the Pali word 'Metta', meaning kindness and goodwill. This form of meditation appears in one of the oldest Buddhist texts, the Pali Canon, which dates back 2,500 years. Metta is also referred to as the first of the four "Divine Abodes" (Brahmaviharas), which constitute a series of virtuous mental states and habits.

The basic principle of Metta meditation is pretty straightforward: it's all about developing a positive emotional state towards all sentient beings. The traditional practice usually follows a sequence, beginning with yourself because, let's face it, sometimes being kind to ourselves is the hardest part. From there, you gradually extend that kindness to others—first loved ones, then acquaintances, and finally your foes and all beings without exception.

Ultimately, engaging in loving-kindness meditation is like planting seeds of compassion and watering them daily. Each time you sit down to meditate, you nurture these seeds. And just as a garden doesn't bloom overnight, the feelings of unconditional love grow gradually—over time, through consistent practice.

How Loving-Kindness Meditation Changes You

How does loving-kindness meditation actually make a change in how you feel and look at the world around you? Let's explore:

- **Boosts Wellbeing:** Regular practitioners of loving kindness Meditation often reports increased levels of happiness and a greater sense of inner peace. This uplift in mood comes from focusing on positive thoughts and wishing well to others, which in turn reduces personal anxieties and fears.
- **Fosters Compassion:** This kind of meditation enhances your capacity to empathize with others, making your heart a little softer each day. You start recognizing that others have the

same needs and desires as you do—they too want happiness and dislike suffering.
- **Promotes Emotional Resilience:** By repetitively wishing others well, you develop a buffer against negative emotions. The next time you find yourself in a tough situation, you might just find it easier to access feelings of patience and understanding rather than irritation.
- **Enhances Connections:** Metta meditation can improve interpersonal relationships. It opens up avenues of patience and empathy, reducing conflicts and deepening connections. Who knew kindness could be a superpower?
- **Encourages Non-Judgment:** In the spirit of universal love, Metta asks us to look beyond our biases and judgments. We learn to accept people as they are, not as we wish them to be.

Starting a loving-kindness meditation practice doesn't require any fancy equipment—just a few moments of your day and a quiet corner. Begin by finding a comfortable position and focusing on your breath to get settled. Then, slowly build your meditation by directing kindness first towards yourself, then a close friend or family member, followed by a neutral person, then perhaps someone you have difficulties with, and finally, all sentient beings.

Feel free to get creative—some people like to imagine sending out light or energy; others prefer to repeat kind words or phrases that resonate with their personal intentions. Whatever helps you channel that genuine vibe of compassion, go for it!

How to Practice Loving-Kindness

Let's take a deeper look at how to weave this beautiful practice into your life, step by step. Imagine it as learning a dance where every step is about opening your heart a little more.

Step 1: Find Your Happy Place

First things first, find a quiet spot where interruptions are like unicorns—rare and magical. It could be a cozy corner of your room, a peaceful park, or anywhere that gives you good vibes. Sit comfortably; you can perch on a cushion, a chair, or even lie down if that's what floats your boat. The goal is to be comfy and alert.

Step 2: Settle In

Close your eyes and take a deep breath. Let's not dive into the 'love' part just yet. Instead, let your body and mind settle. Feel your breath—its natural rhythm. Notice where you feel it most distinctly. Is it the nose? Chest? Belly? Let your breath be your anchor, gently bringing you back whenever your mind decides to go touring somewhere else.

Step 3: Start with Number One—You!

Once you're feeling centered, shift your focus gently to yourself. Start by silently repeating phrases of goodwill like "May I be happy, may I be healthy, may I be safe, may I live with ease." Think of them as little beams of love and kindness radiating from your heart to yourself. Feel each phrase; don't just say it; imagine soaking in these good vibes like a sponge. Why start with yourself? Well, as they say on airplanes, you've got to secure your oxygen mask first before helping others!

Step 4: Visualize Someone You Love

Now that you've sent some good vibes your way, picture someone you love dearly—a family member, a friend, your kindergarten teacher, or even your fluffy pet. Hold their image in your mind's eye and send them the same loving thoughts: "May you be happy, may you be healthy, may you be safe, may you live with ease." Picture their smile, imagine their laughter, and feel the warmth of your love reaching out to them.

Step 5: An Acquaintance Next

After showering your loved ones with kindness, think of someone neutral in your life—maybe the barista who brews your coffee or a coworker you've only smiled at. Although your feelings towards them might not be as deep, send them your newly polished loving-kindness vibes too. It's like flexing a muscle—the more you do it, the stronger it gets.

Step 6: The Challenge—Someone You Struggle With

Here comes the tricky bit. Think of someone you have difficulties with. It's not easy to send warm wishes to someone when there are tensions or hard feelings, right? But give it a try. Remember, this doesn't mean you approve of their actions or give up your feelings—it's about tending to your heart and not harboring negativity. Send them thoughts of loving kindness: "May you be happy, may you be healthy, may you be safe, may you live with ease."

Step 7: Spread the Love Everywhere

Imagine your loving-kindness growing exponentially—a giant wave of warmth and caring expanding outward. Extend these thoughts to all beings on the planet—the grumpy, the cheerful, furry critters, forest dwellers, everyone. "May all beings be happy, may all beings be healthy, may all beings be safe, may all beings live with ease." It's like you're a love-spreading superhero, and honestly, isn't that a wonderful thing to be?

Step 8: Closing Down

Finally, gradually bring your attention back to your own breath. Take a few deep, nourishing breaths. When you're ready, wiggle your fingers, and your toes, and gently open your eyes. How do you feel? A little lighter, a bit brighter perhaps?

Keep Practicing!

Like mastering any skill, from baking perfect cookies to hitting that yoga pose, consistency is key. The beauty of loving-kindness meditation is that it can be short yet sweet. A few minutes each day can make a massive difference in how you feel and interact with the world.

Benefits of Loving-Kindness Meditation

What if I told you that LKM isn't just a beacon for personal peace but also a powerhouse for enhancing empathy, diffusing negative emotions, and fostering nourishing relationships? Let's embark on a delightful exploration of these benefits.

Developing Empathy

Empathy—often flung around like a hot potato in discussions about emotional intelligence—is the ability to step into someone else's shoes so comprehensively that you might as well have borrowed their socks. It is understanding others' feelings and perspectives, and loving-kindness meditation is just the thing to transform empathy from a flickering candle to a mega-watt light bulb.

You see, when practicing loving-kindness meditation, we focus on sending wishes of happiness, wellness, peace, and love to others, starting with ourselves and gradually extending to friends, acquaintances, and yes, even our "I wish they-were-invisible" folks. This gentle stretching of our hearts boosts our ability to understand what others are going through. It's like upgrading from empathy dial-up to high-speed broadband.

Taming Negative Emotions

Navigating through negative emotions can often feel like trying to calm a swarm of bees with no special tools. It's tricky, and, let's be honest, somewhat dangerous. Yet, loving-kindness meditation can be likened to a sweet tune that turns these menacing bees into a bunch of friendly butterflies. When we meditate on loving-kindness, we're essentially rehearsing emotional positivity. We train our minds to default to positive emotions, reducing the space and energy for the negative ones.

Through regular practice, this form of meditation can reduce stress, anxiety, and even garden-variety grumpiness. Imagine being able to see a traffic jam as more of a spontaneous karaoke opportunity rather than a vein-popping, steering-wheel-thumping crisis. That's the tranquility this type of meditation can bring into the bustling chaos of daily emotions.

Improved Relationships

Here, loving-kindness meditation shines brightly as a facilitator of fruitful and enduring connections. When you regularly send out intentions of love and goodwill, not just in your meditation nook but also in real-world interactions, you begin to notice a shift. You become more patient, more understanding, and yes, less likely to erupt over who left the cap off the toothpaste.

This positivity is infectious. It can transform relationships into thriving dialogues filled with mutual respect and affection. Regular practitioners of loving-kindness meditation often find their social environments becoming more positive, supportive, and connected. Imagine your social gatherings buzzing with a newfound vibrancy, where everyone is genuinely happy to see each other, and conversations are nourishing feasts for the soul.

End of Chapter Exercise

This 10-minute loving-kindness meditation focuses on developing feelings of compassion and love for us and others. This practice can be beneficial for reducing stress, enhancing positive emotions, and fostering a sense of interconnectedness with all beings.

Find a comfortable, quiet place to sit or lie down. Close your eyes gently, letting your hands rest comfortably on your knees or by your sides. Take a few deep breaths, inhaling deeply and exhaling slowly, allowing your body to relax and your mind to center on the present moment.

- Begin by focusing on your breath. Feel the natural flow of air entering and exiting your body. With each exhale, imagine releasing any tension you're feeling.
- Place your hands over your heart and feel its rhythm. Silently say to yourself, "May I be happy. May I be healthy? May I be safe? May I live with ease."

- Repeat these phrases three times, feeling the warmth and compassion emanating from your heart with each word.
- Bring to mind someone you care deeply about. Imagine their face in front of you, their smile, the warmth of their presence.
- Direct the loving feelings from your heart towards them and silently say, "May you be happy. May you be healthy. May you be safe. May you live with ease."
- Repeat these phrases three times, imagining your loved one receiving your love and warmth with each word.
- Next, consider a neutral person in your life, perhaps a neighbor or a colleague. Although your feelings for them may not be as deep, they too deserve happiness and peace.
- Silently express the same phrases to them: "May you be happy. May you be healthy. May you be safe. May you live with ease."
- Visualize your compassionate feelings reaching out to them, surrounding them with positivity and peace.
- Broaden your scope further to include all beings in the world—humans, animals, plants, all living creatures. Acknowledge that, like you, they too seek happiness and peace.
- Silently send out the loving kindness to all: "May all beings be happy. May all beings be healthy. May all beings be safe. May all beings live with ease."
- Feel a sense of connectedness and universal love expanding from your heart outward to the world.
- Gradually bring your awareness back to your own body. Notice the rise and fall of your chest, the air on your skin, and the sounds around you.
- Wiggle your fingers and toes, stretch however feels good, and when you're ready, open your eyes.
- Carry this sense of loving kindness with you throughout your day, reminding yourself of your deep capacity for love and compassion.

Chapter 6

Body Scan Meditation

In this chapter, we're doing to delve into the serene world of body scan meditation, a mindfulness practice where relaxation isn't just a possibility—it's a guarantee! Imagine giving your body a much-deserved systems check, akin to how a mechanic would meticulously inspect a beloved classic car, ensuring everything's running smoothly, bumper to bumper.

At its core, this practice is a form of mindfulness that requires you to concentrate on different parts of the body in sequence, typically starting from the toes and moving all the way up to the crown of the head. The goal? It's really quite simple yet profound: to notice what each part of the body is feeling without trying to change or react to it. Think of it as "feeling without interference."

A body scan can be done lying down, sitting, or in other postures that invite comfort and minimal distraction. The practice often ranges from about 10 minutes to as long as 45 minutes or more, depending on your schedule and patience. It's like marinating in your own physical presence!

Now, you might wonder, "What am I supposed to feel?" Everything and anything! Tingling, temperature, pressure, or perhaps an abstract sense of energy. The key here is not to judge or wish these sensations to be different but to simply acknowledge them with friendly curiosity.

Benefits of Tuning into Bodily Sensations

By regularly checking in with bodily sensations, you stand to gain a treasure trove of benefits that go well beyond basic relaxation.

Improved Self-Awareness

First off, body scanning sharpens your self-awareness like a finely honed chef's knife. It nurtures an acute awareness of the here and now, connecting you to the present moment with an almost photographic clarity. This heightened awareness transcends the meditation session, helping you become more attuned to your body's needs and signals throughout your day-to-day activities.

Stress Reduction

If stress were a tangible opponent, body scan meditation would be your elegantly wielded fencing sword. By encouraging deep relaxation, this practice helps dissolve stress and anxiety, blocking those sneaky stress-response hormones that whisper of worry and tension.

Pain Management

Navigating through pain can feel like trying to solve a Rubik's cube in the dark. Body scan meditation turns on the light. It allows people to change their relationship with pain. Instead of tensing up and amplifying discomfort, you learn to meet pain with a softer, more accepting approach, often leading to a natural alleviation of suffering.

Better Sleep

Ah, the elusive realm of restful slumber! Body scan meditation can serve as your personal lullaby. By calming the mind and body before bedtime, the practice sets the stage for a quicker sleep onset and a deeper sleep state. It's like weaving a cozy, comforting blanket with threads of peace and tranquility.

Emotional Resilience

Imagine navigating life's ups and downs with the grace of a world-class gymnast. Regular engagement with body scan meditation cultivates a sturdy emotional resilience, helping you to better manage emotional stressors and bounce back from setbacks with greater ease. It's like installing shock absorbers for your emotions!

Enhanced Concentration

Body scan meditation can improve concentration and focus. Each session trains you to bring your wandering mind back to the sensations in your body, reinforcing your attention muscle each time it lifts those pesky mental weights of distraction.

Whether you're seeking relaxation, deeper sleep, or stronger emotional fortitude, body scan meditation offers a personalized, gentle path to better health and well-being. It's about turning the spotlight inward and listening to your body's subtle whispers of wisdom.

How to Perform a Body Scan

Body scan meditation is not just about finding tension or pain but about greeting each sensation with a kind of friendly curiosity. Let's look at the process more deeply.

Settle In

Find a quiet, comfortable place where you won't be disturbed. You can either lie down on your back on a yoga mat or bed or sit comfortably in a chair with your feet flat on the floor. If you opt for the superhero cape of a blanket, make sure it's snug but not too tight. Take a few deep breaths, let your eyes flutter shut, and give yourself permission to take this time for yourself. No phones, no worries, no rush.

Begin with a Breath

Take three deep, slow breaths. Inhale through your nose, feel your belly rise, and then exhale gently through your mouth, feeling the belly fall. This is your internal dimmer switch turning down the noise of the outside world.

Feet First

Start your awareness at your feet. Notice any sensations here - perhaps the weight of your socks, the feel of the blanket, or maybe a slight chill. Are your feet tense, relaxed, tingly, or numb? There's no right or wrong here; you're just taking stock, like checking the weather.

A Gentle Inquiry

Move your attention up to your ankles, calves, and knees. Ask each area gently, "How are you feeling today?" Whatever you find, just note it. If you encounter tension or discomfort, imagine your breath flowing to that area, carrying a sense of warmth and relaxation. With each exhale, picture the tension melting away, dripping out of your toes like a gentle stream.

Rise Up

Continue the journey upward to your thighs and hips. These areas do a lot of heavy lifting and can often be tight. Extend them the kindness of your attention. It's like soothing an old friend with a warm compress. Breathe into them, relax them, and appreciate them.

Belly and Back Balance

Your abdomen and back are next. The belly is often a cauldron of nerves, especially if we're stressed. Place one hand on your belly, feeling it rise and fall with your breath, telling it silently, "It's okay. I'm here with you." Allow the back, often stiff from hours of sitting or standing, to sink into the mat or chair, inviting it to unclench its tight grasp.

Chest and Shoulders – The Burden Bearers

Ah, the shoulders and chest—these guys really know how to hold onto a grudge...against gravity! Give them a mental nod of thanks for all they carry. Send breath to these areas, envisioning it as a soft, loosening balm, easing the weight off them. With each exhale, let go of something you've been carrying - that argument, that deadline, that nagging worry.

Arms, Hands – The Conductors of Care

Scan through your arms and hands, parts of you that literally reach out to the world. Observe sensations here, including any pulsing, warmth, or maybe a cool detachment. Offer some softness to them, allowing them to relax fully, palms open, fingers uncurled. They deserve a break too.

Neck and Head – The Command Center

Your neck holds up that beautiful brain of yours, and it deserves some TLC. Let your head sway gently from side to side, easing any tightness. Then move up to your face. Smooth out your forehead, un-pinch your eyes, and soften your jaw. Smile slightly; it's like a little hat tip to yourself.

Full Body Embrace

Now, expand your attention to include the whole body. Imagine a gentle wave of relaxation sweeping from your head to your toes, smoothing down the rough edges of tension. Feel grounded and whole.

Thank Yourself

Before you wrap up, take a moment to thank yourself for devoting this time to your well-being. It's no small thing to choose peace in a busy world.

Open your eyes gently, wiggle your fingers and toes, stretch if it feels good, and sit up slowly. Carry this newfound serenity with you, sprinkling a little bit of it on everyone you meet today.

Remember, like any journey, the path of body scan meditation becomes richer and more familiar with practice. Stick with it, and the process will become second nature.

Using Body Scan for Relaxation and Healing

Ever felt like you're carrying the weight of the world on your shoulders? Or maybe your mind is racing so fast it could win a marathon? If you answered "yes," then you, my friend, might just need to unwind and reconnect with yourself.

Before diving in, find a quiet spot where disruptions will fear to tread. Wear comfortable clothes—yes, those pajamas count—and maybe grab a yoga mat or a soft towel. You can lay down, sit, or even perch on a comfy chair. Basically, anything goes as long as you're comfy and your back isn't mimicking our dear hunched friend, Quasimodo!

Once you're all snuggled in, close your eyes (or keep them slightly open if you're not in the mood for complete eye-closure—your game, your rules!). Then, take a few deep, grounding breaths.

Stress Relief: Unknot, Unwind, Unstress

It's no secret: when stress enters the scene, relaxation exits, stage left. But with body scan meditation, you can coax it back to center stage. As you focus on each body part, imagine breathing warmth and relaxation into it. Got a knot in your shoulder? Breathe into it and imagine the tension melting away like ice cream on a sunny day. This practice helps quell the racing thoughts and brings your attention back to the present, aka the secret garden of peace!

Sleep Improvement: Say Goodnight to Counting Sheep

If tossing and turning are your late-night hobbies, body scanning might just be the sleep guru you need. By engaging in a body scan before sleep, you guide your mind to slow down and switch off the day's playlist of worries and to-dos. This mental quietude paves the way for Mr. Sandman to sprinkle his sleep dust.

Body Awareness: The Inner GPS

Most of us go through our daily grind without really checking in with our bodies. Think of a body scan as upgrading your internal GPS. As you notice different sensations—ache here, itch there—you start understanding your body better. This increased awareness is like having a heart-to-heart with your body, gaining insights into what works for it and what doesn't.

Tips to Enhance Your Body Scan Experience

- **Regular Practice:** Just like you can't expect to nail a gourmet dish on your first try, mastering the body scan takes practice. Make it a regular part of your routine and watch your stress levels go down and your sleep quality go up!
- **Mix It Up:** Sometimes, the same old script can get boring. Switch up your start point—maybe start at your feet instead of your head. Or throw in some mindfulness phrases like, "May my feet feel relaxed," to spice up the journey.
- **Use Guided Recordings:** Not in the mood to lead your own meditation? No problem. There's a plethora of guided body scans out there in the wild world of meditation apps and websites. Pop in your earbuds and let a soothing voice whisk you away to relaxation town.
- **Journal Your Journey:** Keep a little log of your body scan experiences. What did you notice today? Any recurring themes? This can be a treasure trove of insights into what your body is telling you!

Like any good thing, body scanning is simple but mighty. Whether it's easing into a restful night, melting away the day's stresses, or tuning in to your bodily whispers, a body scan is a tool that promises a lot and delivers more.

End of Chapter Example

This journey will help you connect with every part of your body, bringing awareness to the present moment and melting away tension. Let's begin.

- Find a quiet, comfortable space where you can lie down – on a yoga mat, a bed, or a soft carpet. Let your body stretch out flat, with your arms at your sides, palms facing up, and legs naturally apart. Close your eyes and take a deep, cleansing breath, filling your lungs with air, then exhale slowly, feeling a sense of release. Repeat this three times.
- On the broad expanse of your forehead. Envision it as a smooth canvas, stretching wide and clear. Release any creases as if smoothing a sheet of paper with your mind.
- Soften your eyes. Imagine the gentle weight of a feather resting on your eyelashes, encouraging them to remain closed and relaxed.
- Notice if your jaw is clenched. Allow it to slacken as if you're about to yawn, easing all tension.
- Turn your attention to your neck. Picture a warm stream of water flowing from the base of your head down your neck, washing away stiffness and strain.
- Imagine your shoulders as boulders that begin to crumble and soften with each breath. Let the imaginary river carry away the sandy grains, leaving you feeling lighter.
- Sense any heaviness in your upper arms and envisage a gentle breeze lifting and carrying away this weight.
- Notice the air touching your forearms and focus on the sensation of your clothes against your skin – featherlight and soothing.
- Lead your awareness to your hands and fingers. Visualize each finger being caressed by a soft, gentle zephyr, uncurling any tension.

- Pay attention to your chest rising and falling with each breath. Picture each breath as a wave that washes over you, bringing calmness.
- Focus on your abdomen, feeling it expand and contract gently. With each exhale, imagine stress flowing out of your body, leaving peace behind.
- Walking down your spine, feel each vertebra like a stone in a serene path. Envision a warm, comforting glow tracing down this path, reinforcing each stone, relaxing your back deeply.
- Acknowledge any weight or pressure in your thighs. Imagine it seeping deep into the earth beneath you, rooting you securely and comfortably.
- Focus on the curve of your calves and the flex of your ankles. Each breath invites more ease; each exhale releases a layer of fatigue.
- Shift your attention to your feet. Picture each toe as a bud blossoming with relaxation, spreading softness upwards through your body.
- Slowly bring your attention back to the room. Wiggle your fingers and toes. Roll your shoulders and maybe stretch gently.
- When you're ready, open your eyes. Take a moment to notice the calmness in your body and the alertness of your mind.
- Carry this feeling of renewed serenity and wakefulness into the rest of your day.

Chapter 7

Mantra Meditation

In this chapter, we'll jump into the world of mantra meditation.

There is a lot of misunderstanding about mantras, but it's actually a very easy process. A mantra can be as simple as a word or phrase—think of it as your mental anchor, keeping your thoughts from sailing away on a sea of distractions. In these pages, you'll learn how to choose a mantra that resonates uniquely with you and integrate this practice into your day without feeling like it's just another to-do.

Understanding Mantra Meditation

At its heart, mantra meditation involves the repetitive chanting of specific syllables or phrases that hold spiritual significance.

These vibrating sequences are believed to clear the mental clutter, opening up the floodgates to higher consciousness and tranquility. Do you remember the last time you found yourself humming a tune absentmindedly and feeling oddly at peace? Mantra meditation builds on that simple concept but turns the dial-up on intentionality and spiritual connectivity.

Historical Relevance: Hinduism and Buddhism

Mantra meditation has been used through the ages in different areas. Let's explore a little.

Hinduism

The use of mantras has been connected to Hinduism since ancient times. Sacred texts like the Vedas, which date back to around 1500 BCE, are brimming with references to mantras as tools for spiritual, mental, and physical advancement. Within Hindu practice, mantras are more than just focal points during meditation; they are venerated as divine entities themselves. For instance, the 'Gayatri Mantra' invokes the universal Brahman as the source of wisdom and enlightenment.

Buddhism

In Buddhism, the rhythmic chant takes a slightly different, albeit related, path. Emerging during the 1st millennium CE, mantra practice in this tradition is often linked with Mahayana Buddhism but is not exclusive to it. The chanting here is aimed at achieving heightened states of awareness and compassion. The famous "Om Mani Padme Hum" encapsulates the essence of Buddhist beliefs, each syllable a stepping stone to deeper understanding and empathy.

The Symphony of Sound and Vibration

Let's pause here. Close your eyes for a moment, and hum, "Om". Feel that? The vibrations tingling through your body aren't just imagined—they're real and impactful. This essence of sound and its vibrating power is at the core of why mantras are profound meditative tools. Each sound in a mantra is believed to have a unique frequency; when vocalized, it promotes energy flow throughout the body, tapping into the chakras or energy centers.

Modern science, ever the skeptic, has turned its precise eyes towards mantra meditation, and interestingly, it's nodding in approval. Research suggests that chanting mantras helps lower stress, improves concentration, and promotes emotional health. It's akin to tuning a musical instrument; mantra meditation fine-tunes your body at a cellular level, fostering an inner orchestra of wellbeing.

Starting with mantra meditation can be as simple as choosing a quiet spot and a mantra that speaks to you. Sanskrit mantras are popular, but the language is less important than your connection to the sound. It's your personal spiritual mixtape—make sure it resonates with you. Begin with just a few minutes daily, gradually increasing as you find your rhythm. Remember, the key is consistency—you're training your neural pathways to dance to a new vibration.

Choosing a Mantra

Looking for a mantra that resonates with your spirit can be like searching for the perfect pair of shoes: it might take some trying out, but when you find the right one, you just know it clicks! Let's explore how to select a mantra that fits you beautifully and examine the powerful effects of repetitively chanting this chosen magical phrase.

How to Select a Meaningful Mantra

When it comes to selecting a mantra, it's a bit like picking a new favorite coffee flavor – what works wonders for one person might not hit the mark for another. Here's your step-by-step guide to choosing:

- **Start Simple:** If you're new to the mantra game, kicking things off with tried-and-tested syllables like "Om" or "So Hum" might be the perfect starting point. "Om" isn't just a trendy symbol on yoga mats; it's considered the sound of the universe, embodying calm and unity. Meanwhile, "So Hum" literally translates to "I am that", encompassing a deep philosophical dive into identity and existence.
- **Connect with Your Needs:** What are you seeking? Peace? Courage? A nap? Just kidding about the nap (kind of), but truly, your intention can lead you to your mantra. For

instance, if you seek inner peace, a mantra like "Shanti" (peace in Sanskrit) might become your mental melody. Need a boost in self-confidence? Try something like "I am strong, I am capable" to fuel your inner fires.

- **Make it Personal:** While classical mantras are powerful, don't shy away from crafting your own. Personalized mantras can be incredibly potent. Perhaps something like, "Flow like water," if you're working on flexibility and adaptability in life (and maybe also in yoga class).
- **Give it a Test Drive:** Just like you'd check out a new playlist before committing to it for your entire run, try chanting your potential mantra during meditation or a quiet moment. Notice how it feels. Does it uplift you? Soothe you? If not, it's totally okay to go back to the mantra menu!
- **Consult the Experts:** Still unsure? It might help to talk to a meditation instructor, spiritual leader, or a pal who's well-versed in the world of mantras. Sometimes, a little guidance is all you need!

The Significance of Repetition and How it Affects the Mind

Now, why all this talk about repeating a phrase over and over? Is there some kind of magic spell involved? Well, not exactly magic, but definitely some mind-bending science.

Building Mental Muscle Memory

Just as repeating a physical exercise strengthens muscles, repeating a mantra strengthens neural pathways associated with the feelings or intentions behind it. This means the more you chant, the more your brain becomes attuned to, say, feelings of peace if your mantra revolves around tranquility.

Focus Factor

In our ultra-busy world, concentrating on a single thing is nearly as challenging as turning down a free trip to Hawaii! Chanting a mantra can help train your brain to focus. Each repetition helps bring back wandering thoughts (which we all have), sharpening your attention skills.

Stress Be Gone

There's scientific backing that repetitive speech – like mantra chanting – can help decrease stress and anxiety. It's like hitting a mental reset button that not only helps clear the mind but also replenishes your emotional energy.

Positive Vibes Only

Regularly repeating positive phrases can transform your mindset over time, fostering an overall positive outlook on life. This isn't just feel-good fluff; it's a classic case of "fake it till you make "it"— the more you affirm something, the more real it becomes in your perspective and attitude.

So, whether you're using "Om" to connect to the universe during sunrise or whispering "Peace begins with me" while stuck in traffic, remember that your mantra is a powerful tool. It's your secret weapon for creating waves of changes, both in your mind and in your heart, one repetition at a time.

How to Practice Mantra Meditation

For centuries, various cultures around the globe have embraced mantra meditation to ease the mind, soothe the soul, and achieve spiritual enlightenment. Ready to channel that inner calm? Let's get started!

Step 1: Relax

Sit comfortably, maintaining a posture that feels alert yet relaxed. Close your eyes, take a few deep breaths, and allow your body to settle. Feel each muscle from your toes to your shoulders unclench as you exhale.

Step 2: Introduce Your Mantra

Start repeating your mantra silently. Let it flow with your breath—perhaps chant it during the exhale or inhale, whatever feels natural. The mantra should be effortless, almost like a whisper of wind leaves rustling, gentle yet present.

Step 3: Consistency is Key

Repetition is at the heart of mantra meditation. Keep murmuring that mantra over and over. This repetition is the magic wand that makes thoughts disappear and focus sharpen.

Step 4: Anchor in the Sound

Try to concentrate on the sound of your mantra as you repeat it. Each syllable, every vibration, brings you deeper into meditation. Focus on the rhythm it creates as it intertwines with your breathing. It's like a melodious tune that only you can hear, soothing the mind and centering the soul.

Step 5: Ponder the Meaning

While it's perfect to just dwell on the sound, sometimes diving into the meaning of the mantra can deepen the practice. Reflect on what the mantra means to you or its traditional interpretation. This can transform your session from simple repetition to a deeper personal or spiritual connection.

Step 6: Embrace the Drift

It's totally normal for your mind to wander during meditation. If you find yourself planning dinner or reliving an awkward conversation, gently guide your focus back to your mantra. This is like the "settle down" button for the mind. Over time, these mental detours will lessen, and you'll find staying focused becomes naturally easier.

Step 7: Gradually Wind Down

As your meditation session nears its end, don't rush to open your eyes and leap into action. Slowly lessen the repetition of your mantra, allowing your meditation to thin out naturally. Breathe deeply, bringing gentle movement back to your body. Wiggle those fingers and toes, stretch a bit, and open your eyes.

Step 8: Reflect

Take a moment to soak in the peace and clarity post-meditation. It's like basking in the afterglow of a lovely dream. How do you feel? Lighter, uplifted, harmonious? Carry this serenity with you into your daily life, allowing the essence of your mantra to echo through your actions and interactions.

Incorporating Daily Practice

Like any good habit, consistency is vital. Set a specific time each day for your mantra meditation. Start with just five minutes and increase the duration as you become more comfortable. A daily rendezvous with your mantra not only enhances the meditative experience but also strengthens your overall mindfulness and well-being.

Now, equipped with these steps and techniques, you're all set to dive into the tranquil waters of mantra meditation. Remember, there's no 'right' way to meditate. What matters most is how the practice makes you feel. So, find that mantra that feels like a best friend, create a special space, and let the journey to inner peace begin. Happy meditating!

End of Chapter Exercise

- Find a quiet space where you won't be disturbed. You can sit on a meditation cushion or chair or lie down if that's more comfortable. The goal is to keep your back straight to maintain alertness.

- If you are using a timer, set it for 10 minutes. This helps you not worry about time while meditating.
- Close your eyes gently and take a few deep breaths to start relaxing your body. Notice any areas of tension and consciously try to relax those areas.
- Decide on a simple mantra such as "Om" or "Peace." This will be your anchor during the meditation.
- Inhale deeply, then silently chant your chosen mantra in your mind on the exhale. As you inhale again, allow a moment of silence.
- Continue this cycle: inhale — pause — exhale and chant — pause. Let the mantra flow with your natural breath rhythm.
- Each time you find your mind wandering, gently guide it back to the mantra. This is normal and part of the practice. Your mantra is a tool to refocus your attention.
- Around halfway through, deepen your practice by visualizing that each chant spreads a wave of peace or calm through your body.
- Imagine this feeling expanding beyond you, filling the room, the building, and eventually the wider world.
- As you approach the end of your meditation, allow the mantra to become softer and more subtle in your mind.
- At the last minute, let go of the mantra and sit quietly. Observe any sensations in your body or shifts in your mood or thoughts.
- When the timer sounds, gently open your eyes. Take a moment to reflect on your experience. How does your body feel? Has your mental state shifted? Don't rush to stand up; let yourself ease back into the flow of your day.

Post-Meditation

Hydrate yourself with some water and jot down any significant feelings or thoughts that arose during your meditation. This can help in understanding your progress and experience over time.

Chapter 8

Visualization Meditation

In this chapter, we're moving on to another type of meditation – visualization meditation.

Visualization meditation involves forming mental images or scenarios to bring about a sense of relaxation, peace, or motivation. Think of it as your imagination going on a spa day or gearing up for an adventure, depending on what you need at the moment.

This form of meditation isn't just a modern-day relaxation hack; its roots run deep with a rich historical tapestry. The practice dates back thousands of years, with traces found in various traditions, including Hinduism, Buddhism, and even Western spiritual practices. For instance, Tibetan Buddhism has a profound visualization component involving complex imagery of deities and symbols to guide spiritual development.

Similarly, in ancient Greek civilization, philosophers would use "the art of memory," a technique involving visualizing spaces and objects to enhance memory. From early religious rituals to modern-day motivational hacks, visualization techniques have evolved but have always harnessed the power of visual thinking to focus and calm the mind.

How Visualization Engages the Mind and Enhances Focus

Let's paint a picture to better understand how visualization meditation grips our gray matter and boosts our concentration. When you visualize, you're essentially giving your brain a workout session. Instead of lifting weights, its hoisting images, scenes, and emotions—getting stronger with each mental rep!

- **Creates Mental Inclines:** Practicing visualization forms neural pathways, much like hiking trails in your brain, which become quicker and more efficient with use. Every time you visualize something, these pathways light up, ensuring your brain gets to where it wants with ease.
- **Boosts Media Player Skills:** Ever tried watching a movie in your mind? That's what happens here. Visualization stimulates the parts of the brain involved in processing visual information (like the occipital lobe) even though the eyes aren't seeing those images directly. It's like imagining the taste of chocolate—somehow, the brain savors it without a bite being taken!
- **Harnesses the Power of Emotion:** Visualizing scenes or outcomes can also tap into your emotional reservoir. This connection can supercharge your meditation, associating deep feelings with your mental imagery. For instance, picturing yourself acing an interview and feeling the swell of pride makes the scenario more realistic and motivating.
- **Increases Focus and Presence:** By continuously directing your mind to visualize particular images, you're training it to focus and drown out distractions. It's a bit like training a puppy to stay—challenging at first, but eventually, they get the hang of it! This enhanced focus can help reduce stress and increase your overall mental clarity.
- **Flexes the Creative Muscle:** Visualization isn't just about seeing; it's about creating. Each session can be a creative playground where you get to build and explore new landscapes of your mind, finding innovative solutions to problems or simply providing a mental escape hatch when needed.
- **Promotes Relaxation and Healing:** Picture yourself on a sunny beach, listening to the waves crash. Feel more relaxed already? That's visualization meditation at work! Beyond daily stress relief, these practices have been explored for

deeper healing purposes, helping individuals cope with more substantial emotional turmoil or physical pain through immersive, comforting mental imagery.

Imagine you're the director of a movie called 'My Mind.' Visualization meditation lets you create the ultimate director's cut. You can choose the setting, cast your emotions, script your success, and even control the soundtrack—all within the versatile studio of your mind.

In sum, visualization meditation is more than closing your eyes and seeing pretty pictures. It's an engaging, dynamic form of meditation that encourages your brain to get creative, helps manage your emotions, and sharpens your focus. Whether you're looking to relax, motivate yourself, or even just escape for a bit, picking up visualization could be like finding a new best friend for your psyche.

Common Visualization Techniques

There are several types of visualization techniques, and exploring them can help you find the perfect one for your needs.

Guided Imagery

Imagine being whisked away to a tranquil beach or navigating through a challenging task with ease—this is where guided imagery steps in, your mental GPS to relaxation and success. It's a narrative-driven voyage where a calming voice (perhaps a therapist or an app) leads you through vivid, intentional visuals. Picture it as being the director of your own mental movie where the scenes are designed to relax you or enhance your abilities.

Let's say stress is your persistent, unwelcome guest. Guided imagery can help by changing the mental channel. Visualizing a serene location or a past tranquil experience can shift your body's response to stress, promoting relaxation and giving anxiety the boot. This technique not only helps in managing stress but is splendid for pain management too. Patients in hospitals have been guided through imaginary journeys to help manage their pain levels with remarkable success.

Mental Rehearsal

Next up, let's tune into mental rehearsal—this isn't just for athletes, though they sure do love it! Visualize a gymnast practicing her routine in her mind, each flip and twist rehearsed over and over. When she performs, her body recalls every mental practice session. Here's the kicker: studies suggest that when you imagine performing a task, you engage similar brain regions as when you physically perform it. Mind-blowing, right?

Whether it's nailing a presentation or perfecting a golf swing, mental rehearsal is about visualizing success. By mentally simulating the steps involved, the actual performance can feel more familiar, reducing anxiety and boosting confidence. So, the next time you face a nerve-racking challenge, try rehearsing it in your mind's eye. Your brain doesn't totally distinguish between real and vividly imagined events, so exploit that loophole to ace your tasks!

Visualizing Goals or Peaceful Scenes

Cue the dreamy backdrop of your choice because we're wandering into the realms of visualizing goals or peaceful scenes. Dream big—what do you see? Whether it's the sweet taste of victory after winning a local bake-off or the peacefulness of sipping tea in a sun-soaked garden, these visuals aren't just daydreams; they're a blueprint for your mind to manifest reality.

Goal visualization is the secret sauce for many high achievers. It's not just about seeing the end goal but feeling it. When you emotionally connect with your visualized goals, you turbocharge your motivation. It's like planting a seed in your mind's fertile soil. Moreover, regularly visualizing a calm scene—maybe a quiet forest or a gentle snowfall—can be an excellent tool for emotional regulation and stress reduction. Each visual is a brushstroke in your masterpiece of tranquility.

The Role of Imagination in Visualization Meditation

If visualization techniques were a car, then imagination would undoubtedly be the fuel. It's what powers your mental imagery and breathes life into your inner visions. Imagination in meditation isn't just about seeing; it's about immersing yourself in the experience, using all the senses to create a vivid tableau in your mind.

Delving into visualization Meditation with a rich imagination can transport you from a state of worry to a serene escapade or from self-doubt to a confidence-filled rehearsal. Want to enhance your meditation practice? Stoke your imagination by integrating sounds, textures, and even smells into your visualizations.

The Benefits of Visualization

When you actively engage in visualization, you're sketching out possibilities, exploring different hues and shades of thoughts, and seeing what might spring forth creatively.

Partners with Your Muse

Ever felt stuck on a project or in a rut of old, stale ideas? Visualization acts like a gentle nudge to your muse. It opens a dialogue with your inner creative spirit. By imagining different scenarios, solutions, or ideas, you're unlocking new doors within your mind's endless corridors. It's like letting a breath of fresh air into a stuffy room!

Workshop in Your Mind

Consider each session of visualization as a brainstorming meeting with yourself. Ever noticed how relaxed your thinking is while showering or just before falling asleep? That's your brain in its prime creative state. By deliberately visualizing, you cultivate this state, allowing creativity to flow.

Blueprints of Success

Every great accomplishment starts with a plan. Visualization helps you lay down these plans as mental blueprints. By frequently visualizing your goals—be they snagging that promotion, improving personal relationships, or running a marathon—you reinforce your commitment and boost your motivation.

Training Ground

Athletes commonly use this technique to enhance their physical performance. They visualize winning the race, making the shot, or nailing that routine, which mentally prepares them for the actual event. This method applies universally. Regularly visualizing your goals primes you psychologically to act in ways that lead to their fulfillment.

Rehearse, Relax, Repeat

Feeling anxious about an upcoming job interview or a public speaking engagement? Visualize yourself performing perfectly. This mental rehearsal can significantly reduce anxiety by familiarizing your brain with the success scenario, making the actual event feel less intimidating.

A Safe Retreat

Visualization can also be a tranquil escape. By imagining a peaceful scene, like a serene beach or a quiet forest, you engage your mind in a calming exercise. This not only distracts from anxiety triggers but also influences your physical state, easing tension and slowing your heartbeat.

Making Visualization Work for You

Ready to harness the power of visualization? Here are some effective tips to get you started:

- **Daily Doodles in Your Mind:** Set aside a regular time for visualization. Just like you might doodle to spontaneously spark creativity, regular mental imagery sessions help maintain a steady flow of benefits.

- **Vivid is Vivacious:** The more vivid the visualization, the more impactful. Engage all your senses. What do you see? Can you hear anything? What about smells? The more detailed your visualization, the deeper the experience.
- **Guided Imagery Apps & Tracks:** Sometimes, getting into deeper states of visualization alone can be tough (especially with a mind that won't quit chatting!). Using guided imagery apps or listening to visualization tracks can help direct your thoughts, especially when starting out.
- **Journal Your Journey:** After each visualization session, jot down what you saw, felt, and thought. This not only helps in clarifying your visions but also tracks your progress, giving you a motivational boost.

Visualization is like having a mental lab where all the test tubes are your potential ideas, goals, and peaceful thoughts. The great news is that this lab is all yours, and you can visit it anytime. Whether you want to splash some new colors onto your creative canvas, pave the way to your success, or just chill out under your mind's palm trees, visualization is your go-to tool.

End of Chapter Exercise

Welcome to a guided visualization meditation. This brief, peaceful journey is designed to transport you to your own serene sanctuary, a place designed entirely by you for you. Whether you're looking for a moment of serene calm or needing a gentle escape, this practice will help you achieve a state of deep relaxation and mental clarity.

In this guided meditation, you will visualize the journey of climbing a mountain, representing the achievement of a personal goal. This exercise is designed to empower you and foster a deep sense of accomplishment. Find a quiet place where you can sit or lie down undisturbed, and let's begin.

Visualization Meditation

- Settle into a comfortable position, closing your eyes gently. Begin by taking three deep, slow breaths. Inhale through your nose, allowing your belly to expand fully, then exhale slowly through your mouth, releasing any tension. Feel yourself grounded in this present moment, ready for your ascent.
- In your mind's eye, picture a vast, beautiful mountain. Its peak, majestic and covered with a shimmering blanket of snow, stands against a backdrop of clear blue skies. This mountain represents a personal goal or aspiration you have. Feel the excitement of beginning this ascent, knowing at the top lies your achievement.
- Begin your climb. Envision yourself walking along a well-trodden path surrounded by lush green foliage. With each step, feel your strength and determination growing. Notice the smells of the forest around you, the sound of the occasional bird call, and the rustle of the leaves underfoot.
- As you ascend, recognize the challenges of the climb. Perhaps the path becomes steeper or the air thinner. Instead of becoming discouraged, imagine finding within yourself reserves of resilience and strength you didn't know you had. Visualize yourself overcoming these challenges, one step at a time, always moving upwards.
- As you near the summit, the air clears, and the landscape opens up with panoramic views. The final few steps to the peak are before you, feeling somewhat challenging yet exhilarating. As you reach the summit, look around from this high vantage point—around you stretches a landscape of endless possibility.
- Stand at the summit and take in the view. This pinnacle represents your achieved goal. Feel the joy and satisfaction of accomplishing what you set out to do. Breathe in deeply, absorbing this moment of triumph and letting this feeling of achievement fill you up.
- After taking your time at the summit, begin your journey back down the mountain. As you make your descent, reflect on what this journey of achieving your goal has taught you.

With each step-down, feel yourself bringing back this sense of accomplishment into your everyday life.
- As the base of the mountain nears, bring your awareness back to your physical surroundings. Wiggle your fingers and toes, gently bringing movement back to your body. When you're ready, open your eyes, carrying the summit's strength and serenity with you.
- Congratulations on completing this visualization meditation. Remember this mountain journey whenever you face challenges, recalling the strength and perseverance you tapped into today. You can return to this exercise anytime you need a reminder of your capabilities and to relive the sensation of achieving your goals.

Chapter 9

Walking Meditation

The simple joy of walking is something we often take for granted—the gentle catch of heel against the earth, the rhythmic swing of arms, the quiet breath of air in and out. Imagine transforming this everyday action into a profound practice that not only stretches the legs but also settles the mind and fills the heart.

Welcome to the serene world of walking meditation, a chapter dedicated to guiding you through the art of mindfulness in motion. As we amble through this chapter, we'll uncover the subtle beauties of connecting with our surroundings and ourselves, all at the pace of a leisurely stroll.

Now you might be wondering—how can something as ordinary as walking turn into a meditative experience? Well, as you'll soon discover, it's all about intention and awareness.

About Walking Meditation

Walking meditation, or 'Kinhin' as it's known in the Zen tradition, is a practice designed not only to stretch the legs but also to clear the mind and awaken the spirit. Originally, Zen monks used walking meditation to maintain their alertness during long periods of seated meditation, keeping the circulation going while staying engaged in the practice of mindfulness.

So, how can you structure your footsteps into a meditation? In Zen Buddhism, it involves very deliberate, slow steps, often synchronized with the breath. Picture a scene of monks moving silently through corridors or paths, not merely walking but instead gliding in a tranquil dance, each step a deliberate act of presence.

Differences Between Walking Meditation and Seated Meditation

Now, let's spice things up a bit and dive into the differences between walking and seated meditation. This is where walking meditation can strut its stuff on the runway of mindfulness practices.

Energy Flow

The first thing you'll notice is the difference in energy. Seated meditation is static; you cultivate internal energy in a fixed position. Walking meditation, on the other hand, is dynamic. Your body is in motion; energy flows differently, and this can be particularly invigorating. It's like the difference between sketching quietly at a desk or sketching on a moving train, each bump and turn brings a new streak of creativity.

Engagement with the Environment

In seated meditation, your environment is generally static. You might notice the hum of the air conditioner or the chirping of birds outside, but your interaction with your surroundings is limited. Walking meditation allows for a fuller sensory experience. You feel the wind, hear the crunch of leaves underfoot, and see the dance of shadows and light. Its meditation meets nature hike, which can be a refreshing twist for those who find stillness, well, a little too still.

Focus Points

In seated positions, you are often encouraged to focus inward, on your breath or a mantra. Walking meditation, while also incorporating a focus on breath or internal chant, opens up a field of external focal points. You can concentrate on the sensation of your feet touching the ground, the rhythm of your stride, or the overall fluidity of your bodily movements. It's a bit like being the conductor of an orchestra—every part of you moves in a controlled, aware harmony.

Accessibility

Let's talk about practicality. Seated meditation can sometimes be challenging for those with physical discomforts or back issues, making it tough to sit for prolonged periods. Walking meditation? Lace-up your sneakers, and you're ready to go! It's inclusive, allowing those who find sitting painful to take part in a meditative practice. It also provides a lovely alternative for the days when you feel too antsy to sit quietly.

Integration into Daily Life

Finally, integrating meditation into your daily life might seem more approachable with a walking practice. You walk to your car, you walk to your office, and hey, why not meditate while you're at it? It shifts the perspective from meditation as a secluded practice to meditation as a mobile, integrative part of your daily routine.

How to Practice Walking Meditation

Walking meditation is a form of meditation in motion, a practice that invites us to unify our physical movement with our conscious breath, transforming an everyday activity into a sacred ritual of presence and mindfulness. Instead of sitting still, walking meditation involves moving with deliberate intention, immersing ourselves in the rhythm and sensations of our steps.

If you've found sitting meditations to be a challenge, or if you're simply looking to diversify your mindfulness practice, walking meditation might just be the delightful twist you're looking for.

Preparing for Your Walking Meditation

First things first: find a location. This can be anywhere conducive to a peaceful walk. A quiet pathway in your local park, a serene beach, a tranquil section of your backyard, or even a less trafficked hallway or room at home will work. Where you walk is not as crucial as your interaction with the environment during your practice. Ideally, you will want minimal distractions and a safe place where you can comfortably walk back and forth for 10-20 minutes.

Once you've chosen your spot, take a moment to stand still, feet shoulder-width apart, with your spine straight yet relaxed—imagine a string gently pulling you from the crown of your head to the sky. Roll your shoulders back to open your chest for deep, easy breaths. Allow your arms to hang naturally by your sides or clasp them behind your back or in front if that feels more comfortable. Close your eyes for a moment and tune into your current state of being. Acknowledge any thoughts or worries, and gently guide your mind toward the intention of just walking.

Step 1: Start with Awareness

Now, open your eyes and begin to walk at a slower pace than usual but maintain a natural stride. As you start to move, channel your awareness into the soles of your feet. Feel the texture of the ground through your shoes or bare feet. Notice the coolness or warmth of the air as it brushes against your skin. Be fully present with each step as you lift your foot, move it forward, and place it back down.

Step 2: Focus on Breathing

Your breath is a vital part of walking meditation, acting as an anchor to help maintain mindfulness. To synchronize your breathing with your steps, start by inhaling over two steps, then exhale over the next two steps. Feel free to adjust the pattern based on what feels natural—some prefer inhaling for three steps and exhaling for three steps. The key is to keep your breathing even and steady, allowing it to become a rhythmic complement to your movement.

Step 3: Engage Your Senses

As you become more comfortable with synchronizing your breath with your steps, expand your awareness to include your other senses. What smells are present? What sounds can you discern? Can you feel a breeze on your skin or the sun warming your face? Allow each sensation to anchor you more deeply into the present moment. Observe these with curiosity, not clinging or rejecting, but simply noticing and moving on.

Step 4: Cultivate Gratitude and Compassion

With each step, imagine that you are treading upon the earth with gratitude and kindness. Reflect on your interconnectedness with the world around you. Think about the countless individuals who contributed in some way to the paths you walk on, the clothes you wear, and the life you lead. Practicing walking meditation can become an act of gratitude and a practice of compassion—not only towards yourself but towards the entire world.

Finishing Up

After 10-20 minutes, or however long you've decided to practice, gradually come to a halt. Stand still for a moment and return to just standing as you did at the start. Close your eyes again and reflect on your experience. How does your body feel now compared to before the meditation? What about your mind?

Ultimately, walking meditation is a gentle yet powerful practice that helps us reconnect with our physical bodies and the sensory delights of our environment while also grounding us in the present moment. Delight in every step, and you'll start to find that every path you walk becomes a little more peaceful, a little more joyful.

Incorporating Walking Meditation into Daily Life

Walking meditation: it's like multitasking for the soul. Whether you're pacing through your hallway or meandering in a meadow, this practice can infuse a dash of tranquility into your bustling life. You can also practice walking meditation in different environments.

Indoors

Not everyone has the luxury of stepping out into a lush forest or a breezy beachside for their meditative walks. Indoor walking meditation can be equally enriching. You just need a little space—

like a hallway or even around a table. Begin by focusing on your breath, feeling the rhythm of your inhalations and exhalations.

Take slow, deliberate steps. With each step, mentally note the lifting, moving, and placing of your foot. Rotate through your space, mindful of each movement, each breath, and each moment. The corner of your kitchen can transform into a circuit of calm.

In Nature

Nature, with its intrinsic beauty and natural soundscape, can supercharge your walking meditation. The soft rustle of leaves underfoot, the chorus of birds, and the playful dance of sunlight through the trees can heighten your sensory experience. Begin with greeting the natural elements around you.

As you walk, engage fully with the environment: notice the colors, the patterns of light and shadow, and the textures under your feet. This full-sensory engagement can deepen your meditation, creating a powerful connection between your inner peace and the outer world.

The Benefits of Combining Movement with Mindfulness

Mindful Walking has a range of useful benefits for both body and mind. Let's dig in a little and discover what they are.

Improved Overall Health

Combining movement with mindfulness not only soothes the soul but also boosts the body. Regular walking, especially in nature, can decrease blood pressure, enhance immune function, and improve cardiovascular health. Add mindfulness to the mix, and you reduce stress, increase mental clarity, and enhance emotional resilience.

Cognitive Clarity

Ever felt foggy? Walking meditation can help clear the clouds in your mind. Physical activity increases circulation, sending more oxygen to your brain. Combine this with the mindful focus of meditation, and you've got a recipe for enhanced cognitive function. It's like giving your brain a spa day.

Emotional Equilibrium

Walking meditation also provides a unique opportunity to process emotions gently and naturally. The rhythm of your steps can help pace your processing of feelings, making the practice a moving meditation in emotional balance. With each step, you can literally walk through your emotions, viewing them with clarity and perspective, and then softly letting them go.

So how do you take these insights and turn them into action? Simple! You start small. Maybe it's taking a mindful walk during your lunch break or pacing softly around your home as you wait for the kettle to boil. Let these moments be opportunities to connect with your movements and your senses, turning routine walks into mindful journeys.

Adding Some Personality

To keep the experience light and full of personality, treat your walks like they're mini explorations. You could create little "missions" for yourself during each walk—today, I'll notice every shade of green, or I'll count how many different sounds I can hear. Turn it into a game where the only winning prize is a deeper sense of peace and a smile.

In the end, incorporating walking meditation into your life isn't about piling on another task—it's about transforming what you already do into something richer and more meaningful. Each step is a chance to tread a little lighter, to breathe a little deeper, and to see the usual things in unusual ways. So, lace up your shoes and take your mindfulness for a walk. Who knew being present could actually take you places?

End of Chapter Exercise

Here's a guided walking meditation exercise designed to be completed in about 15 minutes. This practice can help you connect with your body, your breath, and your surroundings, fostering a sense of mindfulness and presence.

- Choose a quiet place where you can walk back and forth or in a circle safely without too many distractions. This could be a peaceful path, a park, or even a quiet room. Wear comfortable shoes and clothing suitable for the weather and environment.
- Start by standing still. Close your eyes gently, take a deep breath in through your nose, and exhale through your mouth. Repeat this three times.
- As you stand, set your intention for this walking meditation. It might be to find peace, connect with nature, or just be present.
- Slowly, bring your attention to your body, from the soles of your feet up to the crown of your head. Notice any sensations, tension, or relaxation.
- Open your eyes and begin to walk at a slower pace than usual but naturally. Concentrate on the sensation of your feet making contact with the ground. Feel each part of your foot roll from heel to toe.
- As you settle into your walk, align your breathing with your strides. Breathe in for three steps, hold for two, and exhale for four steps. Adjust the numbers as comfortable.
- Notice the colors, shapes, and movements in your environment. Observe without labeling or judging them.
- Tune into the sounds around you, whether distant or near. Again, just notice these without forming an opinion.
- Pay attention to the air on your skin, the texture of your clothes, and any scents you can smell.
- If your mind wanders, acknowledge the thought and gently guide your attention back to the sensations of walking and breathing.

- Gradually slow your pace until you come to a stop.
- Close your eyes again and take three deep breaths, fully inhaling and exhaling.
- Open your eyes. Take a moment to feel gratitude for this time you've given yourself. Reflect briefly on your state of mind before and after the meditation.

Chapter 10

Progressive Relaxation

If you ever feel like the world is spinning a little too fast, don't worry. You're about to discover a secret that will help you unwind, and it's called Progressive Muscle Relaxation (PMR). Imagine having the power to dial down your stress levels as easily as turning down the volume on your speakers. Sounds magical, doesn't it? Well, let's talk about this calm-inducing sorcery!

What is Progressive Relaxation?

So, what exactly is PMR? Developed with the idea that the body responds to anxiety and stress by tensing up, making us feel like we're perpetually braced for something awful, Progressive Muscle Relaxation teaches us to turn the volume down on this incessant tension. Imagine your body is a radio, and the stress is a really noisy station—PMR is essentially reaching out and tuning into a calm, soothing melody instead. It involves tightening and then relaxing different muscle groups throughout the body, promoting an overall sense of relaxation. It's like teaching your muscles to speak the language of calm fluently.

And why is this worth your time? Because not only can it help reduce stress, but it can also improve sleep quality, reduce symptoms of chronic pain, and even enhance your concentration. In essence, it helps to reset your body's stress levels and give you a clearer, calmer mindset. Think of it as pressing the 'refresh' button on your browser when it's getting a bit glitchy.

History and Development of Progressive Relaxation Practices

The origins of Progressive Muscle Relaxation are as fascinating as the technique itself. This method was pioneered by Dr. Edmund Jacobson, an American physician, in the early 1920s. Dr. Jacobson was quite a visionary; he noticed that stress caused his patients' muscles to tighten up, leading to all sorts of health issues. He thought, "There's got to be a way to calm down these overly enthusiastic muscles!" And thus, PMR was born.

Jacobson's methodology was straightforward but revolutionary. He asked patients to sit back, close their eyes, and move through their body systematically, tightening and then relaxing each muscle group. He instructed them to focus intensely on the contrast between the tension and the relaxation. It's kind of like watching those before-and-after cleaning videos, satisfying and wholly transformative.

Through years of rigorous research (we're talking about a time when flip phones were still a far-off fantasy), Jacobson refined his technique. In his journey, he was adamant that the method should be easy enough to practice without any fancy equipment or special attire (pajamas for the win!). His philosophy was simple: the more relaxed the muscles, the more relaxed the mind.

Bringing PMR into the Modern Era

Fast-forward to today; PMR has not only stood the test of time but has also been embraced by various fields. It's widely used in psychotherapy, incorporated in sports training regimes, and even recommended in corporate wellness programs. Basically, it's like the Swiss Army knife of relaxation techniques!

Moreover, progressive muscle relaxation has adapted to our digital age beautifully. There are now countless apps and online tutorials that can guide you through the process, accompanied by soothing backdrops and gentle reminders that "Hey, it's okay to take a moment for yourself."

The beauty of PMR lies in its simplicity and the fact that anyone can do it anywhere. Whether you're a stressed-out executive, a tired parent, or a student facing finals week, PMR says, "I've got you!" With just a few minutes a day, it offers pocket-sized peace of mind, and who doesn't need a bit of that?

While we often can't control the external chaos that fills our daily lives, techniques like Progressive Muscle Relaxation give us a handy tool for managing our internal responses to this chaos. It's empowering to know that tranquility can be as simple as tensing and relaxing our muscles.

How Progressive Relaxation Works

Let's explore progressive relaxation step by step and untangle why pairing up the loosening of your body can tune up your mental serenity.

Creating Your Peaceful Sanctuary

Before we start flexing those muscles, setting the right atmosphere is key. Choose a quiet, cozy nook where interruptions are about as likely as a snowball's chance in a sauna. Dim the lights, sit down on a comfy mat or a plush chair, and perhaps play some soothing tunes—think flowing rivers, gentle rain, or a soft symphony serenading your soul.

Welcoming the Calm with Breathing

Begin by taking deep, slow breaths. Inhale the good vibes and exhale the hustle-bustle of your day. This isn't just to get you in the mood; it's like sending out an invitation to relaxation. Your body understands the memo and prepares for the chill fest that's about to unfold.

The Tension Tour—from Toes to Top

We start at the very foundations—your toes. Curl them as if you're trying to grip a pencil with them. Feel the tension? Good. Hold it right there for about 10 seconds (no cheating!), then release it!

Let that tension seep away. Notice the blissful lightheadedness? That's your muscles going from 'alert!' to 'at ease!'. Move up to your legs, thighs, and buttocks, and continue the journey upwards until you've given each muscle group their turn at the tension spotlight.

Hold, Hold, Release

Each muscle group—calves, thighs, abdomen, chest, arms, hands, neck, shoulders, and finally, the face—gets its moment. It's about precision here; tension the focus group, hold for a sweet stretch of 10 seconds, then let go. It's almost as if you're sculpting away the stress, chiseling out the calm.

Repeat the Enchantment

Often, a single run-through feels so delightful that you might be tempted to go for round two, and why not? Repeating the process ensures no sneaky bit of tension remains. It's like double-checking your pockets for keys—better safe than sorry!

End with a Mindful Moment

Once you have toured your entire body, end with a few serene minutes of just breathing and being. Feel your body—lighter, like a feather ready to float away with the slightest breeze. Revel in this quietude.

The Link Between Muscle Ease and Mind's Peace

It's not just a feeling; there's some solid science backing the blissful connection between relaxing your body and clearing your mind. Ever heard of the fight-or-flight response? It's our body's primitive, automatic, in-built system designed to protect us from harm. Your heart pumps fast, your muscles tighten, ready to battle or bolt. But let's face it, in our daily lives, we rarely face wild beasts.

What Progressive Muscle Relaxation does is smartly use this system by flipping it. By tensing and then relaxing, you're essentially training your body to switch off the alarm system. It's like telling your body, "Hey, false alarm! It's all chill here." When the body relaxes, it communicates to the brain that all is well. Your brain, happy to oblige, dials down the stress hormones, and thus, a state of calm envelops you.

This practice doesn't just stop at achieving a one-time Zen. Over time, you're teaching your brain to reach for this calm more easily and maintain it. It's like building a mental muscle—flex it regularly, and it gets stronger and more resilient. Plus, the more relaxed you are, the happier and more productive you become—imagine breezing through tasks because you're no longer a bundle of nerves.

In the cozy entwine of loosening muscles and a peaceful mind, we find a practice both simple and profound. Progressive Muscle Relaxation is like a daily spa for your soul, tucked neatly into your routine. It's an invitation to slow down, a gentle reminder that in the mellow rhythm of tensing and relaxing lies the path to tranquility.

Applications of Progressive Relaxation

Dr. Edmund Jacobson discovered that physical stress is closely linked to muscular tension. So, by reducing this muscular tension, the overall sensation of stress dissipates like morning fog under the sun. Engaging in progressive relaxation can feel like giving your body a gentle nudge, saying, "Hey, let's take it down a notch."

Sleep Improvement

Now, let's talk about sleep—our nightly recharging ritual. For many, a good night's sleep can sometimes be elusive. With thoughts buzzing like a hive of bees, it's tough to hit that snooze mode. Here's where progressive relaxation swings in like a superhero. By systematically relaxing your muscles, you send a signal to your brain that it's time to switch from "daytime hustle" mode to "nighttime chill" mode.

As you focus on each muscle group, your mind is distracted from those buzzing thoughts and focuses instead on the calming process of relaxation. It's like telling those bees to buzz off because it's time to rest. By the time you work your way from your toes to your head, you're often ready to drift into the land of dreams—peacefully and naturally.

Transforming Anxiety into Calm

Stress and sleep aside, there's another giant that progressive relaxation helps to tame—anxiety. Anxiety can feel like a relentless drill sergeant, constantly barking worries and what-ifs into your psyche. Progressive relaxation steps in as the soothing diplomat, promoting a peace treaty between your mind and body.

When you start feeling anxious, your body's natural fight or flight response can go into overdrive. But with progressive relaxation, you can reclaim the driver's seat. By slowly relaxing the muscles, you are practically demonstrating to your body that there's no real threat out there. This process helps to dial down the body's alarm system—your heart rate decreases, breathing deepens, and your mind clears. It's like applying the brakes gently and smoothly on a speeding vehicle.

Tips to Cast the Relaxation Spell

- **Regular Practice:** The key to mastery? Regularity. Make progressive relaxation a routine—perhaps a 10-minute session in the morning or evening. Over time, it's like training your body's chill muscles, making it easier to invoke relaxation whenever you need it.
- **Comfort Zone:** Ensure you're in a comfortable position, either lying down or sitting in a cozy chair. Reduce distractions—phones on silent, dim lights, an orchestra of calm, perhaps some soothing instrumental music.
- **Guided Imagery:** If you're venturing into the relaxation journey alone, guided imagery can be a helpful companion. Picture yourself in serenity—a quiet beach, a sunny meadow, your ideal spot—and link this imagery with the relaxation of each muscle group.

- **Breath Buddy:** Combine muscle relaxation with deep breathing. Think of each breath as a wave washing over you, carrying tension away from the shore of your mind.
- **Progress Check:** Sometimes, keep a log of your sessions. Note how you felt before and after, and any improvements in your sleep or anxiety levels. This can be incredibly affirming and motivating!

In the bustling world we inhabit, finding peace can sometimes feel like searching for a quiet corner in a rock concert. Progressive relaxation offers a practical and effective method to turn down the volume of life's stressors, improve the elusive art of slumber, and transform anxiety into tranquility. The best part? You can start right now, right where you are—no fancy gadgets needed. Just you, your body, and a journey to relaxation.

End of Chapter Exercise

Begin by finding a comfortable, quiet place where you can sit or lie down without distractions. Dim the lights if you can, and consider playing some gentle, soothing background music or nature sounds. Take a moment to settle in, making any adjustments to ensure you are completely comfortable.

- Begin by closing your eyes gently. Allow your breath to flow freely.
- Inhale deeply through your nose, filling your lungs fully and expanding your abdomen.
- Exhale slowly through your mouth, letting all the air out and relaxing your body further with each breath.
- Continue this deep, rhythmic breathing for about one minute, focusing on the rise and fall of your chest and abdomen.
- Focus on the muscles in your forehead. Inhale deeply, and as you exhale, imagine the tension releasing and smoothing out.

Progressive Relaxation

- Move to your eyes. Soften the muscles around your eyes and across the bridge of your nose. Feel your eyelids becoming heavier.
- Relax your cheeks and jaw. Let your teeth slightly part, relaxing the tongue and the area around your mouth.
- Bring your awareness to your shoulders. Lift them slightly as you inhale, then fully relax them downwards as you exhale, feeling the weight being released.
- Gradually move down to your upper arms, elbows, forearms, wrists, and finally, hands. Tense each muscle group slightly as you breathe in, and then release as you breathe out.
- Focus on your chest area as you breathe in deeply. As you exhale, feel your chest relax and let go of tension.
- Shift your attention to your upper back and then slowly down to your lower back. With each exhale, release any tightness or stiffness you're holding in your back.
- Gently draw your attention to your abdominal muscles. Breathe into them and feel them relax and soften with each out-breath.
- Then, focus on your hips. Feel them sinking deeper into relaxation, letting go of stress and tightness with every breath.
- Now bring your attention to your thighs. Notice any tension, and with your exhaling breath, let it melt away.
- Move down to your knees, calves, and ankles, and finally focus on your feet. Tense and release each part, from your thigh down to your toes, gradually letting go of all tension.
- Now imagine a wave of relaxation slowly spreading from the top of your head down to your toes. With each breath, this wave deepens, relaxing you more profoundly.
- Allow yourself to feel the full weight of your body being supported. Enjoy this deep state of relaxation for a couple of minutes.
- When you're ready, gently wiggle your fingers and toes, slowly awakening your body. Take a deep breath in, gently stretch if you like, and then exhale slowly as you open your eyes.

Chapter 11

Guided Meditation

By now, we know that there are many types of meditation, but a common issue is not knowing where to start. That's where guided meditation comes into play, like a friendly hand reaching out to show you the ropes in the vast sea of your own consciousness.

So, what exactly is guided meditation? Picture this: instead of trying to navigate a complex subway system in a foreign city without a map, guided meditation offers you a seasoned tour guide. This guide doesn't just know the paths through the noisy mind but also knows the quiet alleys where peace likes to hang out. In simpler terms, guided meditation is a process wherein you meditate in response to the guidance provided by a trained practitioner or a recording. This guidance can be delivered in many forms—be it through words, soothing music, or even visual cues in some cases.

Guided meditation also has plenty of benefits:

- **Ease of Use:** Jumping into meditation can often feel like learning a new language. A guided approach eases this learning curve, providing a voice that helps navigate through the thought traffic.
- **Stress Relief:** It's a biggie! As you're guided through relaxation and mindfulness exercises, the mental chatter decreases. This is like putting down heavy shopping bags after a long day—refreshing!
- **Improved Focus and Concentration:** Regular practice under guidance can enhance your ability to concentrate, much like working out at the gym but for your brain muscles.

- **Emotional Resilience:** Tuning into guided meditation can equip you with armor against emotional turmoil. It's like having an emotional first-aid kit!
- **Accessibility:** Whether you're in a bustling city apartment or a quiet country house, guided meditation can be accessed just about anywhere. All you need is a comfortable spot and perhaps a pair of headphones.

These are just starters in a full-course meal of benefits that guided meditation serves up!

Role of the Guide in Leading Meditation Practice

The role of the guide in meditation is pivotal. Think of the guide as your personal mindfulness coach. They're not just there to read a script but to lead you through a mental and emotional landscape that might sometimes feel like a labyrinth.

- **Navigator:** First and foremost, the guide serves as your navigator. They help you focus on the present moment, often guiding your attention back when it wanders off to yesterday's troubles or tomorrow's anxieties.
- **Educator:** They also act as educators. As you start your journey, the myriad techniques of meditation—from breathing exercises to visualizations – can seem daunting. A knowledgeable guide can teach these techniques in an understandable and relatable way.
- **Support System:** Beyond the technicalities, a guide is there to offer support. They create a safe, welcoming space where all feelings are valid and where each breath brings you closer to inner peace.
- **Motivator:** Let's face it, maintaining a regular meditation practice isn't always a walk in the park. On days when you feel less motivated, the guide's voice can be the gentle nudge you need to keep going.
- **Innovator:** Lastly, a creative guide can make each session unique, tailoring it to meet your evolving mental and

emotional states. They spice up practices by incorporating stories, different thematic meditations, and perhaps some humor to keep you engaged and interested.

In essence, while meditation is often viewed as a solitary activity, having a guide can be like having a wise friend who walks the path with you, shines a light on the stones to avoid, and highlights the scenic views you might otherwise miss.

Different Types of Guided Meditation

There are several different types of guided meditation, let's take a look at the main ones:

Relaxation-Oriented Meditation

Let's start with everyone's favorite – the relaxation meditations. This format is like the soft, fluffy pillow of meditation types. Designed to help you let go of the day's stress and tension, these sessions often start with deep, rhythmic breathing to calm the nervous system. You might hear soothing instructions like, "Feel your arms getting heavier," drawing your attention to relaxing different parts of the body. Before you know it, you're more noodle than human.

Stress Reduction Meditation

Next up, for the warriors battling daily stress, stress reduction meditation comes to the rescue. These sessions are tailored to help unpack the mental backpack of worries. They often incorporate visualization techniques; imagine packing your stresses into a balloon and watching it floats away (bye, worries!). Or they might guide you through a progressive muscle relaxation sequence. Perfect for those days when deadlines are piling up and you need someone to say, "It's okay, just breathe!"

Healing and Self-compassion Meditation

Healing meditations are warm, comforting soups for the soul. These guided sessions focus on fostering self-compassion and promoting emotional and physical healing. Whether it's guiding listeners through forgiving themselves or others or envisaging healing energies soothing aches and pains, these meditations are about nurturing the mind and body. They're akin to a verbal salve, reminding us that it's okay to take care of ourselves first.

Mindfulness-Based Stress Reduction (MBSR)

Developed by Dr. Jon Kabat-Zinn, MBSR is like the Swiss Army knife of meditation – versatile and practical. This program is structured (typically spanning 8 weeks) and combines mindfulness meditation, body awareness, and yoga. It's particularly good for those who like a bit of structure in their Zen-seeking endeavors and are dealing with conditions like anxiety, depression, or pain.

Visualization and Journey Meditation

These meditations are the virtual reality of the meditation world. They transport you to different places—imagine sitting by a crackling campfire or standing on a serene beach as the waves gently lap at your feet. These guided "journeys" help in visualizing peaceful scenes, which can be incredibly soothing and invigorating for the imagination.

Concentrative Meditation

Ever wanted to really focus on something but found your mind wandering to that embarrassing thing you did in 2009? Concentrative meditation is all about focusing on a single point – be it a sound, object, or even your own breathing – to train your attention. It's great for those looking to enhance their concentration and enjoy a deeper, perhaps even spiritual, connection with the meditative process.

Choosing Your Meditation Match

Finding the right guided meditation can feel a bit like dating – you might have to meet a few dudes before you find "the one." But when you do, it's magical. Here's a little cheat sheet to help you narrow down the search:

- **What's Bothering You?** Pinpoint what you're trying to fix. Is it stress? A scattered mind? Emotional baggage? Different meditations cater to different needs.
- **Personality Clicks:** Just like in real life, the tone and voice of the meditation guide can be a make-or-break factor. Look for someone whose voice and delivery style resonate with you.
- **Time Constraints:** Consider how much time you can devote. If you're always on the go, maybe a series of short 5-minute sessions will work better than hour-long epics.
- **Methods Matter:** Some people love vivid visualizations; others might prefer straightforward mindfulness practices. Experiment to find what genuinely helps you connect with the experience.

Use your guide-time wisely—it's about finding a space where your mind feels at ease, and you can grow into the practice at your own pace. Whether it's pooling tranquility or navigating emotional gales, guided meditation offers a beautifully supportive space to anchor down and explore the vistas of your inner self.

How to Use Guided Meditation

Let's get you settled into the art of guided meditation with a sprinkle of charm and a dash of practical ease.

Set the Scene

Find a quiet spot where interruptions are as unlikely as finding a snowflake in the Sahara. This could be a cozy corner of your bedroom, a sunny spot on your living room floor, or even a peaceful park bench. Just make sure it's somewhere you can sit or lie down comfortably without turning into a modern art exhibit of cramped limbs.

Choose Your Guide

Platforms like YouTube, Spotify, or meditation apps like Calm and Headspace are like the Netflix of guided meditation—they have a vast selection of guides ready to whisk you away from anxiety and stress. Pick one whose voice resonates with tranquility for you—it could be deep and slow, or perhaps light and cheerful. It's like choosing your barista for the perfect coffee blend of calm!

Plug In and Zone Out

Using headphones is a game changer. They can not only block out external noise but also help deliver the soothing tones of your meditation guide directly into your ears, making it easier to focus.

Eyes on the Prize

Close your eyes. This helps shut out any visual distractions and makes it easier to turn your focus inward.

Breathe Like You Mean It

Often, your guided meditation will start with a focus on your breath. Try to sync your breathing with the rhythm of the instructions—deep and deliberate inhales followed by easy, unhurried exhales. Feel the stress melt away with each breath, like butter on a hot pancake.

Integrating Guided Meditation into a Regular Practice

Integrating meditation into your daily routine might sound as challenging as convincing a cat to take a leisurely bath, but with some creativity, it's perfectly doable:

- **Make It a Ritual:** Maybe it's right after your morning coffee or right before bedtime. Whenever it is, try to stick to this spot in your routine—it'll help your mind automatically prepare for some quality me-time.
- **Use Short Sessions:** Even on a crammed day, a 3-minute guided meditation can be squeezed in. It could be during your commute (no, not if you're driving!), during a lunch break, or

while waiting for your laundry. Small snippets of calm can contribute significantly to your overall well-being.
- **Connect with Community:** Sometimes, sharing the journey can make the path easier. Join online groups or local meet-ups that focus on meditation practices. Sharing insights, tips, or even challenges with like-minded folks can reinforce your commitment.
- **Variety is the Spice of Life:** Keep things interesting by changing your guided meditations. Explore different themes like gratitude, forgiveness, or mindfulness. It's refreshing and keeps the practice from going stale.
- **Set Milestones and Celebrate:** Set small, achievable goals (e.g., "I'll meditate daily for a week") and reward yourself when you meet them. Perhaps a new meditation cushion, a book, or a nice cup of your favorite leafy green tea!

Remember, progression in meditation is not linear and varies enormously among individuals. So, bear with your wandering mind, and give yourself a generous pat on the back for embarking on this journey to a calmer, more introspective you.

End of Chapter Exercise

Whether you're at your desk, on a break, or in the comfort of your home, this session is designed to help you let go of stress and find a moment of peace.

- To begin, find a comfortable position. You can be seated on a chair, on the floor, or lying down. Adjust yourself gently to ensure your back is straight yet relaxed. Allow your hands to rest softly on your knees or by your sides. Whenever you're ready, softly close your eyes.
- Inhale deeply, filling your lungs completely. Now exhale slowly, letting all the air out. As you continue to breathe deeply, pay attention to how the breath feels entering and exiting your body. Perhaps you feel the air moving through your nostrils, or

- maybe your chest or abdomen is rising and falling. Continue to focus on this natural rhythm: inhale deeply, exhale fully.
- Imagine that with each inhale, you are drawing in a sense of peace and calm. And with each exhale, imagine releasing any tension or stress you may be holding.
- As we move further into relaxation, picture yourself in a serene environment. It could be a quiet beach, the gentle, early morning woods, or a cozy, sunlit corner of your garden. Visualize this place with as much detail as you can. The sights, the sounds, the smells. Are there any particular colors that stand out? Maybe the gentle lap of waves, the rustle of leaves, or the serene silence enveloping your space. Take a moment to really embed yourself within this peaceful place.
- As you continue breathing deeply and evenly, let your body relax. Starting at the top of your head, imagine a wave of relaxation slowly spreading downwards. Relax your forehead and your eyelids. Feel any tension in your jaws released. Let this feeling of relaxation flow down your neck and shoulders. Release any burdens you carry. Let this relaxing wave move further down to your arms, all the way to your fingertips, down your torso, relaxing your chest, your belly, down to your legs and knees, all the way to your feet.
- With each breath, you feel more relaxed. With each imaginary sensory experience, your stress responds by diminishing more and more. Remind yourself that this place is available to you anytime. It's a sanctuary created by your mind, for your mind.
- Now, very gently, start to bring your awareness back to the physical space you are in. Notice the surface beneath you. Begin to wriggle your fingers and toes, slowly awakening your body. Take one more deep breath in, hold it for a moment, and then exhale completely.
- When you feel ready, gently open your eyes. Take a moment to pause and feel grateful for taking this time for yourself. As you continue with the rest of your day, carry this feeling of calm and relaxation with you.

Chapter 12

Developing a Sustainable Meditation Practice

Building consistency in your meditation practice is akin to nurturing a plant; it requires patience, care, and a smidgen of dedication to bloom beautifully. A regular meditation routine is essential for both budding enthusiasts and seasoned meditators alike, enabling the practice to deepen and becoming as natural as breathing. This journey, although filled with its own set of challenges such as squeezing meditation time into a jam-packed day, finding motivation, and warding off the ever-persistent distractions, can be embarked upon with a scoop of commitment and a sprinkle of creativity.

The Importance of Regular Practice

Imagine your meditation practice as a cozy, delightful café that you visit every day. Just as the comfort and warmth of the café soothe you, consistent meditation enriches your mental landscape, providing clarity and tranquility in the otherwise chaotic hustle of daily life. As you drop by this mental café regularly, you begin to cultivate a sense of inner peace, heightened awareness, and an overall sense of well-being. Isn't that a stop worth making daily?

Regular meditation practice reinforces neural pathways that aid in enhancing focus, reducing anxiety, and improving emotional health. This mental training cultivates an environment where stress does not overrun your mind's garden but instead finds a small, manageable space in the corner.

Establishing a Meditation Routine

Creating a meditation routine is like setting up a dance playlist—it has to resonate with your rhythm. Begin by setting realistic targets; perhaps start with as little as five minutes each day and progressively groove into longer durations as you become more comfortable. The key is consistency, not intensity. It's better to dance for five minutes daily than to aim for an hour and step back after the first song!

- **Time It Right:** Identify a time of the day when you can consistently spare a few minutes. Are you a morning lark or a night owl? Align your meditation with your natural inclinations. Maybe in the morning, when the world is just waking up, or in the evening, as the sunlight dims, calibrating a perfect backdrop for winding down.
- **Create Your Space:** Dedicate a comfortable spot for your practice; it doesn't have to be an elaborate setup – even a quiet corner with a comfy pillow will do. Add personal touches like a scented candle, a soft mat, or even a stack of serene pictures. This little nook will soon start calling out to you, "Hey, let's meditate!"
- **Equip Yourself:** There are bountiful resources to scaffold your practice. From meditation apps, which are like having a personal meditation coach in your pocket, to soothing playlists and guided meditation videos. Equip yourself with these tools to keep the practice engaging and structured.

Overcoming Common Challenges

Just when you thought you could cruise along on your meditation journey, challenges like lack of time, dwindling motivation, and pesky distractions pop up. But don't worry, as you can navigate these with some flair.

- **Lack of Time:** Everyone has the same 24 hours, yet some manage to find time for what rejuvenates them. It's not about finding time but making time. Could you wake up 15 minutes

earlier? Or spend less time on your phone? Sometimes, time isn't lost; it's just misplaced!
- **Motivation:** Keep a little meditation journal. Note down how you feel after each session, what worked and what didn't. Over time, you'll have a personalized blueprint of what brings you inner peace. Remember, motivation is like fire; you need to keep adding little bits of kindle to keep it alive.
- **Distractions:** First, identify what distracts you. Is it noise, physical discomfort, or perhaps wandering thoughts? For noise, a pair of earplugs or a white noise app can be golden. If it's comfort you seek, arrange your meditation spot with cushions or invest in a comfy meditation chair. As for the buzzing bee of thoughts, visualize them as clouds passing in your sky of mindfulness, observing them without attachment.

Building a consistent meditation practice is a rewarding adventure, peppered with its own twists and turns. As you tune into the rhythm of regular practice, you'll find the cadence that suits you best, turning challenges into opportunities for growth.

Customizing Your Meditation Practice

Embarking on a meditation journey can be a bit like cooking your favorite dish for the first time. You've got your basic ingredients—basic breathing techniques, a quiet space, and perhaps a comfy pillow to sit on. But just as in cooking, the magic happens when you start tweaking the recipe to taste just right for you. Customizing your meditation practice isn't just helpful; it's essential for making it a sustainable and enjoyable part of your life. So, how do you mix and match meditation styles to suit your unique flavor? And how do you adapt your practice as your life seasons change?

Choosing and Combining Techniques: Your Personal Meditation Menu

The meditation choice is vast and varied, offering everything from mindfulness meditation and focused attention to progressive relaxation and loving-kindness meditation. The key is to not get overwhelmed by the abundance but to start sampling small bites of different techniques.

- **Start Where You Are:** If the idea of sitting in silence for an hour is about as appealing to you as a cold shower, you might start with just five minutes of guided imagery or a few moments of deep breathing. It's perfectly okay to start small. Think of it as the equivalent of sprinkling a little salt into your dish—you can always add more as you go.

- **Mix and Match:** Maybe on Monday, the simplicity of focusing on your breath feels right, but by Friday, you're energized and craving something more vibrant, like a walking meditation in the park. Or perhaps morning calls for a gentle body scan, while evenings are perfect for jotting down things you're grateful for. Listen to your mood and energy levels—your meditation "menu" can be as flexible as the day's meal plan.

- **Theme Your Sessions:** Just as you might choose a culinary theme for a dinner party, you can theme your meditations around your current life events. Facing a big decision? A session of guided reflective meditation on clarity and decision-making could be your go-to. Needing a boost of joy? A loving kindness meditation focusing on happiness and gratitude might just be the recipe.

Adapting Meditation to Changing Life Seasons

Life is as dynamic as a dance floor—sometimes you're in the groove, moving effortlessly, and other times it's more of a clumsy shuffle. As your life circumstances change, so too should your meditation practice adapt to fit.

New Chapters

Whether you're starting a new job, moving to a different city, or entering another significant life change, these transitions can be the perfect time to reassess your meditation needs. A practice that once soothed you might now feel redundant, or maybe you discover you need more time in meditation rather than less. It's okay to rewrite your meditation menu to match your new life chapter.

Busy Bees

During particularly hectic periods, it might seem impossible to carve out time for a 30-minute session. This is when "meditation snacks" can come into play. Just a few minutes of deep breathing or a quick mindfulness exercise while waiting for your coffee to brew can make all the difference. Think of these as grabbing a quick healthy snack to keep your energy up through the rush.

Emotional Seasons

Just as we crave hearty soups in winter and crisp salads in summer, our emotional landscapes might need different meditative approaches. In times of grief or sadness, gentle, nurturing practices such as metta or yoga nidra can be comforting. Conversely, in moments of high energy or anxiety, more structured techniques like mindfulness or mantra-based meditations might help channel your energy more effectively.

Like a quilt that becomes more beautiful with every patch added, your meditation practice too will grow richer and more nuanced with each adjustment and addition. The beauty of meditation lies in its flexibility—there are no rigid rules, only guidelines, and a multitude of options to tailor it precisely to your needs.

Be patient with yourself as you experiment and adjust. Some techniques will resonate immediately, while others might take time—or may never fit quite right. And that's perfectly fine. After all, no chef ever mastered their signature dish on the first try!

Long-Term Benefits and Progress

Have you ever tried to learn an instrument, say, a guitar or a piano? At first, your fingers might feel like they're doing a little dance of their own, definitely not the one you're trying to teach them. But with practice, something magical happens. Suddenly, you're making music, and the notes that once tangled under your fingertips flow smoothly. Well, meditation isn't much different. Like any beautiful symphony, its effects get better with time and practice.

With consistent practice, meditation nourishes you in numerous ways.

Stress Reduction

One of the most celebrated powers of meditation is its ability to reduce stress. Initially, you might find yourself just a tiny bit less frazzled when things go awry. But as months and years pass, you might discover that what once made you go 'Arrgh!' now only makes you go 'Hmm.' That's your meditation muscle at work, making you more resilient against the storms of stress.

Emotional Health Elixir

Consistent meditation is like an elixir for your emotional health. Each session helps you understand your emotions better, allowing you to navigate through your feelings like a skilled captain in the sea. In the long run, this means fewer days sunk by sadness and more days sailing smoothly, basking in the sunlight of a well-managed emotional state.

Enhanced Self-Awareness

Do you know how you feel more familiar with a route the more you travel through it? Similarly, as you meditate more, you become more attuned to the highways and byways of your own mind. This enhanced self-awareness is a treasure. It helps you discover not just who you are but who you can be, paving the way for personal growth and self-improvement.

Attention Span: Your Personal Bandwidth

Fancy giving your attention span an upgrade? Meditation is your go-to tool. Regular practice helps increase your focus, similar to how a jogger gradually increases stamina. Over time, this can lead to better performance at work or school, making you the MVP of managing tasks.

Kindness Overdrive

Here's a lovely ripple effect: regular meditation is linked to increased kindness. Not just towards others, but towards yourself too. This nurture stems from practices like metta meditation, which focuses on developing positive feelings, first towards oneself and then towards others. Picture it as planting flowers of kindness in your mind, which bloom and spread their sweet fragrance in all your interactions.

Reflecting on Personal Growth and Continued Learning in Meditation

Journeying through the landscape of meditation is a continuous learning experience. Each session is unique, and there's always something new to discover about the technique or yourself—like unwrapping little gifts of insight every day.

The Beginner's Mind

Even as you advance, retaining a beginner's mind is a gem. It keeps the curiosity alive, fueling your practice. You learn to approach each session without baggage, ready to explore and accept whatever comes your way.

Peaks and Valleys

It's essential to acknowledge that progress in meditation isn't always linear. You'll have days when meditation feels like a breeze and others when it feels like a chore. These peaks and valleys are part of the journey. Recognizing and accepting them teaches you the art of equanimity—remaining calm and even in various situations.

Meditation as a Lifestyle

Eventually, meditation becomes a lifestyle. This profound integration affects how you live, work, and play. It becomes less about 'doing' meditation and more about 'being' meditative in your daily activities. Whether you're washing dishes, attending meetings, or chatting with friends, the presence and peace learned on the cushion come to shine in all corners of your life.

Never-ending Journey

Lastly, know that the path of meditation doesn't have a final destination. With each step, you peel back layers, discovering newer depths in your consciousness. It's an ongoing adventure, one that keeps the mind ever young, curious, and agile.

Ultimately, think of meditation as one of those gifts that keep on giving. Its benefits accumulate and blossom beautifully over time, helping you build resilience, emotional intelligence, and a profound sense of well-being. It's a tune you get better at playing, one whose music enriches not just your moments but your entire life.

Resources for Further Exploration

Embarking on your meditation journey can be like stepping into a serene, mysterious garden—there's so much to explore and discover! Whether you're a bright-eyed beginner or a seasoned meditator looking to deepen your practice, the right resources can light the way like twinkling lanterns on a dusky evening. Here are some handpicked goodies—books, apps, and online resources—that will keep you inspired, informed, and, yes, impeccably Zen.

Books to Explore

- **"Wherever You Go, There You Are" by Jon Kabat-Zinn:** Consider this book your gentle hand guide. Kabat-Zinn, a sage in the realms of mindfulness, makes meditation as approachable as chatting with an old friend over a cup of tea.
- **"The Miracle of Mindfulness" by Thich Nhat Hanh:** Written by one of the most revered Zen masters in the world, this book is a gorgeous tapestry of stories, practical advice, and foundational techniques that illuminate the art of mindful living.
- **"10% Happier" by Dan Harris:** If you've ever been a tad skeptical about meditation, this book is your new pal. Harris provides a no-nonsense look at how meditation can be a game-changer, and he does it with a hefty dose of wit.

Apps to Anchor Your Practice

- **Headspace:** Think of Headspace as your meditation mentor tucked neatly in your pocket! The app is full of guided meditations tailored to every mood and need—perfect for sneaking in some tranquility on your lunch break.
- **Calm:** As the name suggests, Calm is like a deep, soothing breath for your mind. With a variety of meditation exercises, sleep stories, and breathing techniques, it's a great tool for those nights when your brain won't stop buzzing.
- **Insight Timer:** With an impressive library of over 45,000 free meditations, Insight Timer is like the all-you-can-eat buffet of meditation apps. Dive in and explore teachings from thousands of meditation instructors and musicians.

Online Platforms to Keep You Engaged

- **The Chopra Center:** Dive into the deep end of meditation insights with a dash of holistic wellness. Their website offers a broad spectrum of articles, meditation programs, and workshops that are just waiting for your curious click.
- **Mindful.org:** Whether you're looking for articles to skim through or intensive courses to tackle, Mindful.org offers a plethora of resources that cater to both the heart and the mind.
- **Tara Brach's Website:** Tara Brach blends psychology and meditation in her teachings, making her website a treasure chest for those who seek to deepen emotional healing through meditation.

So, there you have it—your toolkit for an enriching meditation practice. Each book, app, and website is a stepping stone to greater mindfulness, peace, and self-discovery. Whether you dip into these resources between sips of coffee or allocate dedicated time each day, they're here to guide you through your meditation adventure.

Conclusion

As we close the pages on this introductory voyage into the world of meditation, let's take a moment to look back on the journey we've traveled together. We began by demystifying meditation, brushing away the cobwebs of misconceptions that often shroud its serene facade. We explored its numerous benefits—reduced stress, enhanced concentration, and a general boost in well-being, just to name a few.

Remember when we unpacked various meditation techniques? From the focused attention of mindfulness meditation, where we witnessed our thoughts and feelings like clouds passing in a grand, blue sky, to the dynamic movements of walking meditation that grounded us in the rhythmic symphony of our own steps—each practice introduced a unique flavor to our meditation feast.

We've also tackled challenges together, like finding time in our busy schedules and coping with the wandering mind, always with a gentle nudge to approach each obstacle with kindness and a dash of humor. Did anyone else find themselves planning dinner in the middle of a session, or is it just me?

Whether today marks your first or hundredth meditation, there's always a new depth to explore, a new understanding to reach. Keep the curiosity of a beginner, and let your practice be a constant invitation to delve deeper into the mysteries of your mind and the universe.

Remember, meditation is not a race, nor is it a magic pill; it's more like slowly sipping your favorite tea, savoring each unique note and aroma. Sometimes you'll encounter bitterness or an unexpected tanginess, but with patience, you come to appreciate each nuance. Similarly, each meditation session is a separate layer in your journey.

Compassion, too, is paramount—not just for others, but for yourself. It's perfectly fine if some days your meditation feels like a juggling act between calm and chaos. Smile, take a deep breath, and remember that every meditator, whether novice or sage, has been there too. Be gentle with yourself; celebrate the small victories and embrace the lessons in the stumbles.

Finally, I invite you to view meditation not as a task to be completed but as a lifelong journey. This path offers not just fleeting moments of peace but a profound transformation that permeates every aspect of your life. It's about discovering the boundless possibilities within yourself, finding tranquility in the turmoil, and fostering an unwavering friendship with your own mind.

References

Grabowski, S. (2021, November 24). *23 Meditation Techniques: A beginner's guide to the many styles of practice*. THE MINDFUL STEWARD. https://themindfulsteward.com/mindfulness/23-meditation-techniques-a-beginners-guide-to-the-many-styles-of-practice/

Meditation for Beginners - Headspace. (n.d.). Headspace. https://www.headspace.com/meditation/meditation-for-beginners

Nash, J., PhD. (2024a, September 17). *What is Loving-Kindness Meditation? (Incl. 4 Metta Scripts)*. PositivePsychology.com. https://positivepsychology.com/loving-kindness-meditation/

Nash, J., PhD. (2024b, October 4). *The History of Meditation: Its Origins & Timeline*. PositivePsychology.com. https://positivepsychology.com/history-of-meditation/

Pmp, H. J. B. C. (2021, November 5). *Which type of meditation is right for me?* Healthline. https://www.healthline.com/health/mental-health/types-of-meditation

Ross, A. (2016, March 9). How meditation went mainstream. *TIME*. https://time.com/4246928/meditation-history-buddhism/

Staff, M. (2024, October 22). *How to meditate*. Mindful. https://www.mindful.org/how-to-meditate/

Thorpe, M., MD PhD. (2024, August 15). *How meditation benefits your mind and body*. Healthline. https://www.healthline.com/nutrition/12-benefits-of-meditation

Vogel, K. (2022, March 10). *10 types of meditation and how to do them*. Psych Central. https://psychcentral.com/health/types-of-meditation

Wikipedia contributors. (2023, July 8). *Visualization*. Wikipedia. https://en.wikipedia.org/wiki/Visualization#:~:text=Visualization%20(graphics)%2C%20the%20physical,of%20complex%20data%20and%20information

Wikipedia contributors. (2024a, October 18). *Meditation*. Wikipedia. https://en.wikipedia.org/wiki/Meditation

Wikipedia contributors. (2024b, October 20). *Mindfulness*. Wikipedia. https://en.wikipedia.org/wiki/Min

Dear Valued Reader

We hope you enjoyed your 5-book bundle on Reiki, Chakra Healing, the Vagus Nerve, Ayurveda, and Meditation! If you found these guides helpful, we'd be eternally appreciative if you would take a few moments to leave a review so that it can help others discover these Holistic Practices.

Here are the links:

Amazon.com/review/create-review?&asin=B0DLYDSBMX

Amazon.co.uk/review/create-review?&asin=B0DLYDSBMX

Thank you in advance for your support and for being part of our wellness community!

Warm regards,

Monika Daniel

https://www.reikisoulacademy.com